LIBRARY MANAGEMENT

(A MANUAL FOR EFFECTIVE MANAGEMENT)

Dr. Anil Kumar Dhiman
and
Smt. Yashoda Rani

Ess Ess Publications

4837/24, Ansari Road, Darya Ganj,
New Delhi-110002
✆ : 23260807
Fax : 23274173
E-mail: info@essessreference.com
url:http://www.essessreference.com

First Published 2004

ISBN : 81-7000-388-1

Price : Rs. 950/-

Published by :

Ess Ess Publications

4837/24, Ansari Road, Darya Ganj,
New Delhi - 110 002
Phone : 23260807
Fax : 23274173
E-mail: info@essessreference.com
url:http://www.essessreference.com

Printed at :

Mehra Offset Press, New Delhi

To

our son

AMAN

CONTENTS

Preface

Library is the essentiality of the society not the luxury. It has finished its long journey started from clay tablets to papers and now to the paperless society. There is a paradigm of shifting from printed materials to paperless, from ownership of documents to access of the information and from specific libraries to virtual libraries.

Management is a process that brings several varied resources like physical, human and financial along with techniques and technologies together to accomplish a task or a series of tasks. If we manage our organization well the results will be fruitful but if the management fails, the entire organization will held up. In past, the libraries were managing with traditional techniques of management but the introduction of computers and information technologies has brought the remarkable changes in the library scenario. Information and Telecommunication technologies have boosted up the production of information at such a terrific speed that the Libraries and Information Centres cannot cope up with the traditional methods of management. Now, library professional are expected to keep pace with these changes, so there is an urgent need of adequate training and exposure on modern and scientific techniques of management.

This book is an attempt to provide a concise account on different management techniques along with traditional methods of management to train the library professional in the new environment. The entire book is divided into twelve chapters. Its first chapter Introduction gives a general idea of management. Second chapter deals with the development of management thoughts. A complete chapter is retained on Elements and Principles of Management. In the modern environment of ICT, it is essential to train the library professionals to cope up with the changed scenario, hence a chapter on Human Resource Development, giving overview of this aspect comes next. New concepts in the management field like Management by Objectives, Total Quality Management etc., are discussed in the next chapter. Separate chapters are given on Personal Management, Financial Management, Space Management and Collection Management. Staffing pattern, job analysis and organizational chart are given under Personnel Management. Chapter on financial management covers financial estimation and the various methods of budgeting etc. The chapter on Space Management deals with the building planning and the planning of furniture and various sections in the library. Collection Management deals with the various aspects of the library collection viz., document selection, document processing and effective usage of the documents. A separate chapter is retained on the 'Maintenance. Preservation and Stock Verification' covering the preservation, binding and different methods of stock verification in the libraries. As the role of authorities and committees, is very crucial in the management, the next chapter is given on Library Authorities, Committees and the Library Rules. We can establish a Management Information System (MIS) with the help of computers for effective management. So, the last chapter is designed on Computers, Internet and the Library Management, where the role of computers in library management is discussed. An exhaustive bibliography is also provided for the general readers for further reference.

We believe that this book will be useful for the library professionals for effective management in their libraries and the students of library science as well.

In preparing the book, various works of authors have been consulted for which the authors are grateful to them. We are also thankful to Mrs. Sheel Sethi and Mr. Sumit Sethi, the owners of Ess Ess Publications, New Delhi for publishing this book in nice form. Dr. Dhiman is indebted to his parents Mr. Ramlal Dhiman, and Mrs. Kamla Devi for their blessings and moral encouragement and to his sister Ms. Alka Rani for her help in writing of this work. Yashoda Rani is indebted to his parents Mr. Chandra Dutt Sharma and Mrs. Kamla Devi for their blessings.

Dr. Anil Kumar Dhiman
Information Scientist
Gurukula Kangri University
Hardwar - 249 404 (UA)
and
Smt. Yashoda Rani
197, Maktool Puri
Rookee - 247 667 (UA)

August 2004

1
Introduction

Management is a mental process. Right from the dawn of civilization man has been acquiring and sharpening the principle of management for better understanding of nature, better exploitation of resources, better human relations, better organisation and governance. Scientific management though is of fairly recent origin, it has cought the attention of scientists; planners and policy-framers; officers and decision-makers, and in fact every one in every field.

Management is essential for ail kinds of organisations, whether they be business, organisations or non-business organisations, because every organisation requires the making of decisions, the co-ordination of works, the handling of people or personnel, and evaluating the output of work. This managerial task is performed by the officer called Manager. Every organisation, therefore, appoints managers. They may be called by different designations-such as—supervisors, directors, superintendents etc. In a Library also we find so many designations as Librarian, Chief Librarian, Director, Superintendent etc. The management takes place at all levels in the organisational set-up. Every manager performs essentially the same function whether he belongs to the top, or middle or first line management. The only difference is the scope, quality and degree of authority. Qualified managers, therefore, are boon to their firms and to the society. Similarly in a library we find top level, middle level and lower level management. The Librarian with the help of middle level and lower level staff manages a library. Therefore a qualified and professional librarian is an asset to the library as well as to the society.

MEANING AND DEFINITION OF MANAGEMENT

There is a difference of opinion about the meaning and nature of management. Some consider it as a vital function concerned with all aspects of the working of an enterprise. In an enterprise, there is a group of people having certain goals and objectives to achieve. They try to achieve the goal with the help of physical factors of money, machines, materials etc. Similarly in a library, the Librarian tries to achieve the goal with the help of physical factors of money, mechanical tools, men and materials. In general usage, the word management means a special group of people who direct effort towards common objectives through the activities of the people.

Before describing the Library management, it is essential to know the general term of "*management*" which is variously defined by different scientists. Some of important ones are :

C.W. Wilson: "Management is the process of realising and directing human agencies towards attaining a different goal."

John F. Mee: "Management is the art of securing maximum results with a minimum effort so as to secure maximum prosperity and happiness for both employer and employee and give the public the best possible service."

Henry Fayol: "To manage is to forecast and to plan, to organise, to command, to co-ordinate and to control,"

Lawrence A. Appley: "Management is the development of people and not the direction of things."

E.F.L. Brech: "Management is the process of planning and regulating the activities of an enterprise."

Kimball & Kimball: "Management is the art of applying economic principles that underly the control of man and materials in the enterprise under consideration."

Stanley Vance: "Management is simply the process of decision-making and control over the action of human beings for the express purpose of attaining pre-determined goats."

E. *Peterson & E.G. Plowman:* "Management is a technique by means of which the purposes and objectives of a particular human group are determined, classified and effectuated."

James L. Lundi: "Management is principally a task of planning, co-ordinating, motivating and controlling the efforts of others towards a specific objective."

Oliver Sheldon: "Management proper is the function in the execution of policy within the limits set up by the administration and the employment of the organisation for the particular objects set before it."

Rose Moore. "Management means decision-making."

D. E. Mcfarland: "Management is that process by which managers create, direct, maintain, and operate purposive organisations through systematic co-ordinative, co-operative human effort."

Spriegel and Launsburgh: "Management is essentially an executive function. It deals particularly with the active direction of the human efforts."

Sir Charles Renold: "Management is the process of getting things done through the agency of a community."

Donald J. Clough : "Management is the art and science of decision-making and leadership."

F. W. Taylor: "Management is the art of knowing what you want to do and then seeing that it is done in the best and the cheapest way."

George R. Terry: "Management is a distinct process consisting of planning, organizing, actualing and controlling, performed to determine and accomplish the objectives by the use of people and resources."

From the analysis of the above definitions and discussions we come to the conclusion that good management achieves a social objective with the best use of human and material energy and time and with satisfaction for all. Hence management is significant to every organisation, public or private, governmental or business, because it deals with a natural function of human society, namely, the fundamental endeavour of achieving objects.

ADMINISTRATION AND MANAGEMENT

The terms administration and management has been controversial issue in the management literature. Some writers do not make any distinction between the two terms, with others maintain that administration and management are two different terms.

This has led to a great deal of confusion. A few statements by eminent writers of different schools of thought are given here to enable the reader to understand them clearly. Those who held administration and management distinct include *Oliver-Skeldon, Florence and Tead, Spriegel and Launsburgh*, etc. According to them management is a lower level function and is concerned primarily with the execution of policies laid down by administration. Administration determines the organisation, management uses it. Administration defines and the management strives to achieve it. Administration frames the policy; management executes it. Administration is, thus, legislative or determinative. *Breech* states, "management is the total process of executive control" and administration is "that part of management which is concerned with the installation and carrying out of the procedures by which the progress of activities is regulated and checked against plans." Similarly authors like *Walter* and *Haimann* are of the opinion that administration involves broad policy-making and management involves the execution policies laid down by the administration". This can be illustrated in the following way : -

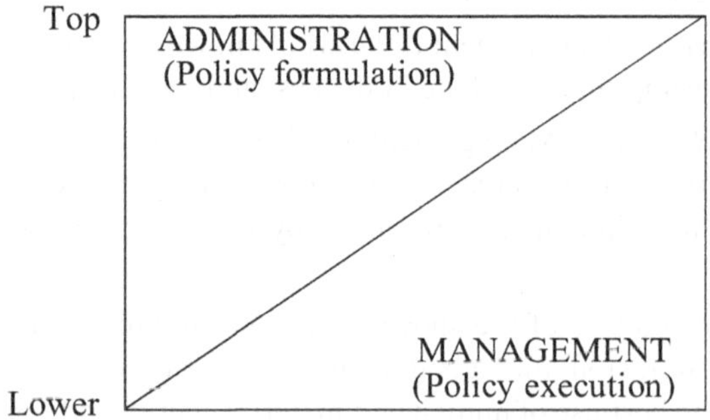

Functions in a organisation

Some of the scholars are of the view that the administration is a part of management. They treat management as having more comprehensive function which includes administration also. *E.F.L. Breech* has viewed management and administration in the following way:-

Management is a generic name for the total process of executive control in industry or commerce. It is a social process entailing responsibility for the effective and economical planning and regulation of the operation of an enterprise, in the fulfillment of given purpose or task. Administration is that part of management which is concerned with the installation and carrying out of the procedures by which it is laid down and communicated and the process of activities regulated and checked against plans.

According to the third approach management and administration are the same. Both involve the same functions, principles and objectives. There is no difference between the two terms in their usage in different countries or different fields of human organisations. *Albert Lepawsky* has observed that "The British conception seems to be the general European usage in which management is given a broader meaning administration". The American usage, administration includes management and organisation.

The distinction between the two terms may be drawn by analysing the origin of the words administration. Its origin is found in the bureaucratic structure of government or in the regulation of the same laws. The government often uses the word administrator, instead of manager, to handle and manage its affairs. In law also, administrators are appointed to look after the estate of a deceased person. While handling the government affairs, administrators are to execute the board policies-laid down by the government, though they may also participate in policy formulation. Similarly, the estate administrator keeps intact and manages the estate according to some specific mandates of law. On the other hand, management is normally used in business sphere. However, whether administration is used in non-business fields or management is used in business fields does not make a fundamental distinction between the two because of the similarity of the process involved in these. Infact, even this distinction is also disappearing.

The basic point of controversy between management and administration lies in terms of coverage of activities. The controversy arises because people call the various level management functions differently. But generally people do not care and they assume that these two words are the same. But the contention of the use of these two words is true. After a careful analysis of the definitions and views of the scholars given against the distinction between these two words, it leads to the conclusion that the top or upper level management may be designated as *'Administration Management'*. Both administrative and managerial functions must be balanced properly if the business is to grow and be able to the meet changing conditions.

LIBRARY MANAGEMENT

ALA Glossary of Library and Information Science defined library management as the process of coordinating total resources of an organisation towards the accomplishment of desired goals of that organisation through the execution of a group of inter-related functions such as planning, organisation, staffing, directing and controlling.

Further the *glossary* differentiates administration and management in the following way:

"So defined management is usually used synonymously with administration in current literature. Administration may be considered to be a broader term, emphasizing the planning function, involving goal setting and major policy; formulation, with management variously limited to the process of coordinating certain functions and activities of an organization toward the accomplishment of its goals."

Administrators are regarded as superior class of peoples in the hierarchy who formulates, goals and objectives as well as the procedures. Where as, managers are executives, who execute the policies and programmes decided by the administrators.

A modern library is considered to be a service oriented but a non - profit organisation. As a matter of fact, it is that part of management which is called "service management" which is more important to libraries than the management of industrial and profit-oriented organisations.

At this juncture, it is necessary for us to have a quick look at some of the basic characteristics of service and not-for-profit organisations. Four important characteristics of service are:

Intangibility (or impalpability) : Services often may not directly appeal to the senses of customers.

Inseparability or customer participation in service production : Service is usually produced in the presence of customers and service production and consumption are inseparable.

Heterogeneity (variability): Service rendered cannot be fully standardised and as a result there will be variations in the quality of service rendered to deficient customers.

Perishability (non-inventoriability) : Many times service cannot be stored and an inventory developed for later physical distribution.

In addition to the above four of fundamental characteristics of service, the other characteristics of the service for not-for-profit organisations are worth noting. It is difficult to measure and compare performance of service organisations. It is equally difficult to inspect quality, determine and implement specifications, take samples and try in advance as well as determine the cost of a service. The relationship between costs and benefits (i.e. inputs and output/outcome) is blurred. Output is often a mix of physical facilities and mental or physical labour. There is no title or ownership transfer when a service is rendered. Service organisations are labour (personality) and equipment intensive and are dominated by professionals. In service organisations, excellence is rare and mediocrity common and, surprisingly, dissatisfaction is rarely conveyed by customers. Service organisations are usually small and operate at a single location. Lastly, market forces play a less significant role in service organisations. The characteristics of service organisations are by no means exhaustive. But these are most basic and have their own impact on the nature and style of service management.

LIBRARY ADMINISTRATION & MANAGEMENT

Library administration, as mentioned in *Harrods* 'Librarians Glossary and Reference Book', is the force behind the machinery of its working routine. To oversee the work of a library in all its relations, and to plan for and promote its usefulness, is the work of the library administrator, and it embarrasses the supervision and development of the work of all departments and the solution of their various problems; "library administration must of necessity begin where library organisation ends". Library management means the skill or manner of handling, controlling and directing the working of a library. In the words of *Girja Kumar* "there has been a qualitative change during the transition from Library administration to library managements. The former is a narrower concept concerned with the set of rules to run the administration. It is atleast concerned with achieving results, improving the quality of human beings, raising the out put and generally improving the environment in which the system operates. The latter is much broader concept viewing all operations strictly in term of results so that a given input brings about maximum output and constantly results in improvements." The principles that govern library management are drawn much from management science as library administration was influenced in the beginning the principles of public administration.

Library management is not merely administering the routine works of the library, rather it is for achieving or accomplishing the objectives of the library. Therefore, a modern library requires more purposeful managerial concept rather than applying some traditional and outdated norms. Hence new kinds of tools, techniques and procedures has to be adopted for satisfactory performance of library Service.

Management of a library as a service organisation is accomplished by a combination of basic management functions and skills as well as management of roles. We can think of three important roles for a library manager:

(i) Interpersonal role: (a) library manager as a figurehead with duties of a ceremonial nature, (b) leading role, (c) liaison role.

(ii) Informational role: (a) perpetually scanning and monitoring information, (b) disseminator role, (c) specific role of informing and satisfying various groups.

(iii) Decisional role: a) As entrepreneur looking out for new ideas and adopt them for change, (b) solving unanticipated problems and handling disturbances, (c) resources allocation role of dividing' work and delegating authority, (d) negotiator role.

Libraries have grown with times in the social, cultural, scientific and technological environments in which they have been developing and operating. Modem libraries are not merely storehouses of knowledge and information but are also live and active institutions involved in a vital service to society. Today knowledge and information are considered as important as energy and biotechnology and hence have to be taken care of and managed well. Scientific management theories, principles and practices are, therefore, increasingly being applied to manage libraries to provide effective and quality service.

Some potential areas of library activities in which modern management techniques and methods could be applied are given below. The list is indicative and not exhaustive. The important point to note is that library managers and workers should develop an attitude and approach to scientific management and cultivate a culture so essential to proper library management.

As modern library is regarded as a big business concern and its management requires not only managerial ability of the highest order but also a highly cultured and sophisticated skill to solve the multi-dimentional problems of a library its Professional Library Manager (Librarian) is expected to possess fundamental knowledge of concepts, principles and theories of management. However it is different to a

Applications of Management Techniques to Library Functions

Library functions	Management techniques	Purpose served
Information and Documentation services such as CAS, Indexing and Abstracting, SDI, etc.	PERT/CPM	To streamline publication schedules and connected operations
Document delivery	Operations Research techniques like queuing theory, linear programming	To develop an effective service delivery system
Information products and services	Marketing techniques	For promoting use & sale
Planning and plan implementation	Network analysis	To develop a plan model
Forecasting	Delphi technique	For planning activities and service
General management	Management information Systems, principles and procedures	For operational efficiency and decision making
Evaluation of operations	Cost benefit analysis and cost effectiveness analysis	For economical operation
Budgeting	PPBS, ZBB	For preparing activity and performance oriented budgets
Housekeeping routine operations	Computer simulation techniques	For streamlining operational efficiency and work output

great extent from the other organizations especially because a library is a non-profit making organisation and usually provides free service to its users.

2
Managements Thoughts and Their Developments

Though the management practice is as old as human civilization when people started living together in groups yet the systematic study of management as a separate branch of knowledge is of recent origin and is largely the product of twentieth century.

Before the-systematic study of management which started close to the 19th century, contributions in the field had come from a variety of sources. For example, the concept of organisation and administration existed in Egypt in 1300 BC. *Confucius's parables* included suggestions for proper public administration and admonitions to choose honest, unselfishness and capable public officers long before Christ. Kautilya had offered sound principles of state administration in 320 BC. *Roman Catholic Church* introduced the concept of staff personnel in church administration which was further carried on by military organisations. The Camera lists, a group of German and Australian public administrators and intellectuals, emphasised systematic administration as a source of strength during the 16th to 18th centuries. These contributions provided some insights about how resources could be utilized more effectively. However, these contributions were outside the field of business and other economic organisations.

The first systematic approach to the study of administration during the 20th century was legalistic. The beginning was made by Weber around 1900 and later by F.W. Taylor by propounding a theory of Scientific management which was confined to the study of organisation, functions, powers and activities, etc. of the public authorities. Later, attempts were made to determine rules for effective and efficient administrative organisation on the basis of empirical evidence.

After the two World Wars, the situation on the global level started changing and the people started thinking of solution to the problems and of using the limited sources in a better way. Growing competition and complexity of managing large business organisations further provided impetus to the development of systematic management concepts and principles, Complexity of managing business organisation has also increased due to (i) increasing size of business organisations (ii) high degree of division of labour and specialization, (iii) increased government regulations and controls to make business more socially-oriented, (iv) organised union activities to put pressures on management, and (v) pressure of various conflicting interest groups to meet their demands from the organisations. The growing competition and complexity in managing business have demanded the efficiency in management process which by and large forced to develop the sound management principles.

MANAGEMENT SCHOOLS OF THOUGHT

There are different schools of thought. Each school centres the management concept around various elements involved. For example, the classical school centres round the concept of 'universalist' or 'traditional nature'; the scientific management school links rewards and motivation for work; the social system school deals with 'contribution-satisfaction equilibrium'; the psycho-sociological school tries to relate 'individuals to their abilities' and the human emotions and other factors that underlie the process of organisation; human behaviour and motivation school is of the view that working conditions have a great role to play in production; and management styles group is of the opinion that a complex of issues like leadership, motivation, decision-making, right and timely communication play an important, role in management process.

The schools of management thought are broadly divided into three parts, they are:

(1) Classical Management Theory (1880's-1920's) which is organisation-centred and has dealt with the economic "rational man", and included scientific management, administrative management, (Henry Fayol, C.I, Barnard, L Urwick) and bureaucratic organisation (Max Weber).

(2) Neoclassical Theory (1920's-1950's) which is person-centered and human-oriented and has emphasised the needs, behaviours

and attitudes of individuals (i.e., "social person" view) and included human relations schools (Elton Mayo, F.J. Roethlisberger, W.J Dickson) and behavioural schools (Maslow, McGregor, Argyris, Herzberg, Lickert, Lewin).

(3) Modern Management Theory (1950's-) which emphasises the complete employee view by revisionist researcher (Litchfield) which includes systems theory, contingency theory, organisational humanism and management science.

Modern management is characterised by a scientific approach, which involves:

- the application of scientific methods and analysis to managerial functions and problems;
- serious consideration of human elements in management, based on psychological studies and behaviour analysis in different situations;
- increasing emphasis on economic effectiveness in all management functions;
- a systems approach, focusing equal attention on all functions of management; and
- use of electronic computers for analysis and studies.

Major schools of management theory may be classified as follows :-

1. Bureaucracy Management School
2. Scientific Management School.
3. Classical School.
4. Human Relations School.
5. Decision Theory School.
6. Systems Theory School
7. Contingency Theory School.

1. Bureaucracy Management School

The first pillar in the classical organisation and management theory was systematically provided by Max Weber (1864-1920), a German Sociologist. He offered bureaucratic model for management of any large and complex organisation in any branch of human activity. He considered bureaucracy as the most efficient form for a complex organization.

Elements of Bureaucracy: The elements of bureaucracy are vital parts of modern business, government, educational and other complex organisations. These elements are: (i) Hierarchy of authority involving superior-subordinate relationship and chain of command; (ii) Clear-cut division of work, based upon competence and functional specialisation. An ordered hierarchy takes the advantage of specialisation; (iii) A system of rules, regulations and procedures. A bureaucrat seeks rationality, routine, objectivity and consistency for his organisation. Behaviour is subject to systematic discipline and control; (iv) A rule by law leads to impersonality of interpersonal or mutual relations. Interpersonal relations are based on positions and not on personalities. We have mechanical and impersonal behaviour; (v) A system of work procedures involving standardisation of methods; (vi) Selection and promotion of employees based upon managerial and/or technical competence; and (vii) Authority and power rest in the office. Bureaucracy recognises only legal *power and authority* given to each office or position in the organisation. The power does not belong to an individual. It is a part of the office.

Bureaucracy provided a rigid machine model of an organisation. It could not account for humanistic model of an organisation which could recognise importance of human, interpersonal or mutual relations in an organisation. Bureaucratic organisation may be preferred where change is not anticipated or where rate of change is slow and it can be predicted. In a stable or static organisation, bureaucracy can work and may be preferred. It is usual in government and in many stable large businesses. But in a dynamic business organisation which can be considered as an open system, we cannot use bureaucracy. There are many glaring disadvantages in bureaucratic organisations: rigidity, impersonal and mechanical or dehumanised environment, higher cost of controls, tendency to forget ultimate goals of the organisation, self-perpetuation and empire building, difficulty of co-ordination and communication, blind faith in rules, regulations and procedures. Above all, bureaucracy cannot offer satisfaction of higher level wants of employees and to that extent it fails miserably to exploit fully the human potential. It offers limited scope for the development of human resources or for management development. Many of the problems of bureaucracy probably would be reduced if the individual needs and characteristics of all people are remembered and are duly considered in making managerial decisions. In other words, we must humanise bureaucracy.

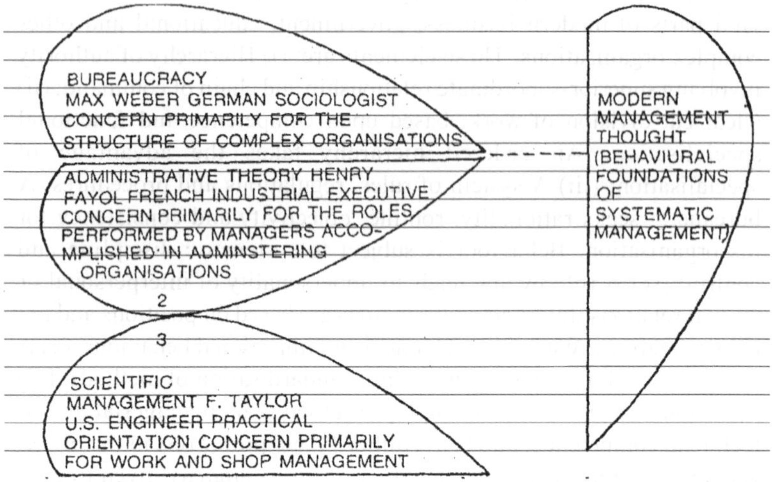

Fig. 1. Emergence of Modern Administrative Thought

2. Scientific Management School

The term scientific management was coined by Louis Brandeis in 1910 in his appearance before Interstate Commerce Commission. "The basic assumption of this school", according to Robert D. Stueart and J.T. Eastlick, is the philosophy that workers are economically motivated, and they will respond with their best efforts if material rewards are closely related to work efforts. The emphasis is on maximum output with minimum effort by eliminating waste and inefficiency at the operative level. The primary emphasis of scientific management was on planning, standardizing and improving human effort at the operative level in order to maximize output with minimum input. F.W.Taylor (1856-1915) eventually became acclaimed as "the Father of Scientific Management." He provided a base upon which much of our current thinking about management is firmly established. He published his famous book *The Principles of Scientific Management* in 1911 and his other contribution was 'Testimony before the special house committee' presented in 1912. These two works combined together published in a book form entitled '*Scientific Management*' in 1947 by Harper and Brothers, New York.

The scientific management involves a complete mental revolution on the part of workers and management, and without complete mental revolution on both sides, scientific management cannot exist. Hence co-operation is essential from both sides for maximising output. Any kind of confrontation, hostility and suspicion between the employees and the employer be avoided to the maximum possible extent.

Scientific management revolutionised the entire shop or plant management. It led to the development of time and motion study, and it refined wage incentive plans. It provided necessary foundation for industrial engineering. If we take a broad view of Taylorism or scientific management, the contributions of Taylor and his eminent followers were truly outstanding and many features of their contributions have proved to be enduring and classical. The basic theme of Taylor was that managers should study work scientifically in order to identify "One best way" to get the job done. Taylor codified his ideas in terms of certain principles which were very popular.

The essence of positive view of scientific management was described by Taylor as follows:

(i) All jobs can be observed and analysed in order to determine the one best way of accomplishing them. Management must use scientific, rather than the rule of thumb approach. (ii) The best man for the job can be scientifically selected and trained. (iii) You can insure that the one best way is followed by paying the man on incentive basis tying his wage or salary to how much he produces, (iv) Put a manager in charge of analysing, planning, preparing and inspecting work. The worker simply carries out the directions and instructions issued by the manager, (v) Harmonious organisation can be obtained by assigning the appropriate man to each set of operations. This will prevent any discord, (vi) Management has to choose the best means of economical production. Specialisation of workers is essential to increase efficiency of production. (vii) Co-operation between labour and management can be achieved. This will ensure maximum output, in place of restricted output by workers, (viii) striving for enterprise and the development of each man to his greatest efficiency and prosperity must be accomplished, (ix) Workers must be inspired or trained to use the scientific methods developed through time and motion study, (x) Management must organise in such a way that it can properly manage and carry out its duties.

Henry L. Gantt (1816-1919), an ardent advocate of scientific management, made four important contributions to the concerns of management : (i) Gantt Chart to compare actual to planned performance, (ii) task and bonus plan for remunerating workers indicating a more humanitarian approach, (iii) psychology of employee relations indicating management responsibility to teach and train workers. (iv) emphasis on service rather on profits. Gantt's contributions were more in the nature of refinements rather than fundamental concepts. They made scientific management more humanised and meaningful to devotees of Taylor. H. Emerson (1853-1931) coined the term *efficiency engineering* to describe his brand of efficiency. He announced twelve principles of efficiency - five relating to employer-employee relations and seven relating to systems in management. He was one of the America's first consultants, thus bringing emphasis to the staff principle. He was the first to codify a set of principles to guide management. D.H.S. Person was called Mr. Management. He was in the education line. Person's contribution was to give scientific management a new academic respectability and to vigorously spread the idea that scientific management was not dedicated to the stop watch and speed-up but rather dedicated to the purposive and scientific determination of effective ways to accomplish given tasks.

Principles of Scientific Management :

For scientific management, Taylor has given some basic principles which are as follows :-

1. **Replacing Rule of Thumb with Science :** He stressed that organised knowledge should be applied which will replace rule of thumb.
2. **Harmony in Group Action :** Taylor has emphasised that attempts should be made to obtain harmony in group action rather than discord.
3. **Co-operation :** Scientific management involves achieving co-operation rather than chaotic individualism. It is based on mutual confidence, cooperation and goodwill. Cooperation between management and workers can be established through mutual understanding and change in thinking.
4. **Maximum Output :** The objective of the scientific management is continuous increased in production. Taylor advised the management and workers to "turn their attention towards increasing in size of the surplus until the size of the surplus becomes so large."

5. **Development of Workers :** In this principle the workers should be developed to the fullest extent possible for their own and for the company's highest prosperity.

Scientific management is also called Taylorism. It emphasized detailed, precise planning of work to achieve efficiency, standardisation, specialisation, simplification. It relied on formal top-down budgeting which led to centralised control system. Scientific techniques of management were employed for the management of physical resources rather than for human resources. Primary emphasis was on the analysis, planning and control functions related to performance of basic tasks. It was assumed that normal economic incentives were enough for implementation of plans and policies. It aimed at improving the efficiency of human work but it considered human being as a rational economic man and he can act just like a machine. It assumed that industrial efficiency can be improved through the application of the methods of science and the movement to high wages for higher productivity. It advocated that standardisation of working conditions, work methods, time study, motion study, standardisation of work, planning of daily tasks. etc., can promote industrial efficiency. Taylor emphasised five concepts on which management theory and practice could be based: (1) research. (2) standards, (3) planning, (4) control and (5) co-operation.

Scientific management certainly used systematic experimental techniques; on the other hand, it showed mechanistic assumptions about human behaviour. To Taylor, human behaviour was indeed a component of a large productive machine. Only those individuals who acted like machines had a place in his productive system. He failed to understand the complexities of human behaviour.

The essence of positive view of scientific management was described by Tailor as follows :

Science, not rule of thumb, Harmony, not discord. Cooperation, not individualism. Maximum output, in place of restricted output. The development of each man to his greatest efficiency and prosperity.

3. Classical School of Management

This school developed in France. Sometimes, this school is referred to as the "traditional" or "universalist" school or administrative management theory.

Scientific management was launched in the U.S.A. by Taylor, and his followers at about 1910. At about the same time administrative theory of management (process management) was initiated by H. Fayol, a French engineer-cum-manager in Europe. Sheldon, Mooney and Reiley, H. Simon, L F. Urwick, L. Gullick, C. Barnard were the followers of Fayol and they contributed a lot to the classical theory.

This pattern of management was established by Henry Fayol. The pyramidal form of organisation, scalar principle, departmentation, delegation, unity of command, exception principle, span of control, authority-responsibility, etc., are some of the important management concepts set forth by the advocates of process school of management principles. He pointed out that technical ability is more dominating on the lower level of management whereas managerial ability is more important on the higher level of management. He also stressed the value of staff to assist line managers in complex organisations.

Fayol proposed that all operations in business organisations can be classified under six headings: (i) Technical (production), (ii) Commercial (purchase and sales), (iii) Financial (finding and controlling capital), (iv) Security (protection of property and persons), (v) Accounting (stock-taking and balance sheet, costing, records), and (vi) Administrative activities (planning, organising, commanding, co-ordinating and controlling). He further noted that with regard to administrative operations: (i) to plan means to study the future and arrange the plan of operations, (ii) to organise means to build up the material and human organisation of the business, (iii) to command means to make to staff do their work, (iv) to co-ordinate means to unite all activities and (v) to control means to see that everything is done in accordance with the rules that have been laid down and instructions given.

Other contributors: J. Mooney (1884-1957) and Alan Reiley were the advocates of process management school. These two management experts identified and elaborated principles of organisation such as coordination, scalar principle, line and staff duties, etc. Two other individuals L. Urwick and L. Gulick also emphasised the functional or process approach to management. They synthesized the ideas of various writers on process management theory and indicated the probability of the science of management.

Fayol has observed that the most important and ability for a worker is technical; the relative importance of manager ability increased as one goes up the scalar chain, with insight becoming the most important ability for top level executives. On the basis of this conclusion, Fayol recognised a widespread need for principles of management and for management teaching. He held that managerial ability should be acquired first in school and later in the workshop. In 1916 in his famour book, '*General and Industrial Management*' he described a number of management/organisation principles. These principles constitute the theory of management or administration of business enterprises. They are enumerated below :

1. **Division of Work :** Fayol has advocated division of work to take the advantage of specialization. As division of work takes place, it leads to development of specialization.
2. **Authority and Responsibility :** Responsibility is corollary of authority. He finds authority as continuation of official and personal factors. In order to discharge the responsibility properly, there should be parity of authority and responsibility.
3. **Discipline :** The personnel serving in an organisation should be disciplined. Discipline may be of two types : *self imposed discipline and command discipline.*
4. **Unity of Command :** Under this principle, the sub-ordinate should receive order from one senior only. It considered as an important aspect in managing an organisation.
5. **Unity of Direction :** According to this principle, each group of activities with the same objective must have one head and one plan. Unity of direction provides better coordination among various activities to be undertaken by an organisation.
6. **Subordination of Individual to General Interest :** This principle advised that common interest is above the individual interest. Individual interest must be subordinated to general interest when there is conflict between the two. Any kind of self interest must be reduced.
7. **Remuneration of Personnel :** Remuneration of employees should be fair and provided maximum possible satisfaction to employees and employers.
8. **Centralization :** Everything which goes to increase the importance of subordinate's role is decentralization, every thing

which goes to reduce it is centralization. So, there should be centralization of authority.

9. **Scalar Chain :** There should be scalar chain of authority and of communication ranging from the highest to the lowest. It suggests that each communication going up or coming down must flow through each position in the line of authority and it should be unbroken line of authority. For this purpose, Fayol has suggested *'gang plank'* which is used to prevent the scalar chain from bogging down action.
10. **Order :** According to this principle there should be a place for every thing and every thing should be in its place.
11. **Equity :** Equity is the combination of justice and kindness. In dealing with subordinate equity is essential.
12. **Initiative :** Within the limits of authority and discipline, managers should encourage their employees to take initiative. Initiative is concerned with thinking out and execution of a plan.
13. **Stability of Tenure :** No employee should be removed within short time. Unnecessary turnover is both cause and effect of bad management.
14. **Esprit de Corps :** This principle emphasises team work and the importance of effective communication in achieving the same.

Other Principles of Management: Followers of H. Fayol gave other principles of management such as universality of management, control by exception, decision by exception, equality of authority and responsibility, power and accountability, and coordination.

By introducing two modifications to Fayol's concepts, we could easily install the foundation of modern management theory; (1) Management is the planning, organising, command, co-ordination and control of technical, financial commercial, accounting and security activities. (2) It is not command *but* motivation and leadership which can help us to understand why men and women work and how to secure from them maximum productivity. Thus, we substitute motivation and leadership for command. Direction and command have outlived their utility to get things done through people. The manager today has to encourage, communicate, develop, guide and stimulate his employees to secure higher output. Modern management places the greatest emphasis on leadership and motivation as keys to productivity.

The pattern of management that developed in Du Pont Company had a far reaching influence on modern business enterprise. The writings of Taylor and Fayol stimulated further investigations into the theory of management and its application to business. The example of Du Font provided a pattern that was followed with great success by many other companies.

The works of Taylor and Fayol - the two pioneers in the evolution of managerial thought are in reality complementary; (i) They both pointed out that the efficiency and effectiveness of management must act as the master-key to industrial productivity and progress. (ii) Both implied scientific approach and scientific method to solve the managerial problems. (iii) Taylor was a management engineer. He worked primarily on the operative level from the bottom of the organisation hierarchy upwards. Whereas Fayol concentrated on the Managing Director and worked downwards on the organisation hierarchy. Fayol was a management philosopher. (iv) Both, however, stressed on the technical or professional aspects of the management and both are responsible for the managerial revolution which took place after 1940.

In short, Taylor introduced scientific plant management whereas Fayol and Du Font company introduced the foundation of the pattern of theory and process of management.

Social scientists described administrative theory as an ideal bureaucracy. It places heavy emphasis on the power and authority structure of an organisation. It enjoys all the advantages of bureaucracy such as order, stability and certainty. It also suffers its disadvantages such as rigidity, impersonality, and excessive categorisation. It is institutionally power-centred and cannot give greater scope for individualism. Hence, it can not provide democratic organisations. Administrative theory is a way to achieve bureaucracy. If you desire bureaucracy administrative theory will also be valued. If you desire more democracy, you will have to modify administrative theory considerably.

4. Human Relations School :

The human relations or the behavioural approach to management began with the Hawthrone Plant of the General Electric Company Chicago, who experimented in 1927 to 1932.

Elton Mayo (1880-1949) with his associates in his "Hawthorne studies" pointed out that workers were not simply '*cogs in the machinery.*' Instead, the employee morale both individually and in groups - could have profound effects on productivity. Managers should adopt a more '*people-oriented*' approach to management. Management should recognise that people are essentially social beings and not merely economic beings. As social beings, they are members of a group and management should understand the group attitudes and group psychology also in determining solutions to management problems.

Human relationists made very significant contributions to management thought by brining into limelight human and social factors in organisations, but these concepts were carried beyond an appropriate limit. Later on, it was proved that there is no direct and deep connection between morale and productivity. Morale is an elusive quality and it is not a very meaningful concept of management thought. There are many other factors which influence productivity directly. Productivity is influenced by plant efficiency, work environments, managerial style, job contents, man-machine system financial resources, marketing efficiency and materials movement, etc.

Frederick Herzberg studied the motivation factor in management. According to him, hygienic and psychic factors determine the motivation to work. Hygienic factors are those relating to working conditions, salary and fringe benefits, policies and the type of administration. The psychic factors include the desire for achievement, recognition, challenge, job satisfaction, a sense of sharing responsibility and belongingness. Abraham Maslow viewed the needs of workers and their relative importance or hierarchy in terms of psychological needs such as belongingness, esteem and self-actualization, and physiological needs like food and shelter.

The human relations school of thought has since then been vastly enriched by systématic researchers and the deductive contribution made by so many thinkers.

Human relations, together with the behavioural sciences constitute the neo-classical theory of management which opened the door for deliberate shift from bureaucratic to participative and democratic leadership or managerial style.

Distinction between Human Relations and Scientific Management

Human Relations	Scientific Management
1. No universal principles	1. Principles for universal application
2. Focus on man behind the machine	2. Focus on the machine
3. Interpersonal relations among the people working together	3. Standardised and the best way of things
4. Use of the concepts of group dynamic, motivation, morale, job satisfaction	4. Use of time and motion study, the wage plans, functional foremansh
5. Man is social animal	5. Man is an economic animal
6. Application of the knowledge of psychology, sociology and anthropology	6. Use of the knowledge of physics, chemistry and mathematics
7. Improvements in attitudes and morale	7. Improvements in productivity and efficiency

5. Decision Theory School

These schools perceive management in terms of decision-making. These are primarily concerned with the study of rational decision procedures and also the way managers actually reach decision. Major contribution in this approach has come from Simon. Other contributor are March, Cyert, Forrester, etc. The major emphasis of this approach is that decision making is a decision-making unit. Therefore, the basic problem in managing is to make rational decision. From this point of view, decision theory approach has the following features :-

1. Management is essentially decision making.
2. The members of the organisation are decision-makers and problem-solvers.
3. Quality of decision affects the organisational effectiveness.
4. All factors affecting decision-making are the subject- matter of study of management.

In decision-theory, the inbuilt assumption being that mathematical models and quantitative processes can serve as a basis of all management

6. System Theory School

Chester I. Barnard (1886-1961) reviewed the manager's functions and pattern of functioning as a system of cooperative effort in a formal organization. An understanding of the functioning of human society, why people cooperate, and the evolution of the system of such cooperation and related areas may contribute to the theory of management, which is a human group activity. Barnard analysis brought out the following facts:

1. Physical and biological limitations of individuals lead them to cooperate when they work in groups. While the basic limitations are physical and biological, once people cooperate, psychological and social limitations of individuals also play a part in inducing cooperation.
2. The act of cooperation leads to the establishment of cooperative systems in which physical, biological, personal and social factors are involved. The continuation of cooperation demands on its effectiveness and efficiency.
3. Any cooperative system may be divided into two parts: an *organization* which includes only the interactions of people in the system, and 'other elements'.
4. Organizations can, in turn, be divided into two kinds : the *formal* organization, which is a set of consciously coordinated social interactions that have a deliberate and joint purpose, and the *informal* organization which refers to social interactions without a common or consciously coordinated joint purpose.
5. The formal organization cannot exist unless there are persons who are able to communicate with one another, are willing to contribute to group action, and have a conscious common purpose.
6. Every formal organization must include the following elements:
   (a) A system of functionalizations so that people can be specialized.
   (b) A system of effective and efficient incentives that will induce people to contribute to groups action.
   (c) A system of power authority which will lead group members to accept the decisions of executives.
   (d) A system of logical decision-making.

Systems Approach to Management

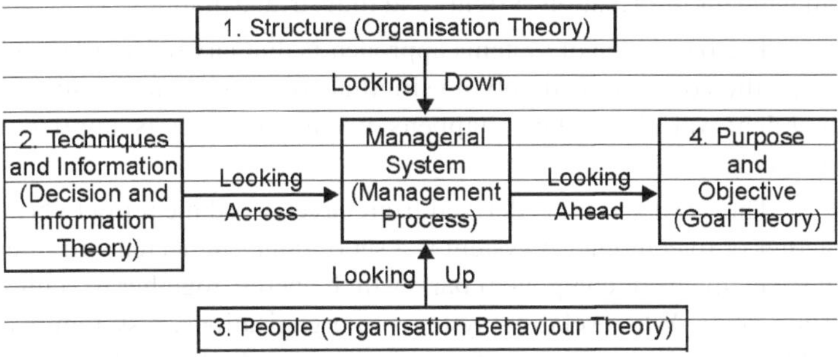

Fig. 2. Systems Approach to Management

7. The functions of the executive in this formal organization are:
   (a) Maintenance of organization communication through a scheme of organization, together with loyal, responsible and capable people, and a compatible executive informal organization.
   (b) Securing essential services from individuals in the organization.
   (c) Formulation and definition of purpose.
8. The executive functions enter the process through the work of the executive in integrating the whole and in finding the best balance between conflicting forces and events.
9. To make the executive effective requires a high quality of responsible leadership. As Barnard emphasizes, "cooperation, not leadership is the creative process; but leadership is the indispensable fulminator of its forces".

The systems approach to management and organisation indicates a new stream of management thought under modern theory of management. Since 1950, we have a period of refinement, extension and synthesis of management thought and practice. While the behavioural and quantitative schools were developing new concepts and techniques of management, a new direction in management thought appeared which is usually called as the systems approach. Basically it took up where the process management school left off in attempting to unify management theory. It stresses the inter-relatedness and interdependence of all activities within an organisation. It includes operations research, behavioural sciences, social technical systems, management information systems and industrial dynamics.

The basic idea of systems approach is that any object must rely on a method of analysis involving simultaneous variations of mutually dependent variables. This happens when approach is applied is management.

The word system is derived from Greek word meaning to bring together or to combine. A system is a set of inter-connected and inter-related elements or component parts which operate together to achieve certain goals. When relating systems to organisations, a system is an established arrangement of components which leads to the accomplishment of particular objectives as per plan.

This definition has three significant parts: (i) Every system is goal-oriented and it must have a purpose or objective to be attained. The objective provides the basis for evaluating functions performed within the system. (ii) In designing the system we must establish the necessary arrangement of components. This is nothing but organising function of management. (iii) Inputs of information, material and energy are allocated for processing as per plan so that the outputs can achieve the objective of the system *viz.*, productivity and satisfaction.

When systems approach is applied to an organisation, we have the following features of an organisation as an open adaptive system: (i) It is a subsystem of its broader environment. (ii) It is goal-oriented people with a purpose. (iii) It is a technical subsystem — using knowledge, techniques, equipment and facilities. (iv) It is a structural subsystem — people working together on interrelated activities. (v) It is a psychosocial system people in social relationships. (vi) It is co-ordinated by a managerial subsystem creating, planning organising, motivating, communicating and controlling the overall efforts directed towards set goals.

Elements of environment include persons, physical resources, climate, economic and market conditions, attitudes, competition, and laws. The environment offers both opportunities and risks. Management overcomes risks and exploits opportunities.

An organisation and its environment are interdependent. The environment of an organisation provides inputs, *i.e.*, resources and opportunities and limits which determine the nature of success of an organisation. The output is goods and services desired by its environment. The activities of an organisation must be acceptable to the environment. An organisation has also a feedback. The environment, reacts to the output of an organisation. On this reaction, the environment determines its future inputs into the organisation. The environment, is dynamic.

7. Contingency Theory School

It was found that behavioural approaches worked in some situation, but not in all. The same was true for quantitative-approaches. Neither of these approaches could claim universal applications in the real world situations. This was more apparent since 1980. Many management experts now believe that a systems-based theory could solve the quantitative/behaviour dilemma. Open and adaptable systems approach is called Contingency Approach. A business organisation is now regarded as an open and adoptative system which alone can cope with the increasing complexity and changing environmental influences. Contingency or situational approach seems better suited to lead management out of the present management theory jungle.

Systems approach emphasises that all subsystems of an organisation along with the supersystem of environment are interconnected and interrelated. Contingency approach analyses and understands these interrelationships so that managerial actions can be adjusted to demands of specific situations or circumstances. Thus contingency approach enables us to evolve practical answers to the problems demanding solutions. Organisation design and managerial actions most appropriate to specific situations will have to be adopted in order to achieve best possible result *under the given situation.* The performance of each managerial function is closely connected to an analysis of the total situation.

The basic theme of contingency can be viewed in these words "when a system in an organisation behaves in response to another system or sub system, we say that response is contingent on environment. Hence, a contingency approach an approach where the behaviour of one sub unit is dependent on its environmental relationship to other units or sub units that have control over the consequences desired that subunit."

MANAGEMENT THOUGHT IN THE LIGHT OF INDIAN ETHOS AND INSIGHT

Western management thought could not produce the true holistic and integrative principles for management philosophy. Ancient Indian wisdom provides value-based holistic approach to link our ancient culture and modern management so that we can have a new and authentic philosophy of management.

The essential link is found in holism starting with the course of subjective management, new movement in management thinking and practice, a movement that will make "the managerial revolution" of 21st century. The holistic or integrative principle is a goal that unites all the different aspects of business into one common social, economic and ecological goal. Business organisation based on objective terms was concerned exclusively with what is *prays* or socially desired in contrast with what is socially and ecologically desirable or needed, *i.e., Sreyas* (which is conveniently ignored).

Under holism, we have to develop unity and harmony between: (i) spirit and science, (ii) values and skills, (iii) subject and object, (iv) left-brain skills and right-brain skills (v) subjective and object, (vi) management of self and management of other people for getting things done through and with them. (vii) man and machine, (viii) economic development and human/ecological development, (ix) profit motive and social responsibility, (x) individual benefit and public benefit, (xi) internal development and external development, (xii) quality of life *i.e.,* standard of life and quantity of life or standard of living. We want enriched quality of life for all. Wealth is not merely for rising consumption. It is essentially a means for public good.

Under the Western management thought business is created by society as its instrument of wealth and welfare, functioning for socially desired goals, through *result-oriented means,* in short-term success and continuous conflict between individuals and businesses.

Under Indian ethos and insight, business was created by society as an instrument of wealth *for* welfare, to attain socially desirable or needed goals (*i.e., shreyas* and not *preyas* goals), through ethically worthy means (*i.e.* value-driven means and value-driven goals), resulting in a generation of healthy, wholesome individuals who carry human and ethical values and positive impulses in their community.

If management adopts value-oriented holistic management as per ancient Indian insight, the practice of management will surely acquire a new look or appearance. Developing Macro Vision is the practical need of the day. The times are rapidly changing. It will no longer be a purely objective exercise to achieve of external results even at the cost of internal disharmony and unrest. On the other hand, it will give equal emphasis on subjective and objective aspects of development of individual, organisations and society. Indian insight wants individuals to emerge as important positive, wholesome, harmonious individuals with a sense of growing towards their own total fulfillment. In this way, managers will be able to create a healthy, wholesome, harmonious and happy community, of which the managers themselves will be satisfied members. We can have both increasing standard of life and also increasing standard of *living* of all members of the society and the nation. We shall assure *enriched quality* of life and also *enriched material* prosperity. Individuals, organisation and society all will have sustained economic growth without ecological damages, *e.g.*, pollution of environment.

The Indian wisdom insists on concepts such as *yajna* spirit (sacrificing individual desires in favour of social benefits), *sreyas* (preferring long-term benefits over short-term *preyas* gains), sharing in joy and a sense of cosmic harmony. Here, business is regarded as a means for the evolution of human society towards its own perfection, with all its activities being supplementary to and justifiable only in terms of perfection. *Means and ends both will honour human and ethical values.*

In spite of many streams of management thought in the West, we have still the unstable state of management theory. We need a modern *synthesis* to pull together ideas from all stream of thought. Indian Insight can bring about synthesis through holistic approach and reconcile all dualities. Holistic approach alone can give us the Macro Vision of Life as ONE expressing MANY diverse forms.

Eastern Insight can introduce integration or synthesis in management theory and practice.

The tables given depict briefly the comparative picture of the present and the future management thought and practice.

Table 1. Management Today & Tomorrow

Items		Management (Oriented by Science and technology, Western Approach)	Management (Oriented by Values and adopting holistic approach Indian and Eastern)
1.	Belief	Production, Productivity, profit at any cost.	Material gain, with belief in achieving human and social welfare also.
2.	Guidance	Management guided by mind only, led away by ego and desire. Soul-less management.	Management by consciousness, power beyond mind i.e.. soul. Interiorised Management.
3.	Emphasis	Worker development, Management of Others, Profit maximisation. Human being given only lip sympathy.	Development of Man Integrated Growth Harmony, Happiness and Health, Management of Self.
4.	Tools	5 Ms as Resources - men, money materials, machines, markets. Science & Technology, Information for decision making.	Men, Machines, Materials and Methods as Conscious Partners–all having consciousness whether manifested or dormant. Information and intuition for decisions. Ethics and values combined with skills.
5.	Problem-solving	Conflict resolution by negotiation, compromise, arbitration liquidation of differences only for a temporary period. No reference to higher consciousness.	Conflicts resolution through integration and synthesis on stressing superordinate common-goals so that enduring harmony and unity is assured. Self-intro-spection, stepping back aids for solution.
6.	Decision making	Brain-storming (Round the table approach).	Brain-stilling (Room of silence).
7.	Development process	Physical Vital and Mental only. Soul or Spirit ignored. Material development only even at the cost of man and Nature.	Integrated Development, Whole-man approach, breath control and meditation emphasised. Human Enrich-ment and Total quality.
8.	Approach	External Behaviour Mental, Material, Selfish only, Soulless.	Noble Attitudes, Inner guidance, Team spirit, Total Harmony, Global good.

Table 2. Management Thoughts Redefined

	Term	General Definition	I.E.M. Definition
1.	Management	Gettings things done.	Helping other people to produce extraordinary results.
2.	Productivity	Related to plant capacity.	Related to men's capability.
3.	Planning	Management by results.	Management by strategy.
4.	Effective supervision	Concern for task and not for people.	Produce performers. Help the subordinates to develop leadership quality.
5.	Motivation of People	Maslow's theory of needs with some modifications.	Emphasis on self-motivation by subordinates to have creative joy and autonomy.
6.	Resources	Reliance almost on external resources.	Reliance almost on Internal resources.
7.	Health of the Company	Balance Sheet and Profit/ Loss A/C money-oriented,	People oriented performance, environment friendly. Private Public benefit.
8.	Profitability	In terms of money, Social costs not included in Balance Sheet.	In terms of good public image, Social costs internalised. Trust of customers and society.
9.	Hygiene factor	Attention only on job enrichment.	Primary emphasis on mind enrichment.
10.	Rights and duties	Emphasis on taking not on giving. Rights become primary. Duties become subsidiary.	Emphasis on giving not on taking. Duties given great importance and right assume secondary value.
11.	Marketing	Keen competition to capture and retain demand: market driven economy.	Through co-operation by playing complementary role. Social awareness in marketing.
12.	System	Set of inter-related elements working as a whole. Hardware aspect. More emphasis on quantity and objective aspect.	Pattern of particular response expressed through organisational functioning. Software aspect. Equal emphasis on quality/quantity with emphasis on subjective aspect.
13.	Structure	Hierarchical.	Organic evolution, autonomous.

14.	Growth	Ultimately dependent on turnover of goods.	Co-ordinating private and public benefit.
15.	Job satisfaction	Hygiene factor. Creativity ignored.	Through innovation uniqueness, extraordinary result, trouble shooting.
16.	Training	Functional skills not value oriented and holistic.	Value oriented, Holistic approach and equal emphasis on both i.e., values/skills.
17.	Man-Machine equation	Machine dominates man as human being receives lip sympathy.	Man behind the machine given due regard. Healthy Philosophy of life. Emotional stability.
18.	Man Placement	As per qualifications and experiences.	More stress on natural inclination and character.
19.	Quality	Product quality by I.S.O., TQM., Q.C., Human value, quality plays minor role. Crises of Values, Adulteration is widespread.	Human quality, values, character, mind-enrichment, whole-man approach. Mind and matter are given *equal* treatment.

3
New Concepts in Management

MANAGEMENT BY OBJECTIVES

The latest thinking about management is that best results can be achieved through Management By Objectives and as such it has now been accepted as the best management approach. The principles of this system were propounded in 1954 by Peter Drucker. It is based on two main principles :

(i) Results Orientation ; and

(ii) Particular view of human behaviour.

This system helps in realization of an organisation's goals by its members as if those are their personal goals. The mechanism used to achieve the aims is that goal—setting process is made not only an open secret but all the members of the organisation are also made to realise the importance of the goals, thereby resolving the various inconsistencies and misunderstandings before these take firm roots. Any MBO system has four basic components :

1. Setting Objectives.
2. Developing Action Plans.
3. Conducting Periodic Reviews, and
4. Appraising Annual Performance.

This system has been based on Maslow's theory of hierarchy of needs', and Herzberg's theory of identification of motivators and hygiene factors in the work environment. The former theory identifies the factors i.e. responsibility, achievement, and recognition while the latter takes into account better salary and other conditions of service. Besides McGregor's theory of management system and Likert's theory of participation fortify MBO theory. The first theory states that if employees are properly motivated to work, they are sure to be achievement—oriented. The second theory provides the mechanism of participative style of leadership and thus fosters commitment to objectives of an organisation.

Merits of the System

The MBO system has the following benefits.

1. Improvement in Management Performance : It ensures managerial efficiency because manager's commitment to organisation's objectives increases as the members are made responsible for the achievement of their set objectives.

2. Improvement in Planning : This is possible because each manager's individual goals are made consistent with those of each other and with those of the organisation because these are decided in the presence of their superiors.

3. Improved Co-ordination : Improved planning and agreement on tapping of resources needed for the purpose result in better co-ordination of the organisation as a whole.

4. Improved Control : Improved co-ordination results in improved control.

5. Improved Flexibility : Each manager knows fully well his own objectives and those of the organisation and their priority for them, so improved flexibility is possible.

6. Improved Superior-Subordinate Relationships : It provides increased opportunities for communication between the superiors and subordinates at various stages, such as at the time of objective-setting and performance appraisal.

7. Improved Personal Development : It provides better opportunities for personal development as it fosters personal responsibility.

Demerits of the System

Many writers have challenged MBO theory as enunciated by Maslow and Herzberg. These include Victor H. Vroom and Edwin A. Locke.

The main attack against the MBO theory is that it has been oversimplified and that the theory as enunciated by Herzberg is a theory of job satisfaction and not a complete theory of work motivation and improved job performance.

Second plank of attack is that MBO theory does not take into account other variables which affect job performance. For example Victor Vroom gave three variables i.e. Valence (preference), expectancy and force while according to Porter and Lawler, these include efforts, performance, reward and satisfaction. Similarly, Smith and Cranny have proposed a three-pronged approach i.e. effort, satisfaction and reward.

The merits detailed above outweigh demerits because an organisation's inputs, outputs and processes are critically examined through self-analysis. This is the main reason why MBO theory is respected inspite of severe criticism against it.

MBO's Relevance to Libraries

Libraries can benefit from MBO though in a limited way. MBO is relevant to various technical and procedural operations in Libraries such as acquisition processes and technical services. MBO is beneficial to middle management of library. In other words, it is relevant to Sectional and Departmental Heads. It is useful for libraries because a library can be managed by sharing responsibility among those who are responsible for managing a library. However, those benefits which are likely to accrue from MBO approach should be carefully weighed keeping in view the staff and monetary costs.

PERFORMANCE APPRAISAL

When we look back at the history of management, we find that management has undergone several changes and it can be divided into Pre-scientific Era, Scientific Era and Human Relation Era. Human relation is the process of effective motivation of individuals in a given situation so as to achieve greater human satisfaction and accomplishment of desired goals. As stated earlier, there are various techniques of management which can be applied to any organisation, such as Bureaucratic Management. Participative Management, Management by Objectives and Total Quality Management etc.

Employee appraisal techniques are said to have been used first time by the Walter Dill Scott, the US Army Officer during first world war when he adopted the "man-to-man" rating system for evaluating military personnel. During the 1920-30 period, relation wage structures for hourly paid workers were adopted in industrial units. Under this system, the policy of giving grade wage increments on the basis of merit was accepted. These plans were called merit rating programmes which continued to be called so upto the mid-fifties. In the early fifties, however, attention began to be paid to the performance appraisal of technical, professional and managerial personnel. Since then, as a result of experiments and great deal of study, the philosophy of performance appraisal has undergone several changes. Now, the so called merit rating is changed to performance appraisal. It is a continuous learning and development through the performance of jobs and it cannot be denied that organisations can use staff appraisal to control their size. Indeed it is the most powerful tool in rationalising the resources and goes on to suggest that by linking appraisal schemes to selection, training, and career planning, an organisation can control employee behaviour and organisational directions. But, it is one of the most neglected techniques in library and information centres despite its advantages in ensuring the efficient and effective running of the services.

Performance appraisal or PA is the process by which an employee's contribution to an organisation during a specific time period is assessed. And it can be effectively used to improve employee motivation and performance, if used properly and can lead to disastrous conditions if used inappropriately. It is a multicomponent process of identifying, observing, measuring and developing human performance in organisations. Where, the identification is the process of determining what areas are to be focused on which job analysis is required as a means of identifying performance scale. The observation indicates that all appraisal criteria must be sufficiently observed so that a fair and accurate judgement can be made. Observations on infrequent and non-performance characteristics may lead to poor ratings. The measurement is the central feature of appraisal. The evaluator must somehow translate the observations into value judgement representing the level of subjects. The development suggests that performance appraisal should also focus on improving future performance.

Objectives of PA

The following are the objectives of good performance appraisal system:

- Facilitating integrated growth of employee.
- Helping employees to know their strengths and weaknesses and

thus enable them to improve performance of self and organisation.

- Helping the creation of an enabling organisation where opportunities are available for fuller utilisation of the known potentials of the employees. The climate of such an organisation is one of the mutuality, trust, collaboration and openness, etc.
- Generating valid data about employees for personnel functions like training, placement, selection and promotion etc.
- Providing feedback and guidance by the superior to the employees for improvement of their performance.

Purposes of PA

The following may be the purposes of performance appraisal in any organisations:

- Administrative decisions, such as promotion, transfers and allocation of financial rewards etc.
- Employee's development, i.e., identification of training needs and performance feedback etc.
- Personnel research, such as generation of manpower information for salary and wages determination, career planning, man job matching promotion, helping supervisors to know their subordinates and also to help subordinates to assess their achievement and failure etc.

Characteristic of a Good Performance Appraisal System

A good performance appraisal system would have the following characteristics:

- The organisation believes that development of employees is in its own interest.
- The organisation will provide opportunities and conditions for the development and optimisation of human resources.
- The corporate management is willing to invest adequate time and resources for the development of employees.
- Managers have concern for the growth of subordinates.
- Employees are willing to avail the given opportunities for growth and receive necessary help from the managers for their development and improving performance.

Types of Performance Appraisal

There are two types of the performance appraisal system; Cost Centred Appraisal System and Objective Centred Appraisal System. Of these, the first one is meant for profit making organisations and second one is meant for non-profit making organisations. Since, library and information centres are primarily non-profit making organisations, hence the objective centred appraisal can be implemented in these centres.

Measurement of Performance Appraisal

Several methods and techniques are available for measurement of performance of an employee. Broadly, these can be divided into two methods viz., traditional methods and modern methods. Traditional methods lay emphasis on the rating of the individual's personality traits, such as initiative, dependability, drive, responsibility, integrity, leadership potential, intelligence, judgement and organising ability etc. On the other hand, modern methods lay emphasis on the evaluation of work results such as, job achievements rather than personality traits. The result oriented appraisal tends to be more objective and worthwhile, especially for counselling and developmental purposes. Further, both of these are subdivided as shown in Table 1.

Table 1. Methods of Measurement of Performance Appraisal

Traditional methods	Modern methods
Straight ranking method	Assessment centre
Man-to-man comparison method	Appraisal by results
Grading method	Human asset accounting method
Graphic rating scale method	
Forced choice description method	
Check list method	
Free form essay method	
Critical incidents method	
Group method	
Field review method	

Performance Standards

There are some criteria against which individuals' behaviour and output are judged in order to evaluate his performance. Generally, there are three features which define performance standards viz., evaluative component, externally established standards and established entities. The evaluative components serve as criteria for judging effectiveness and established entities usually remain stable over a time and across individuals. As per Locke and Lamam, performance standards are the rule to measure or evaluate things. They distinguish standards and goals, by defining the latter as the aim or end of an action. The standards are usually consistent across individuals, whereas goals are assigned on an individual basis. These are used in a variety of personnel decisions, including but not limited to performance appraisal, training, promotion and reward for performance. But evaluative standards can influence the motivation and job satisfaction of those to whom the standards are applied.

For the development of performance standards, several methods have been suggested:

- production records
- work sampling
- time study data
- standard time data
- subjective standard based on production of fastest worker, group action or personal interview with worker.

Each one of above methods has its own merits and demerits. But the staff formula given by Dr. S.R. Ranganathan contains systematic work, Job analysis and routine works etc. This can be used in library and information centres with some modifications.

Why Performance Appraisal System in LIS Centres?

As stated earlier, this is the most neglected and under-used technique of management in the library and Information fields. But, the following points ensure why performance appraisal is needed in library and information centres:

(i) To ascertain the definition of the work or job to be performed as there is an urgent need for clear demarcation of the jobs.

(ii) Wherever amenable, we should establish acceptable performance standard in terms of specific measurable desired behaviour. This calls for defining units of job, the time taken for doing the job and the modes of performing these jobs.

(iii) To identify the present performance level of the library staff in terms of specific measurable behaviour which is considered to be desirable or acceptable.

(iv) To identify the needed improvement in library staff behaviour consistent with the objective of library science.

(v) To provide a basis of feedback for the performance of library staff in differences.

TOTAL QUALITY MANAGEMENT OR TQM

In earlier days, libraries were considered merely as a store house of books but with the advent and use of modern technology the complete scenario has changed and nowadays these are known as Library and Information Centres because at present they are not only storing and preserving the information but also generating and disseminating them to the users for maximum use and benefits. Information explosion, increasing rate of obsolescence, increasing and complex information needs of the clientele, interdisciplinary nature of scattered .information, continued resource constraints and vide variation in quality and reliability of information have produced a major challenge in front of librarians that how the information should be managed so that a library & information centre could provide right information at right time to the right user. It is rightly stated that 'the library' has to move from the state of being merely a passive customer of knowledge to the level of becoming a platform for generation, exchange and utilization of knowledge.

Librarians must know how to cope intelligently and objectively with the changes in technological advances by adopting a newer technique of management for delivering library product and services. Therefore, the traditional techniques of managing a library centre become helpless and philosophy of participative management involving every member from the team of personnel to achieve total quality in every aspect would now become relevant, meaningful and valuable i.e., TQM.

What is TQM

The concept of quality control emerged around 1920s in United States simply to control the creation of defective items in industrial process. This concept did not immediately take its roots there but it did in Japan after world war II, as a result of which Japan emerged as a world quality leader. The concept central to TQM returned to United

States in early 1980s and quality revolution is continuing to develop there.

TQM is concerned with the integration of all efforts in the organization towards quality and customer care. According to Tenner and DeToro, TQM is based on:

- One objective: continuous improvement;
- Three principles: customer focus, process improvement and total involvement and
- Six supporting elements: leadership, education and training, a supportive structure, communications, reward and recognition and measurement.

ISO has defined TQM as 'A management approach of an organization centered on quality, based on participation of all its members and aiming at long term success through customer satisfaction and benefits to all members of the organization and to society'. Brockman, has defined TQM us a management philosophy, embracing all activities through which the needs of customer, the community and the objectives of the organization are satisfied in the most efficient and cost effective way by maximizing the potential of all employees in a continuing drive for improvement. In TQM, there are no seniors and no juniors but all work as team members to look at problems which are of integrated and cooperative nature.

So, TQM ultimately aims to improve product quality and customer, satisfaction as per their needs and expectations.

According to Joseph and Berk, continuous improvement, prevention rather than detecting defects/customer focus and universal responsibility are four basic elements of Total Quality Management. TQM practice in any organization may lead to the following benefits:

- Creates quality awareness;
- Orients work and workers to customer needs and satisfaction;
- Generates team spirits;
- Improves performance, process and quality and
- Enhance productivity and job security

Principles of TQM

The management scientists have also derived certain principles from the philosophy of TQM concept, which can be described as follows:

(i) Leadership : Effective leadership is the foundation for TQM. Top management should provide the leadership for quality awakening in the organisation. They should evolve effective plans and provide leadership in achieving the objectives.

(ii) Internal and External Customers : The external customers are the outsiders who buy the organisation's products or services. The internal customers are the staff of the organisation including those not in direct contact with the external customers. These staff interact with other staff as may are involved in dispensation of services of the organisation. In this way the customer orientation can pervade the organisation.

(iii) Customer Satisfaction : The customer has to decide what the standards should be and not the supplier/producer. If the organisation decides the standards, the product may not satisfy the customer's requirements. Therefore, quality is customer defined.

(iv) Performance Measurement : Performance measurement needs to be based upon timely measures and feedback on performance through superior quality information systems.

(v) Measure of Success : Every organisation has to define what is the criterion for success in their operations and how to measure it. For instance, one of the measures is sales of products and the resulting profits. Thought it is difficult to measure the customer's satisfaction, it can be measured through indirect indicators such as increased sales, repeated orders, exports, etc.

(vi) Continuous Improvement is the Goal : Continuous improvement should be the responsibility of everyone in the organisation. The organisation should not be satisfied with one-time success. It should aim at sustaining success through continuous improvement, because customers will expect still better services and products.

(vii) Training and Education are Essential : The Manual specifies the jobs and what they are supposed to do and how they can do them. The employee should be educated and trained in their trade; otherwise they cannot understand the documentations and manuals.

(viii) Communication is Essential : Right communication is to be maintained to carry out the jobs in the right way. Manuals and other such documentations help to achieve proper communication. The organisation should also improve communications through newsletters, notice-boards, problem solving sessions and departmental meetings etc.

(ix) Attitudes Towards Quality : Every employee should develop an attitude to improve the quality of the organisation.

(x) Team Work : The organisation has to make every effort to mould the employees to work as a team. It is the only way through which an organisation can achieve its objective and practice. Recognition of achievements is also equally essential for the success of TQM programme.

(xi) Employee Involvement : Employee involvement means that each individual must take the initiative and rely upon someone else. To achieve this, the organisation needs a culture which encourages this behaviour. Everyone must understand that they contribute equally and can only succeed through co-operation and support.

Benefits of TQM

In the light of the aforesaid elaboration of the concept of TQM, the following benefits can be derived:

(i) Work itself becomes more interesting through a greater involvement of employees.

(ii) Increase in general productivity.

(iii) Less absenteeism because of greater interest in job satisfaction to employees.

(iv) Fewer grievances among the employees; and

(v) All-round greater team spirit.

Thus, all these aspects of TQM are to be understood by every employee so that they can create a new culture that leads to a great success of the organisation.

TQM in library and information centres

Although. TQM is a new concept in management but it is equally beneficial to each and every organization including service organization like library. Dr S.R. Ranganathan's fourth law of library science, 'Save the time of the readers' has similar implications to what is advocated in TQM approach. Since the beginning of 1990s, some of Library and

Information Centres had started to think about TQM after a growing awareness of the relevance of quality management methods to provide pinpointed, exhaustive, expeditious and efficient information to the users but still it is not being taken into consideration very seriously. TQM can be seen on two groups of libraries viz., (i) those whose parental organizations are adopting TQM and (ii) the library and information services.

The users are the ultimate judge of the quality of the services being provided by a library & information centre. User satisfaction and continues improvement of the services are the two primary goals of a library. By applying TQM technique, the librarians can not only satisfy the users consistently as per their needs and requirements but also improve quality of their services regularly. TQM in a Library & Information Centre may helps in:

- better product design;
- developing an inventory of all the documents available in a library;
- developing a database which includes records for all types of material held in a library;
- facilitating through a variety of tools that can provide access to universal publications;
- improving quality of information analysis and consolidation product;
- improving skills of end users to profitability interact with information system and services;
- integrating and networking all library resources into serviceable resources to users;
- reduction of user complaints;
- efficient utilization of men, machines and materials, resulting in higher productivity; and
- elimination of bottlenecks and tension free work environment leading to good human relations and improvement of confidence among users.

Implementation of TQM

Various models have been suggested to implement TQM in any organization. Oakland model states that every organization has systems, teams and tools and total quality of its services or products improves when the persons engaged in using systems, teams and tools are able to provide a higher order of work culture, communication and commitment with full understanding of each one's role in each process of work as a supplier to meet the need of internal customer, i.e., his own colleagues. Demming's 14 points programme may also be used to implement the same in Library and Information Centres. Barnard, suggested a ten stage programme for implementation of TQM which may be discussed under four phases as given below.

(i) **Exploration and Decision Making:** This is first phase where librarians or library managers are required to gather information about quality management including literature, conferences, training events, contacting and visiting the other libraries which had already adopted the TOM.

(ii) **Organizing for Qualify:** Second phase consists of a number of series's of planning tasks which provide groundwork on which TQM is to be implemented. This include environmental assessment, seeking deeper understanding of internal as well as external customers and finally a vision needs to be clearly expressed, supported by guide, lines and action, which will enable the organization to move forward upto the expectation.

(iii) **Start up:** In third phase, there is a need to identify the needs and expectations of their users, then measurement of critical process which are being used by library and to set up a pilot project team to tackle these processes and finally to provide training to each and every members of the team to enable them to work.

(iv) **Planning:** The integrated result of the project team, strategic, and departmental planning activity constitute this final phase. An emphasis should also be made there on spreading the expertise of the initial teams to all members of staff and involving them in teams and problem solving activities.

How to Achieve Total Quality Management

To obtain quality management, the following approaches are to be implemented or carried out in the library.

(i) Automation in the Library : Library automation is being applied in all major libraries in India. Libraries are applying information technology to their operations, products and services in order to achieve increased operational efficiency.

Information is now accessible through various electronic media such as disc, tapes, CD-ROM, fax, e-mail, voice mail, video text, e-journals. Internet, etc. International database have been developed and new telecommunication network has been established throughout the world. Now with help of Internet, e-mail, files transfer and remote login, librarians can exploit the catalogues, citation databases etc. easily.

a. Change in the attitude of people that library is not mere warehouse or stock room for books but it is a high technology information center managed by professionals who are in communication business.

b. The profession will continue to be populated with large number of persons, where change is not engineered as the *modus operandi*. Librarianship changes only through massive programmes of retraining, reorientation and redirection which can help to maintain the value of this most vital resource for the benefit of library and its users.

(ii) Commitment to Lead : Librarian should be committed to lead the library and leaders, administrators, managers must bend to make every effort to assure that the wise and the most talented librarians are allowed to make their contribution to new generation of librarian.

(iii) Periodicals in Library : Periodicals have increased dramatically in this country due to proliferation of scientific research. These titles have increased and their subscription prices have also increased tremendously. A large number of indexing and abstracting journals are there which are too costly to be acquired by each and every library. These trends have raised frustration both in librarians and library users. Selection, acquisition and maintenance of periodicals are very important in library. Resource sharing will help in saving multiple subscriptions, on-line availability of periodicals can eliminated many steps in research process of library listing, storage and retrievals. It is for enlightened professionals to outmode practices in order to streamline library process and improve accessibility of valuable contents of periodicals.

(iv) Team Building : Team is a group of people with different background, skills and experience that work together to achieve defined common goals through clear communication and action. Team building

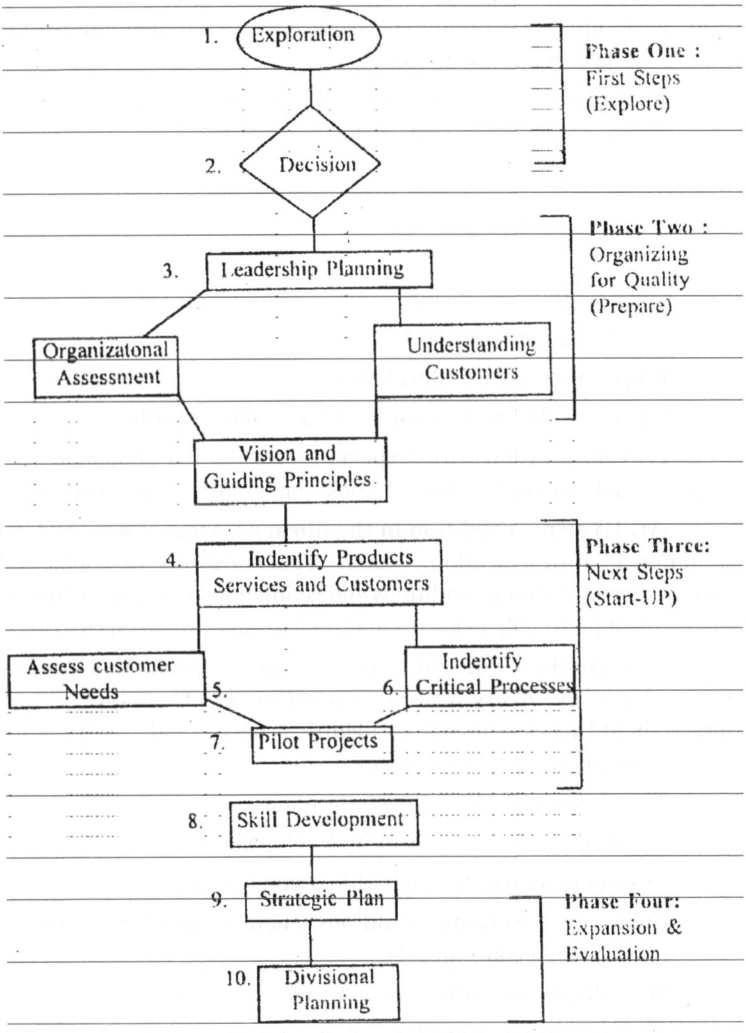

Fig. 2. Total Quality Management Library Implementation Model

is critical element of quality management in library. The key factors in team developing are commitment, trust, purpose and communication involved in process of orientation.

To achieve good team building the requirements are:

- Best recruitment and selection
- Sound organisation structure
- Good administration and organisation
- Proper training of staff
- Good motivation of staff
- Proper management philosophy
- Proper planning and development
- Clear aims in library setup and reasonable rewards.

(v) Consultation with Experts : Consultation of some expert in specific field for the purchase of books and journals is also necessary.

(vi) Hygienic condition in the library : Arrangement of good sanitation facilities, drinking water, regular dusting of books and journals, proper lighting conditions and ventilation are required. Sitting arrangement preferably to keep a marginal distance between two users.

(vii) Quality Control : This is very important in quality improvement. In quality control, a small group of employees from library should meet regularly to identify, analyse and resolve work related to improve quality services.

The philosophy of quality control aims at:

- Contribute to improvement in developed library.
- Respect to humanity and building good rapport.
- Create good working conditions whereby moral of workforce remains high continuously.
- Wide discussion with management.
- Training different levels of employees on the concept.
- Structure and operation of quality control system and circulation of literature on quality control.

Barriers to Implementing TQM

The implementation of TQM in library organisations provides an opportunity to update and enhance the abilities of the staff to work effectively, yet it is still not free from some barriers. These could be listed as under:

(i) **Vocabulary Barrier :** The words "total", "quality" and "management" imply that standards are not already being observed, nor is quality work valued.

(ii) **Commitment Barrier :** TQM requires long-term commitment, perhaps even longer in the service sectors like libraries and information centres. Cultural change which can not be accomplished over night or in a year, may be positive changes, particularly in staff attitudes and learning, but they should occur early in the process.

(iii) **Process Barrier :** Sometimes the process merely represents a desire to postpone decision making or reluctance to resolve the issue. One should learn to define problems better at the outset and then give them the kind of systematic analysis which can lead to lasting solutions.

(iv) **Professional Barrier :** The higher the degree of professionalisation within an organization, the greater the resistance to certain elements of TQM, particularly its customer focus. Professionals simply are mystified by, if not fearful of, the consequences of what they think could mean turning over their services and practices, which are based on tradition, standards and respected bodies of knowledge, to the uninformed whims of customers.

Although different management techniques are in practice among library management but TQM seems to be important one in modem era of information technology. TQM can not change the complete scenario of an organization with in a night but it is a continuous process and according to situations and needs it demands improvement. Today, Librarians are expected to be experts not only in library and information science but also efficient and effective managers to achieve the user satisfaction by using modern management techniques then one can think of TQM.

PARTICIPATIVE MANAGEMENT

Decision making is an important management process in any organization. Without decision, nothing can be properly planned or accomplished. Decisions may be simple— and with sufficient foresight—or complex and with lack of foresight. Modern management techniques encourage the use of participative decision making, stressing that productive and efficient results can come out of this decision making process. This management technique allows its employees, individuals or groups to take part in decision making. This is known as participative management.

The availability of information is vital to the decision making process. Involvement of the staff in the decision making process is a major strength of participative management.

Since participative management publics decision making down to lower levels, the higher level officials need to develop their competence, expertise and experience. It does not believe in punishment as a tool of control. The group is supportive of the individuals/employees comprising it and intended to fulfil the organizational objectives. In the process of decision making, the participation of staff is considered from various aspects such as:

(i) What are the systems of participation at present?

(ii) Are people involved in issues that affect them?

(iii) Are they being consulted specifically when a vital decision is being taken (e.g., Application of Information Technology)?

(iv) Is involvement early enough or regular enough ?

Participative management, being one of the human relations techniques, lays much emphasis on satisfying a greater proportion of people's needs at work. It is considered conducive to high staff morale to provide more delegation, to push decision making lower down the staff hierarchy, and to involve staff in setting their own objectives and in evaluating their achievements. Participative management structures and styles create conditions at work which enable staff to realize their potential, make greater use of their professional training and thus improve the effectiveness of the service offered.

Components of Participative Management

The involvement of staff in the decision making process of the organization and having increased awareness of the organization's purpose, depend upon two important factors: (i) Leadership (ii) Organisational Style.

(i) Leadership : Leadership behaviours lead to highly motivated staff. Subordinates rely upon the leadership skills of their superiors to show them how to achieve their needs of motivation, rewards and ability to perform their allocated tasks. Leaders resolve interpersonal differences. Formal systems are simplified and attempts are made to create a more open, reactive organizational environment. The need for leadership qualities turns more towards the ability to get people to interact. The capacity to mediate is very important, and the ability to plan and analyse feedback is emphasized. The leader's role is not diminished but it is changed in its nature. Participative leadership involves employee participation in management. Subordinates are consulted for their opinions as part of the decision-making process.

(ii) Organisational Style : Whether the participative approach can really work depends upon the type of organisation and its functioning. An open organisation is more likely to encourage participative management than a mechanistic one. The emphasis in organizational communication from top to bottom through informal, group, team and party meetings is laid on self-starting qualities, the capacity of staff to-develop themselves in their own jobs and to grow professionally. The organizational style of functioning should encourage that people at work need to satisfy their higher level needs, for success, self respect and self-actualization, as well as their basic needs for material support and security. Participative decision making has its effect on the organization's objectives.

Participative Management in Libraries and Information Centres

Like most other organizations, libraries and information centres have the dual social responsibility of satisfying the needs of both the employees and the public at large. One of the methods by which this can be achieved is by employee participation in facilitating the accomplishment of the library's goals. Today there is increased emphasis on measuring performance, which usually means efficiency and effectiveness.

Efficiency ensures that the optimum level of service is provided at the lowest possible cost. However the ability to meet the effectiveness criterion is not always easy since the interests of the stakeholder groups are not stable. Stakeholders are those persons who take an interest in the library, or who have the capacity to influence its ability to achieve the objectives. Of course the concept of Participative Management in libraries and information centres has been relatively neglected. Recent theories in management have proved that Participative Management and group decision making appear to have important applications to libraries and to personnel development, it not only affects the quality of decisions but their implications for productivity also. The involvement of library staff in determining the library's objectives and the means to attain these might improve library service.

The availability of information is vital to the decision-making process. The information required to make decisions about an activity within a library system differs from that required to make decisions about a total system, both in degree of detail and comprehensiveness. Library and information professionals often possess relevant, practical information relating to library operations which is not available to senior official because they do not perform the same task. Library staff acquire a lot of information and share it in the decision making process. At the operational level this will result in a more practical solution. This leads to greater creativity in finding a solution. Professionals who have been involved irrespective of their status in the decision making process are more likely than others to be motivated to ensure that the proposals are carried out as there is a feeling of commitment to the decisions.

This sense of involvement also leads to increased awareness of the library's goals after participating in the decision making process.

Advantages and Disadvantages of Participative Management

Advantages: For improving the library and information services, the management follows the technique of participatory decision making which has got the following advantages.

(i) High Productivity: Participative Management assures high productivity in the sense that involvement of staff in the decision making process provides one and all good working condition, motivation, and ability to work and introduce the desired result in time. The outcome of the decisions is always target oriented to meet the goals and objectives of the organisation. It taps the talents, the ideas, the knowledge and the skills of individuals who might not otherwise be included in the decision making process.

(ii) Superior Quality: Participative Management stresses that higher quality decisions and quality of library services often result from these practices. Decisions are found to be superior especially if the group is composed of individuals of different areas of expertise with a common need for a solution.

(iii) **Wider Acceptability :** Group decisions tend to be more readily accepted by the group. Participative decision making is also useful for resolving differences among group members. The decisions are acceptable to all groups or individuals.

Disadvantages : There are also some disadvantages to participative decision-making.

(i) Implementation of the tough decisions taken by the management through participative decision-making sometimes stalls the entire activities taking the problem form one committee to another committee.

(ii) Group decision-making can be expensive in terms of staff time. A group decision normally takes more time than an executive action. In order to estimate the full cost of participative decision-making the decision-making time should be multiplied by the number of people attending the group meeting.

(iii) Lower quality decisions are also expected through participative decision-making which is not truly effective. If superiors are present or if one member has a dominant personality, the decision of the group may in reality not be a group decision. This can have lowering effect on group morale and of a negative factor for motivation making for feelings of frustration and uselessness.

CONFLICT MANAGEMENT

Librarian as Library Managers has dual role of understanding the behaviour of their customers and also their superiors and subordinates.

Katz and Mann have proposed three skill typology of managerial skills. They are

(a) Technical skills,

(b) Human Relation skills, and

(c) Conceptual skills.

Of the three skills, human relation skills are important for establishing effective relationships with subordinates, superiors, peers and outsiders. Unless a Librarian is sensitive to the attitudes, feelings and needs of people, he cannot estimate how they will react to what he says and does. The important human relations are-not only those related to achieving the organisations' objectives, but those related to maintaining the organisation's internal system. Among the killers of interpersonal relationships, conflict is a very influential one.

Despite the best of managerial practices in acting and communication conflicts occur, the term Conflict different things to different people. It may be regarded as a disagreement or hostility between individuals or groups in the organisations. A total absence of conflict would be unbelievable and a strong indication that such conflicts are being suppressed.

When the needs of human beings meet the needs of organisation conflict often occurs. It is quite essential for the manager to examine the fundamental motive of the human resource, integration of these resources in organisations, coping with the inevitable conflicts and ensure the various mechanisms. Lack of understanding between interacting individuals is the root of interpersonal conflict. When human beings set goals that are actually unattainable, conflict occurs. The completely unrealistic expectations of one self or others lead to conflict. Conflict reflects the inner frustration and tension of individuals.

Conflict is the part and parcel of every organisation. Hence, the management should create congenial atmosphere in which it does not grow or it is directed to constructive one. Building views that some optimum level of conflict and associated personal stress and tension are necessary for progress and productivity. Conflict poses the following positive aspects:

- more concrete views are taken
- innovation and new ways of working created
- brings cohesiveness in groups
- used as a device to overcome frustrations
- it indicates, the short-comings in the organisation thus overcoming them.
- provides a challenging working environment. It also has the following dysfunctional aspects:
  (i) It may lead to organizational disequilibrium.
  (ii) It affects contribution-inducement relationship.

Conflicts in Libraries

Libraries which are peoples' institution cannot escape from the clutches of conflicts. The Library Manager or Librarian should identify the areas of conflicts in a Library. The areas may differ from library to library depending upon the nature of the library, type of users served and the objectives of the Library. The following are some of the general areas where conflicts could arise:

- When authorities insists on more service and satisfy more number of readers with minimum resources.
- When a change is introduced either in the infrastructure or in the pattern of services inside the library the subordinates resist exchange in the working time or introduction of computers.
- When the authority or Librarian fails to recognise the special efforts taken by subordinates to improve the out-look of the library.
- When allocation is very much limited but readers demand better service.

When the Librarian or the authorities fail to be aware of conflicting conditions a hostile relationship is established.

Identifing conflicts in Libraries

The first step in the resolution of conflicts is their discovery and exposure. The following procedures are generally adopted. Librarian can choose any one of the methods suitable for him:

(i) Grievance Procedure : Individual submits a complaint to the superior for discussion. Hiding behind the complaint is usually a suppressed conflict.

(ii) Direct Observation : Librarian should be sharp enough to note the change in the attitude and behaviour of the individual towards his superior and working environment.

(iii) Suggestion Box : Anonymity may provide courage to submit a dissatisfaction which will otherwise go unnoticed.

How to Solve Conflicts

Conflict Management is the extent to which the superior or authority restrains subordinates from fighting and arguing encourages them to resolve conflicts in a constructive manner and helps to settle disagreements between the individuals.

It can be resolved or managed in the following ways:

- Personal approach
- Participative decision making
- Better understanding and co-operation
- Creating trust

Setting a personal example of behaviour, integrity of the superior, a feeling by the subordinates that their legal interests are safeguarded and delegation of powers would lead to mutual trust.

Apart from the above the change in the structure of the organisation or some part of it reduces conflict. Such organizational changes should debit in the removal of obvious differences in the status symbols, between hierarchical interest groups and opportunities to subordinates in completing tasks and sharing in organizational rewards.

4

Elements and Principles of Management

Every organisation or institution has a set of goals to achieve. For this an organisational structure is raised, an administrative machinery is created and management authority is appointed. The basic policies of the organisation are laid down and management staff is appointed by the administrative machinery for achieving the desired goals. Libraries are generally a part of a big organisation except the public libraries. The operation of libraries are based on the guide lines, rules and regulations framed by their parent body. If it is a public library in that case the rules are framed by the some committees. According to prevailing customs and procedures, the librarian representing the executive committee, a policy making body. In that case he may be directly participating in the decision making by the highest body. Even otherwise, a manager can always send a proposal to the top management and also canvass for it. In this way a manager plays an important role in the formulation of rules and regulation. To ensure better functioning and smooth running of an organisation, Luther Gulick propounded some basic elements of management on the pattern of Fayol principles of management. These are known as 'POSDCORB' which stands for the following seven elements.

1. Planning
2. Organising
3. Staffing
4. Directing
5. Co-ordinating
6. Reporting
7. Budgeting

Planning

Planning is a process which involves the determination of future course of action. To achieve better and desired objectives from an institution, the administrator should first plan and forecast the goals of an institution. These outlines are given concrete shape and a regular frame work authority is established in such a manner that maximum work of best quality is ensured at a minimum cost with minimum efforts.

It is very closely associated with the goals or objectives of the organisation. The goals may be express implied, however, well-defined goals lead to efficiency in planning. Planning presupposes the stock taking of the existing conditions and the relevant causes. The solutions are suggested for removing the defects by a phased systematic programme. Economic planning is concerned with the production of maximum input. In planning, entire wastage is avoided and every constituent factor is made to contribute its own share. The efforts are made to remove the basic defects and their future implications are taken care of.

The special features of planning can be identified as under:

(i) Planning is the process rather than behaviour at a given point of time.

(ii) Planning is primarily concerned with looking into future.

(iii) Planning involves selection of suitable course of action.

(iv) Planning is undertaken at all levels of the organisation because all levels of management are concerned with the determination of future course of action.

(v) Planning is flexible, as commitment is based on future conditions which are always dynamic.

Planning requires wide knowledge and experience of works. It is the most basic of all managerial functions and is considered as a rational approach to preselected objectives.

A systematic planning involves the following steps :

(i) The problem exists and need for action is recognised.

(ii) Collect all the available information regarding the problem.

(iii) Assess the possible alternative solutions and method to solve the problems.

(iv) Take decision to act.

(v) Put decision into action and;

(vi) The evaluation on the basis of experience.

Organising

Organising means establishing of a formal structure of authority, which is well defined and coordinated towards the attainment of specific objective. The structure of formal organisation denotes a system of well-defined jobs, each bearing a definite measure of authority, responsibility, and accountability, and the whole things consciously designed to enable the people of the organization to work most effectively together in accomplishing their objectives. It is an important process which starts after the planning is completed. Its objectives are achieved by the combined efforts of different specialists belonging to the organisation.

Planning, to be fruitful needs of a sound organization, which means that such a structure of authority is established which is capable of achieving the set goals. After finalysing the creative phase of planning through which librarians define what is to be done, the next step comes before them is who will do it. Since the work of library is done by number of persons working together, librarians have to define who will do what and what will be relationship among these persons. This aspect is taken up by the librarians in the form of organising which basically involves analysis of activities to be performed for achieving organisational objectives grouping them into various divisions-departments, and sections so that these can be assigned to various individuals and delegating them appropriate authority so that they are able to carry on their work effectively.

What pattern of organisation should be adopted in the library is another important aspect. The pattern of organisation varies from library to library depending upon the objectives, nature of users, type of staff, kinds of documents available in the library, financing, building and more important thing is the attitude of higher authorities.

Generally there are two types of administration, viz. centralised administration and decentralised administration so in the choice of a pattern these two points should be considered first. Since an organisation is a man based structure, therefore, flexibility must be considered as the alteration should be possible when it is required. The library is a growing organism so the organisational structure will become large and more people will join it and the structure will become complex.

Staffing

Like other organisations, library requires the services of a large number of technical and non technical personnels to perform the works of different sections. The persons posted in the different sections of the library must have sufficient ability to meet its requirements. Staffing basically involves matching jobs and individuals.

The management function of staffing involves managing the organisation structure through proper and effective selection, appraisal and development of personnel to fill the roles designated into the structure. The managerial function of staffing is defined as filling positions in the organisation structure through identifying work force requirements, inventorying the people available, recruitment, selection, placement and promotion, appraisal, compensation and the training of needed people.

Staffing is an essential element of management process. It is the process of acquiring, developing, employing, appraising, remunerating and retaining people so that right type of people are available at right position and right time in the organisation. Within each function, there are various sub-functions. For example acquiring of reading materials, personnels are involves in ordering the books, section of reading materials and process of books and its bills for the payment.

An organisation for its efficient working is totally dependent upon proper staffing and recruitment policies. The staff appointed in the library should have the special aptitudes and capabilities for doing the particular job. With the introduction of electronic machines, computers and other sophisticated instruments in the library operation, the personnel must be acquainted of these equipments. The practical experience of various jobs at the credit of applicants for various posts should be taken into consideration at the time of their appointment.

Directing

Everyone of us, perhaps, may be aware about the concept of directing and role of director or manager when the works of a big organisation is in progress. The manager direct their sub-ordinates how to they should do the work for achieving organisational objectives. A superior directs his subordinates as to how and when they have to perform various duties assigned to him.

Once planning, organizing and staffing have been achieved, then action is required. To execute the action successfully, the direction is involved. Direction is defined as the continuous task of taking decisions and incorporating them in specific and general orders and serving these orders. New man and Warren have defined directing in the form of activating as "Activity deals with the steps a manager taking to get subordinates and others to carry out plans.

Direction has some special features which are as under :-

(i) It is an important managerial function.

(ii) Its function is performed at every level of management.

(iii) It is a continuous process and it continues throughout the life of the organisation.

(iv) It initiates at the top level in the organisation and follows to bottom through the hierarchy.

(v) It has dual objectives.

In a library, the harmony and efficiency of the staff depends upon the personal qualities of the Librarian. He should be capable of performing his duties as a leader. Besides, he should be able to infuse confidence amongst the staff members. He should be able to boost up their morale. He should also be an example to be followed by his subordinates. In other words, he should not be frustrated with his job leather, he should do his job with zeal. He should be ready to sacrifice his personal comforts for the sake of library work and library staff. He should prove an ideal leader by dint of his hard work and sincerity for the staff welfare.

Coordinating

Coordination is an important function of a manager, which deals with task of blending efforts in order to insure successful attainment of an objective. Though some writers do not regard coordination as a separate activity of the manager, but some have the opposite views and they considers 'Coordination' as a separate function of management. Haimann considers coordination as the part of all the managerial functions of planning, organizing, staffing, directing and controlling.

Coordination may be defined as an on-going process whereby manager develops an integrated, orderly and synchronised pattern of group effort among the sub-ordinates and tries to attain unity of effort in the pursuit of common purpose. It is a harmonious combination or interaction. It is concerned with interrelating of the various parts of an organisation.

The coordination can be achieved if the head knows well all the jobs and effects such an automatic administrative machinery that he feels practically no necessity to interfere. It depends upon the kind of organization which has been brought into being i *e.* as to whether he introduces Line Type or Line and Staff Type of structure or Functional Type of organization. In other words, there should be delegation of powers but the staff members in whom the powers are vested should also be made responsible for their jobs. They should be answerable to the Chief. An automatic procedure should be effected by means of introducing a practice of getting periodical reports from the various Section Heads. He should allow these Heads to use their initiative but whenever there is some difficulty or misunderstanding, the Chief should thrash out the problem in periodical staff meetings.

Reporting means keeping the authorities informed about the progress or regress of work and also keep them abreast. To perform this duty efficiently, the executive head has to keep himself and his sub ordinates informed about their jobs and performances through research, records and inspection. It is a sound principle of organisation that a periodical report is asked from a head of an enterprise. Such report will base on factual and real statistics. The librarian has to submit the annual report to the executive committee for this librarian issue a direction to the subordinates to prepare the report of their concerned section. On the basis of report received from different sections of the library, the librarian is able to prepare a comprehensive report. Report is the only authentic device for evaluation of library procedures and service. Librarian often use it because it is a continuous process and its costs are not apparent being hidden under general expenses of library.

Budgeting

Budgeting is an effective management tool in the hand of librarian or manager. Budget, means formation of plans for a given future period in numerical terms. It includes fiscal planning, accounting and control. No organisation can function properly without adequate finances. But it is very difficult to get adequate finance or funds for all kind of organiations, especially libraries which are fully depends on the parents institution or government aid. Libraries do not earn any revenues in the physical sense. Their services, though essential for the well-being of the individual, the society and the government, are not considered apparently indispensable. Consequently, the legislators and bureaucrats alike reject the demands of libraries on one or the other pretext. The libraries are given almost the lowest priority in matter of allocation of funds. The librarian has to muster strength and acquire necessary skill and tact for securing adequate funds.

The available funds should be spent properly and very carefully. Under this situation budget helps a lot to the librarian. Careful planning, accounting and control are necessary in budgeting. The librarian should have to examine the needs of library on the basis of users requires. Since budget is an important item the librarian should himself participate and guide the budget formulation.

Mohinder Singh has added a few more elements.

1. Creating (before planning)
2. Motivating (after staffing)
3. Communicating (before directing)
4. Controlling (after coordinating).

Briefly, these are discussed below :

Creating

Creativeness is one of the vital functions of management. A creative manager can make an organisation itself creative. Through his creative approaches of logical thinking, idea linking and problem solving, he can create new and better ways of achieving objectives. Creative function adds innovation and improvement in the activities and procedures of the organisation.

Motivating

Motivation is a valuable function of management. Motivated people only achieve set goals. In an organisation, people at all levels should be motivated by way of giving proper stimuli to them so as to achieve desired behaviour. Only desired behaviour leads towards accomplishment of organisational objectives. Individuals are motivated by satisfying their five-tiers of needs as recognised by A H Maslow. Physiological Needs relating to maintenance of life (e.g. food, air, water, rest, etc.); Safety Needs relating to security from physical danger (e.g. fire, accident, criminal assault, etc.) and economic security relating to job protection, salary deduction, fine, etc.; Social Needs relating to form associations, friendships, etc.; Esteem Needs relating to enjoyment of status, recognition, appreciation, self-respect and freedom; and Self-realisation Needs relating to self-fulfillment or continued self-development.

Communicating

Communicating is also an important element of the management. Communication creates coordination and participation in the management. Through communication, managers transfer the message, may it be facts, ideas, attitudes or opinions in all directions, to all concerned executives and subordinates to influence a particular course of action to achieve a pre-planned common goal or objective. The communication may be formal or informal. It may flow in any direction upwards, as suggestion from subordinate to superior, downwards as orders or instruction from superior to subordinate and laterally as an information flow for necessary action or correction among concerned executives across the lines of an organisation.

Controlling

Controlling is yet another essential part of management. Controlling is the process by which management gauges the progress of work against set targets. In other words, controlling compares events with plans and makes necessary corrections where events have deviated from plans. In management, budget provides inherent control over plans. In a business type management, break-even analysis, where profits or losses are measured at different volume levels of sales, is another controlling technique. This concept in the form of cost-benefit analysis can also be profitably applied to a service-type organisation, like a library or information centre. Leadership of a manager also plays an important role in controlling employee's behaviour in an organisation. He feeds checking, regulation, verification and overall supervision to actions for achieving desired objectives.

LEVELS OF MANAGEMENT

In an organisation there exists a chain of command or scaler chain from the ultimate authority to the lowest rank. This chain is made up of superior-subordinate relationships. Various managers are linked with, one another through the vertical chain. This chain or hierarchy of management consists of a series of managerial positions called 'levels of management'. The level of management determines the authority and status of managers. Thus, the term 'level of management' refers to a line of demarcation between various management positions in an organisation. There is no fixed number of management levels. The number of managerial levels depends upon the size and complexity of the organisation. "As a company becomes larger and more complex, there is a natural tendency for the chain of command to lengthen. Even though the company makes no effort to limit span of control to any given number, if there is an extensive growth there comes a time when command at various levels have to be split up and another layer of supervision is inserted".'

In practice, it is often difficult to slice management hierarchy into specific levels because various layers of authority constitute an integrated pyramid. However, the different levels of management may be classified into four categories as shown in Fig. 1.

(1) Top Management;

(2) Intermediate or upper middle management

(3) Middle management; and

(4) Supervisory or operating management.

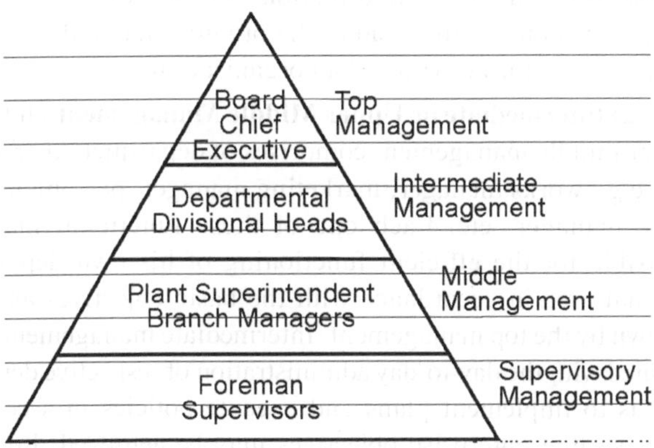

Fig. 1. Levels of Management

(1) Top Management : Top management of a company consists of the board of directors and chief executives. Chief executive may be an individual or a committee. It is known by different names, e.g., managing director, general manager, president, chairman-cum-managing director, etc. Top management is the ultimate source of management authority and it is accountable for overall management to the shareholders of the company. The main functions of top management are as follows:

(i) to analyse, evaluate and deal with the external environmental forces;

(ii) to establish overall long-term goals strategy and policies of the company including the master budget to allocate resources;

(iii) to create an organisational framework consisting of authority responsibility relationships;

(iv) to appoint departmental and other key executives;

(v) to provide overall leadership to the company;

(vi) to represent the company to the outside world, e.g., trade associations, government, trade unions, etc.;

(vii) to exercise overall review and control on the company's operations; and

(viii) to coordinate the activities and efforts of different departments.

Thus, top management of a company is the policy-making group responsible for the overall direction and success of all company activities. It stands at the head of the organisation and gives purpose and direction to the activities of an organisation.

(2) Intermediate or Upper Middle Management : Intermediate or upper middle management comprises of departmental or divisional heads, e.g., works manager, marketing manager, personnel manager, finance manager, etc. Each one of these functional managers is responsible for the efficient functioning of his own department or functional area in accordance with the basic objectives and policies laid down by the top management. Intermediate management is largely concerned with the day-to-day administration of respective departments. Its job is to implement plans and execute policies in a coordinated manner so that enterprise objectives may be achieved. Intermediate managers are concerned with priorities and specific results. At upper middle management, departmental operational plans are established and targets of achievement are laid down. Departmental heads exercise the usual functions of management in respect of their own departments. They plan operations, issue instructions, assemble the required resources, design operating policies and operating routines, evaluate results of their respective departments, programme efforts and control the work of people in the departments. They interpret the policies framed by top management, prepare departmental organisational setup, select suitable supervising personnel, motivate the personnel and collect information. They are responsible for the efficient utilisation of resources placed at their disposal. They translate the objectives and strategies of the organisation into specific decisions and actions. They are more concerned with the internal management rather than the external environment of the enterprise. Thus, this group is responsible for departmental performance.

(3) Middle Management : This level of management consists of deputy heads of departments and sectional officers such as plant manager, area sales manager or branch manager, office manager, chief accountant, purchase officer, etc. These executives serve as a means of coordination between top management and operating management. According to Marry C. Niles, "they often share in the difficulties of their superiors in arriving at decisions and they necessarily take part in the efforts of their subordinates to carry out policies. They transmit orders, decisions and guidance downwards; they also take problems, difficulties, and suggestions upward. The lines of communication meet in them". They are involved less in physical activity and more in paper work and meetings than the operating managers. While top management is concerned with conceptual thinking middle management deals with operations.

The middle management usually performs the following functions:

(i) To interpret and explain the policies framed by top management.

(ii) To compile and issue detailed instructions regarding operations.

(iii) To maintain close contacts with operating results so as to evaluate performance.

(iv) To participate in operating decisions.

(v) To cooperate among themselves so as to integrate or coordinate various parts of a division or a department.

(vi) To motivate supervisory personnel to work for organisational goals.

(vii) To develop and train supervisory and operative personnel.

4. Supervisory or Operating Management : Supervisory management is the lowest level of management. It consists of plant superintendent, senior foremen and front line supervisors, sales officer, accounts officer, etc. They are concerned with technical routine and day-to-day problems. They maintain personal contacts with operatives. It involves management of rank and file and is directly concerned with the mechanics of jobs. Operating managers are expected to get work done from the staff under their control. They lead an active, hectic, often .interrupted work-life, spending most of their time communicating and caring for problems of the moment. They are the only managers who do not manage other managers. They are caught between labour and management. According to Davis, supervisory management "refers to grades of executive leadership whose work has to do largely with personal oversight and direction of operative employees". The operating managers plan, implement policy, organise, instruct and guide personnel and control performance. They serve as the link between management and workers. Their authority and responsibility is limited but the quality of workmanship and the quantity of output depends on their efficiency and effectiveness. They are responsible for directly managing operatives and resources.

The functions of supervisory management are as follows:

(i) To plan day-to-day production within the goals laid down by higher authorities. .

(ii) To assign jobs to workers and to make arrangements for their training and development.

(iii) To supervise and control workers and to maintain personal contact with charge hands.

(iv) To arrange materials and tools and to maintain machinery.

(v) To advise and assist workers by explaining work procedures, solving their problems, etc.

(vi) To maintain discipline, morale and good human relations among workers.

(vii) To report feedback information and workers problems which cannot be solved at the supervisory level.

SKILLS OF MANAGEMENT

In modern business, the job of a manager has become very complex. Different types of skills are required to manage effectively a large organisation in a dynamic environment. These skills of a manager have been classified into three categories, namely technical, human and conceptual skills.

1. Technical skill : Technical skill refers to the ability and knowledge in using the tools, equipment-processes, techniques and procedures involved in performing specific tasks. These skills require specialised knowledge and proficiency in the mechanics of a particular job. Ability in programming and operating a computer is, for instance, a technical skill. Managers need technical skill to guide and train subordinates. They cannot manage the activities of then-subordinates if they do not know how the jobs are done. People with technical skills are recognised as experts at what they do. There are two things a manager should understand about technical skills. In the first place, he must know which skills should be employed in his particular enterprise and be familiar enough with their potentiality to ask discerning questions of his technical advisers. Secondly, a manager must understand both the role of each skill employed and the inter-relationships between the skills. The nature of technical skill is twofold. The manager should have developed some expertise in the work being owner. Secondly, there are skills involved in the work being done.

2. Human skill : Human skill consists of the ability to work effectively with understanding and motivating other people both as individuals and as members of a group. Such a skill is required to win cooperation of others and to build effective work teams. Such skills require a sense of feeling for others and capacity to look at things from others' point of view. Human skills are reflected in the way a manager perceives his superiors, subordinates and peers. A person with human skills is sufficiently sensitive to the needs and motivations of others in his organisation so that he can judge the possible reaction to and outcome of various courses of action. With human skills, managers can resolve intra and inter group conflicts. An awareness of the importance of human skills should be part of a manager's orientation and such skills should be developed throughout the career. While technical skills involve mastery of inanimate objects or 'things', human skills are concerned with understanding of 'people'.

3. Conceptual skill : Conceptual skill comprises of the ability to see the whole organisation and the inter-relationships between its parts. This skill refers to the ability to visualise the enterprise as a whole or to consider a situation in its totality. These skills involve understanding abstract ideas, constructing models and relationships, and anticipating consequences of planned actions. It is the mental ability to coordinate and integrate all of the organisation's interests and activities. It involves the manager's ability to see the organisation as a whole and to understand how its parts depend on each other. It also involves the manager's ability to understand how a change in any given part can affect the whole organisation. Such skills help the manager to conceptualise the environment, to analyse the forces working in a situation and to take a broad and farsighted view of the organisation. Conceptual skill also includes the competence to understand a problem in all its aspects and to use original thinking in solving the problem. Such competence is necessary for rational decision-making. A manager needs enough conceptual skill to recognise how the various factors in a given situation are inter-related so that the actions taken will be in the best interests of the total organisation.

Thus, technical skill deals with jobs, human skill with persons and conceptual skill with ideas. These three types of skills are interrelated and they are required by all managers. But the proportion or relative significance of these skills varies with the level of management as shown in Fig. 2.

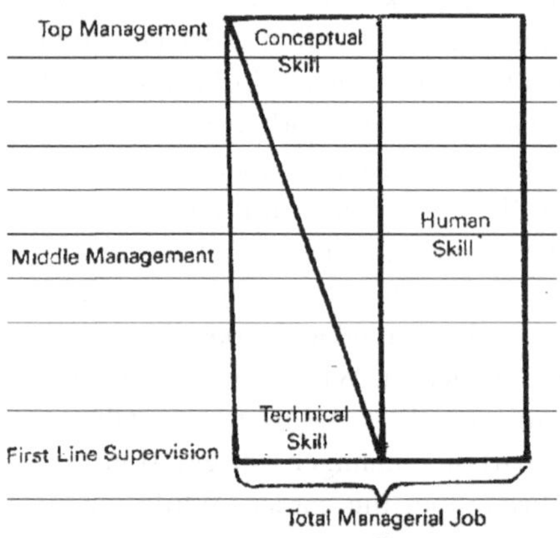

Fig. 2. Managerial Skills at Various Levels

Technical skills are most important at the supervisory or operating level where a close understanding of job techniques is necessary to guide workers. As one moves up the management hierarchy, technical skills become less important. Higher level managers deal with subordinate managers and specialised technical knowledge is comparatively less important for them.

Conceptual skills are most important for top management which is responsible for formulating long-range plans, making broad policy-decisions, and relating the total business enterprise to its industry and the economy. Thus, the relative importance of conceptual skills increases as we move to higher levels of management. Human skills are important at all levels of management. This should be self-evident as management is the process of getting things done through and with people. At every level managers interact and work with people. Probably, the human skill is the most important at the lowest level, where the greatest number of superior-subordinate interactions take place.

Thus, all the three skills are essential to effective management, but their relative importance to a specific manager depends on his or her rank in the organisation. Similarly, Librarian and its deputies should possess such skills for effective management in Libraries.

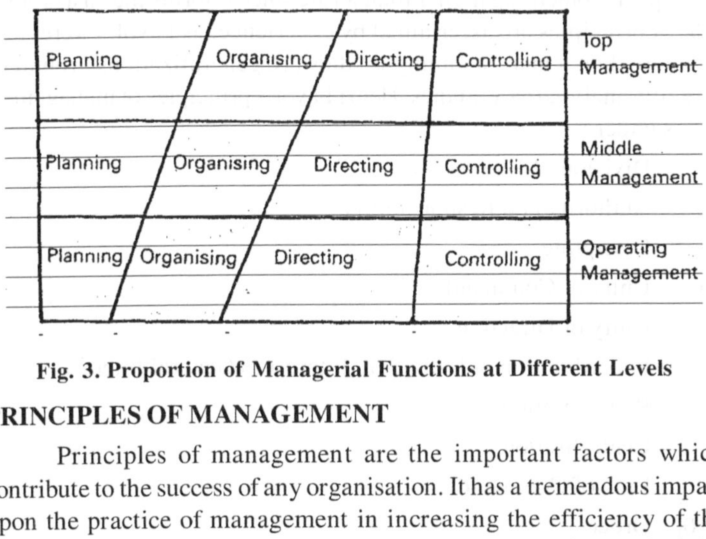

Fig. 3. Proportion of Managerial Functions at Different Levels

PRINCIPLES OF MANAGEMENT

Principles of management are the important factors which contribute to the success of any organisation. It has a tremendous impact upon the practice of management in increasing the efficiency of the organisation. The responsible administrator must know those principles and apply them with judgement in terms of his immediate situation. In view of its importance, scholars or management scientists have offered some view and propounded some fundamental principles. The principles of management are generalizations based on experience and careful analysis of case studies and are universally applicable. These are not rigid, but are changeable in circumstances.

The principles in management are fundamental truths explaining relationships between two or more sets of variables, usually an independent variable and a dependent variable. These management have tremendous impact on a working of institution or organisation as it increase managerial efficiency, crystallise the nature of management, encourage research and help in attaining the social objectives. If the management is efficient, the resources of the society and the quality of life of people is improved.

As the principles of management are generalization based on experience and careful studies and these are applicable in every sphere, therefore, principles are flexible and capable of being adopted to every need. It is a matter of knowing how to make use of them which is a difficult and require intelligence, experience and proportion.

The principles may be defined as a set rule for action. But principle is something higher than a rule since it forms the basis for the rule. If principles are ascertained by experience, as Fayol's were, they are more than a mere summing up they are generalizations ground on carefully analysed case studies. Henri Fayol's principles of management are as under :

1. Division of Work
2. Authority and Responsibility
3. Discipline
4. Unity of Command
5. Unity of Direction
6. Subordination of Individual Interest to General Interest
7. Remuneration
8. Centralisation
9. Line of Command
10. Order
11. Equity
12. Stability of Tenure
13. Initiative
14. Esprit de Corps

1. Division of Work

Division of work means distribution of work load for the smooth running of the institution. In a small library where the affairs of the library is dealt with one man, he will carrying out all the functions such ordering, acquisition, classification, cataloguing, preparation, shelving, servicing, etc. there would be no division of work. But in a big library if the works of the library are divided into sections and sub-sections and the work of these sections are carried out by the technical personnel, it would be definitely increased the efficiency. On the other hand if all the professionals carry out all these works, then this would led to inefficiency and confusion. The division of works makes a worker specialised on that particular work and the worker concerned always with same matter acquire an ability, sureness and accuracy which increase their output.

2. Authority

Authority means the legitimate right to give orders and get these orders obeyed. Max Weber has defined authority as, "The willing and unconditional compliance of people, resting upon their belief that it is legitimate for superior to impose his will on them and illegitimate for them to refuse to obey". Simon has defined authority as the power to make decisions which guide the actions of another. It is a relationship between two individuals; one superior, another sub-ordinate. The superior frames and transmits decisions with the expectation that these will be accepted by the subordinate. The subordinate executes such decisions and his conduct is determined by them.

Authority to give orders may be delegated by the head of a department to his first assistant. Possession of authority must also involve responsibility for action. The organisation must have a supreme authority, and clear lines of authority should run from that person down through the hierarchy. The word hierarchy in an organisation is pyramidical in structure and has a broad base with a top having graded levels. The principle defines and distinguishes sub-ordinate relationship; and tries to bring coordination and teamspirit in the organisation. The line of authority and responsibility flow along the path of hierarchy. Though link after link, the chief executive is united with each individual employee. The scale or hierarchy extends in an unbroken line from the chief executive to the lowest employee. This line serves as a means of communication orders go down the line and information and appeals go up it.

Authority can be either statutory or personal. Statutory authority belongs to a person due to his position. Personal authority is achieved due to qualities of leadership. Possession of authority means responsibility for action. Actual work in library may be done by different persons but the ultimate responsibilities are with the chief librarian for all that goes on. He can delegate authority for a certain job or task, and he should also be deligated authority to take necessary action to fulfil the job or task successfully.

When an individual is assigned the responsibility of accomplishing a particular task, he must correspondingly be delegated proper authority to carry out or discharge such responsibility. Responsibility cannot function in the absence of authority, rather they move together for the achievement of a goal.

3. Discipline

Discipline is an important factor for the success of a management. Discipline creates culture and order in the organisation. It sets the limits of acceptable behaviour in terms of obedience, application, energy and respect. It unifies all efforts of a team towards the accomplishment of a planned task.

Discipline may be of two types : Self imposed discipline and Command discipline. Self imposed discipline which springs from within the individual, is in the nature of spontaneous response to a skilful leader. Command discipline stems from a recognised authority and utilize deterrents to secure compliance with a desired action which is expressed by established customs, rules and regulations.

Discipline can be maintained by providing incentive to the workers and punishment if requires in terms of remuneration, warnings, suspension, demotion, dismissal, etc. the best way to establish and maintain discipline is to good leadership to staff, dissolve disputes with fair justice.

4. Unity of Command

Unity of Command means that no individual employee should be subject to the orders of more than one immediate superior. If he is, he might receive conflicting orders from them, and his position may become an impossible one diversity of command may also result in the sub-ordinate playing off one superior against another or others. All this may cause confusion and blurring of responsibility.

The concept of unity of command requires that every member of an organisation should report to one, and only one leader. A worker should not be put under two bosses. Proper work at the lowest cost in the best manner is possible only if a person is put under the command of one boss. There should be only one supervisior or the officer to supervise over him and the worker should be given the understanding that he is under the command of only one and not many. Under this system there will be no conflict of orders and hence would ensure smooth working to the library. The command deligated from more person will always creates confusion. This situation can be elaborately presents through this diagram :

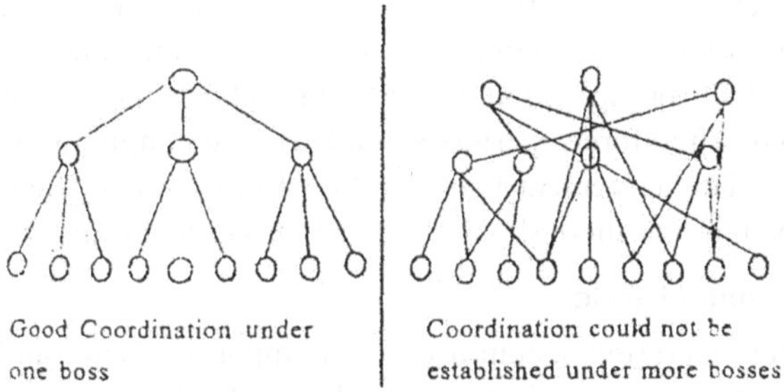

Fig. 4. Unity of Command

Dual command always creates confusion, bring indiscipline and disturbs order and stability of library. The unity of command ensures efficiency and quick decision. Each worker should know as to from whom he has to take orders and to whom he has to give orders. Ultimately, every body should be responsible to one executive head. Any order by the chief librarian to a professional assistant should be transmitted through an Assistant Librarian, who is incharge of the section.

5. Unity of Direction

Unity of direction means each group of activities with the same objective must have one head and one plan. It is different from unity of command in the sense that the former is concerned with functioning of the organisation in respect of its grouping of activities or planning while the latter is concerned with personnel at all levels in the organisation in terms of reporting relationship. Unity of direction provides better coordination among various activities to be undertaken by an organisation.

There should be only one or a single point of guidance or direction for each organisational objective. For each plan there must be a specific guide or a supervisor, whose direction is sought for accomplishing a particular task in a particular way. He is a person finally responsible for the acceptance of a job or a task.

6. Sub-ordination of Individual to General Interest

Common interest is above the individual interest. The principle individual interest must be subordinated for the sake of common good, when there is conflict between the two. However, factors ambition, laziness, weakness, etc. tend to reduce the importance of general interest.

There should not be any allowance for an individual interest at the cost of organisational interest. Under all circumstances, the overall interest of an organisation should come above the interest of any individual. Therefore superiors should set an example in fairness and goodness. The agreement between the employers and the employees should be fair and there should be constant vigilance and supervision.

7. Remuneration

Remuneration of employees is an important factor and it should be fair and provide maximum possible satisfaction to employees and employers. Depending upon the nature of job, there should be adequate compensation in terms of money. Pay should be fair and accurate, affording maximum satisfaction to both employee and employer. This creates stability in the work force. Under such conditions, talent is retained in the organisation, and at the same time attraction of the workers to their respective jobs is also maintained.

8. Centralization

Centralization, means systematic reservation of authority at central points within the organization. It implies that a majority of decision regarding the work are made not by those doing the work but a point higher up in the organisation. Centralization is the retention or concentration of managerial authority in and at relatively key managerial positions of nerve centre of an organisation, viz., at the top level. In short, every thing that goes to reduce the subordinates role in decision making is centralization.

Delegation of power can be divided into two group, i.e. centralization and decentralization. In management centralization refers to concentration of authority and decentralization desperation of authority. As far as possible, the authority of making policy, rules and procedures should be centralised in order to provide better control. This is more true in smaller organisations; however, to maintain better efficiency, some decentralisation of authority is necessary in larger organisations.

9. Line of Command

There should be an unbroken chain of command from top to bottom in terms of authority and responsibility for carrying out various functions in an organisation. This creates dynamism, order and smoothness in the flow of communication. The principle of scalar chain is very important for any organisation. It is a chain which explains the relation between different employees, right from the supervisors enjoying the ultimate authority to the lowest rank. It is the hierarchy of jobs and line of authority starting from the chief executive to the immediate person in subordination and so goes down to the lowest person in the organisation. The scalar chain consists of a series of steps, extending in an unbroken line from chief librarian to the lowest employee. This line serves as a means of communication orders of down along the line travelling from top to bottom. However, in cases where this hierarchical arrangement of positions hampers the progress of work, it is necessary to establish some direct communication at lower level positions.

10. Order

This principle can be referred to the best possible arrangement to achieve the most efficient operation of the organisation. There should be some logical order or system in creation of activities, positions and placements in an organisation. All organisations should be based on an orderly plan throughout. The positions should be created in a logical and rational manner, so that everyone gets his specific place in the organisation.

In the library management, this principle has a special value. Library deals with reading materials which should be kept in proper order as well the office or the sections deals with the users need should be located at the nearest approach. As regards movement of materials, it would be economical if Book Order Section should be kept near the Cataloguing Section. Similarly in the case of the work allotment to the employees of the library it must be considered that a right job may be given to suitable person who like to do the work seriously. A person whose interest is in the classification may not be posted in the Reference Section.

11. Equity

This is the combination of justice and kindness. Employees must be viewed as individual persons, rather than a set of things to be manipulated. Equity in treatment and behaviour is linked by every-one and it brings loyalty in the organisation. The application of equity requires good sense, experience and good nature for soliciting loyalty and devotion from sub-ordinates. Salary scales must be based on educational, ability, experience and level of responsibility. Preferential treatment should be based on the question of superiority of a person in terms of the factors mentioned above.

12. Stability of Tenure

This principle is related to the staffs benefit. There should be stable and efficient work force for the survival of an organisation. Frequent leaving of persons is expensive for the organisation and reflects bad management. It must be corrected to ensure stability of efficient employees for longer duration in the organisation. In the library, it will better to fill up some positions in a library with medicore persons, who will stay with the library relatively for long period. At the same time there should be promotional avenues for competent persons.

13. Initiative

It is concerned with thinking out and execution of a plan on the part of a manager or a worker, which minimises the period for completion of a particular project or a task. Initiative promotes innovation, creativity and efficiency in the organisation. As a positive gain, initiative must be encouraged at all levels in the organisation.

14. Esprit de Corps

Sense of belongingness, unity and team spirit on the part of workers and managers is vital for an organisation. All successful organisations survive only when there is a feeling of unity and team spirit among its workers and managers while working for the achievement of organisational objectives.

In general it is not possible to supervise more than five or six subordinates whose work is interlocking. However, there is no criteria to determine how many persons one manager can supervise with efficiency. Some one have the view that the number may be increased in certain situations more than nine supervisors can be attached with one manager. In case the nature of activities are similar allocated to the different units, the number of supervisors can be increased. Any how at all costs, this culture must be created and promoted in all sides of an organisation.

These principles are basic for the efficient functioning of an organisation and are to be kept as tools in the 'managerial kit' to solve variety of managerial problems and malfunctioning in an organisation.

5
Human Resource Development

One of the important and the key roles of human resource in modern libraries is development of human resources. This function is centered on individual's roles, teams, inter-teams and the total organisation. Development of human resources means "Employees of an organisation are helped to acquire essential skills, knowledge and other capabilities required by the organisation according to its standards in a planned process to meet the-present and future expectations of the organisation on human side in a conducive environment with result orientation".

Human Resources Development is a process of helping employees in an organisation to acquire new skills and competence on a continuing basis. The organisation should provide facilities to the employees in a planned and systematic way to:

- acquire and sharpen skills and capabilities to perform various tasks associated with their present and expected future roles;
- develop their general capabilities, discover and exploit their inner potential for their own and/or organisational development purposes;
- help bring about an organisational culture in which collaboration among sub-units is strong and contributes to the supervisor-subordinate relationships, team work and the professional well-being and pride of employees;
- facilitate upgrading of skills through mechanisms and instruments; and
- improve abilities by the introduction of strategic and operational HRD planning and execution.

HRD, is necessary for any type of organisation for:

- survival and stability;
- growth and development;
- change and diversification;
- retuning the activities to become more effective;
- providing highest quality in products and services;
- playing a leadership role in the field; and
- obtaining goodwill and reputation through customer satisfaction.

COMPONENTS OF HRD

An HRD programme for an organisation is a planned activity, which should include a clear statement of objectives and goals, strategic and operational planning, and appropriate means, mechanisms and instruments for execution. Important of them are discussed briefly as :

(i) Strategic and Operational Planning

Strategic and operational planning is largely confined to defining the objectives of the organisation, preparing policy guidelines, evolving pragmatic plans and strategies for executive actions, and establishing appropriate procedures, rules and regulations for implementation at all levels. This would ensure:

- professionalism;
- personal involvement in work in achieving set targets;
- formalisation;
- enhancement of work skills ;
- increasing application of information technologies;
- evolution of a corporate culture; and
- continued progress and development.

This approach would encourage organisations to plan their future staffing structures and to take into account changes in services and technology. Exercised properly, and on a continuing basis, it should eliminate problems of over supply or under supply of particular skills within an organisation. It also aids the determination of training needs in relation to new skills required.

Operational planning takes care to implement and execute the activities and programms to achieve the targets set by the objectives and goals of an organisation. Further it handles personnel recruitment, selection, placement and development, and personnel skill development through training and hands-on experience. The distribution of personnel to the various units, divisions and departments is done through task analysis, job analysis, job description, job specification, competencies etc. The implication of this exercise is that the right person should fit into the right job that would not only ensure work efficiency and quality but also give job satisfaction to the concerned person.

Mechanisms

The first step towards HRD is to set up a unit to deal exclusively with personnel development programmes. The mechanisms to implement these programmes are to introduce a process of performance evaluation of staff at all levels, assess deficiencies or under performance, and such other shortfalls in performance. Corrective steps are to conceive and design specific instruments to set things right and get maximum productivity through the optimum efficiency of the staff. The HRD unit should concern itself with the following aspects:

* performance appraisal;
* role analysis;
* training policies;
* communication policies;
* job rotation;
* organisation development;
* awards, rewards and incentives; and
* organisational and work culture.

(i) Performance appraisal: It is a periodical evaluation of employees' performance. Proper evaluation is carried out with appropriate yardsticks; data on performance review and feedback from the employee are estimated with reference to the employee's optimum potential. Performance coaching and counselling would enable employees to contribute to their optimum potential.

(ii) Role analysis: Role is the position an employee occupies as defined by expectations of different significant persons have for the person. Role analysis is concerned with optimum stress, linkages and autonomy. Optimum stress refers to tuning a person to raise his contribution to the optimum level. Linkages provide for intra and inter relations between individuals and teams within the units and outside.

Autonomy permits an individual to display initiative in dealing with a new problem and finding a solution to it.

(iii) Training policies: These are widely laid down and practised in most organisations to build up staff skills. Training has to be with reference to the types of training required by an organisation, in-house training or training by professional bodies or institutions, evaluation of trained employees and utilisation of the training obtained.

(iv) Communication policies : These contribute substantially to the health of the organisation. Through inappropriate internal communication channels, the organisational activities can be authentically reported. This would prevent unnecessary faith in grapevine and gossip among the employees. The employees would also be properly informed about the activities and progress of the organisation.

(v) Job rotation: Judicious transfer of persons to pick up experience and expertise in different areas of work in different units of an organisation also would contribute to the health of the organisation.

(vi) Organisation development : An organisation has to be dynamic and should positively respond to changes in the environment, advances in technology, and diversification of products and services. Growth, impact in the field and self-developing mechanisms are important for organisation development.

(vii) Award, reward and incentives : Another important aspect relates to awards, rewards, incentives schemes, both for individuals and groups, which would generate greater involvement of employees in work and contribute to quality assurance. This scheme needs very judicious implementation, i.e., only after a foolproof method has been evolved. If this precaution is not taken, undesirable results detrimental to organisational growth may follow.

(viii) Organisational and work culture: For the development of an organisational culture, an appropriate environmental climate is necessary. Communication within the organisation that permits top-down, bottom-up, horizontal, circular and external communication has to be built into the organisation. This would ensure smoothness in employee–employer relationship. This also would create the right atmosphere to develop a work culture, contributing positively to the organisation.

The above aspects would be influenced by factors like management style, environment, technology, resource availability, background and past history of the organisation, nature of business, and others.

If properly attended and successfully implemented, this is likely to be reflected in organisational effectiveness like higher productivity, growth and diversification, cost reduction, more profits and a better image of the organisation.

HRD Process

HRD is a continuous process and not merely a set of planning, and setting of mechanism, instruments, techniques, etc. The mechanism and techniques such as performance appraisal, counselling, innovations in organisational development, etc., are meant to initiate, facilitate and promote the process of implementation. These mechanisms, instruments, and techniques need to be constantly reviewed for their effectiveness. The organisation can facilitate this process of development by the conscious application of ideas described earlier.

Every work-related issue should be examined at periodic intervals and at every level — managerial as well as operational. Task analysis, quality of work life that includes work place democracy, autonomous work groups, active participation, etc., productivity oriented activities, and quality assurance of the products and services are some aspects that would demand considerable attention.

A healthy atmosphere contributes the success and growth of an organisation. Activities, methods and techniques will have to be reviewed constantly to improve the impact and effectiveness of the organisation. This is done through organisation development which is concerned with the development of competency through effective teams to diagnose problems and initiate the process of collaborative work to deal with them. Process competence is improved, aiming to monitor and maintain sound organisational health, assisting non-performing units, helping healthy units and departments in self-renewal, conflict management and creation of strong teams, etc.

Organisational learning is a process of obtaining new skills through involvement, thereby picking up valuable experience. This is a sure way of adding value to every function in the organisation. This is very greatly helped by a research wing in the organisation which would collect data on different issues, analyse such data, interpret, evaluate and apply positive results to solve problems.

So, discussions on strategic and operational planning, mechanisms, instruments, techniques and all other ideas are to be taken in their integration and not in isolation. Concepts such as appraisal, career orientation, training, work analysis, organisational and work culture, self-renewal, etc. are to be superimposed on organisational planning and operational analysis and planning.

Usually it is the top management that is responsible for a well defined programme, for evolving strategies and for achieving targeted goals and objectives, but it is persons' operating at lower levels of management who have the responsibility of implementation.

HRD IN INDIAN LIBRARIES AND INFORMATION CENTRES

HRD may seems to be somewhat irrelevant to the conditions prevailing in Indian libraries and information centres. The large majority of LICs are small in terms; of staff deployed and budgetary provisions. There are, of course, national library and information centres operating as independent and separate institutions. Universities, institutes of technology and such other academic and research institutions have large libraries and information centres. But even in these larger institutions, these ideas of planned HRD are not operative. As it stands now, in most LICs personnel aspects are handled, by and large, by their respective parent bodies. The administrative departments of these parent bodies deal with personnel, mostly in relation to salary and allowance, discipline and control, training and deputation to conferences, performance appraisal in a limited way and such others. Moreover Some of the limited personnel developmental avenues are available only to certain levels of staff, seldom percolating to lower levels. No personnel/ HRD departments seem to be exclusively existing to take cars of all personnel aspects.

The relevance of HRD, however, is with reference to future possibilities, apart from the exposure it provides to comprehend HRD concepts and issues. Libraries and information services at the national level and at the higher education and research level are growing in terms collection, size, variety, and services with computerisation and networking. Personnel problems, not necessarily to deal with the large number of employees but some of the other aspects like designing appropriate instruments for performance appraisal, training to all levels of employees, development of organisational and work culture, are sure to crop up. These aspects and others that might help even smaller LICs? To design and develop high quality products and services may include:

- personnel planning;
- orientation towards modern information products and services;
- productivity;
- customer satisfaction;
- quality of products and services;
- acquisition of new skills and knowledge;
- task analysis for deployment of personnel;
- performance appraisal, counselling and coaching;
- motivational aspects;
- organisational development; and
- R & D.

Stress should be on quality and value added information systems and services, aiming at excellence. HRD is one and an important strategy to build up a cadre of highly competent professional staff.

KAIZEN - INEXPENSIVE WAY TO DEVELOP HUMAN RESOURCES IN LIBRARIES

Gemba Kaizen is the inexpensive way to improve human resource continuously. 'Gemba' means the 'real place' where the action occurs and 'Kaizen' means 'change for the better'. In libraries ' Gemba to the real place is the place where the user meets the service provider and the place where different library activities are carried out. Kaizen culture talks about simple way as the best solutions for improving the attitude of the employees. It does not include sophisticated technology or any complex procedures the success of a library lies in the satisfaction of the users. Kaizen helps to improve the attitude of the people through simple processes. The satisfaction of the users depends on the positive and courteous behaviour of library personnel to a large extent.

The pillars of Kaizen are standardisation, 5S (for house keeping) and muda (waste) elimination.

Standardisation

Libraries are non-profit service organisations. The criteria for gauging the efficiency of a library depends entirely or users' feedback.

The jobs of the library professionals can be considered having no slur if there is no negative comment by the user. The next step of kaizen is to improve further. For example, the professionals in the circulation desk may provide more prompt service than he has been providing, to save the time of the users. The reference librarian may provide pin-pointed information to the user instead of providing only the source. The quality of the service is thus improve if there is a complaint from any user the root cause is to be detected and has to be eliminated accordingly. For example, if a user complains about non-availability of the desired book in the specified position the employees should identify the reason behind it. Whether the book is issued or misplaced and even if it is misplaced, why is that so, these are the pertinent problems most of which commonly occur in libraries. The solutions of these perennial problems can certainly improve the quality of the library services. The solutions must involve the improvement in process also. One time solution can not improve the situation.

Five S for Good Housekeeping

These can be described in the following way.

Seiri means sorting of all unnecessary items and eliminating them. The process is to distinguish between necessary and unnecessary items in gemba and discard the latter.

Seitor means straighten i.e. to arrange all items remaining after seiri in orderly manner.

Seiso - scrub *i.e.* to keep the work environment clean.

Seiketsu or systematise, the process which extends the concept of cleanliness to oneself and continuously practice the above steps.'

Shitsuke means to standardise the 'four steps to make the process that never ends and can be improved upon.

Five S in relation to libraries

Seiri, the first step of housekeeping involves identification is necessary and unnecessary items and removal of the latter. In traditional libraries, it is observed that some books are lying unused. They do not attract any user. Eventually, those books and their information content become obsolete. In the field of science and technology the rate of obsolescence is much faster than in other fields. So the old books can be removed from the main stack area so that place for new books can be made available. Sometimes the new edition of some volumes may replace the old ones if the latter are not needed. The library professionals can also identify the books which are not issued for quite some time. A strategy can be taken up by the top management that kind this books or study materials can be removed from the main stack area 'Gemba'. Thus, the unnecessary books or study materials are identified and removed from the area where only the necessary items are kept for effective use.

Incase of library furniture also some extra racks, tables, chairs, catalogue cabinet are seen lying unused, these are also unnecessary. Removal of extra furniture is necessary to keep a library neat and clean.

The second step in gemba kaizen is seiten (straighten). Once the seiri is carried out, the unnecessary items are removed and then the process of organising the necessary items in an orderly manner comes into picture. The 'straighten process involves keeping the necessary things in their proper place'. If the book is misplaced, it may not be traced by the users or by the employees. Misplaced books or study materials may be missed forever. To avoid this, a thorough seiten is the answer. Seites also demands a clear indication of the address of the materials. For example, the call numbers have to be written legibly and pasted very carefully so that the users do not have any problem in identifying the material. The title of the book the authors' name the volume number if written on the spine of the book should not be hidden by the call number sticker.

The third step of gemba kaizen culture is seiso which means cleaning the working environment. Cleanliness is missing in most of the big libraries. Keeping the books and study materials dust-free, is a major challenge for the libraries. The library manager can motivate other people in clearing the racks and the work place by involving themselves in the activity. Everybody likes clean workplace and the employees feel motivated if they work in a clean library. The employees will try to keep the place clean if they themselves are involved in the cleaning process. The work should not be thrust only on the employees who are supposed to do it, for example, the peons. Everybody including the library manager should participate in the activity.

The fourth step is seiketsu implying the continued effort to work on seiri, seiton and seiso. These three steps can be carried out everyday. Kaizen does not work if it is practiced only once. The continuity is needed. For example, if seiri is carried out once in 5 years, the problem of the burden of unnecessary items will be rolved initially. But again the accumulation will start after sometime. So the steps are to be continued. A clear-cut strategy- can be taken by the top management for carrying out the steps for gemba. Like other quality strategies, the top management commitment is a must for kaizen also.

The final stage is 'shitsuke' the self discipline. People Performing the four steps continuously will acquire self-discipline ultimately, and then they will sustain the culture in their daily work. Self-disciplined people will automatically practice 5S in gemba. The attitude of the people, in the workplace will certainly change.

Appriasal of 5S : There are certain ways to appraise the level of the steps of housekeeping in gemba.

* self-evaluation;
* Valuation by an expert consultant;
* evaluation by the superiors;
* evaluation by the customers (users);
* competition among gemba groups;

The library authority can organise the appraisal activity. Ready-made appraisal tools are available with publishers like AMA, BTD, Par-Training etc. The library managers can also develop their own assessment tool. It does not cost much. The situation can be understood with a view to initiate the improvement processes.

Muda (waste) elimination

The third pillar of kaizen is the muda *i.e.* waste elimination. In seiri, we have seen the elimination of the unnecessary items. Muda elimination includes not only the items but different activity also. Thaichi Ohyo was the first person to recognise the enormous amount of muda that existed in gemba. Muda refers to items as well as activity which do not add value. Ohno's categorisation for muda elimination can be seen with reference to the libraries in the following way.

(i) Muda of processing;

(ii) Muda of motion;

(iii) Muda of excessive order;

(iv) Muda of waiting; and

(v) Muda of transport.

(i) Muda of processing : It indicates the unnecessary work which is carried out in organising the library. The work which does not add any value to the work is considered as muda. While processing a book the elements used in bibliographic description such as author, title etc., are to be used carefully. Any elements which does not add any value for the users have to be eliminated. In a computerised library, when database is created extra precaution has to be taken to remove the muda.

(ii) Muda of motion : It means the unproductive movement of the people inside the workplace. Any movement which is not required for actual work purpose is to be removed. Walking from one section to the other to convey messages sometimes become unnecessary and unproductive.

(iii) Muda of excessive order : It in libraries denotes unwanted lag between the delivery of books in the library and its availability for use. If processing can not keep pace with the orders, the processing section becomes a dumping peace for new books. Gemba kaizen says that the number or new books coming into the library should be processed at once. There should not be much gap between the time when the books or study materials are delivered to the library and their availability in the stack area.

(iv) Muda of waiting : It relates to the idle time when the hands of the people engaged in stack area becomes idle as the processing of books lags behind. If there is a synchronisation between the ordering section, processing section and the circulation section the muda of waiting can be eliminated.

(v) Muda of transport : If the order section and processing section and the stack area are situated away from each other, the unnecessary burden of transport of books is inevitable. That can be avoided by simply keeping the inter-related sections in close proximity to each other.

It is clear that the standardisation, 5S of house keeping and muda elimination in relation to different library activities are the pillars of gemba kaizen.

Masaaki Irai has suggested some basic rules for practicing kaizen in gemba.

(i) Discard conventional rigid thinking;

(ii) Think of how to do it, not why it cannot be done;

(iii) Do not seek excuses, start by questioning current practices.

(iv) Do not seek perfection. Do it right away even if for only half of the target.

(v) Correct mistakes at once.

(vi) Do not spend for kaizen.

(vii) Wisdom is brought out when faced with hardship.

(viii) Ask why? Five times and seek the root cause.

(ix) Seek the wisdom of ten people rather than the knowledge of one.

(x) Remember that opportunities for kaizen are infinite.

In libraries being non-profit organisations, the user satisfaction is the criteria for evaluating the library services. Inter-personal communication is the building stone for carrying out services. Inter-personal communication can only be successful if a highly motivated and self-disciplined team of people work in the libraries. Self-discipline can be acquired by practicing kaizen in gemba. The top management has to build a self-motivated team by selecting the people with positive attitude. The team may start work with a clear-cut objective and strategy. They can initiate activities which will motivate others. Finally, most of the employees will become self- disciplined and practice gemba kaizen. Eventually the libraries will become nicer places for the scholars to learn on.

6
Personnel Management

The staff, the books and the readers make up-the fundamental trinity of a library. The success of a library largely depends upon the persons who are responsible for the effective use of a good collection of books in the hands of the readers. A library having good collections can not render best services to its readers without efficient and trained personnel. Thus, for the fulfillment of desired objectives of any library sincere and organised human effort is essential. The basic aim of the library staffs should be to place the right book in the hands of right readers at the right time. They should ensure that no reader who requires help either in the choice of books, or in getting information from documents should so without it. According to Clara W. Herbert, "The organisation of a library is, therefore, of fundamental importance in the consideration of personnel administration. It is the house in which the members of a like profession live and should partake of the characteristics of a happy home. It should be well regulated, smooth running cooperative, comfortable in which each member of the stall may find his rightful place".

Personnel management typically encompasses, at the very least, recruitment and classification of employees; salary administration: training and staff development: performance evaluation; personnel policies, including grievance procedures; and possibly unionization.

PERSONAL POLICIES

The personnel policy of a library includes the ranking and grading, job analysis and job description, condition of service, recruitment, selection and training and strength of the staff.

Ranking, duties and grading of the staff

The entire staff structure of library usually consists of certain ranks of employees of different grades. The "ranking" of employees is determined according to the type of works they perform. In other words, it relates to the number of posts at each level. The "grading" of the staff is made according to different classes of personnels blazing on their salaries and wages. The first requirement in getting the best out of a library staff is to make a clear-cut a separation as possible between professional and semi-professional work, as it will not economical to burden professional employees with non-professional duties or vice-verse. So all the employees in a library are divided into three categories— professional, semi-professional and non-professionals.

The professional staff are engaged in performing professional duties whose minimum qualifications should be graduation with at least one year training in library and information science leading to post graduate degree or diploma. The semi-professional staff of a library consists of employees who perform library routine and techniques under the guidance of professional staff and have received alternative training in library science. Also some none professional as clerical workers and unskilled workers are appointed to perform certain library works.

Job analysis

As our modern library is complex affair it becomes very necessary to define duties and responsibilities of the library staff working in different sections. Therefore, an analysis shall be made embodying a general description of level of work and the responsibility of each grade or level of work. A detailed job analysis of each section of a library also needs to be attempted so that each member of the staff knows what he is supposed to do and what is expected of him. In deciding on the grade of the post, the general level of work and responsibility for a particular post should be laid down. Thus it can easily be determined what specific duties appropriate to each post, and what qualifications, knowledge, skill and aptitudes are necessary to perform the job.

Advantages of Job Analysis : It

1. Defines labour needs.
2. Specifies duties and responsibilities in each
3. Assists in organizational planning.
4. Helps in determining job opportunities.
5. Provides a scientific base for fixing wages.
6. Helps in using scientific principles of management.

Job Description

Job Analysis leads to Job Description which implies the recording of the following data concerning, each analysed :

1. Principal duties to be performed and responsibilities involved are outlined.
2. Operations involved in each job are listed in proper sequence.
3. Requisite materials, equipment, machinery etc. are listed.
4. Conditions of work i.e. surroundings, the time of work etc. are stated.
5. Relations of various related jobs are indicated.
6. Mental and physical abilities for performing operation are listed. The kind of training an length of experience required are also indicated.
7. Wages payable alongwith other fringe benefits are stated.

Job Evaluation

Job Evaluation means job-rating. By it the value of each job is specified vis-a-vis another job or a group of jobs. This is, perhaps, an objective method of measuring the value of a particular job. This process may imply the following essential steps:

1. Determination of requisite elements or factors involved in all jobs carrying monetary remuneration.
2. Using these elements and factors for comparing one job with another.
3. Knowing the relative value of each job.
4. Fixing the money value of each job.

Condition of service

Service condition is an essential ingredient of staff management. It includes such matters as hours of work, service regulations, pension, retirement and resignation policies and procedures, policy relating to educational and welfare facilities. Conditions of service in state and central government managed both public and academic libraries are laid down on a state or national basis. In order to relate the salaries of the staff to their work performed and responsibility attached, the chief librarian or the Director of Libraries must use his professional knowledge to assess these. Also through joint consultation or negotiation between staff and management, the gradation, working conditions and scales of pay of the library personnel should be determined.

Recruitment, selection procedure and training

The recruitment policy of a library is planned considering the nature of its services. Thus, the recruitment policy of a public library differs from a school or college or University library or from any special and research library. Hence the recruitment of the library staff should be made by certain tests like aptitude test, personality test, interest test, intelligence test, etc. The tests are necessary and helpful in assigning the right job to the right person so that he can be able to develop his interest as a scholar, cultivate a real intellectual awareness and assist the research scholars, teaching staff and students to save their time in bibliographic search and information retrieval.

Recruitment and Selection Procedures' steps include :

1. Ascertaining vacant jobs;
2. Finalising the qualifications;
3. Inviting applications;
4. Receiving applications;
5. Deciding interview dates:
6. Sending interview letters;
7. Laying down interview criteria;
8. Inviting opinion of referees;
9. Interviewing candidates;
10. Selecting candidates;
11. Settling pay-scales, salary; etc;
12. Issuing appointment letter, etc.

The recruitment of library staff should be proceeded by job analysis and job description. An analysis should be made to decide the number of posts required, types of jobs to be done, to specify the responsibilities implied in each job and to determine the qualifications required by a staff member to enable him to do the job satisfactorily. The minimum basic and professional qualification should be laid down for each job.

According to the report of the Library Committee of the University Grants Commission, India, the academic qualifications of the Library staff should be at par with those of the Professors, the Readers, the Lecturers and the Tutors. Apart the from general academic qualifications of a high order, the librarian and his professional staff should also have professional qualifications of an equally high order.

The selection and appointment of library staff is to be done very carefully because much of the success of the library staff member on the job in a library depends upon skillful personnel administration. The staff of the library should be well organised so that each member can contribute his highest abilities and skills to the cooperative effort. The usual method of selections either by open advertisement or through the Employment Directorate for the posts and prescribing the qualifications, experience and scales of pay. The head of the library or the chief librarian should be selected through a higher power selection committee consisting of Library experts. The librarian should be the person chiefly responsible for personnel administration, and he should be called for an interview and the selection committee should prepare a panel of names in order of merit of performance so that, if the candidate placed, at the top does not accept the job, an offer is sent to the next one. Thus the appointments to the different posts are made on the recommendation of the selection committee which should be very fair and honest.

After appointment, .the library needs to ensure that new staffs are trained in their duties and that other staff improve their activities, so that they becomes more efficient and may quality for promotion. The existing staff should be trained in the use of new appliances and machines like computer, photocopier, microfilm reader, electronic stencil cutter etc. Training may be imparted through (a) apprentice system, which equips the trainee with a practical knowledge of actual library work; (b) in-service training for those who are selected for promotion may also be required to take additional courses in Library and Information Sciences or it they are in non-professional positions, so attend the library science courses over a particular period of time; (c) under study method which enables an employee to work under another trained experienced employee; (d) study tour which provides scope for an educational visit to big modern libraries; (e) extension lectures, workshops, refresher course, seminars, conferences and meetings.

For the purpose of training in librarianship or library and information science education, schools colleges and departments are established either by Government or by the library associations. The training for the semi-professionals is a undergraduate course where as the training for the professionals should be of the university standard and a postgraduate course, leading to B.Lib.I.Sc and M.Lib.I.Sc. degrees etc.

STAFFING

Staffing is the function concerned with employment and training of employees, and maintenance of conducive environment, for accomplishing the' objectives of an enterprise. According to Mac Farland, "Staffing is the function by which managers build an organization through recruitment, selection and development of individuals as capable employees." It covers both managerial and rank-and-file positions. Staffing aims at building up an organizational structure, which can deliver goods for the present and the future.

Staffing is an important function. The future of an enterprise would greatly depend upon the quality of personnel. Staffing function has become more and more complex during the recent years. There is a need to employ competent personnel, provide continuing training and education to them and make available favourable environment for their effective performance.

Categories of Staff

As stated earlier, according to nature of job, we may classify the personnel in library into the following categories :

1. Professional - Senior & Junior
2. Semi Professional or supporting (Administrative)
3. Non - Professional.

1. Professional Staff

Professional staff consists of those, who possess a decree or post-graduate diploma in Library and Information Science in addition to a degree in some other discipline. In a university library, the positions such as Professional Assistant, Assistant Librarian, Deputy Librarian, and Librarian are considered as professional positions. Similarly, in a college library, a Professional Assistant and a Librarian constitute professional staff. In a school library, a Librarian would very often belong to this category.

Some of the jobs performed by professionals are given below:

* Book selection
* Book order
* Classification
* Cataloguing
* Indexing
* Abstracting
* Reference service
* Information service and
* Planning etc.

In the public library system Director of Libraries, State Central Librarian, Deputy Librarians and Assistant Librarian and other technical assistant are placed in this category.

2. Semi Professional Staff

This category of staff can be compared with para medical staff who also hold technical knowledge of medicine and other respective works of hospital. In library, this category of staff played an important role. They possesses library qualification of the level of certificate or diploma in library science. The semi-professional staff, generally, be designated as - Duplicate Checking Assistant, Order Assistant, Catalogue Assistant. Typist, Issue/Return Assistant, Periodical Assistant etc.

3. Non-professional Staff

Other staff of the library such as clerical, secretarial and peon, attendant, janitor, gardener, watchmen are belongs to this category.

The following is the list of some of the jobs, which are usually performed by the supporting staff or administrative staff.

- Secretarial assistance to the librarian and other senior staff.
- Maintenance of personnel records (personal files, service books, confidential records, etc.)
- Maintenance of stores (Purchase of stores, maintenance of stock registers for both consumable and non-consumable articles, etc.)
- Typing (except that of catalogue cards, bibliographies, documentation lists, etc.)
- Housekeeping and janitorial duties.

Staff Pattern

Adequate staffing is essential for effective library service. According to A.L.A. standard measure a public library needs one full time staff member for every 2,000 - 2,500 persons in its service community. Thus, a library serving 10,000 people should have a minimum of four full time staff members. The staff should be provided in adequate number to avoid placing too heavy a work load on any one employee.

According to the report of the Library Committee of the U.G.C. (1965) a University Library should determine the strength of the different section on the basis of the following staff formula :

Section	Jobs	Staff
1. Book Section	Charged with the selection, ordering and accessioning of purchased as well as donated books.	One person for every 6,000 volumes added in a year.
2. Periodical publications Section	Charged with ordering, weekly receipts, preparation and display of current periodicals, their compilation and preparation for binding on the completion of volume.	One person for every 500 current periodical taken.
3. Documentation Section	Charged with the preparation of the documentation list and of the abstracts of the relevent articles in current periodicals.	One person for every 1000 entries-prepared in a year.
4. Technical Section	Charged with the classification and the cataloguing of the books,	One person for every 2,000 volumes added in a year.
5. Reference Section	Charged with helping the students, the teachers, and the research workers, in the choice of books and articles in periodicals appropriate to their interest at the moment.	One person for every 50 readers in a day.
6. Circulation Section	Charged with the charging and discharging of	One person for every 1500 hours for which

Section	Jobs	Staff
	the books needed for study by readers, all through each day.	one wicket gate of the Library has to be kept open in a year.
7. Maintenance Section	Charged with the maintenance of the books and the periodicals in the correct sequence on the shelves, the maintenance of the gangway guides, the bay guides and the shelf guides in the stack-room in order to facilitate open access, the daily placement of the books returned by readers, and the preparation of books for repairs and binding week after week.	One person for every 6000 volumes added in a year, one person for every 500 volumes to be replaced in day and one person for every 100000 volumes in the library.
8. Administrative Section	Charged with the usual office functions such as accounts, budget, correspondence work, steno typist work, and maintenance of the buildings, filings and furniture.	Minimum of one library accountant, one steno-typist and one correspondence clerk.
9. Supervisory Section	For two shifts for supervision, organisation, and solving the difficulties cropping up in the work of different sections.	One Librarian and One Assistant or Deputy Librarian.
10. Unskilled staff	One cleaner for every 30,000 volumes in the library, one attendant each for every 6000 volumes added in a year, for every 500 current periodicals taken, and for each of the shifts in the circulation section, besides unskilled and the semi-skilled workers normal to any institution.	

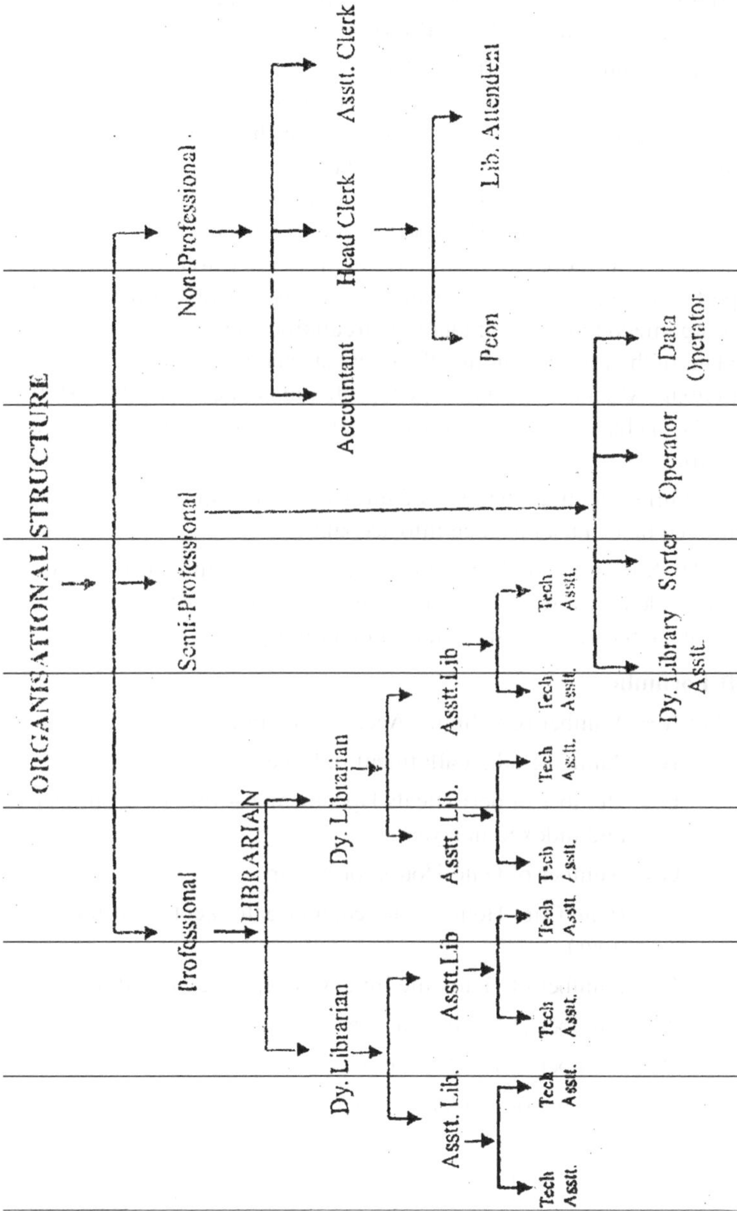

Fig. 1. Typical organisational structure of a Library

Thus, it is clear that the development and improvement of libraries is intimately bound up with the provision and maintenance of library staff according to the staff formula.

The number of staff members in a public library should be sufficient to provide consistently efficient service at all hours when the library is open to the public, and to perform the duties involved in assembling, organizing and interpreting the materials required by the programme of the Library. The size of the staff for any given library or library system must be based upon the programme of service adopted by the library, the populations and size of the service area, the financial support, and more specially, the number of departments, branches and other organized units, the amount of circulation and reference service, the plans of the library building, the hours of opening, and other factors. At all hours when the library is open, professional members of the staff should be in charge of public services requiring professional preparation and skill.

While deciding the size of the staff of the library the above mentioned facts must be taken into account.

Dr. S.R. Ranganathan in his book "Library Administration" has recommended the following staff formula for estimating the number of different categories of posts required in a library:

Staff Formula

Let A = Number of volumes Accessioned in a year.

B = Annual Budget allotment in Rupees.

D = Number of periodicals Documented—that is, abstracted and indexed in a year.

G = Number of Gate-Hours for a year.

(One Gate-Hour = One counter gate, kept open for one hour).

H = Number of Hours the library is kept open in a day.

P = Number of Periodicals currently taken.

R = Number of Readers per day.

S = Number of Seats for readers.

V = Number of Volumes in the library.

W = Number of Working days in a year.

[X] = X, if X is one integer.

= The Integer just greater than X, if its fractional part is greater than .25.

= The Integer just smaller than X, if its fractional part is not greater than .25.

SB = Number of persons in Book Section.

SC = Number of persons in Circulation Section.

SL = Number of persons as Librarian and his Deputies.

SM = Number of persons in Maintenance Section.

SP = Number of persons in Periodicals Section.

SR = Number of persons in Reference Section.

ST = Number of persons in Technical—that is Classification and Cataloguing—Section.

Formula for Different Staff of the Different Sections

SB = A/6,000	Book section: 1 person for every 6,000 volumes added in a year.
SC = G/1,500	Circulation section; 1 person for 1500 gate hours.
SL = HW/1500	Librarian and his Deputy: 1 person for 1500 working hours in a year.
SM = A/3,000	Maintenance section. For shelving and repairing 3000 volumes.
SP = P/500	Periodical Section: 1 person for acquiring and recording 500 periodicals in a year.
SR = (R/50) W/250	Reference Section: 1 person for 50 readers in a day.
ST = (A 40 D), 2000	Technical Section 1 person for classifying and cataloguing and documenting 40 books per day on an average.

Formula for Total Professional Staff

SB + SC + SL + SM + SP + SR + ST

= {3 (A + 20D) + 2(G + 3P) + 2W (H + 6 [R/50]} /3000

Formula for Non-Professional Skilled Staff

B/30,000 + (S/100)

Formula for Unskilled Staff

SB/4 + SC/2 + SL + SM/4 + SP/2 + SR/8 + A/20,000 + D/500 + B/60,000 + [S/100]/4 + V/30,000

= {27A + 2(B + 120D) + 40(G + 3P) + 30,000 [S/100] + 4V + 2W(40H + 3[R/50]}/120,000

According to Dr. S.R. Ranganathan this staff formula is applicable for all types of libraries with adjustments and additions. The Advisory Committee for Libraries which was appointed by Government of India in 1958 under the Chairmanship of Shri *K.P. Sinha* has given the following recommendations regarding designations, qualifications and status in various categories of public libraries:

Table 1. Library Posts, Qualifications for the Posts and equivalent Educational Posts

Sl. No.	Library Units/Library posts	Librarians qualifications	Equivalent in Educational Service
1.	Village Library— A library which serves a village or group of 4 or 5 neighbouring villages (Designation: Village Librarian)	Volunteer who is atleast Middle pass or a teacher willing to work honorarily or on a small allowance.	Literacy teacher of adults.
2.	Small Town Library— A library of a town with 2500 to 5000 population (Small Town Librarian)	Matric with Elementary training.	Primary School teacher.
3.	Small Area Library — A library of a town with 2500 to 5000 population with 3 or more deposit stations. (Small Area Librarian)	Matric with elementary training, and atleast a year's experience.	Headmaster in a primary school
4.	Medium Town Library — A library of a town with 5,000 to 20,000 population. (Medium Town Librarian)	Matric with elementary tradining, and at least a year's experience.	Middle School teacher.

Sl. No.	Library Units/Library posts	Librarians qualifications	Equivalent in Educational Service
5.	Medium Area Library — A library of a town with 5,000 to 20,000 populations and 3 or more deposit stations (Medium Area Librarian)	Graduate with Training and atleast a year's experience.	Headmaster Middle School.
6.	(a) Large Town Library— A library of a town with 20,000 to 50,000 populations (Large Town Librarian)	Graduate with a full year's training in Library Science.	High School training graduate teacher.
	(b) Professional Assistant — A person who performs work of professional nature requiring formal training in Library Science. (Reference Assistant, Cataloguing Assistant).	— do—	—do—
	(c) Branch Librarian or Branch Inspector	—do—	—do—
	(d) Block Library. (A library for serving the inhabitants of block area) (Branch Librarian)	Graduate with a full year's training in Library Science with some experience.	High School trained graduate teacher with some allowance.
7.	(a) Head of Department — An officer in charge of an administrative division of a library or of a particular type of work which employs not less than 4 workers including the Head. (Reference Librarian, Head-Processing)	Second class Graduate with at least second class in Library Science and at least with 5 years' experience.	Headmaster of a High School.
	(b) Superintendent of Branches—An officer of the district headquarters library responsible to the District Librarian for the	—do—	— do—

Sl. No.	Library Units/Library posts	Librarians qualifications	Equivalent in Educational Service
	efficient administration of the libraries within the district. (Superintendent of Branches)		
8.	Small City Library—A library of a small city of 50,000 to lakh population (Small City Librarian)	Second class Graduate with a full year's course in Library Science and at least 2 years experience.	High start in the same grade as Headmaster of a High School.
9.	(a) City Library—A library of a city of 1 to 3 lakhs populations. (City Librarian)	Second class Graduate with a full year's course in library science and not less than five years experience.	Junior class II (Educational Service).
	(b) District Library—A library which serves the district headquarter's town and is a Central Library for block and town libraries in the district (Designation—District Librarian)	—do—	—do—
10.	State Central Library—(Designation—State Central Librarian)	As above with 10 years' experience or original publication in Librarianship.	Class I Service (Educational)
11.	Director of Libraries—An officer in over-all charge of the administration of Libraries in a state either through an independent Library Department or Sub-Deptt. within the Education Deptt. (Designation—Director of Libraries)	—do—	If he is the head of an independent Deptt. he will be equated with other heads of the Deptt. If not, he should be class I officer of the rank of Deputy . D.P.I. with a special allowance.

The Advisory Committee for Libraries (1959) has made the following some important recommendations regarding the Library personnel:

1. State Government should accept the responsibility of public library service in their areas. The Librarians of these libraries, should be State Government employees.

2. Library Departments in the state should make clear-cut separation between professional and semi-professional work and entrust professional work to trained staff only.
3. After recruitment, the semi-professional staff should be given elementary training during their probation period.
4. As far as possible, librarians should not be transferred too frequently.
5. State Government should freely grant study leave to librarians going in for ordinary higher training in the profession.
6. It should be the responsibility of the State Librarian to see Librarians in the public library system to keep up with the professional literature after leaving the library schools.
7. Every State Government should give at least one opportunity in a year to State and District Librarians to come together for one to four days camp.

The Committee has further mentioned in its recommendations regarding powers of the Director of Libraries, State Librarians and District Librarians.

Duties of the Staff

In the libraries, the librarian and his staff should make themselves familiar with the wave front of knowledge in which research is in progress. They should serve the staff with the nascent thought expeditiously, exhaustively and pinpointedly. They should keep close touch with the progress of class room teaching programme and in collaboration with the teaching staff of different subjects should plan for the students to pursue, preparatory, parallel and follow up study by mobilising the resource of the library. Also they should specialised in the bibliography of different subjects for book selection just to build a balanced book-collection in close-correlation with the current and future of research workers and students. Thus the Library staff should render their services to the research workers, teachers and students.

Generally the staff of a modern library has many duties to perform but the most important one being they way in which information is channelised to the staff members. This is done through staff manuals containing standing instructions, occasional memoranda, dealing with day to clay changes and regular staff meetings to pass on information to all the employees of the library. The staff of Library should perform their duties in order to achieve its objectives. The main aim of a library is to utilise its resources to the best advantage of its readers. So the staff should investigate the reading interests and needs of the readers. They should attend sincerely the technical and processing work such as classification, cataloguing, documentation, circulation, preservation and maintenance of the reading materials. They should extend their special services to the children and youths. The other important duties of the library staff are- Ordering and Accessioning of Books and other documents, processing payment of bills, salaries and sanction of leaves of the staff members, initiation and filing of correspondence, maintenance of staff records, the preparation of budget, annual reports, committee reports and proceedings, assembling statistical data, checking and certification of accounts, as discussed earlier.

Staff Manual

The manual is a book that gives information or practical instructions. Library manual gives guidelines to the staff of the library as to the sections, levels of staff, their functions, work-flow, records to be maintained, coordination among staff, preparation of reports, etc.

It is advantageous to have a staff manual prepared for each library which spells out the various jobs and help as a guide for reference in the hour of need. Such a manual should give a detailed chart of various positions indicating coordination and subordination, line of control, job specification of each employee, etc. These manuals should also specify, the procedure for recruitment, qualifications, age limit and other service conditions as well.

The major areas that need to be specified includes:

1. **Job titles**–Assigning job titles.
2. **Distribution of work** - Distribution consulting, Distribution communicating, Distribution reporting, etc;
3. **Work Assignment** - Casual jobs-Assignment consulting, communicating, assignment adjusting, etc.
4. **Discipline Work** - *Immediate jobs*, control of Class IV employees, Attendance watching, Reporting abnormalities; *Daily jobs*-Scrutining attendance register. Absence intimating, etc; *Weekly* Jobs-Obtaining explanations for memos, Forwarding explanations, transmitting decisions, etc; *Monthly jobs* - Writing attendance register, work report of various employees: sectionwise-qualitative as well as quantitative;

5. **Time** - Table-Finalization, Reconciling, etc.
6. **Staff Order Book** - *Casual jobs* : Staff order writing, order circulars, instructions to new recruits, etc.
7. **Diaries** - *Daily job* of scrutinizing, intimating abnormalities, weekly and monthly totals scrutinizing, etc.
8. **Junction Moments** - Watching, Adjusting if necessary. Avoidance of conflicts, etc.
9. **Progress Report** - Correspondence, disposal of pending items, rounding of routines etc.
10. **Accounts** - Financial diaries. Monitoring expenditure. Payments, Maintenance of accounts and correct figures etc.

Coordination of library work

Librarian as the chief personnel manager of a library should exercise his leadership within the Library. He must inspire confidence among his staff and should guide them properly to improve efficiency and attain best library service. He must delegate the authority of personnel function to the Deputy Librarian, Assistant Librarian, Sectional Heads and other Supervisors. Also he should discuss the problems of different sections with its heads to ensure smooth functioning, and proper co-ordination. Thus, delegation of duties amongst the staff members is most essential for running a library smoothly and efficiently. Basing on the principles of scientific management, the line and staff method of organisation is a suitable approach for co-ordination of library work with some modifications and adjustments according to the needs and requirements of particular library. The line staff officers are jointly responsible for the achievements of a library. A line officer discharges his responsibility by taking direct action but a staff officer discharges his responsibilities by furnishing information and advice to the line officer. C.W. Herbert has suggested the following guiding principles to ensure co-ordination and efficiency of library work.

1. The organisation should be as simple as possible; it should not be over organised with unnecessary overheads or under organised so that too many conflicting duties are placed on to few officers.
2. Authority must always go with responsibility, and these lines should be so clear as to be reading and generally understood.
3. Executives are of two types those who like responsibility for the

execution of work and those who like planning. While the two qualities have to be combined to a certain extent in each executive, a large library needs to provide for both types with corresponding separation of duties,

4. The organisation should be built upon the basis of community needs and be sufficiently flexible to adopt itself to changing demands and conditions.
5. Personnel should be appointed to fit the requirements of the organisation than the other way round. This is one of the difficulties of reorganisation, since libraries must naturally make the most of the capacities of the present members of the staff. But to great consideration, these personal factors make an unbalanced development of the service as a whole.
6. The best organisation is the one which gives the larger number of its members individual responsibility and opportunity for creative work and professional growth.

Thus, library is a service organisation and its existence is justified by the degree of service it renders, to the clients. The Librarian at the helm of its affairs should have ability to command and guide this organisation safely. He should act as an able organiser, co-ordinator guide and controller of the Library staff should play an important role in the set of sound library organisation through co-ordination of their technical efforts.

ORGANISATIONAL STRUCTURE

Library is a social institution. It needs a simple and systematic organisational structure to achieve its goals and objectives. The Librarian should adopt various suitable criteria to structure necessary programmes and activities of a Library. He has to describe and to apply principles, useful for creating an organisational structure, and also to draw organisation charts explaining the inter-connections, inter-relations and inter-dependence among various sections or units of a Library.

For organising the functions of a Library, its activities relating to each function have to be divided into works and jobs and grouped and arranged to form a structure. So it is a practice to divide and group the activities of a Library into desirable sections or units for getting best management results. Some suitable characteristics should be determined for division which would be relevant to fulfill the purpose.

The following characteristics are now being used for creating sections or units in a Library.

(a) Numbers, (b) Functions; (c) Territory (geographical contiguity), (d) Product, (e) Customers (users), (f) Process or Equipment, (g) Subjects, (h) Materials (books, periodicals, microfilms/ forms, maps, etc.)

The most common form of organisational design, is the functional structure. This divides a Library into functional departments/ sections/units such as— Acquisition, Technical, Processing, Circulation, Reference, Documentation, Extension and Maintenance, etc. The public and academic libraries use the criteria '*subjects*' which provides for more-in-depth reference and information services, requiring a higher degree of subject specialisation on the part of the staff. In academic libraries, subject departments are usually broad in scope to include all related subjects. Some libraries also get organised on the basis of materials they do serve such as books, periodicals, micro forms, manuscripts, maps etc. The publication department/section of a library can be organised considering its information products such as Current Awareness Bulletin, Indexing Journals, Abstracting Journals, etc. Special Libraries and. Documentation Centres use the method '*process*' or '*equipment*' for organising their printing and photographic/ micrographic units. In a national library system, regional libraries are organised on the basis of their geographical character.

Principles of structuring

In the process of designing the organisational structure of a library, the dividing and grouping various library activities produce a number of horizontal and vertical units at different levels. So these units need to be structured relating them approximately, to produce a desirable organisational structure for effective administration and efficient management. This structure is essentially an establishment of appropriate relationship between various groups of persons working at vertical and horizontal positions of a Library. Therefore, it is necessary to adopt some useful principles for creating organisational structure such as:

(1) *Span of management :* This refers to the number of activities a manager can effectively manage. This emphasises on the limit to which a Librarian/ Information Officer would be able to supervise, control and manager a number of activities efficiently.

(2) *Scalar principle and the vertical hierarchy :* This needs that there should be final utilise authority and the Lines of authority should clearly extended downward to every subordinate position in a library.

(3) *Unit of command :* This emphasises that each employee is supervised by only one supervisor who should make assignments and assess the employee's performance.

(4) *Delegation of authority and responsibility* : This states that responsibility can not be delegated without accompanying authority. The process of delegation should consider certain facts such as:

(a) Assignment of tasks, (b) the determination of the results expected, (c) degree of delegation of authority for performing the tasks, (d) exact fixation of responsibility for failure or success in performing the tasks of an employee in a Library.

(5) *Line and staff positions:* Line positions or managers are responsible and accountable for the tasks assigned to them in the achievement of organisations aims and objectives. Staff positions are those that provide advice, support and service to the line positions/managers in carrying out their tasks. Usually staff if positions are created in big libraries to streamline operations on the basis of advice given to make right choice from different alternatives.

(6) *Functional authority:* It relates supervisory power exercised on a section or unit by a position/manager/specialist outside the organisational section or unit by a position/manager/specialist outside the organisational section/unit. In libraries, often functional authority is given to specialists who complete a particular project work within specific time; also sometimes they are known as co-ordinators because they have to work with employees involved in their type of speciality.

(7) *Co-ordination and integration:* The employees of a Library work in different positions to accomplish the desired result but these positions are not to be operated in isolation. So they have to operate in close cooperation and coordination with various units of a library. Thus, the final integration of different functions alone will ensure success.

(8) *Centralisation and decentralization:* In a library certain activities

need to be centralised and certain others decentralised. But a judicious combination would ensure best results in most economical way. Therefore, in big libraries house-keeping operations may be centralised and specific services may be decentralised.

Organisational chart

An organisation chart is a useful visual aid for including the horizontal and vertical structure of an organisation. It is a graphic presentation of organisational structure showing different positions, span of control, relationships between line and staff positions, flow of authority and responsibility, relationship with Advisory Committees and such others.

The process of organisation and also its administration must work upto this end. Thus S.R. Ranganathan has formulated his famous five laws of library science just to exemplify this basic approach of library organisation at different stages of its operation. The successive stages in library organisation are as follows:

(a) Planning and construction of Library Building.

(b) Equipping the Library Building with necessary furniture.

(c) Selection, appointment and duties of the staff.

(d) Co-ordination of the work of various departments and sections.

The different types of organisational charts are given in Fig. 2 to 5 for different types of libraries.

STAFF DEVELOPMENT

Once staff is recruited, the next step is to improve their performance and prepare them for new areas of activity. There are several aspects which constitute staff development and contribute to high-performance of staff. These are (i) Probation (ii) Appraisal (iii) Promotion (iv) Induction and Training (v) Staff Records (vi) Welfare.

(i) Probation: Many authorities have a provision of probation for all new appointments. The period of probation varies from organisation to organisation and post to post. At the end of the probation period if a satisfactory report is received from the appropriate head of the department, the concerned member of staff is confirmed. If the report is unsatisfactory, the probation period may be extended or services of the person concerned can be dispensed with.

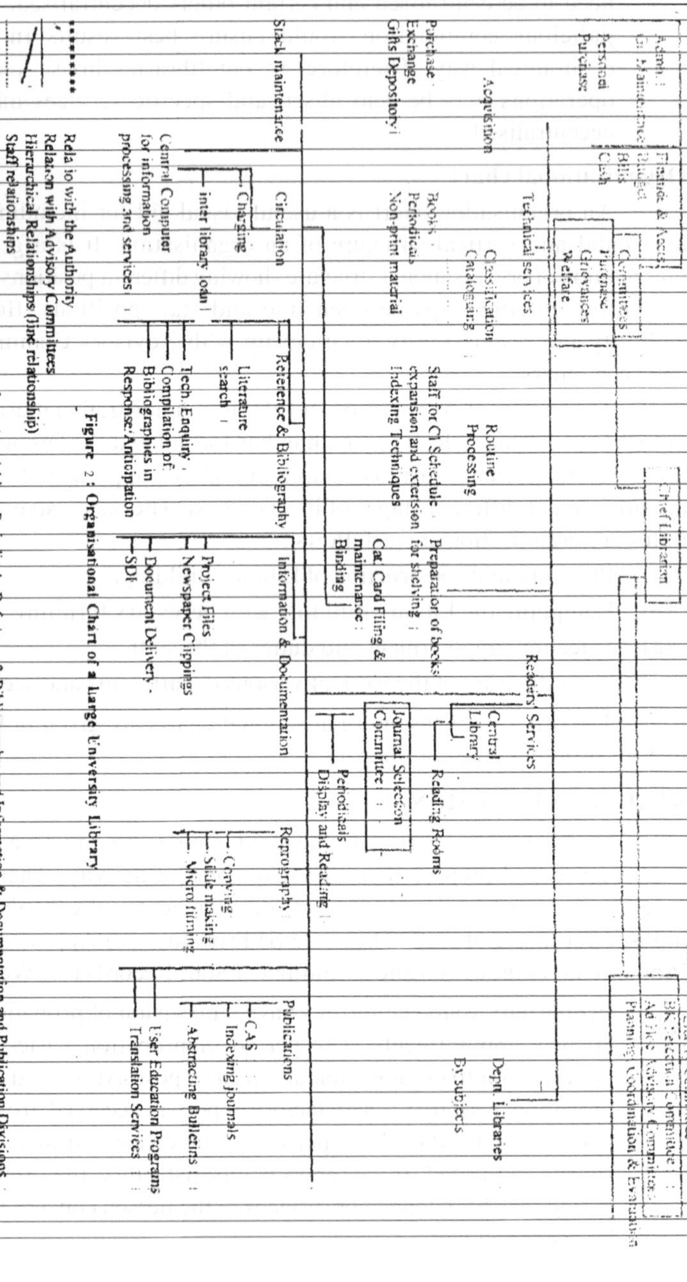

Figure 2 : Organisational Chart of a Large University Library

This journal selection committee may comprise persons from Acquisition, Periodicals, Reference & Bibliography and Information & Documentation and Publication Divisions.

There are many junctions points, which have not been indicated in the chart.

Organisational Chart of a Large Public Library

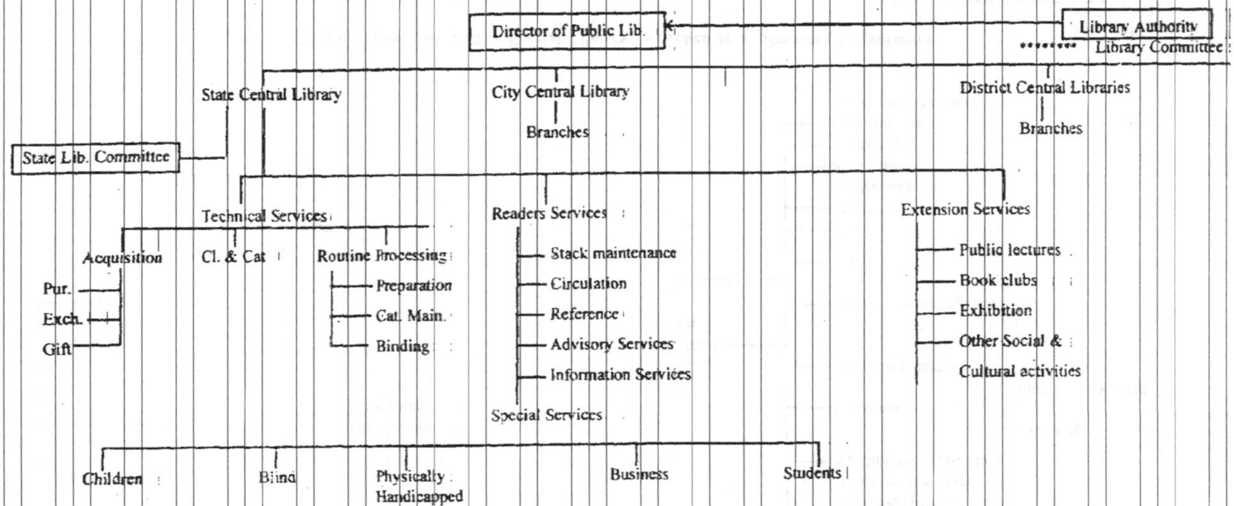

Figure 3 : Organisational Chart of a Large Public Library

******** Relation with the Authority
.... Relations with Advisory Committee
———— Hierarchical relationship (Line)

The other structural relationships may be the same as shown in Figure

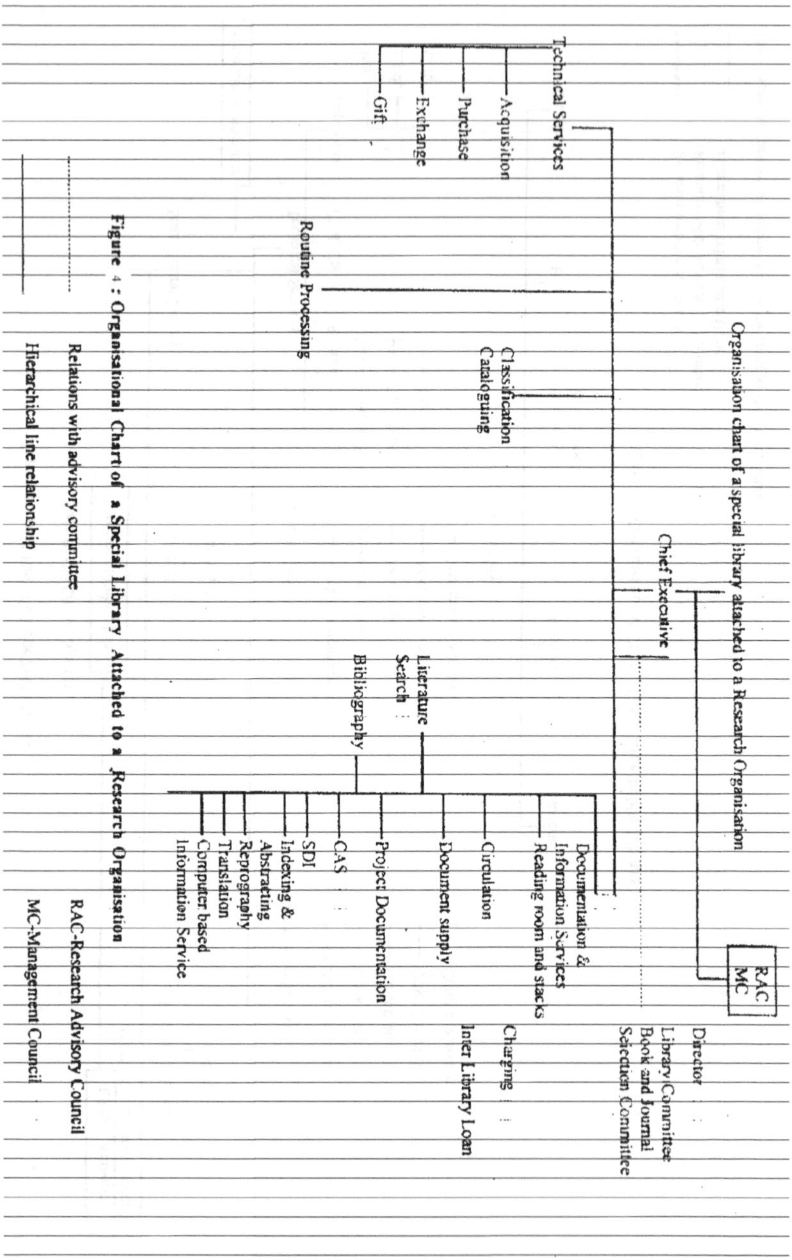

Figure 4 : Organisational Chart of a Special Library Attached to a Research Organisation

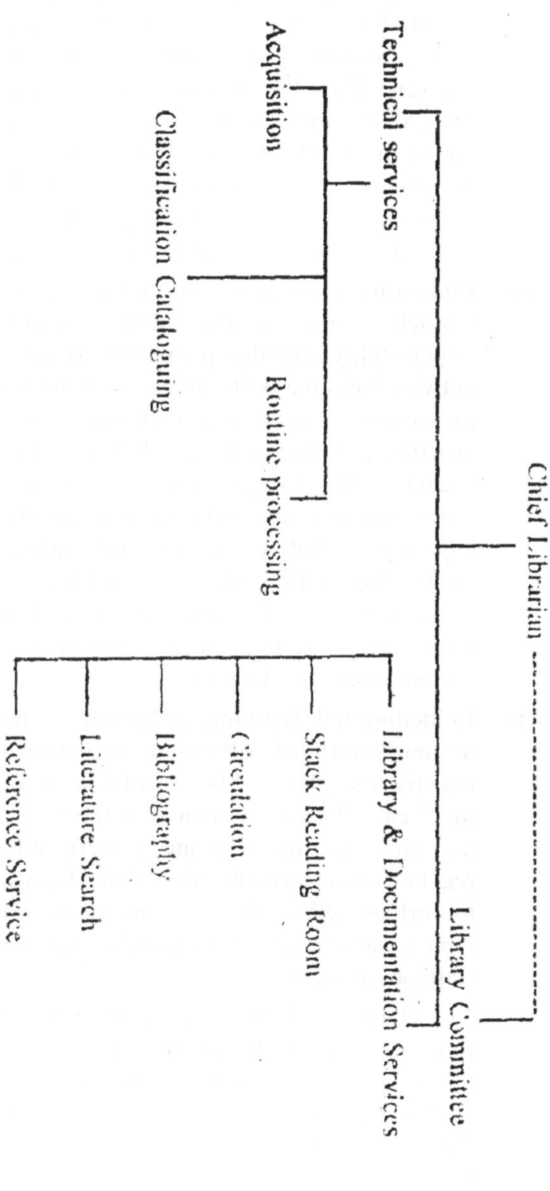

Figure 5 : Organisational Chart of a Small Library, A College Libary or a Library Attached to a Research laboratory

(ii) Appraisal: The probation system sometimes entails performance appraisal or called 'assessment' or 'evaluation'. These are also used for assessing eligibility of each member of staff at periodic intervals. The self appraisal report serves as a basis for rewarding who have rendered excellent service and the management makes use of his capabilities and potential for the interest of the organisation. Since such reports are confidential in nature and the authorities make use of this, it could contribute to achieving higher levels of staff performance.

(iii) Promotion: Promotion is one of the ways of staff development. It usually entails an increase in the salary, higher status, greater responsibility and other perquisites on the expectation that the individual has the skills, preparation and personality necessary for success in the new job. Besides the qualifications, past experience, annual confidential Character roll for promotion, is taken into consideration partially on the basis of involvement in professional activities at the local, regional and national levels. Papers presented at seminars and conferences, offices held, awards received are all taken into account. Participation in continuing education, involvement in research activity and contributions to books and book reviews are all granted a place in committee considerations.

(iv) Induction and Training: Induction is aimed at familiarising the newly recruited staff with the new surroundings, colleagues, organisation, place of library within it and the basic regulations involved. Thus, the newcomer will be given an introduction to his immediate supervisor and the staff with whom he is to be in regular contact, brief function of the department in which he is to work as well as other sections, introducing Library's union representatives, the conditions of service, working hours, leave, staff facilities etc.

Training to the newcomers in the library (a) reduces learning time for tasks to be performed on the job; (b) improves performance on a job in which the employee is already engaged (c) develops the attitude towards their work, largely by giving them a better understanding of what and why they are doing and (d) solves the operational problems in the performance of certain tasks. Training should be regarded as a continuous process involving experience and courses, both within and without the library which keep up with the constant changes in librarianship. This sometimes provides an opportunity to acquire an additional skill and leads to improved chances of promotion.

(v) **Staff Records:** An efficient system of personnel management presupposes that within any concern, a systematic record will be kept of every member of staff from appointment to resignation or retirement. All staff records should be treated as highly confidential and staff in charge of personnel matters should ensure that no unentitled person has access to such records.

(vi) **Welfare:** General welfare of the staff at all levels means both physical and mental well-being. Responsibilities of this nature need the co-operation of both the employers and the employed. The library authorities have a duty to ensure that adequate attention is given to staff working conditions and that potential sources of danger are limited. Provision of fire regulations by installing alarms and fire extinguishers, emergency exists, emergency lights, steps and ladders, regular servicing of boilers, proper training to the janitors, lifts and hoists, polishing of floors regularly, keeping the library environment free from air pollution, chemicals and other similar hazards, adequate ventilation etc. should be made available to the library staff to take adequate precautions against creating potentially dangerous situations for others through sheer carelessness and ignorance.

LEADERSHIP

Leadership is the ability to influence the behaviour of others in a desired direction. Managers have to be effective leaders with the ability to influence subordinates and colleagues to work willingly towards the attainment of enterprise objectives. The ability to comprehend the behaviour of people and the motivating force to which they respond, the ability to inspire, and the ability to create an environment responsive to motivation are considered to be the most significant attributes of a leader.

Theories of Leadership

Following theories are well known and these are briefly discussed here.

(i) **Leadership by trait.** Before the advent of psychological studies of leadership, it was the view that leaders are born and not made, which emphasizes in born qualities of leadership. Subsequent researchers have stressed that, except for physical characteristics, most of the traits of leadership are acquired and can be consciously developed. Intelligence, self-confidence, ability to supervise, respect for and interest in people, social participation, and strong motivation to achieve are some of the traits found in leaders.

(ii) **Situational theory.** This theory postulates that a given situation throws up forces, which create leaders. Such leaders reflect the mood of the situation and the aspirations of those led.

(iii) **Contingency theory.** According to this theory, the effectiveness of leadership depends on the style, personality and traits of the leader to fit the group in a given situation. Leadership is contingent upon the power or formal authority inherent in the position held, the defined nature of the task with fixed responsibility, and the leader-follower relationship.

Contingencies are very popular in organization theory today, a contingency theory suggests that the appropriate behaviour is contingent on some variable. For example, a leadership contingency theory states that the managerial style of a leader depends on the type of organization in which the leader is working. A leader who is a general in the army faces a different situation than the head of volunteers for the local Red Cross.

What kinds of contingencies influence leadership? The first are the personal characteristics of subordinates. Consistent with discussion of motivation and with preceding discussion of supportive and participative leadership styles, one would expect the characteristics of those being led to influence the leader. Are the needs of systems analyst the same as those of computer operators?

A second contingency factor is the environment or situation. Continuing the preceding example, the systems development environment is a creative one characterized by uncertainty. The environment in computer operations is more frenetic and is characterized by deadlines and pressure to meet operating standards.

Combining the two contingencies suggests a different approach to management based on the characteristics of individuals and the environment in which they work. The systems analyst has to reason conceptually and deal with a great deal of ambiguity; the operator has to execute tasks and respond quickly to problems.

(iv) **Behavioural theories of leadership:** There are a number of behavioural theories of leadership which focus on the behavioural patterns and philosophies of managers, Filley, House and Kerr (1976) summarize much of the research on leadership style. Three of their categories are important.

The first is *supportive leadership,* in which the leader gives great consideration to the needs of subordinates. The leader is concerned with the well-being, comfort and satisfaction of subordinates. A supportive leader expresses appreciation when a subordinate does a good job, he or she does not demand more than the subordinate can do. Supportive leadership means not criticizing workers in front of others, leaders also provide rewards for jobs that are done well. A supportive leader treats subordinates as equals and is willing to make changes.

The second behaviour category is *participative leadership.* Here is a great deal of sharing of power, information, and influence between the leader and followers. In true participative leadership situations, the leader makes sure that all parties have an opportunity to influence the any decision.

The third category is *instrumental leadership,* a category associated with the mechanics of a particular job. Here the focus is less on personality characteristics than on the managerial tasks associated with leadership. Can the leader plan, organize, control and coordinate the activities of subordinates? In a technological task, does the leader understand the technology well enough to manage the work? Instrumental leadership also involves the ability of the manager to acquire and marshal resources in the organization.

(v) **Great Man School of Leadership :** A significant amount of popular literature is written from the perspective of the "great man" school of leadership. The basic belief of this view is that an individual rises to a leadership position at a critical time for the organization. The talents of the great man fit well with the needs of the organization.

Because there are so few great men, and because the situation in which each finds himself is unique, it is very difficult to generalize. Great men may also be very appropriate at the highest levels of the organization or government, however, there are also many senior and middle-level managers on whom the firm depends. This need a more conceptual and insightful view of leadership to learn how to manage the firm better.

Styles of Leadership

Styles of leadership vary depending on the behaviour of the leader. Some of the prominent styles are as follows:

(i) **Authority-based styles.** Leadership categorized according to the use of authority is of three types: (a) autocratic, (b) democratic or participative, and (c) *laissez-faire* where all initiative and actions are left to the subordinates. Within these main styles further variations are found. For example, an autocratic leader may be benevolent or despotic. Similarly, a participative leader may be supportive of subordinates.

(ii) **Likert's systems of management.** The studies of Likert (1961 and 1967) on leadership and management, have led to the identification of four systems: (a) exploitive-authoritative, (b) benevolent-authoritative, (c) consultative, and (d) participative. He concludes that of the four styles, the participative style is the most rewarding. This is because of the two-way relationship existing between the manager and subordinates. Subordinates are made to become involved, cooperate and communicate more freely in various aspects of work and management. The system is based on complete trust of the manager in his subordinates.

(iii) **Fiedler's contingency style.** Fiedler (1967) expressed the view that leadership styles conform to two broad categories, viz. those that are primarily task oriented and those that are people oriented. He concludes that in "*very favourable*" and "*very unfavourable*" situations the task-oriented leader will be most effective. In contrast, where the situation is neither very favourable nor very unfavourable, the human relations-oriented leader will be most effective. An unfavourable situation is considered to be the one in which the job structure and responsibility are diffused and ill-defined, and the leader-follower relations are poor.

(iv) **Immaturity - maturity continuum :** Argyris (1957), recognized the fact that disparity between individual needs and the organization needs leads to disharmony. This can be overcome by providing challenging tasks and opportunities as motivators, and training, which leads to maturity. For example, the dependent outlook of an employee, a characteristic of immaturity, can be turned into a state of independence, a mature characteristic.

(v) **Managerial Grid.** Blake and Mouton (1985), formulated a graphic device that depicts management styles. They have taken a manager's concern for production and concern for people as the determinants of style. The device can be used to assess the style of any manager. By studying the causes for a particular managerial style, remedial measures to improve the style can be tried.

The theories of leadership and leadership styles give an insight into the different styles of leadership and help in self-assessment. However, what ultimately determines leadership and leading is a manager's perception of people, situations and goals, personality qualities, and the environment-both organizational and outside. The success of a manager as a leader is measured by his or her ability to develop a symbiotic relationship between the fulfillment of individual goals and the organization goals over a long period of time.

7
Financial Management

Financial management is a diagnostic technique for detailed analysis of future oriented activities of persons and groups of persons responsible for administration. The word 'finance' is used to express any statement of monetary accounts or comparison of income with expenditure. It is essential for effective functioning.

The *Encyclopaedia Americana,* describing finance states that, "the economic activity of individuals, business, nations in the modern world require the use of funds for their completion." It also explains that both proper amount of means of payment and right kinds of funds are important for successful achievement of economic aims... It characterises finance as the study and practice of providing funds for economic activities.

Broadly speaking finance is concerned with obtaining funds and making the optimal use of these funds. But each firm treats this as a special problem within the limitations of its specific environment. There is a lot of difference between the funds of a firm and those of educational institutions especially the libraries. Basic difference lies in the fact that firms raise their funds by sale of products which is not true in case of the libraries. Instead libraries are normally maintained by public funds collected in the forms of taxes etc. and granted to university libraries by the government. Libraries by their nature are spending institutions, not having their own income source. Libraries have certain peculiar characteristics which must be kept in mind whenever we talk of finance in libraries.

CHARACTERISTICS OF LIBRARY FINANCE

The following characteristics of library and library finance are of worth consideration in determining library finance -

1. Spending Institutions : Libraries are public welfare, nation building institutions. Unlike other public sector departments these are spending agencies rather than revenue fetching ones. Mostly documents and services are rendered free of charges to readers and they have nothing to sale for fetching some money. Libraries spend on staff, documents and introduce new services to satisfy their information needs. About 50% of its funds are spent on the staff only.

2. Growing Institutions : As a result of continuous investment the libraries grow constantly. The fifth law of library science, "Library is a growing organism" implies that library grows multifocally i.e. in documents, staff building and furniture. Literature is coming in different physical forms. With floppy diskettes, audio and video cassettes, microfilms, CD-ROM etc., we are marching towards a paperless society. All these forms are necessary for users of library and thus have to be purchased.

3. Recurring Financial Demands : Establishing a well-equipped library with sufficients funds only once is not sufficient. The financial demands of libraries are of two types viz. recurring and non-recurring. It requires annually continuous and recurring grants and some non-recurring grants time to time for continuing the on going services handsomely, e.g. non-recurring grant is required for purchasing back volumes of journals, for establishing core collection in a specific discipline as and when it is started in a university.

4. Price-rise : Though libraries get constant recurring and non-recurring grants yet these become insufficient due to many reasons. Price-rise is one of the most important points among them which must be kept in mind before allocating the funds to a university library. Price - rise in respect of periodicals subscription, books, furniture, equipments etc. are the pointers. For example, the rates of American journals have doubled in the last few years. On an average the increase is from $59.70 in 1985 to $ 117.11 in 1992. In India average increase in 1990 was 25.61 percent to 36.40 per cent in 1991 and 54.24 per cent in 1992. These are the results of a survey made by National Physical Laboratories (NPL) library on 76 journals in physics and chemistry.

5. Devaluation of Money

Devaluation of Rupee is another reason which contribute in shrinkage of the existing funds. Library has to pay more money for the same documents due to devaluation at different stages.

PRINCIPLES OF FINANCIAL MANAGEMENT

For effective financial management, some guiding principles are necessary, the understanding of which is useful. These are :

1. Effective Control
2. Simplicity
3. Regularity and Farsightedness
4. Economy
5. Flexibility

1. **Effective Control :** Financial management can work efficiently only when it is controlled properly. The method of financial control should be simple and easy. Control is also necessary for the economical use and chanelisation of resources so that there is little wastage and the limited financial resources can be put to maximum use.
2. **Simplicity :** The procedures for financial management should be simple and easy to operate as simplicity results in efficiency and economy.
3. **Regularity and Farsightedness :** Financial management programmes should have a typical timetable so as to acquaint everybody with what he is expected to do at a particular point of time. For example, in the preparation of the budget for a library, inputs should come from the heads of sections who would in turn expect cooperation from their staff. The preparation of the budget would be time-bound and the budget should be submitted to the authorities in time so that the budgetary sanctions can be obtained in time to operate it. Similarly subscriptions to current journals should be sent to the publishers at a particular time of the year. Sticking to a timetable facilitates advance thinking and preparation. Not only present needs but future requirements should be kept in view when making provisions for finance.
4. **Economy :** Economy should be effected in any activity and every activity, more so in financial matters. All precautions should be taken to avoid unnecessary expenditure and wasteful use of scarce finances.
5. **Flexibility :** Financial management should keep in mind the virtues of elasticity so as to learn scope for adjustment according

to circumstances. Only then can it be successful in times of emergency and crisis. But this does not mean that one should take undue advantage of its flexible nature. There are provisions and practices in utilising or diverting funds appropriated for a certain item of expenditure to the purchase of books or any equipment, but this flexibility should be within the framework of financial rules and procedures. This type of adjustment usually is done at the fag end of the financial year when unutilised funds are available in other items. While these principles are useful in operating and managing finances in libraries, there are statutory financial rules and procedures laid down by the executive authorities. Libraries have no option but to follow financial rules.

The other related fields which need to be kept in mind by library and information professionals include cost accounting and economics various tools and techniques of financial management, economics and cost accounting like funds flow analysis, ratio analysis, break even analysis, operating and financial averages. Financial forecasting, capital budgeting, economic theory, theory of production, costing, etc. have adequate scope for application in library and information centre management.

FINANCE ESTIMATION

Keeping in view the above characteristics, proper financing is possible on the basis of correct and effective estimation of finance. These estimates are always made for the coming year. The financial requirements of a library also depend on the following factors:

(a) Age
(b) Jurisdiction
(c) Quantity and quality of reading material
(d) Number of readers
(e) Number of research scholars
(f) Seating capacity
(g) Staff
(h) Services provided by library
(i) Other factors relating to that particular library.

Various methods have been suggested and used for estimating/ determining the library finance. Actually there is no full proof method which can be adopted for determining finance to be allocated to a library. *Kothari Commission and Carl M. White* were also of the opinion that there is no formula for estimating with precision how much money a university should invest in its library but *Carl M. White* has suggested three methods of estimating university library finance as under :

(i) Ratio of library expenditure to total educational expenditure.

(ii) Ratio of library expenditure to university registration.

(iii) Library performance requirements.

Dr. Ranganathan suggested almost the same methods under different names :

1. Per capita method
2. Proportionate method
3. Method of details

Per capita method is similar to the method (ii) above, proportionate method is in the line of (i) i.e. some percentage of the total expenditure on education may be determined for libraries, and the last one is same as (iii) suggested by Carl M. White. In this method all the expenditures are enumerated and accordingly funds are allocated.

1. Per Capita Method

In this method, a minimum amount per head is fixed which is considered essential for providing standard library services, keeping in view future expansion of library needs, average cost of reading material etc. Radhakrishnan Commission, Ranganathan committee and Kothari Commission recommended norms for determining funds with this method. Their recommendations are discussed below :

1.1. **Radhakrishnan Commission** (1948-49) suggested that we can calculate the annual grant of a library @ Rs. 40 per student. A special non-recurring grant, once in five years, was also recommended so that the library may purchase books which it could not acquire within the recurring budget allowed to it.

1.2. **UGC Library Committee** under the able Chairmanship of Dr. S.R. Ranganathan (1957) suggested that Rs. 15 Per registered student in a university and Rs. 200 per teacher may be given to university library as a grant. These are very low norms than those suggested by the 1948-49 Education Commission. This allocation rate was raised slightly by the Kothari Commission.

1.3. **Kothari Commission** (1964-66) recommended that "- as a norm, a university should spend each year about Rs. 25 per student and Rs. 300 per teacher" on its library.

1.4. According to **Dr. Ranganathan** per capita expenditure of university library should be @ Rs. 20 per student and Rs. 300 per teacher, or Rs. 50 per student for purchase of books and reading material. An equal amount be paid for expenditure on staff and other recurring items. Thus in total provision for student community other than research community would be Rs. 100 per student.

All universities do not follow this method for allocating funds to their libraries. Some libraries adopt the proportionate method for the purpose.

2. Proportionate Method

In this method a particular minimum limit of library budget is fixed and some adequate percentage of the institutional budget is allocated for library purposes. Various norms have been suggested for deciding this limit.

2.1. *UGC's Parry Committee* (U.K.) suggested that 6 per cent of total university budget may be provided to university libraries.

2.2. For determining library finance according to proportionate method *Radhakrishnan Commission* recommended that 6.25 per cent of total budget of a university be provided to its library.

2.3 The *Kothari Commission* recommended provision of 6.50 to 10 per cent from university's budget for library, depending on the stages of development of the university.

2.4. *Working Group on Libraries (of Planning Commission)* (Chairman Dr. K.N. Raj) in its report (1980-81) to the state government recommended setting apart of as much as 20 per cent of total universities budget for maintenance and development of their libraries. Other states should also adopt these norms while allocating funds to libraries.

2.6. *A.I.C. Report on National Policy on University Libraries* provided 10 per cent of universities total budget for libraries. But the suggestions made for adding 25,000 volumes per annum at the rate of Rs. 200 per volume works out to Rs. 50,00,000 for books every year. The report suggested that this book grant should be 25 per cent of total library budget. Thus total budget for a university library will be Rs. 2 crore per annum, which no university will be able to afford.

Alongwith these, some special recommendations have also been made viz. *Ranganathan library Committee* (1957) suggested that in case of a newly started university which is not more than five years old, an additional grant upto a sum of Rs. 3,00,000 may be given to build up initial stock of reading material. It further says whenever any university is allowed to start new courses i.e. post-graduate departments, some assistance should be given for purchase of reading and kindred materials.

Dr. C.D. Deshmukh, Chairman UGC in his inaugural address of the seminar on "From Publisher to Readers : Work-flow in university/ College Libraries" (1959) said that a new university library should have at least one lakh volumes of books on its shelves. Then there is question of yearly addition to libraries if they are to continue to be up-to-date.

3. Method of Details

In this method all the items of expenditure are accounted for while preparing financial estimates for a library. These items, besides others, include salaries/ wages, reading materials, books, periodicals and newspapers and other kindred materials; binding and repairing heading; cooling and lighting, rents and interests, posts, telegrams and telephones, stationery etc. The finance is divided in two types -

(i) Recurring or current expenditure ; and

(ii) Non-recurring or capital expenditure.

U.G.C. Library Committee (1957) suggested a staff formula for finding out the quantum of library staff members and also gave their pay scales but for books and journals, it suggested the per capita and proportionate methods.

In another approach i.e., functional approach library finances are determined by taking into account number of teaching departments, number of students, research scholars and faculty members and nature of study and research in the university. It also takes into account regular increase in the cost of input-books, journals, non-book material, equipments and maintenance cost.

The proportionate method with the help of percentage of total university budget to arrive at the expenditure of university library seems better as compared to per capita rate because it has a tendency to remain static despite rising cost of books and periodicals.

Despite all these recommendations and suggestions there are no consistent and standard norms according to which finance may be allocated to universities. The authorities are not following these recommendations at all.

Kothari Commission found the situation of Indian university libraries most unsatisfactory. It recorded "... only in 4 universities expenditure on books and periodicals is more than 5% of the total expenditure. The remaining universities spend less than 5% ... there are 5 universities which spend even less than 1% of the total budget on their libraries."

Based on the data of a survey of library budget of 99 universities given in *University Hand Book*, 1985-86 has revealed that 67% and only 14% of them have budget of 8.10% and above. The lowest allocation is 0.13% and the highest 24.15% of total university's budget.

Successful achievement of main goals and functions of a university viz. teaching and research mainly depend on the material available in its library. All forms of literature are important for the readers but due to financial crunch libraries are unable to feed its users as efficiently as they are supposed to do. This naturally impinges on academic and research programmes of universities.

SOURCES OF FINANCE

A. Academic Libraries

Sources of finance means the funding sources of libraries. In India main source of finance of universities is government grants that may be provided by respective state government or central government, and sometimes by both. It depends firstly on the nature of university and secondly the funding plans of government. On the basis of funding agencies we can divide universities in three types :

1. Central Universities : These are funded by central government (Ministry of Human Resource Development) through University Grants Commission (UGC).

2. State Universities : For maintenance grants they depend on the state government but they also get some special grants from UGC under various schemes.

3. Private Funded Universities : Though in West, most universities are privately funded universities, but these are also started recently in India by now. There are also some universities, those have been provided with the status of "deemed universities" but they mostly look at the centre or state government for funds. They send different plans which if approved, get grants from state or central government.

The state university libraries are starving for want of funds. The reason being most of the UGC/MHRD (Ministry of Human Resource Development) grants are swallowed by central universities and the IITs. Around 1980s total grants with UGC were 250 crore or so per year. Out of this, central universities received around 80 crore and all state universities got twice as much. A decade later, out of an aggregate of 400 crore or so, central universities received around 300 crore and state universities only on third of that i.e. 100 crore. Clearly, share of central universities has been increasing steeply while that of state universities has been declining equally steeply.

Keeping in view the above discrepancies UGC took a strong decision to freeze recurring grants of central universities for some time and suggested to generate their own resources to meet the growing demands. It created a great concern among academicians and as a result, this decision has been withdrawn for the time being. The gate-ways open for universities to meet such situation are as under :

1. Self Financing : UGC suggested universities to raise their own finance. Education in India is a social welfare activity but now the concept seems to be changing slowly. It has given a way to the privatisation of education. Concept of free library services is vanishing and soon marketing of library services, like in the West, will start. It has already started in case of different computerised and on-line services. Besides government organisations like INSDOC and DESIDOC, private organisations are imparting some such services on payment. Similarly academic libraries should also charge for special services.

2. Fees and fines : Almost all university libraries charge fees from their students for its use but it is so meagre that it cannot be considered as a dependable source of finance. This is because charges for education in India as compared with West are very low. In West education is available to all but charges are so high that everyone cannot pay for it, so one who can pay it, can get education. But in India fees had been stagnating for nearly 50 years which was quite an unrealistic occurrence and moveover students succeeded in gaining concessions after organising demonstrations. But now universities are thinking in this direction and perhaps library fees will also be increased to improve their services.

The fines are also charged in library for late return of books or against losses or misuse of books. But it is not enough to be considered as a source of finance, because its main aim is to compel the user to return borrowed books in time and not to damage it.

3. Self-paying education : Many institutions were charging capitation fees which were controlled by Supreme Court. They have introduced new scheme of 'self-paying' education which has not yet got full governments approval. Similarly libraries may launch special schemes if they want to improve their economic health.

Wilson and Tauber, Lyle, Gelfand considered the following sources of income of university libraries including fees and fines -

(i) Funds allocated from the university budget

(ii) Endowments

(iii) Gifts

(iv) Miscellaneous sources.

The financial demands of universities are of two types viz.

(i) Recurring grants

(ii) Non-recurring/Ad hoc grants

The recurring grants are given generally for the purpose of purchase of books and periodicals, maintenance of regular services and for anticipated contingent expenditure. The non-recurring grants are given for specific purposes e.g. for preparing special collection, purchasing equipment and furniture etc.

In India central universities get different grants from central government i.e. Ministry of Human Resource Development through UGC. The state universities depend for maintenance grants on the state government. But they also get different types of grants directly from UGC or other Central Government agencies CSIR, ICSSR. These provide finance for establishing collections for a newly started department. Equipment grants e.g. UGC is funding universities for purchasing computers to establish local network and later become part of INFLIBNET which is fully supporting automation programme of university libraries. UGC also gives non-recurring grants for construction of library buildings etc.

4. Endowments and Gifts : These are not permanent sources of finance and the University libraries cannot depend on these. Some libraries were really benefitted from the Ford Foundation, Rockefeller Foundation and PL 480 (US Government's funds under India Wheat Loan Programme) funds etc. but all these were temporary help and supported very selective libraries only. Truly speaking these are not very common in India.

The libraries may encourage passing out students and research scholars and retiring and desirous teachers to donate their books to the respective library which will prove to be a great help to them. But libraries should make a policy to receive only rare books which are of permanent use. Otherwise they will increase their problem instead of enriching their collection. Problem in the sense that they are short of space and money will be wasted on staff, maintenance etc. on the trash material.

5. Caution Money : Many libraries receive caution money from its readers. It is refundable and rounded when a reader ceases library membership, but its interest becomes a handsome source of income.

6. Miscellaneous Sources : Alongwith the above sources of finance, libraries have some more areas of making funds. Libraries help university in some publications and some libraries have their own publications. Their sale helps library in fetching money to some extent. Similarly libraries to charge subsidized rates for translation and reprographic services but now they should raise their charges, of course, not equal to market rates, at least to meet the maintenance charges of those equipments etc. In some universities prices recovered for lost books, for lost reader's tickets, unclaimed library security (if any) are transferred to university funds which should be treated as library income.

B. Public Libraries

The sources of finance for public libraries are not fixed and permanent like other institutional and governmental libraries. Generally it comes from different sources. The financial resources should be made available in a such way that growing financial requirements of libraries are to be met adequately and the users need can be fulfilled easily. The main resource of finance for public libraries are :

1. Subscription from the members : The public libraries receive funds from the different external and internal sources, among them the subscription of membership fees received from the members are important. The person who want to use the library is essential to get the membership of the library. For this he must acquired membership of the library after submitting a nominal fees prescribed by the library authorities. These nominal fees also to be considered a source of revenue. But some body have the viewed, that especially the modern Library Scientist, that this is a wrong tradition. They opined that the membership fees charged from the users may harms the cause of libraries and this practice will discourage the person who are already unwilling readers of library. Moreover, **Dr. S.R. Ranganathan** has also opposed the system. He has very strongly advocated in many of his books that library should provide free services to its clientele. He declared 'the Bill of Rights of Library Readers' as early as in 1931 when he published his first book on library science, viz. Five Laws of Library Science. The Advisory Committee for Libraries, Government of India, has strongly protested in its report that considering subscription of membership of library as a source of revenue is not a healthy practice and this should be stopped.

2. Endowments and Donation : The next popular financial resources of public libraries are endowments and donation which comes from the private agencies, but this is not dependable source. Library has some recurring expenditure and being the uncertainty of its nature the library should not depends on it. Endowments and donations can never be expected regularly, more over the amount received under this head are insufficient and dependence upon endowments would tantamount to signing a suicidal pact. The funds received under this head can be used to meet non-recurring expenditure of the library. This can be utilized to meet the cost of building construction, its repair, purchase of equipments, books and other electronic equipments which are necessary for the library.

3. Library Taxes : Library taxes can be said a principal financial resources for Public Libraries. Taxes levied at the Government level bring amount. Since the direct library taxes are levied by the government after the enactment of a law, its collection has become cheaper. Tax payment are subject to essential to every one, hence it is not depended on the wills of people. An uniform rates of taxes can be levied there by making it easier to provide standard and uniform library service in all parts of the country. The library taxes can be charged either directly to the public or be a surcharge on existing taxes or a fresh tax can be levied. Generally such type of taxes are imposed on the immovable property after the assessment by the local authority.

Of the States of the Indian Union which have library legislation, some, viz., Tamil Nadu, Andhra Pradesh and Karnataka, have provision for a library cess. Tamil Nadu and Andhra Pradesh Library Acts have provision for a cess in the form of a surcharge on land and property tax at the rate of six per cent. The Karnataka Act has provision for a library cess in the form of a surcharge at the rate of three percent not only on Sand and house tax but also on octroi duty, vehicle tax and professional tax. In addition to the library cess, Karnata public libraries receive a grant from the government equivalent to three per cent of the total land revenue collection. The other two states i.e., Maharashtra and West Bengal, have not proposed any library cess. In these states the respective governments have made provision for grants for public libraries. But experience shows that library cess/rate alone cannot be sufficient to meet the continuously growing needs of public libraries. Besides, the taxable capacities of various local areas differ, thereby making standard and uniform public library service throughout the country difficult.

4. Library Cess/Rates : Library cess/rates is a local tax system. After assessment of the property of the local people, the authority imposed a local levy or the library cess to meet the expenses incurred on the library management. The library cannot depend on this sources, but to some extant, they can meet the receiving expenditure of libraries. More over most of the local area cannot bear the taxes because of their taxable capacities. According to **Dr. S. R. Ranganathan** on the basis of his personal observation, library rates alone cannot be sufficient to meet the daily growing demands of Public Libraries.

The library cess is very popular among the Western countries and have adopted this system of tax pattern. Their library system is fully based on local rates since there library service is considered as local service.

5. Government Annual Grants : This type of source can be treated as the main source of finance of libraries. The government provides some annual grants to meet the annual expenditure, which is called budgetary annual grants to the libraries. The noted Public Libraries of India have got such budgetary provisions. The library submitt its annual budget and government after the considerable discussion, pass the budget after a few alteration. All the recurring expenditure of Libraries can be meat out from this grants. In which state the library legislation is enacted, the state governments are liable to provide the annual grants to the Public Libraries to meet the annual expenditures of libraries on the similar pattern under which the other Government Departments receive the annual grants. However, as per view of the library scientists the government should also encourage local authority to collect more funds by giving them incentives under the provision of local taxes for the library facilities.

6. Gifts : Libraries oftenly receive gifts in terms of cash or kind from the various resources. Generally the persons who are charitable minded donates a fixed amount to the libraries with a view to encourage the learning among the common people. There are numbers of charitable agencies who are constantly increasing the libraries facilities by providing aids to the libraries both in cash or other kind. Some noted persons who have their own libraries with a special collection also donates to the libraries. The ideas behind such donation are to put the books to better use by other also, and books can be saved bitterly after the death of the donors. But this kind of resources cannot be treated as dependable source. It can be only treated as complementary and supplementary aid to the library.

7. Fines : With a view to fulfil the objectives of the first law of library science, books are lent out to the borrowers for a fixed period. Libraries, generally, realized a certain amount as a fine from the members who have borrowed the books and not returned on due date. Some time books are lost by the member, in that case the current prices of books and other cost incurred on the head of getting the lost books from the publisher are charged from the borrower. But this is not accountable income of the library and the income from this source will be very meagre. Mostly the readers do not like to pay the overdue charges and the Public Libraries are not in favour to punish the readers. Such practice discourage the reading habits, so it cannot be considered as a proper source of revenue.

8. Miscellaneous sources : Other sources of revenue can be Interest of bank, Rents from library property, Sale of publications, Sale of catalogues, Sale of used papers, news papers, etc and the Income from Library estate.

C. Special Libraries

Special libraries get their funds from appropriations made by their respective parent organisations. Whenever the parent body takes up a new project or programme, which needs library and information support, adequate finances may be provided to the library to meet the special support facilities. The library is expected to ask for funds for any additional or special services which are usually examined before funds are provided for such services. In addition, ad hoc grants from governmental agencies are obtained for specific purposes. Of late, special libraries have been seriously considering the ways and means of generating part of their own resources.

BUDGETING

The term 'budgeting' refers to the process of budget planning and preparation, budgetary control and the related procedures. The formal presentation of the plan is called budget. Budget is a written statement of income and expenditure during the year. It covers all items of work to be taken up over a specified period of time in future. Thus an overall budget covering the institution as a whole is also known as 'master budget'.

A library budget is an estimate of expected income and expenditure of the library for the coming year. Being merely an estimate, it can be altered, due to change in the circumstances. Budgeting is usually done on yearly basis.

Preparation of budget lakes a great deal of time. Generally, during the middle of a current financial year, budget estimates for the next financial year are called by the office of the parent body. The librarian is expected to submit the budget estimates in the proforma approved by the institution on the basis of the past experience, present demands and future expectations of requirements.

Objects of Library Budgeting

The overall objective of library budgeting is to plan different phases of library operations. Co-ordinate activities of different departments of the library and to ensure effective control over it. Thus specific objectives may be outlined as follows:

1. To predict library's future services, service costs and other costs to achieve desired goal.

2. To anticipate library's future financial condition and the future need for funds with a view to keeping the library active and up-to-date.
3. To co-ordinate the efforts of different departments of the library towards the common objectives.
4. To accelerate the efficiency of operation of different divisions and departments of the library.
5. To fix responsibilities of different departmental heads.
6. To have effective control over the library's funds.
7. To facilitate centralised control over the library through the budgetary reports.

Budget Affecting Factors

Budget may be affected by the factors mentioned below:

* Size of the Library—collection, staff, users and service points.
* Location.
* Kinds of library services.
* Types of users.
* Rising costs.
* Period covered (one year or more).

Budgeting Techniques

Some of the budgeting techniques are given below:

(i) Line-item budgeting
(ii) Lump sum budgeting
(iii) Formula budgeting
(iv) Performance budgeting
(v) Programme budgeting
(vi) Planning programming budgeting system (PPBS)
(vii) Zero-based budgeting (ZBB)
(viii) Strategic budgeting.

(i) Line-item Budget

Line-item budget is the most commonly used kind of budget. Each line is increased a little each year. No questions are asked.

Here the 'items of expenditure are divided into the broad categories as below:

Items	Revised budget	Proposed budget
Salaries and wages	Rs. 400,000	Rs. 420,000
Reading materials such as books, periodicals etc.	Rs. 200,000	Rs. 220.000
Equipment	Rs. 10,000	Rs. 10,500
Binding	Rs. 10,000	Rs. 10,500
Heating, lighting, water and telephone	Rs. 10,000	Rs. 10,500
Stationery, printing and supplies	Rs. 4,000	Rs. 4,200
Insurance	Rs. 10,000	Rs. 10,500
Miscellaneous	Rs. 10,000	Rs. 10,500

The current budget is prepared, increasing each item over the previous year's allocation. The increase may range from 5 to 10 per cent. The salaries and other items are increased by 5%, keeping in view the minimum of 5% rise in general prices. Prices of reading materials have gone up by 10% (the library acquires a large number of reading materials published abroad). The authorities would understand the reason for increase in the allocation of each item.

In this kind of budget, there is no relationship between the request made and the objectives of library. The reallocation of funds can be done provided the authorities agree in this regard.

(ii) Lump sum Budget

In lump sum budget, a certain amount of money is allocated to the library. The library is given the necessary freedom to decide as to how the amount is going to be allocated to different categories.

(iii) Formula Budget

In formula budget, predetermined standards are applied for allocation of money. Such a budget is technical and easy to prepare. It does not require special skills to prepare the same.

(iv) Performance Budget

The concept of performance budget is not very old rather it is new one which was originated in the USA around 1960s. Later on it became quite popular in many government departments out side the United States America. Now the performance budget is being used in business and other organisations also. The expenditure allocated is based on the performance of the activities. The emphasis is laid on the efficiency of operations. The quantitative data about all activities are collected carefully over a period of time. The management techniques like cost benefit analysis are applied to measure the performance. The norms are established. For instance, one can determine the manpower, money and materials required to carry out-classification and cataloguing work. However, this would require expensive and complicated techniques.

Performance budget gives justification for and description of the extent of services to be achieved by means of the proposed programme. The resources like men, materials and money require to fulfil the proposed programme during the next fiscal year are described.

(v) **Programme Budget**

It is concerned with activities. The amounts are allocated to programmes or services rendered. Suppose, a university library may decide to start an indexing service in the field of social sciences. In such a case the expenditure on staffing, materials, postage etc. is to be estimated and the budget is to be prepared on the basis of programmes or services programmed .

Performance budgeting and programme budgeting have some similarities. The emphasis in the first is on performance but in the latter one it is on programmes.

Programme Budget Sheet

Organisation	University Library	
Programme	Indexing service in social sciences (monthly)	
Objective	To provide free indexing service to teachers and research scholars in the university and also to leading social science libraries.	
Costs	Personnel	
	(salary of 1/2 professional and 1/2 typist)	Rs. 60,000
	Materials (paper)	Rs. 12,000
	Postage	Rs. 6,000
	Others	Rs. 2,000
	(per annum)	Rs. 80,000

Note:

(i) It is assumed that the equipment available in the library would be used. These include typewriter, duplicating machine, etc.

(ii) Each year, the library decides, whether or not to continue the programme or modify it. The budget is, therefore, prepared accordingly.

(vi) Planning Programming Budgeting System

Planning Programming Budgeting System (PPBS) is a technique, which takes into consideration the best of programme budgeting and the best of performance budgeting. Here the focus is on planning.

The important steps in PPBS are:

(a) Identifying the objectives of the library.

(b) Presenting alternative ways to achieve those objectives with cost benefit ratios presented for each.

(c) Identifying the activities that are necessary to each programme.

(d) Evaluating the result so that corrective actions can be taken.

The library manager enumerates programmes and costs of these points. PPBS enables the authorities to be able to examine the programmes in proper perspective. As a consequence, they would be able to realize the effects of reducing or increasing the funding. The table given below gives data about a college library. The library serves 1000 students and 50 teachers. On an average 200 books are issued and returned per day.

Use of Lending Service in a College Library for the Period March to August, 2002.

Input-cost	Kind of Service	Objectives of the programme	Output total	Cost per output
Rs. 25000 (Salaries, cost of equipment stationery etc.)	Lending service	lending of documents for home use	24000 documents	Rs. 1.04
Rs. 15000 (salaries, stationery, etc.)	Cataloguing and classification	To classify documents and prepare catalogue cards, filing of catalogue cards, stamping and pasting	1200 documents	Rs.12.50

(vii) Zero-based Budget

Zero-based Budgeting (ZBB) was developed by Peter Pliyor so as to achieve greater effective planning and fiscal control. ZBB requires that costs of current and new programmes be justified at the beginning of each budgetary cycle. The library manager is expected to "look for services and activities of the library which can be offered at funding levels below the current one, at the current level, and at some prescribed amount above the current level. The resulting programmes or packages are then arranged in priority order, from top to bottom, with their costs. At the point where expected or actual funds run out, programs below the line are dropped entirely". The request for financial support for every programme and activity is, therefore, worked out on fresh basis every year without reference to the past.

(viii) Strategic Budgeting

Strategic budgeting is comparatively newer concept of budgeting and is used as a look of resource allocation to various strategic business units and other units of an organisation. Under strategic budgeting, in determining the resource needs of various units- the basic question that is put in, "what sort of performance and results does the organisation want to generate"? This should be followed by another question," what are key activities organisational units, task and job needed to be set up and organised to produce these results? The answer should suggest the kinds of skills, expertise, and funding which will be needed to allow the various organisational units to accomplish the designated results. Therefore, jobs and tasks should be defined in terms of the desired strategic results and performance rather than in terms of the functions to be performed. Specific objective should be developed not only for the organisation as a whole but for each major organisational submit and through the efforts of subordinate managers, for each job.

Allocation of Budget

Allocation of budget is an important aspect of a successful budgetory procedure. The success of a library budget is largely depends upon the sound principles of allocation of budget to the different heads. The committees and commissions on libraries appointed by the government have aptly suggested norms and principles for the allocation of funds amongst different heads of library budget. It was a time when the services of libraries were ignored and it was not considered that the library is an important tool for accelerating educational pursuit and contributing a lot for socio-economic development of a developing nation. With the emergence of *Information* as a powerful weapon on the global basis, the library has find a suitable place in the national developments programme. With a view to realising the importance of library services in the national prospective, the Government have appointed a number of committees and commissions, at the both State and Central level, to draw a guide line for the proper development of library services in the country. They strongly suggested a number of ways and means to determine the right proportion of funds for the libraries in the budget allocation. With the phenomenon development, the entire concept of library services has been changed. The authorities began to feel the necessity of library as a result a notified and trained personnel are appointed in the library.

(a) University Library

Indian Universities have not made any clear cut division of the budget on three major items. A very part of the library budget is spent on books and journals and a little for the other items. It affects library service as sufficient manpower is not there to organise and maintain the book resources. The budget also includes library supplies, such as catalogue cards, stationary communication, telephone charges, printing, duplicating, travel, entertainment, membership fees of Library Association, library organisation, freight and postage, insurance maintenance of building, etc. And a major portion of budget on books and journals affects library services. Most of the Universities provide 50% of the total budget on staff salaries. Moreover, these days the University authority is bound to divert 90% of the total budget to staffs salaries. Although H. F. Dammers has presented a tentative statistics relating to the actual current operations of the British University Libraries.

–	Salaries	50%
–	Books	25%
–	Periodicals	13%
–	Building	6%
–	Sundries	6%

Colleges of Great Britain, it, however, besides other recommendations on better methods of library orgranisation and library co-operation, suggested that a special allocation be made in each University for purchase of text books @ 3 pound per under-graduate. This committee, better known as Parry Committee, (1967) laid down some other standards also. It, first of all gave a definition of a model University i.e., a University which had 3,000 under-graduates, 1000 research students and 500 teaching staff members, then the following standards were laid down for university library.

- Book stock (Total of Volume) 5,00,000.00
- Finance -

  Percentage of Library expenditure to the total expenditure of the University. 3.8%

  Expenditure on staff of the total library's 50%
- Expenditure

  Expenditure on books, periodicals etc. of the total library's expenditure 50%

  Expenditure on Binding to the total book fund 25%

  Expenditure on Sundries of the total library's expenditure 10%

But in our country, prior to the Education Commission there was no standards and norms for the allocation of budget for University Library. The University Education Commission' (1948-49) in its report recommended that Universities and Colleges should spend up to an optimum of 6.25% of the total budget or Rs. 40 per student as the annual grants for their libraries. This should be supplemented by a non-recurring grant once in ever, five years to cope with arrears of books and journals.

U.G.C, Library Committee (1957) has laid down the following standards :

- *Book Stocks* :

  University Central Library- 100,000 to 300,000 vols.
- *Finance* :

  Total book fund per ceptia- Rs. 15 per student and 200 per Teacher and Research fellow.

  Expenditure on staff of the total library expenditure - 50%

  Expenditure on books etc, of total library expenditure - 50%

  Staffs salaries- U.G.C.'s share- 80%

  State Government's share - 20%

Apart from the above allocation, capital expenditures are kept separate. Building and maintenance costs are usually treated by the University as separate budget items. The second thing is that the preparation of budget is a full one year's job. It cannot be prepared at random. The sectional heads of the various departments of the library should go on recording their needs and demands during the course of the year and present the statement of expenditure along with a statement of justification of demands of the various teaching departments and research faculties and on the basis of their needs should compile a statement of expenditure for the purchase of books and other reading materials.

(b) Public Library

The annual recurring expenditure on Public Library System, according to Dr. S.R. Ranganathan, are :

Staff salary	50%
Cost of reading materials binding, and other expenses	50%

(c) Special Library

In case of special libraries, as mentioned by Prof. A. Neelameghan and others the percentage of expenditure should be as follows:

Expenditure on reading materials (2/3 on periodicals and 1/3 on books)	35 %
Staff Salary	50%
Equipment other expenditure—Binding	9%
Distribution of documentation list	6%

It can be accepted that the budget allocation should be flexible and not rigid so that re-appropriation of funds from one head to other is possible, if required.

ACCOUNTING

The purpose behind maintaining financial accounts is to know easily and conveniently the positions about income, expenditure and balance in various heads. Its other advantage is that it restricts excess expenditure. It helps and guides the Librarian to spend the amount within time limit. The other benefits of maintaining financial accounts is to ensure adequate and accurate data for the preparation of annual budget, for controlling the budget operations for deciding future programmes and for supplying financial statistics in annual reports.

For proper accounting the factors to be considered are:

- Kind of financial information required.
- Kinds of financial records to be maintained.
- Preparation of financial records.

In order to advice efficiency in financial administration a library should set up separate accounts section and the following important records be maintained and kept up-to-date:

(a) Cash Book

This is a record in which details of daily cash transactions regarding income and expenditure of an institution are entered. But in many libraries, the librarian does not maintain a cash book, because the financial transactions generally take place through the administrative office, and not directly through the librarian. However, the libraries which take some amount towards contingency expenditure do maintain a record in the form of a cash book.

RECEIPTS					EXPENDITURE				
DATE	PARTI-CULARS	NO. & DATE OF VOUCHER CREDITED	HEAD OF ACCOUNT	AMOUNT Rs. Ps.	DATE	PARTI-CULARS	NO. & DATE OF VOUCHER DEBITED	HEAD OF ACCOUNT TO BE	AMOUNT Rs. Ps.
Total:									Total:

Specimen of the cash book of a library

(b) Ledger

A ledger is a book in which the budget provision or income is given at the top and expenditure on all items and subjects is entered one after the other.

Name of the library: Year:

Budget provision: Rs. Head:

SL.No.	Name of vendor	Bill No. & date	Amount	Amount passed for payment	Progre-ssive total	No. of books	Subject mark	Signature of librarian
1	2	3	4	5	6	7	8	9

Specimen of a ledger

(c) Allocation register or Allotment register

In the allocation register, accounts are maintained headwise and subjectwise. Separate financial records are maintained in the library for books, periodicals, binding, stationery, contingency, postage, etc. under approved budget heads. It helps us in knowing, at any point of time, how much money under what head and on which subject is spent and how much remains as balance to be spent. Technically speaking, though the ledger and the allocation register are two different records but their purposes are the same.

Sl. No.	Name of vendor	Bill No. & date	Amount	Amount passed	Progre-ssive total	Bal-ance	No. of books	Sub-ject	Sign of inch-arge	Sign of librar-ian
1	2	3	4	5	6	7	8	9	10	11

Specimen of Allocation Register .

(d) General invoice register or Bill register

In this register, the serial numbers given in column one are termed as the voucher number of this bill. The office copy of each bill is arranged in a serial number in a separate file after the same has been processed and paid for. This arrangement helps the library staff in finding out any information regarding any item at any time as the voucher number of the bill links it to all registers in library sections and relevant records.

Sl. No.	Bill No. & Date	Name of firm	Amount	Sign of librarian	Sign of bill receiver	Remarks
1	2	3	4	5	6	7

Specimen of Bill Register

(e) Monthly expenditure statement register

This statement helps the operator of each head of expenditure to know the latest position of the grant at the end of every month. A specimen of the monthly expenditure statement is given below.

Name of library: Year :

Allocation: Rs.

Month	Expenditure	Cumulative expenditure	Balance	Signature	Remarks
April					
May etc.					

Monthly expenditure statement register

(f) Salary bill register

The salary bill register of the library staff is a detailed document of the salaries during a particularly year. It contains information relating to salary and deductions of library staff. In this register all the entries are made by the accounts section except the leave record of the library staff, which is filled in by the librarian.

(g) Record of Petty cash

In general, petty cash accounts are handled in two ways: (i) Turning fine and replacement money into petty cash directly, (ii) Fine and replacement money are collected directly by the accounts office and this amount is made available to the library in the form of petty cash.

(h) Equipment record or History card

Another record for the library is a card file of major equipment. This should be made in duplicate, one copy to be kept in the main administrative office and the other in the library's files. It should indicate the name of the item, the date of purchase, the cost, and such information as serial numbers. This record facilitates equipment purchase and replacement, makes possible a more considered judgement in placing replacement orders or in deciding repair versus replacement, and also provides an accurate inventory for insurance and other purposes.

AUDITING

The word audit has derived from the latin 'audire' which means to hear. In old days the auditor was a person appointed to hear the explanations given by those responsible for financial transactions.

Auditing means the an examination of the account books, the relative documentary evidence and vouchers in orders to ascertain the accuracy of the figures appearing therein.

The objects of an audit are:

- Verification of financial statement,
- To detect clerical errors and errors of principle,
- To detect fraud, if any exists, and
- To prevent fraud and errors.

Now the auditing has become an important and integral part of library's financial administration. Libraries and information centres normally have post-audit by external/central/statutory auditors, who usually look into the loss of reading materials, irregularities in procurement processes and outstanding, advance payments and supplies. Even though two types of audit systems are prevalent in our country, government departments and libraries generally follow post-audit. Post-audit means that the drawing and disbursing officer prepares the bills, signs them and sends them to the treasury/bank/principal for payment. The drawing and disbursing officer is responsible for the correctness of the bills. The officer or the librarian must satisfy himself fully before signing the bill. In the post-audit system, only random audit is resorted to, after the financial year comes to a close, Every item is not checked, but some months are selected at random. Payment items occurring during these selected months are thoroughly and minutely verified. Mistakes, if any, are pointed out. The person concerned is advised and warned to be cautious in future.

The pre-audit system is generally followed in autonomous bodies in which the audit is under the local fund account. In case of pre-audit, no item can be passed for payment unless it has been first audited. The pre-audit system reduces the responsibility of the drawing and disbursing officer in the sense that all the necessary verifications such as checking of items, accessing of items, charging of approved rates, correctness of calculations, debiting to proper heads of account, etc. have already been done by the audit section in advance. Here instead of the drawing officer, the auditors satisfy themselves before the bills are passed for payment. Auditing is carried out both by an internal audit team as well as an external/statutory audit team. The problem of collecting and noting of vouchers does not arise in pre-audit procedures. This simplifies matters somewhat and reduces the auditing responsibility of the librarian.

8
Space Management

There are three important constituents of the library - *books, readers and staff*, which are called as the trinity of librarianship and these are expected to grow exponentially in many directions. In order to meet the resultant growth, it is necessary to think about the idea of exploring the ways and means to provide and allocate space for books and other reading materials. Infact a library is a combination of documents and different categories of users and large numbers of staff are working tirelessly and efficiently to provide better service. The success of a library is largely depends on its building which should be design to accommodate all these very conveniently. So the most important aspect of the library management is the space management.

LIBRARY BUILDING

The process of organisation of a library starts with the planning of its building. Irrespective of big or small, luxurious or plain, broad or tall, the library building must be primarily functional and it must suit the purpose for which it is planned and created. It must be built in keeping with the cultural need and taste of the local community but not merely as an architectural show piece for visitors. Hence J.P. Boyd has rightly stated, since a library is the cultural centre of a community, it has to render some specific services to the community. A library building has to be designed keeping in view its functions.

Libraries come in various types and sizes to fulfil certain specific needs of the community it is established to serve. Thus we can have a single room village panchayat or school library to gigantic edifices spread over acres of national library. It may handle a couple of reluctant readers a day or may have to cope with a huge rush of knowledge seekers as in a public or university library. The range is enormous, demands are endless and variety limitless. Needless to say, planning for providing services to this diverse clietele has to be different, to suit the needs of a particular group of clientele. It is not possible to frame rigid guidelines which will be equally applicable under all conditions. Here are some guiding principles which should be kept in mind while planning a new library set-up.

Preliminary Considerations or Preplanning Activities

The task of creating physical facilities and environment involves broadly pre-planning activities followed by preparation of a programme, allocation and utilisation of space, selection of equipment, furnishing and moving into facility. The pre-planning activities include gathering information including internal information through visiting other libraries, discussing with colleagues and experts, attending seminars, exhibitions, conferences and reading literature. One should not be surprised or scared at issues cropping up, rather one should try to discuss with colleagues and experts. The proposal should incorporate general features like objectives type, status and location of the library, nature of users and use of library, special construction features of the facility, statistics regarding existing library and composition of planning team, resources required and the implementation schedule, etc.

Physical facilities and environment can be viewed from three important points, namely, marketing of services, quality of services and customer (user) studies. Before going to create physical environment and facilities in libraries to gear up the quality services, it is necessary to identify and understand the nature and characteristics of services. Characteristics of service organisations like intangibility (impalpability), non-invention ability (perishability), variability and inseparability of production and consumption of services call for an extended marketing mix with emphasis on physical evidence, people (service personnel), process, PR and social marketing. The role of '*Place*' and '*Physical evidence*' in the new strategy for marketing of services is to be emphasised while creating physical facilities and environment. Physical environment is packaging for services and hence it need to be improved for the following reasons and ways :

(i) customer judges the service quality through the process of deduction.

(ii) Creation of service environment should not be left to chance.

(iii) Both dominant and peripheral physical evidences should be coordinated to achieve uniformity in projected service image.

(iv) Peripheral evidences arc small to trival but have impact on customers.

(v) Perception about services are sources of competitive differentiation.

(vi) When it comes to perception *"feelings are facts"*.

(vii) Help to reinforce the proposed position and image of the organisation, i.e., tangibilise the intangible service through physical environment.

Clientele

Any effort to create physical facilities and environment should take into account the unique needs and ways of seeking, gathering, using and communicating information by the target users. In other words, understanding the users in terms of their characteristics, styles, idiosyncrasies, needs, opinions, priorities, preferences, evaluations, attitudes and behaviour is essential. A number of findings in the areas of user research provide clear and direct input for creating appropriate physical facilities and environment. The type of library, nature of users, pattern of usage, age and status differences, psychological and behavioural patterns of clientele are to be given due consideration in planning a library building.

Based on the nature of clientele, three broad groups of libraries are recognised *academic library* (a school, college or university library), where the users are the students, teachers, or research scholars; *public library*, established by a local authority or a philanthropic body or a private or subscription library where the clientele are a cross section of the community both literate and semiliterate; and *special library* established by industrial concerns, commercial organisations, business enterprises, Government or Quasi Government bodies or learned societies where the clientele constitute industrialists, entrepreneurs, businessman, officials, scientists, technocrats, professionals, politicians, literate and others.

Location/Sites

Location is important for homogeneous services, site selection and choice of community, region, etc., depend on the factors like convenience, operating cost, proximity to competitor, availability of support system, geographical or environmental factors like noise, traffic, communication networks, transport facilities, channels/distribution/ service centers, etc.

Ideally, a library should be centrally located so that it is easily accessible to its clientele. It should be set up in serene surroundings, insulated from din and dust. However, in practice, this ideal condition seldom prevails and there will be competitors within the organisation for better location. Quite often, one room in a building is designated as a library. Sometimes aisle vacated by another department is handed over to the library and at times building donated by a philanthropic person or a body serves as a library. If one is fortunate to have the opportunity to plan a library building right from the beginning, one should select a location which is most convenient for the clientele it is going to serve. It should be large enough to have provision for future expansion-both horizontal and vertical, and it should form an integral part of the overall campus plan and should not appear to be an appendage or an after thought. Finally, it should lie in accordance with various governmental codes.

Various factors determine the site that is ultimately selected for a library building. While a central location is of paramount consideration in an academic campus, the same consideration may not be applicable in the case of a special library. Sometimes safety and other considerations like hazardous chemical factory, noisy establishment etc., may dictate the positioning of the library in a remote corner. In addition to safety, aesthetic and cost factors may also be considered. In the process of selection of location and site, not only the adequacy of the size be ensured but population distribution, relation to neighbouring buildings, traffic flow, orientation, elevation, scope for future expansion, shape of the land and nature of the soil and ground are to be taken into consideration.

The following general considerations as stated by I.S.I, may apply in regard to the location of different kinds of Libraries:

(i) **Public Library :** It should be centrally situated alongwith other community buildings so that the reading public will find convenient access to it.

(ii) **Academic Library:** An academic library should be located centrally with respect to class rooms, research rooms and laboratories. There should be convenient access from these to the library.

(iii) **Institutional Library :** An institutional library should be located centrally with respect to the work places of its members,

(iv) **Dormitory Library :** A dormitory maybe located in an area where land is inexpensive and available for future extension. It should have unobstructed access, all the year round from the service library concerned.

Resources

It is obvious that the size and architecture of a library will be determined by the volume of its activity, the number of clientele it is going to serve, variety of services it will offer, and above all the prestige of its patrons. The issue is finally decided by the amount that is available to translate the dream into reality. The librarian should have clear idea about the capital budget available for the library building. In other words, money, land, expertise of librarian, consultant, architect, engineer, contractor, interior decorator, etc. are the crucial resources required.

Team Work

A planning committee for the library building should be constituted consisting of Engineers, Architect and Librarian. The library authority or the management committee is responsible for the selection of a knowledgeable, qualified and experienced librarian, the appointment of a suitable building coordination committee, involvement of senior library staff members, the appointment of a qualified architect, preferably one who has planned or supervised a library construction before with clear mandate, acquisition of a suitable site and the provision of adequate funds for the building project after knowing the costs involved, special items, if any, affecting the cost and financial implications of the new construction.

If it is an University library building, the faculty members and representative of the students may also be included in the committee. The decision of the committee will be final in case of any dispute arises during the construction of the building. The committee will also liable to supervise the construction work. If the committee feels any lacking it would be useful to appoint a library consultant to committee. Galvin and Buren consider the authority, the librarian and the architect as the basic elements of the planning committee. But Metcalf has the opposite view that many competent architect do not have their staff engineers who are capable to designing difficult foundation, heating, airconditioning, plumbing and electric lighting installations, for a large and complicated library building. However, committee is essential to meet the situation, which should determine the local needs. The committee should also draw the experiences of other libraries by studying plans of existing buildings. If needed, the committee may depute some one to visit the recently constructed library buildings and make available the study of the needs of different units of library in performing essential services.

Role of Librarian in building planning

We know any library, small or large, is a growing organism and they play a key role in advancing the cultural, social and educational activities of the nation. Building of such important institution should be planned very carefully. The objectives of the library building is to provide adequate space and safely to the reading materials, users facilities and staff accommodation. A librarian only knows these things and he can able to guide the architect and explain the requirements of the library. It is imperative that before planning library building a experienced and qualified librarian must be appointed as he has the knowledge of the requirements of library and its activities. To plan a library building is a complex thing and librarian can make sure that what architect actually want to know and what is that the library is being created to do so. This may seem so obvious that it is not always taken seriously, the complexity of the task, which lies before the architect and the enormous range of problems which has to be solved, mean that he must have a very clear picture of the proposed library building.

The appointment of librarian will be the first step in the direction of planning of a library building. He will able to do the spade work necessary for planning and equipping the library. A brief note of the librarian for the architect can be valuable in drawing the map of the building. The full information on all aspects of the scheme will certainly lead to the right direction, but an effective brief must be factual, clear and concise. According to R.E. Ellsworth the librarian brief should include the information in the architectural programme for each department or activity, viz (i) "a brief description of the nature of the work performed by the department and ways it relates to the other departments or services in the library, (ii) space requirements including the physical needs of each department in terms of heating, lighting, acoustical levels, access to utility and terminals; (iii) Staff work space requirement when these involve placement of work stations in relation to other staff and library materials, to supervision of reading rooms, to nearness to materials, to the use of hardware, elevators, etc.; (iv) layout and flow charts are desirable; (v) library materials.

The notes given by the librarian to the architect for planning of building is valuable, therefore, he should be associated with the team of planning in all the stages. He will liable to prepare a note on building programme explaining the requirements of the library building to the architect, management, etc. An experienced librarian would be in a position to translate his knowledge concerning library needs into written statement of instructions. This note is extremely important for library planning and design of a library building. In brief the involvement of librarian in the construction of building can be as under :-

1. Librarian is a best consultant of library building.
2. Librarian is the co-ordinator of library building project.
3. Coordinator of publicity campaign.
4. Consultant with the architect in the supervision of construction.
5. Coordinator of procedures for starting library services in new building.
6. Co-ordinator of delegation and opening ceremonies.

The librarian's brief pertaining to the planning of library building seems to be cardinal as the librarian suppose to be the expert of the planning. Therefore, his brief may contains the following information.

1. Activities of the library containing a brief description about the functions and objectives of the library.
2. Clienteles

   (a) Regular

   (b) Potential

   (In case of the University and college library, the categories of users).
3. Automation

   (i) Computer system

   (ii) Networking
4. Size of the library

(a) Location.

(b) Site

(c) Access

5. Space requirement

    (i) Stack

    (ii) Reading room

    (iii) Staffs room

    (iv) Seminar and meeting hall

    (v) For Non-Book materials.

6. Front Elevation.
7. Interior design.
8. Exit and Control.
9. Entrance and Gangways.
10. Airconditioning and Lightening.
11. Equipments & Furniture.
12. Future Extension.
13. Location of Different Sections.
14. Librarian's and Deputy Librarian's Office.

Besides, a very crucial role is played by the architect who is able to transform the requirement plan drawn up by the librarian into a functionally elegant interior and aesthetically pleasing exterior of a library building within the limitations of resources provided. This is possible if there is a good rapport between the librarian and the architect, each understanding the other's strong points and limitations. The librarian and the architect may also need to consult other specialists-interior decorators, equipment and furniture manufacturers, illumination and air-conditioning consultants before drawing up a final plan.

In addition, the team of planning committee may have consultants, field representatives, users, library staff, other staff in the organisation, construction coordinator, telecommunication staff, engineering staff, interior decorator, facilities planners, etc.

A good library building is the outcome of a close relationship between the librarian and the architect. An ideal library is a happy combination of both function and design. The librarian not only draws up the preliminary plan based on the considerations explained earlier; but he is also in touch with the architect at every stage of the plan.

Preparation of a Library Programme or Proposal

A written building programme or proposal is must for any library. It is a basic statement about the need of the community and can be used as a legal document of requirements to the architect. Further, building programme forces the library to make basic decisions and go through a process of soul-searching. It helps to establish the criteria for a site and aids site selection. It also helps lo estimate the potential cost requirements. It enables architect to know the requirements in specific terms of space, function, relationship of areas and minimise friction between librarian and the architect. A written building programme is useful to governing bodies, citizen's groups, the library staff and the architect. It needs to be prepared by librarian and senior library staff in consultation with experts, consultants, users, authority and architect. Steps involved in preparation of a library building programme or proposal are:

(a) The contents

The contents of a library programme for building should reflect the following :

(i) General features

- Objectives of the library
- Type of the library
- Status of the library
- Location of the library and competitors within the organisation

(ii) Nature of library users

- Number, types and composition of users
- User activities
- Use of library and user-interactions with the library i.e. pattern of usage, movement and interaction

(iii) Construction features

- Useful life of the facility

- Unusual construction features
- Environmental controls
- Space for special users; for example for handicapped
- Space requirements
- Services offered
- Future expansion

(b) **Gathering statistics**

(c) **Tin; planning team**

- Library planners
- Consultants, architects, Tick representatives
- Users
- Library staff and other staff in the organisation
- Construction coordinator, telecom staff, engineering staff, facilities planning, interior designers, etc.

(d) **Resource required**

(e) **Implementation schedule**

Some tips for preparation and execution of a library building programme are:

* Know existing constraints
* Compromises are inevitable
* Have a (base) year of reference
* Estimate annual growth rate
* Trade off of aesthetic, functional, safety and cost factors is inevitable
* Forsee the impact of emerging technologies and anticipate impact of new technologies on building, layout and space

- Have a floor plan with 3-dimensional model racks and furniture
- Plan use of appropriate sign boards

Some illustrations of input from user studies for the programme are:

- Inverse square law of use of library.
- Psychological distance between user and library

- Almost one-third of users visit libraries for work space and one-eight exclusively for work space
- Inhouse use, seat occupancy, length of stay, user movement/ traffic flow pattern
- Distance zone studies
- Browsing and current awareness needs, etc.

Size

The size of the library building is determined by, the number of clientele it is going to cater to, variety and range of services provided, document type, total present collection and the rate of growth, staff strength, extension and oilier activities. While the Fifth law of Library Science states that library is a growing organism, there is a limit to growth as far as building space is concerned. Normally a library building is planned with a 15-20 years growth in view. But since the library activity cannot come to a standstill at the end of 20 years, just because funds are not available for a new building, every library should have an active 'de-acquisition' policy along with a healthy acquisition policy. There are a lot of ephemeral materials accumulated in the library over the years-old catalogues and brochures, news bulletins, old text books, outdated reference books, torn fiction books, and many other materials which occupy valuable space in the library. These should be periodically weeded out to make space for the new. In essence, one should ensure that the size of the building is adequate from all perspectives.

Architecture

Library activity is a specialised activity and it should be designed so as to carry out this activity efficiently in a congenial environment. The library design should be based upon and correlated with the functions and services of the library. Just as a temple, a church, or a hospital has a distinctive architecture-both internal and external, the library is also a specialised institution, and its individuality should be reflected in its architecture. But above all its design should aim at bringing about economy in administration and optimise its operation. For the sake of economy the stack area's may have low ceilings, compared to the other areas. For effect, the lobby may have higher ceiling. Above all, library requires floor stronger than other office buildings to withstand load of stocks. While planning and execution of plan for a library building, it should be ensured that load bearing capacity of floor (1500 kg/sq m), floor height (not less than 8 ft), avoiding interior load bearing walls, quiet comfortable and attracting reading rooms, simplicity, efficiency, economy, contort, flexibility and functional usefulness of the building are as per standards. The preliminary considerations should lead to a proper written proposal or programme and that in term should get translated into working drawings and specifications for the requisite building.

Space Allocation, Utilisation and Management

Library planning constitutes correct estimation of space required for various activities, logical juxtaposition of space earmarked for various activities and optimal use of the space available. Since it is within the confines of a library building that most library activities take place, rational estimation of space requirement and optimal utilisation of space is '*sine qua non*' of successful library management. For operation, the library needs space for, books, users and staff. Books are to be stored and displayed in specific areas and in special furniture, equipment has to be housed in special rooms, readers are to be provided with tables and chairs located in congenial reading rooms or study carrels. The staff needs space to work undisturbed. Provision of these space requirements is vital in the planning of a library building.

Mainly the following four broad areas along with their allied and subareas are identified as common service areas in a library:

(a) Circulation area, which includes:
   (i) Stack rooms or halls
   (ii) Charging Desk
   (iii) Public Catalogues
(b) Reader Activity Area, which includes:
   (i) Reading rooms
   (ii) Microform leading room
   (iii) Study carrels
(c) Staff Activity Area, which includes:
   (i) Acquisition section
   (ii) Technical section
   (iii) Reference section
(d) Other Areas, which include:

(i) Senior professionals rooms
(ii) Space for library staff
(iii) Seminar room
(iv) Binding section
(v) Reprography section
(vi) Internet browsing section
(vii) News Paper Section
(viii) Periodical Section etc.

Tips for space management

Some important tips for space management in library building are given below :

* Flexibility is the catchword.
* Function is more important than the beauty.
* Evolutionary steps in orientation and shape of building are I, T, L, U & O.
* Shape : a 3 : 2 rectangle with door half way along long wall of not more than 100 ft. long and not more than 4 floors is ideal for best ratio of assignable to gross area, most direct traffic and transportation, and ease in organising, integrity and adding or enlarging.
* Primary floor and entrance should be on grade.
* Primary floor should be larger than other floors.
* Building perimeter should be as straight and uncluttered as possible.
* Security and fire safety should be incorporated on priority.
* Minimise RCC.
* Avoid space stealers like balconies, air wells, light wells, etc.
* Minimise interior walls.
* Don't overuse glass.
* All assignable space should take a floor load of 150 Ib/sq.ft. and 250-300 Ib/sq.ft for compact storage.
* Simple open forms should be preferred.
* Informal comfortable atmosphere need to be created.
* Accessibility and convenience are very important.
* Noise control should be looked.

- * Space allocation is an important activity which need to be done logically and scientifically. It is better to consider floor as a series of concentric circles with the centre being the place where elevator, main stair case and entrance arc located. Even considering space three-dimensionally, the same principle holds. Then proceed with radial assignment of space to various activities.
- * The relationship between units has to be decided in a heuristic method by drawing charts with different intensity of relationships between units like essential, important, desirable, not important and undesirable.
- * Seating economies like size of tables, and stealing space from aisles to be given due consideration.

It is here that the finding of the past studies both in librarianship as well as other areas like behavioural science and psychology have to be noted. For example, it has always been reported that users prefer to occupy empty tables even if it is little away in the reading hall. The next preferred seat in a four sealer table is diagonal position and the last chance is sitting by the side of another user. Similarly the distance zones of privacy reported by psychologists given below should help us to determine the sealing arrangements in different areas.

intimate	<1 1/2 ft
personal	1, 1/2 ft - 4 ft
social	4 ft - 12 ft
public	12 ft - 25 ft
public domain	>25 ft

CIRCULATION AREA

The stack rooms, issue and return counter and public catalogue constitute the circulation area. Along with the reading room, the circulation area is considered the most important part of the library, since it is in these places where the readers come in direct contact with the library personnel and facilities, hence great deal of thought and attention should be given to their planning.

(i) Stacks

The storage of reading materials posses serious problems of housing them at a safe yet conveniently accessible place in the physical

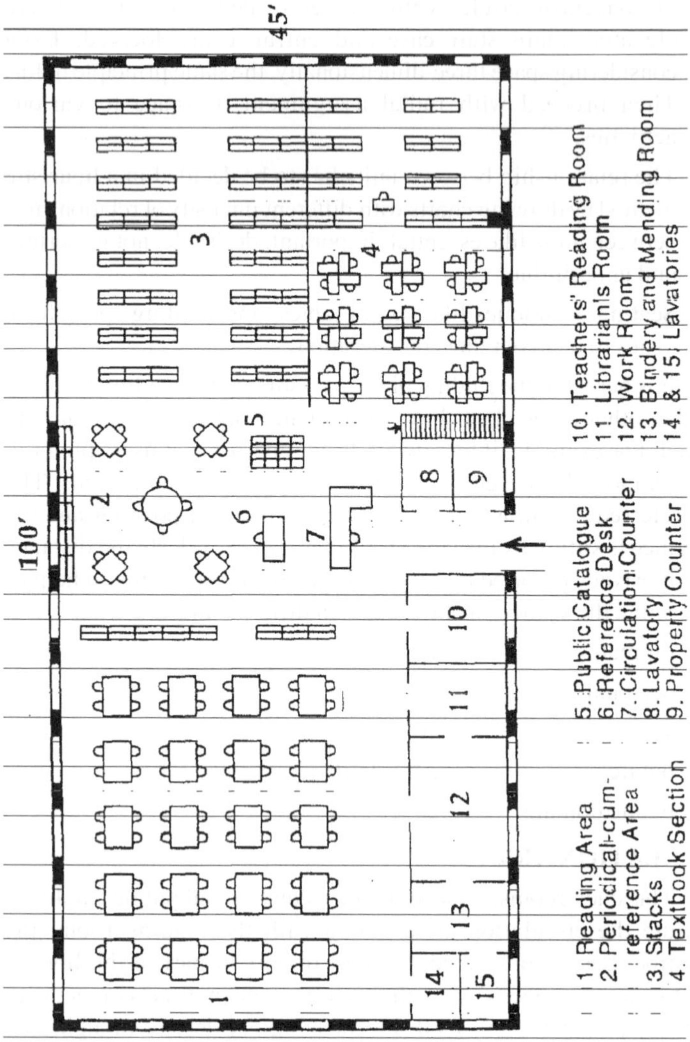

School/Small College Library

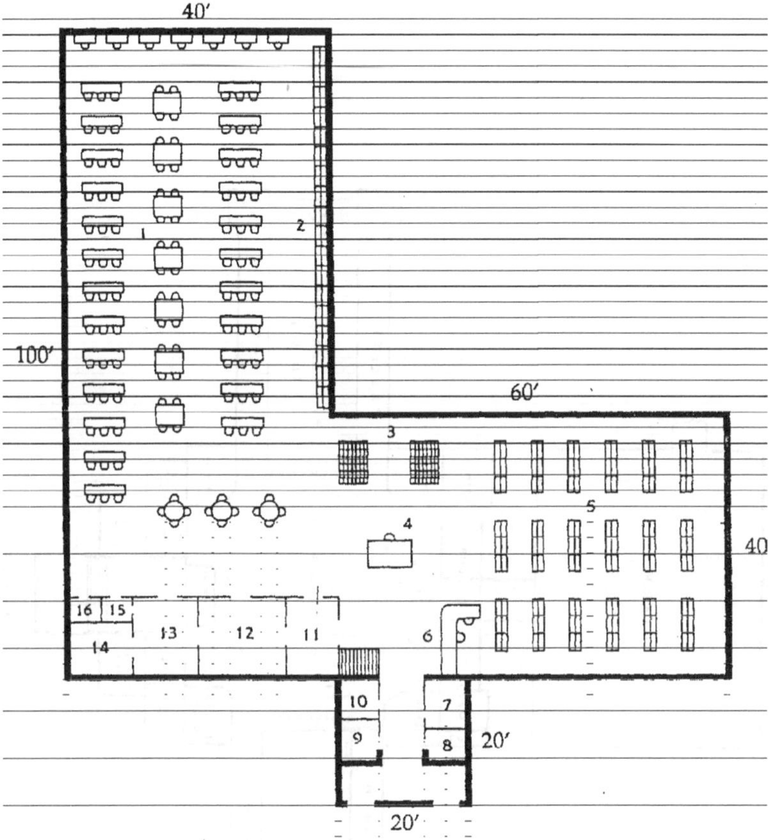

Medium Size College Library Building
(Ground Floor)

1. Reading Area
2. Reference Collection
3. Public Catalogue
4. Reference Desk
5. Stacks
6. Issue Counter
7. Lavatories
8. Watchman's Room
9. Property Counter
10. Store Room
11. Assistant Librarian's Room
12. Work-room
13. Librarian's Room
14. Staff Lounge
15. & 16. Lavatories

Medium Size College Library

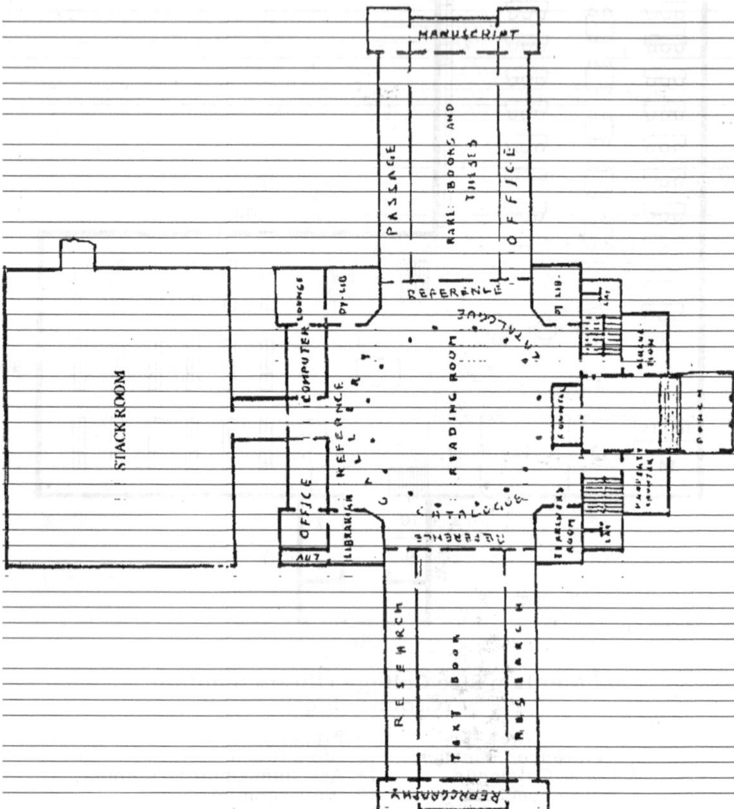

University Library

Research Library

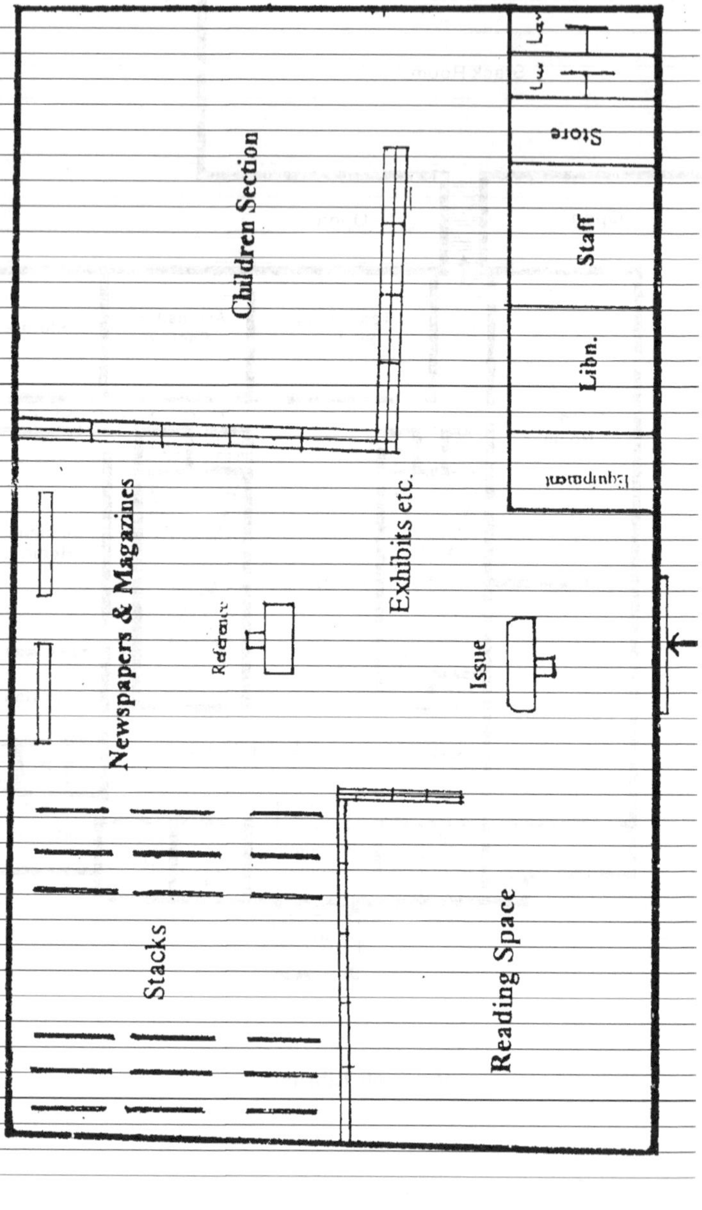

Small Public Library

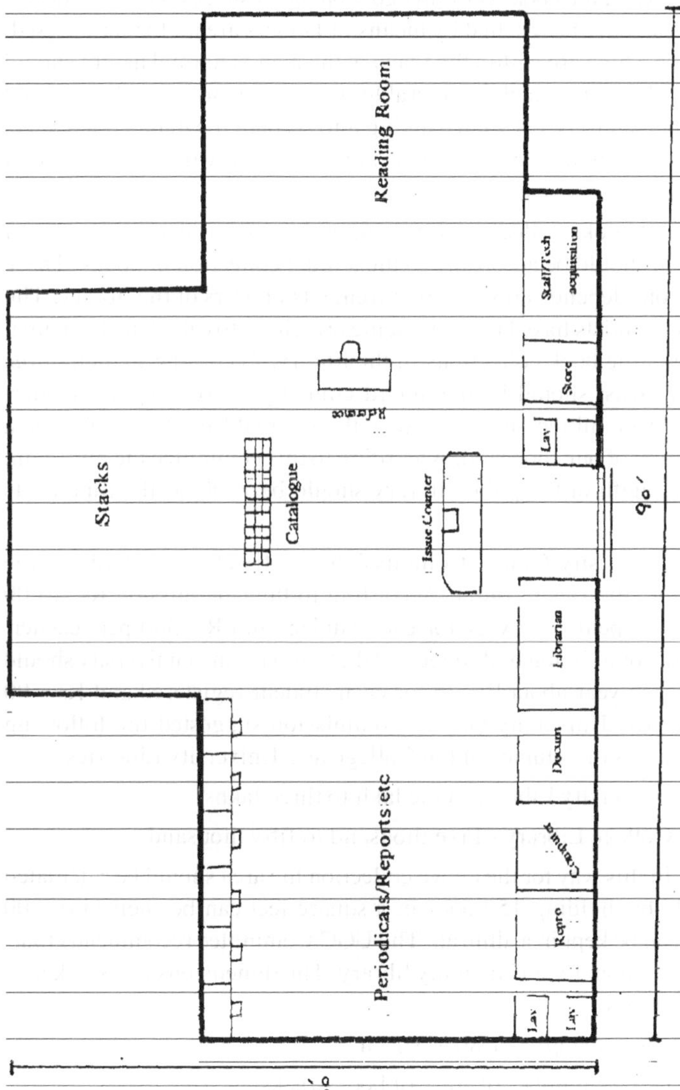

Small Special Library

set-up of the library. As library is growing organism so provision should be made for vertical as well as horizontal expansion of the books stacks, as the stock of the books certainly goes on increasing every year. Shelves which can only be reached by means of ladders are no longer advised, but these which are within the reach of the man of normal height should be provided in the stacks. Preferable stack cum reading is always good for readers must be calculated taking into account the number of readers presently using the library and the anticipated growth of readership in the next 20 to 30 years.

All books collection are stack in the stack room, so the size of the stack should be according to the annual collection of books. These collections depends upon the requirements of users of the library. The library scientists have laid down some principles to calculate the annual adding of the book collections in the library. According to them three books at least should be purchased annually for one regular reader. Roberts Committee suggested that there should be 250 books for a population of one thousand. According to this committee the minimum book strength of the public library should be 7200 at, the time of its starting.

University Grants Commission has fixed a standard for the academic libraries of India. According to the Commission Rs. 15.00 should be spent each year for each student and Rs. 300 per teacher. Kothari Commission had suggested that "as a norm, a university should spend each year about Rs. 25 for each student registered and Rs. 300 per teacher. University Grants Commission suggested the following the numbers of volumes of the College and University Libraries.

- University Library - One lakh to three lakhs.
- College Library - Five thousand to fifty thousand.

In this way for the above collection the area should be calculated roughly by dividing 15 books in a square feet can be shelved or 300 books can be kept in a almirah. The UGC Committee recommends four-tier stack room for a University library. The dimensions of a stack may be as follows:-

(a) *Clear Length* :- 1.80 + 3.15 n

n = the number of rows of books racks.

(The centre to centre distance between consecutive rack is 1.80 m)

(b) *Clear Width* :-

- 3m (on the basis of one rack 2m long plus one longitudinal gangway of 1m) close to a longitudinal wall.
- 5m (on the basis of 2 racks each 2m long plus longitudinal gangway of 1m) longitudinal wall.
- 8m (on the basis of 3 rows each 2m long plus two longitudinal gangways of 1m each) close to each of the longitudinal walls, and
- 10m (on the basis of 4 racks each 2m long plus two longitudinal gangways of 1 m each) close to each of the longitudinal walls.)

  Note: Three meters and five meters widths are generally only in the case of stack- spaces, as the stack room and the reading room may be combined into a single room, in such cases.

(c) *Clear Height* :- Floor to ceiling 2.40 m

Note 1 : The height of rack is 2.20 m and allowance for bay guides is 0.20 m.

Note 2 : The stack room should be combined with necessary devices for effective verification.

If the library is fully computerised and issue and returns are computerised then its size depends on the computer nodes provided on the counter otherwise a small place is sufficient for the purpose.

Circulation counter is an expensive item of furniture and cannot be replaced very often. It has to perform four kind of functions:-

- Register of new readers.
- Charging or issue of books.
- Discharging or receiving books back.
- Reservation of books lent out.

(ii) Charging Desk

The location of charging and discharging desk should be at the entrance of the library. So its location, size and shape of the issue and return counter should be decided before the building plans are finalized. Adequate space, close to main entrance, must be provided for this activity. The issue system used will also affect the size of the counter.

The size of the counter depends on its numbers of member of seats is twenty- five percent of the total number of students.

As per UGC Committee recommendation, the size of the reading room is to be determined as under:-

"The average area per reader- in the reading room should be 2.33 m^2 minimum.

Note: The size of reading table is 2.4 × 0.6 m the centre to centre distance between two consecutive rows of reading tables is 1.8 m with seating arrangement on one side of the table only.

Other Library Scientists have also suggested space required for the accommodation of readers in the reading room. The length and width of the reading hall depend on the number of the readers who use the reading hall. Metcalf has suggested that in a University Library space accommodation for readers should be made on the basis of 25 sq.ft. area for each undergraduate, 30 sq.ft. for each graduate and post graduate and 36 sq.ft. for each one engaged in dissertation writing. For faculty member, he suggested a research cubicles of 75 net sq.f.t. area. Lyie and Burchard have suggested that readers capacity in a College and University libraries may vary from 25-50% of the total enrolment of the students. The UGC Committee has also suggested that 20% of the students population and 10% faculty members be provided reading seats in the university library. On the basis of formula stated above the area can be calculated required for the reading hall.

Indian Standard Institute (ISI) has given the following formula for providing the space for reading room. The size of reading room should be as follows:-

(a) *Length 1.5 m*

(excluding the control region where n is the number of rows of reading tables.)

2. *Width 5 m*

(On the basis of two tables 2 m long plus central gang way 1m wide); or 7.5 m (on the basis of three tables each 2m long plus central gangway 1.5 m wide); or 10 m (on the basis of four tables each 2 m long plus central gangway 2 m wide).

Note: Size of the reading table is 2 × 0.70 m. The centre to centre distance between two consicutive rows of reading room tables is 1.5 m with seating arrangement on one-side of the table only.

(iii) Public Catalogue

Public catalogue is the key to the document collection in a library and is frequently used by the readers as well as the library staff. This should also be placed near the entrance and not far from the counter. Sufficient space should he left near the catalogue cabinets to make consultation easier. A few high stools may be placed near the catalogue cabinet, to make lengthy consultation comfortable. Provision is usually made in the cabinet for small drawout writing board where the readers can note down the contents of the catalogue cards. As catalogues grow with the book stock, hence sufficient space should be provided for future expansion. An economy catalogue cabinet require about 1.75 sq. mtr. (20 sq. ft.) area. In recent years many libraries have automated their services and functions and hence they have been able to provide Online Public Access Catalogue (OPAC) to their customers both within the library as well as on campus through Local Area Network (LAN).

In addition to above, this area has to accommodate new arrivals display, stacking of reserved books, circulation staff, personal property counter, computer workstation, etc.

READER ACTIVITY AREA

Depending on the size and nature of the library, there may be one or more reading rooms. A reading room for books and another for magazines and newspapers is fairly common. In many academic institutions and some public libraries, a separate text book room is also provided. In libraries having a sizeable collection of maps and drawings, a room with special devices to study them properly, is set apart.

i) Reading room

Reading room of any kind of libraries have got a prominent place as this is the place where users can study in a calm and quite reading atmosphere. In an academic library a large numbers of students use the reading rooms for the study purposes. The reading rooms of the university libraries keeps open twelve to sixteen hours. Therefore, to accommodate a large numbers of students in reading room, big halls are provided for both to the under graduate and post graduate students. Generally the capacity of a reading hall is to accommodate 150 to 200 students. So the library building planners must be considered this vital and important point before finalise the plan.

Provision of space allocated to reading rooms vary from library to library. It depends on the factors like :- (a) the present and future enrolment (b) the type of readers to be served (c) the character of curriculum and the teaching methods and the amount of the reading they require, (d) number of students who live off campus, and (e) the presence on the campus of other facilities for study as departmental or dormitory libraries. Apart from the above five factors the conventional figure of providing number are as under:-

Suitable provision should also be made for suspending bay guides from the ceiling of each tier of the stack room. For example, at a depth of about 5 cm from the ceiling of each tier of the stack room and at a distance of about 5 cm from either side of a row of books racks, a rod may be run from wall to wall of the stack rooms, so that frames holding the bay guides may be suspended and slide along.

Besides, the above standard for the space provided by the University Grants Commission, it is also suggested that the length of the stack should be from east to west as the books can be protected from direct sun rays and avoid the direct sun through the window.

(ii) Microform reading room, Collection and Production Units

These days, more and more use being made of microforms-microfilm, microfiche, micro opaque cards, slides, video cassettes, etc., for recording and storage of information. The storage of these materials need special care, viewing of these materials need special equipment and a different environment than obtaining in normal reading rooms. Special reading rooms are set apart for such type of materials. Since each reader has to be provided with individual reading area, more space per reader has to be provided than in a general reading room. About 150 sq ft area is required for one unit of microform reader. A library may also have a microform production equipment either in the same section or a separate section.

(iii) Study carrels

Study carrels are exclusive areas, located in quieter and undisturbed part of the library, which are set apart for prolonged use of a research or academic staff. Very often they are located near the reference collection or the bound volumes collection, which are extensively used by the researchers. More generous space allocation has to be made for these study carrels, and preferably they should be insulated against intrusion by others. Most university libraries and some big public libraries provide this facility. Ordinary table size modular study carrels can also be designed and kept along windows in reading room or stacks to provide a sort of semi privacy.

STAFF ACTIVITY AREA

Main activities carried out by the professional staff of the library are: Acquisition, Technical Processing (cataloguing and classification) and Reference service. Besides, a lot of routine activities like typing, labelling, stamping, duplicating arc carried out in areas screened off from public view. The space allocation for professionals and other staff should take into consideration the fact that besides tables and chairs, they would require space for book racks, trolleys, card trays etc. General norm is to provide about 250 sq. ft. areas for librarian, 125-150 sq.ft., for deputy librarian and 50 sq.ft. for clerical staff. The number of staff obviously depends on the size of the library and the range of services provided. The staff areas are organised around discrete work units, and their layout should be such that work flows smoothly from one work unit to the other.

(i) Acquisition Section

The acquisition work consists of selection, approval (by competent authority, Library committee, Department heads, or in some cases the librarian himself), ordering, receipt of books and their transfer to the technical section after accessioning. Adequate space should be provided for all these activities which will include space for a number of shelves for keeping books and various tools required for acquisition work. It should be located near the catalogue and not far away from the main entrance. Sometimes the interlibrary loan activity is the responsibility of this section, since interlibrary loan can be considered as a temporary acquisition activity. It is very responsible task and special cure has to be taken about safe custody so that the document acquired or obtained on loan or on approval are not lost.

(ii) Technical Section

Cataloguing and classification are the principal technical activities after the acquisition process. Besides the technical staff who catalogue, classify and file the cards in the public catalogue, typists or data entry operators, and other supportive administrative staff constitute the members of this team. However, they may be seated separately. In smaller libraries, technical section and acquisition section are merged into one unit.

(iii) Reference Section

Reference activity is one of the most important activities of a library and very often it is the precursor of documentation and information activity. A Reference librarian not only needs to consult the reference collection of the library, but he has also to consult the public catalogue to answer the readers queries. Reference librarian is located in close proximity of the reference collection. For a more active reference service, the reference librarian should regularly scan contents of current periodicals and maintain a file of pertinent information gathered. He needs suitable equipment to file these records. Small card cabinet or Rollodex may be kept handy by the reference librarian.

OTHER AREAS

These include the librarian's room, senior professionals room in bigger libraries, space for supporting administrative staff, seminar room, reprographic unit and bindery. Besides, there are service areas like stairs, corridors, cloak rooms, entrance hall, janitors room, etc. which forms part of nonassignable area of the building.

(i) Librarian's room

The librarian normally has a separate room of his own, adjacent to the work room and opposite to the main counter area. This room should be centrally located, preferably of wood and glass construction, so that he can keep a watch on the activities of various sections. A few cupboards for important reference tools and locked almirahs for important documents are kept in the librarian's room. Usually generous space is provided in the librarian's room so that readers, vendors, and library staff can come and sit for discussion or any help. Some senior professional staff (e.g. Deputy librarian. Systems analyst) are provided with separate rooms of smaller dimensions. The minimum area of the room must be 30 sq. meter as per standards.

(ii) Space for library staff

Some what interior space is provided for the supportive administrative staff like typists, library assistants, etc. They provide support service for all the technical activities.

(iii) Seminar room or Conference/Meeting/Exhibition hall

A small hall or a big room may be set apart for seminars, meetings, discussions, etc. These activities may be organised by the library staff or at the initiative of other faculty members or research departments. This room can also be used as a projection room for slides, videos and films. Size of the room will depend on the expected number of clientele. A 45 m (6m x 7.5m) or 500 sq.ft. room will accommodate 40-50 persons.

(iv) Binding section

This section is generally located in the basement or some other obscure area. Machinery, material and equipment for mending, repairing and binding of books are provided here. Though having a seperate bindery within the premises of the library, has certain advantages, now-a-days in most libraries major binding work is contracted to outside professional binders. Only minor posting and restoration jobs are carried out in the library by the junior administrative staff.

(v) Reprography unit

With the advent of cheap and efficient photocopying machines, provision of photocopy service has become a must in most libraries. In the West, coin operated photocopying machines are placed near strategic collection of materials, to be used by the readers themselves. In our country, this practice is not in vogue. Supervised operation and close check are maintained to by most libraries. With the rising cost of technical and scientific periodical publications most libraries within a city or within a region, resort to cooperative acquisition, and supplement their collection by obtaining photocopies of articles needed by their clientele from other libraries. Depending on the volume of work, one or more light or heavy duty copying machines are provided. Besides photocopying machines, desktop offset machines, microform machines are standard equipment in some bigger libraries. A room with subdued light is preferable for this operation. Size of the room will depend on the number of machines and operators.

(vi) Internet Browsing Section

Internet is changing the traditional library, that is a closed place into a virtual library, a library without walls. However the usage of internet will have a positive impact of the way the information is generated, processed, stored, retrieved and disseminated. A proper space is to be provided for this section as some computer nodes and telephone connection etc. essentional for internet services.

Besides, there are many other areas like new arrivals display, special materials audio-visuals, computer and, CD-ROM workstations, place for carrying out repair and maintenance of furniture and equipment, etc., need to be given due consideration.

(vii) News Paper Section

The provision of newspaper section in the academic libraries is a conventional necessity rather than mandatory, but in the public library and special library, it is essential items. Infact the argument against it is that the newspapers are purchased by the individuals themselves. Information contained in the different newspapers is generally the same, the cost for its upkeep is high, and this section attract a large number of unwanted readers with meaning less interest. This section should be placed at the ground floor.

(viii) Periodical Section

The periodical section in the library especially in a university library has a very vital role to play. Due to knowledge explosion it has been observed that the periodicals are becoming more and more important not only in sciences but also in social sciences and humanities. Libraries subscribe every year new periodicals thereby resulting in increase in number of readers consulting them. Therefore, a separate area allotment in the library for the procurement, display storage and reading of periodicals has become urgent necessity. Usually the periodical section and general reading room are combined together. The desirable limit area for periodical department is around 5000 sq.ft. for upper class university libraries. However, the middle order and even smaller order, the desirable limit may be 4000 to 3000 sq.ft.

LIBRARY FURNITURE

Just as a library building is a specialised structure with specific functions, the furniture for a library has to be custom designed for each function. The needs of furniture and equipment of individual departments and sections should be given careful consideration so that the users and the staff experience ease, comfort, convenience and efficiency in their work. Generally library furniture is of two types wooden and metal. The kind of furniture is to be acquired is either

(i) stock standard available from manufacturers who specialise in library furniture, or

(ii) custom-built or made to order with specification provided by the library

The standard furniture is usually made of metal whereas the ordered furniture is made with wood. These days some firms have also started manufacturing plastic furniture for the libraries. It is advisable to visit some good libraries and some manufacturers of library furniture before deciding on the type of furniture to be ordered.

List of suppliers of stock-standard library furniture:

M/s Curzon & Co.	M/s Methodex Ltd.
M/s Godrej & Co.	M/s Remington Rand Co.
M/s Mehra & Co.	M/s Vinar Systems.
M/s Standard Library Service	

Three important criteria for selection of furniture are function, maintenance and appearance. Before acquiring furniture for the library, care should be taken to:

(i) Decide the kind of furnishing suitable for a particular library.

(ii) Determine what is available in the market and what can be obtained to satisfy the requirements of the library.

(iii) Select and purchase furniture based on type or users, amount of use, kind of material (to be stored, organised and displayed in the library), number of staff members and future growth/changes in the library.

(iv) Consultation with library staff members.

(v) Market prices, comparison of rates, etc.

(vi) Acquiring and checking sample of each furniture item.

Various kinds of furniture required for a library are stack room racks, periodical display racks, card catalogue cabinet, charging desks and some special furniture items. For sitting purpose tables and chairs for the staff and the users are also required. Some of the furniture items required by all the libraries are discussed as under :

Stack Room Racks

The most important piece of furniture in any library is the racks in the stack room which is also referred to as stacks. These are used to store books, periodicals, bound volumes of periodicals, reports, and other kinds of reading materials. Each individual rack (wooden or steel) is usually 180 cm wide, 195/225 cm high and 25/50 cm deep depending on whether it is single sided or double sided. The number of shelves in a rack is usually 5 or 6 depending on the height of the rack. A number of racks can be joined together to make one row.

Some of the popular kinds of stacks are:

Fixed Shelves with double row : They are normal fixed shelves where material can be arranged in double rows.

Hinged Stacks : Here two shelves are joined together with hinges on one side and one shelf fixed while the other is mounted in front of the hinges.

Rolling Stacks : These are metal stack units mounted on ball bearing wheel placed side by side.

Compact Storage : This system consists of units of three stacks, the centre row of fixed double-sided stacks at each side. This helps in increasing the capacity of the storage space.

Multitier Stacks : This kind of stacking consists of stacks from floor to the roof and has become quite popular in very large libraries.

While selecting stacks for any kind of library, main consideration should be to ensure maximum space utilisation, user convenience and easy movement with the stack room. There should also be adequate provision for future expansion both horizontally as well as vertically.

Periodical Display Racks

Libraries usually display periodical for attracting the users which leads to greater use of this category of materials. Methods of display of periodicals are determined by a number of factors which include:

- Type of periodicals acquired
- Floor space available
- Layout of the library
- Types of users coming to the library

Many libraries have a separate reading room where periodicals are housed and displayed whereas in some others a general reading room accommodates all the reading materials.

For displaying periodicals, usually periodical display racks are used. These display racks are of three kinds:

(i) Step type

(ii) Pigeon note type

(iii) Inclined type

The brief details of each type of the periodical display racks are as :

(i) Step (or Gallery) type

In this type the periodicals are displayed stepwise, each step being 5 cm deep and 15 cm high. Length of the rack is generally 90 cm. There may be 4 to 5 steps and on each step 4 to 5 journals can be displayed and on a single sided rack 20-25 journals can be displayed. Double sided racks are not recommended since the unit becomes too bulky. It is better to place two single sided racks back to back if necessary. Journals are better displayed in this type, but one great disadvantage is that back issues cannot be accommodated within the unit. Normally popular magazines are displayed in this type of rack.

(ii) Pigeon hole type

This is the most popular type of display rack in libraries especially in libraries subscribing to a large number of periodicals. This type of rack has two parts, one being a cupboard in the bottom and other pigeon holes at the top. The usual height and width are 7.5 feet by 6 feet. The depth is about one foot in the pigeon hole and about 1.5 feet in the lower cupboard portion. The cupboard portion is for storing the back volumes of the periodicals and the pigeons holes hold about 36 current periodicals.

This type of display rack is very convenient and useful in the library but there is one disadvantage that the periodicals cannot be displayed properly.

Inclined type

This type of display rack is considered to be the best type and is an improvement over the earlier pigeon hole type of rack. This is a box type rack with horizontal shelves, each covered with wooden planks with an inclination to the shelf plank. The shelves can be partitioned into pigeon holes, each hole being provided with a wooden support for-the periodicals. Here the inclined plank provides a better way of displaying periodicals, with the back issues in the space behind the inclined plank. Display space for 25 to 30 periodicals can be provided in one rack.

Catalogue Card Cabinets

The catalogue cabinet is the most frequently used item not only

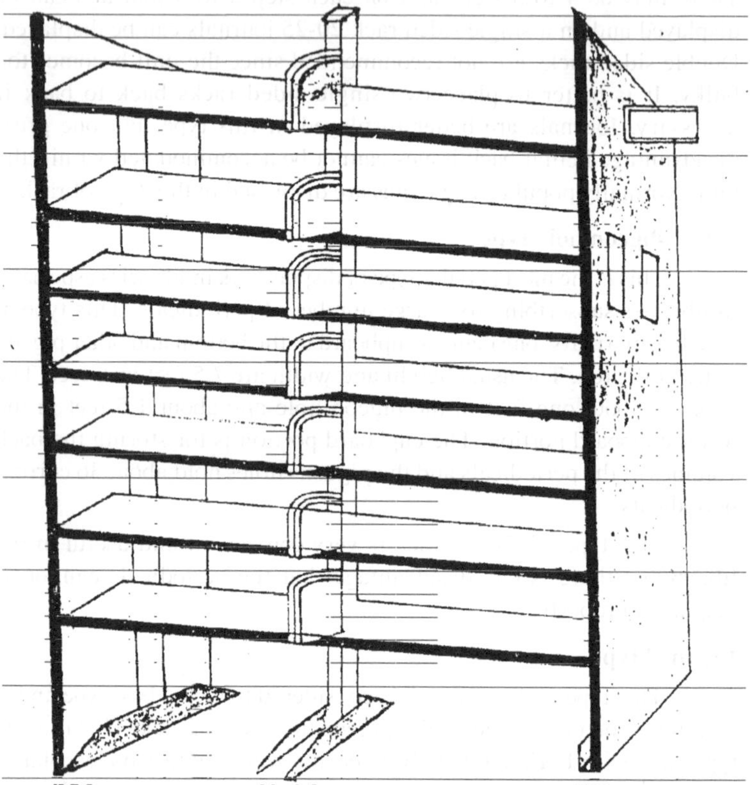

A Conventional Standard Double Faced Steel Book Rack

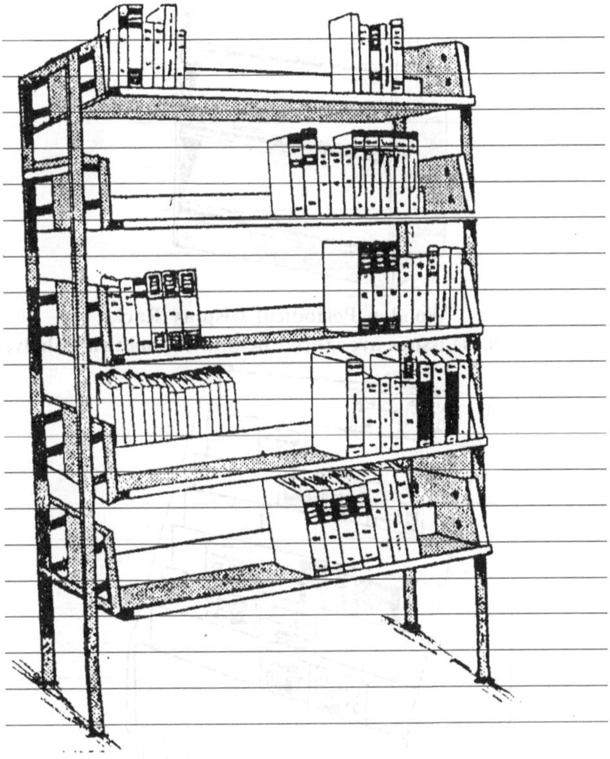

Non Conventional Light Steel Book Rack

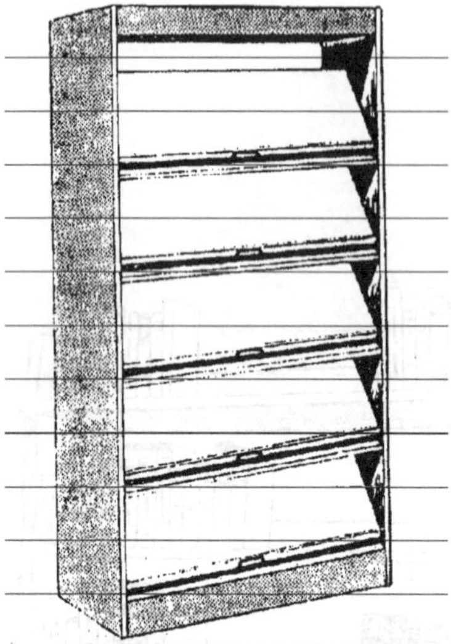

Wooden Periodical Display Rack
(Back loose issues are stored behind the movable shelves)

Stair-type Wooden Periodical Display Rack

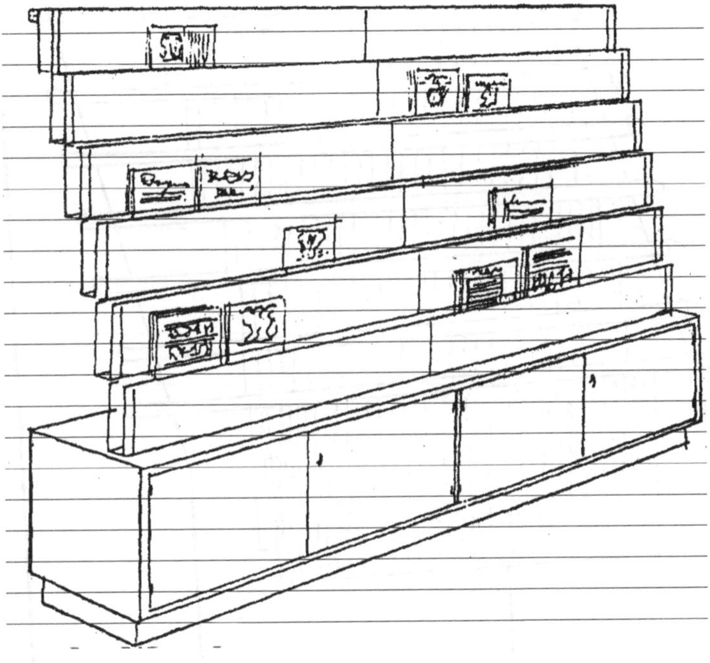

Another type of Wooden Periodical Display Rack (Loose issues are stored in the cupboards underneath)

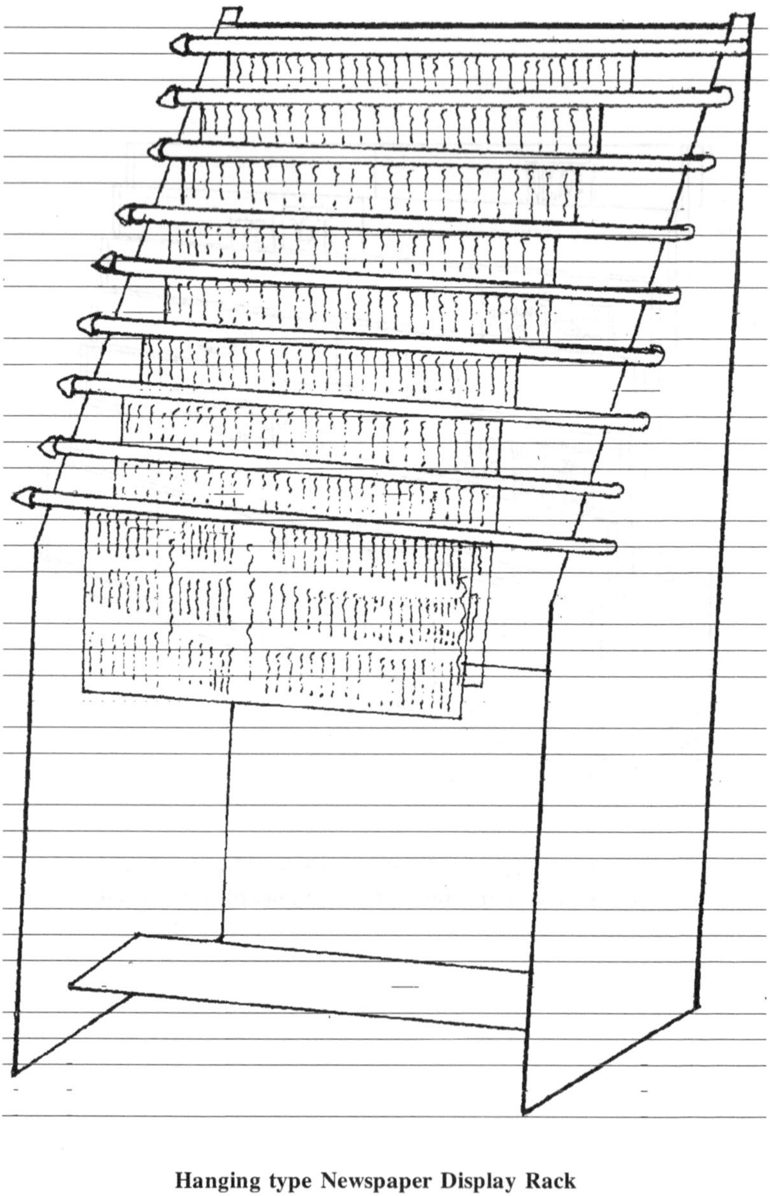

Hanging type Newspaper Display Rack

Catalogue Cabinet with 20 drawers

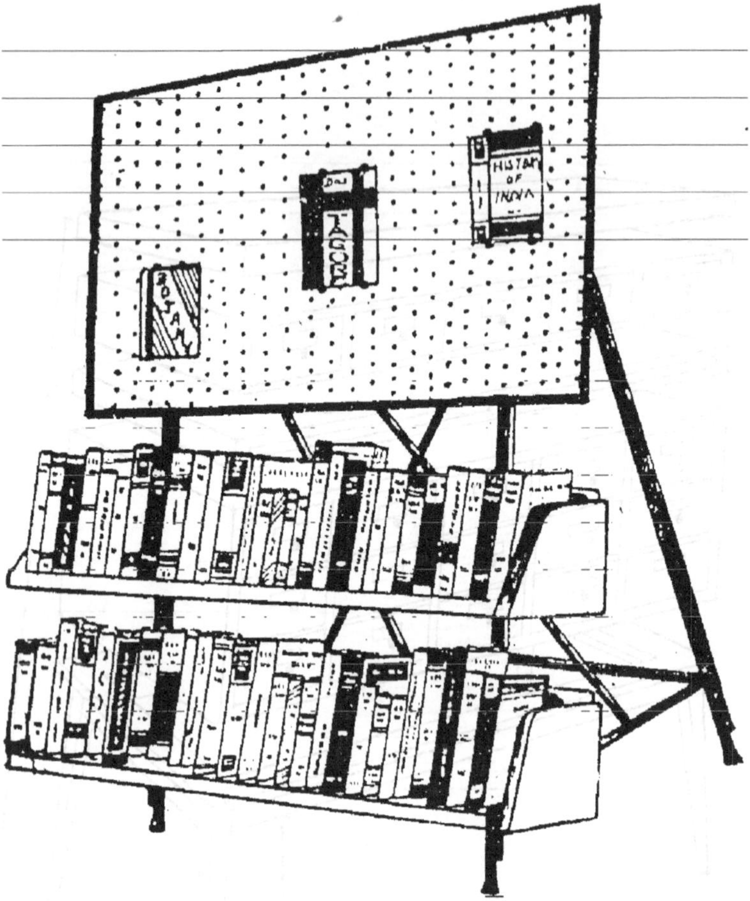

Display System with Shelves and a Board

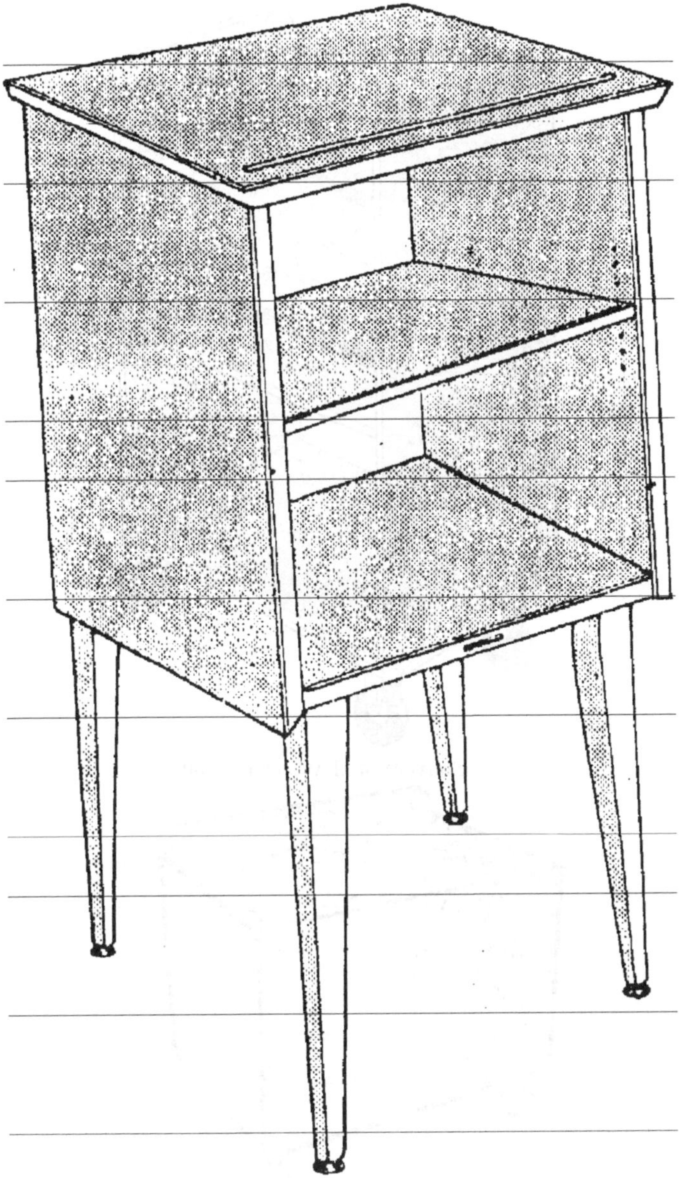

Smaller Dictionary Stand

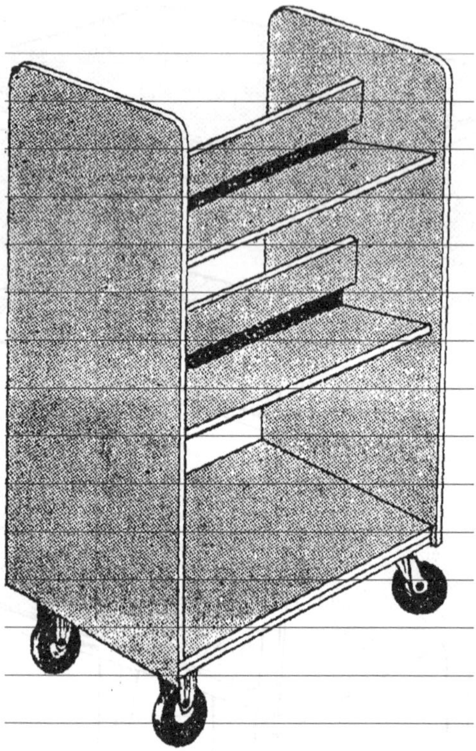

Conventional Wooden Trolley

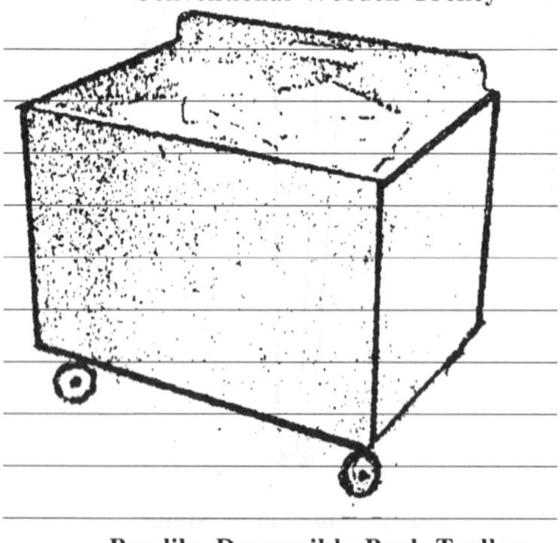

Box-like Depressible Book Trolley

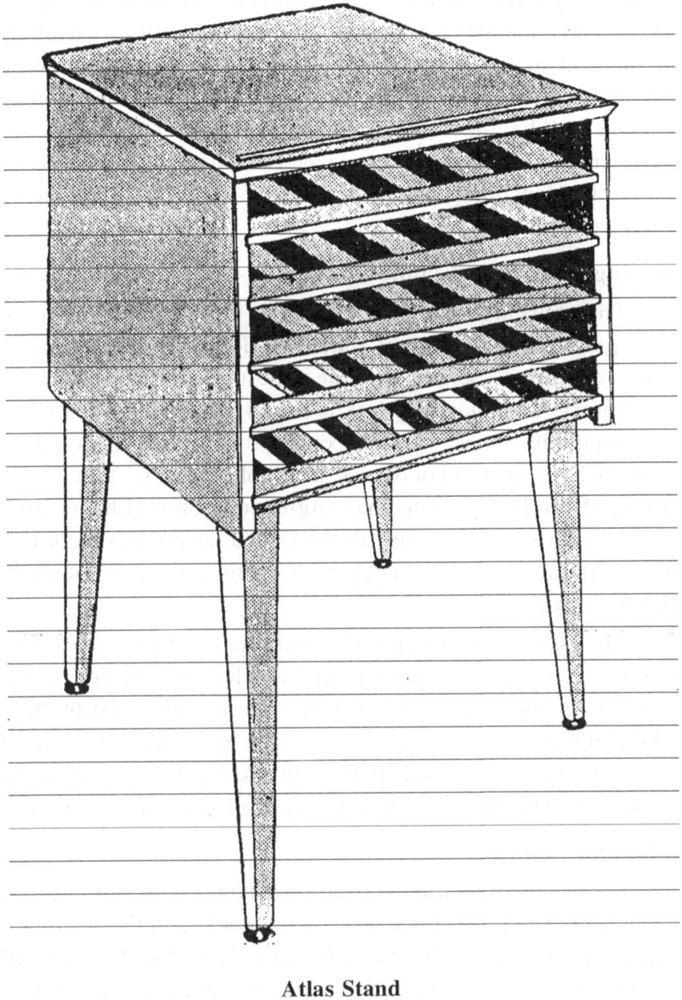

Atlas Stand

by the users but by library staff too. It is a unit of drawers full of cards specially designed to hold library cards (5" X 3") and equipped with a metal holding rods. The catalogue cabinet and its drawers are usually made of wood, metals or plastic material. These units are available in wide range of sizes starting from four drawers to about 60 drawers, For convenience and ease of use the rows of drawers are placed on stands and the overall height of the cabinet alongwith the stand is usually not more than 4.5 to 5 feet that is eye level. Each tray can hold about 1,000 thick cards. Depending on the size of the library the catalogue card cabinet can be acquired.

Charging Desk/Issue Counter

The charging desk also called the issue counter, is the main service point of any library. It should be designed to take care of the various activities associated with the issue and return of the documents of the library. The charging desk is usually specially prepared for an individual library and very seldom bought from the market. It is designed keeping in view the kind of library, available space, specific functions, and size of the library. The charging counter should have sufficient drawer space to accommodate all the issued documents records. -The counter should also have sufficient shelving space for placing books which are returned by the users.

The issue counter is usually designed for two persons to work simultaneously. It is essential that sufficient leg space be provided while designing the counter. As high chairs are usually used by the staff working at the issue counter, a foot stool is also required. Some of the common designs for the issue counter are circular, L-shaped, rectangular or U-shaped. The counter is usually made of good quality wood.

Tables and Chairs

For use by the library staff, proper tables with suitable drawers are required. The tables to be used by the readers in the reading room are larger in size and without any drawers. The table should be atleast 29" high with blunt or round edges. Library tables are usually wooden or metal or a combination of both.

The chairs in any library should be atleast 26" high with a knee height of 17". The chairs are required for reading hall, lounge, staff room, seminar room etc.

Other Furniture Items

In addition to the furniture items mentioned above, a few other item are required in any kind of library. These are:

(i) Display rack for newly acquired books

(ii) Book trolley for moving books from one part of the library to the other

(iii) Stands for over- sized books

(iv) Notice Board

(v) Almirahs for storing new books

(vi) Computer tables

(vii) Foot stools for users in stack room for picking books from upper shelves

(viii) Newspaper stands with sloping top

(ix) Side racks (3-4 feet high) for keeping books, files, etc. for use by the staff

(x) Property counter or racks for keeping users belongings

EQUIPMENTS

The equipment in the library should be suitable for use by the staff and the users. The library should be provided with equipment of standard size and specifications. The kinds of equipment usually found in any library includes:

(i) Record keeping equipment

(ii) Filing cabinets

(iii) Photocopiers

(iv) Computers

(v) Miscellaneous items etc.

(i) Record keeping equipment

Record-keeping equipment in the library is mainly used for keeping records of per current issues as they are received, and the back files of bound or otherwise volumes. The kind of equipment to be selected for this purpose depends on the size of the library, kind of users and the number of currently received periodicals. This kind of equipment is being replaced by computerised record systems in majority of the libraries. The existing manual system in based on a unit card, one for each periodical title, on which complete details of the periodical are available. The cards are filed in transparent holders and placed in an overlapping manner with only the title portion visible. As and when new periodical issues arc received, the details are noted down in appropriate columns. Equipments used for this purpose are Kardex, Linedex or loose leaf binders which are supplied by many companies specialising in the area. Linedex is a metal cylindrical structure of 30 cm height, revolving on ball bearing, and having a known at the top and a number of metal panels these panels where perforated strips of paper bearing the title of the journal subscribed by the library with their location are displayed. A simple loose leaf binder which look like bank ledgers can also be used in place of Kardex.

(ii) Filing cabinets

Plenty of library materials needs to be filed and provision has to be made for keeping these properly. The kinds of material to filed includes - correspondence, newspaper clippings, pamphlets, patents, standards and other types of material with odd sizes. For easy storage and fast retrieval, various types of filing equipment has been designed.

For filing of correspondence, vertical filing cabinets with drawers that can be pulled out are available. Pamphlet boxes of various kinds are available for storing pamphlets, leaflets, standards and patents. These boxes are available indifferent sizes and can open at the top of side. They are made of metal, wood or cardboard. For large drawings and designs, large steel cabinets with pull out drawers are available.

(iii) Photocopiers

Multiple copies of documents, for various purposes, are often needed in a library. For making multiple copies of the documents, every library needs photocopiers. Presently several companies are manufacturing photocopiers with several variation like coloured copies, size-enlargement or reduction and several copies at a time. Depending on the requirements of an individual library and a liability of funds, suitable copier as per requirements can be purchased.

(iv) Computers

The library work involves lot of correspondence, maintaining records and other activities requiring typing work. Typewriters are gradually replaced by computers in most of the libraries. Computers are presently most important piece of equipment in any library as they can be used not only as a replacement of a typewriter but also for preparing automated catalogue record, serials management, maintaining records or correspondence, circulation and easy access of information. Presently, several companies in India are offering computer systems with varied configuration. Care with regard to choice of hardware, vendor and the software should be taken while selecting a computer system. Besides, these days many libraries, which have automated their activities, are bar-coding their documents. For this, bar-coding equipments are also required.

(v) Miscellaneous items

Besides the equipment mentioned above, some more items are required for any library which includes:

(a) Storage cabinets of metal or wooden, for keeping office supplies

(b) Stool or step ladder for reaching high shelves and roofs

(c) Revolving stands

(d) Vacuum cleaners

(e) Air-conditioning

(f) Binding equipment

(g) Electric stylus for writing on spines of book

(h) Microform reading equipment

(i) Non conventional indexing and filing equipments.

Important ones are described below :

Microform Reading Equipment

Micro forms usually found in a library include slides, microfilms, microfiche, microcards and aperture cards. To read their contents special devices are necessary microform reader, reader-printer and projector. Now-a-days many satisfactory microform reading machines are available in the market, and new improved ones are being developed steadily. While some of the simpler ones admit only one type of form-either microfilm or microfiche-most of the machines these days can handle more than one format with only a change of the adapter. There are some which have the facility to make copy of a particular page, by mere press of a button. Catalogues and guides are available which give information about new micro-reproduction equipment being developed and marketed.

Non-Conventional Indexing and Filing Equipment

Use of mechanical devices for sorting information recorded on special kinds of cards like edge notched cards, optical coincidence cards and aperture cards has become absolute with increased use of new computers. The coded cards can be sorted manually or mechanically. Manual systems employ specially designed cards, and some use very simple manupulative devices such as needles. There is a system based on optical coincidence in which the holes are punched in the body of the card, and not on the edges. Some non-conventional systems like Rapid Selector or Filmorex and apertue cards combine the filing and indexing operations usually utilising film copies of documents.

OTHER FACILITIES

Besides the various categories of furniture and equipment mentioned in the previous sections, every library requires some additional facilities, these are:

Stack guides

The users are guided in the stacks by proper guides to find their way through the shelves. For this it is essential that the documents are in their proper places. The following guides are required in the libraries:

i. Tier guide for each tier of stacks
ii. Bay guide for every bay of shelves
iii. Gangway guide in each gangway
iv. Shelf guide with each shelf giving the class numbers contained in the shelf starting number to the last number in the shelf
v. General guide to give an overall view of the library and arrangement of documents

Sign Boards

Besides the above, general instructions should also be displayed in the library for guiding the users to the catalogue, various divisions and floors of the library, location of drinking water, toilets, etc. There should be proper display signs to indicate silence and non-smoking zones.

OTHER ASPECTS

There are a host of other factors going to make satisfactory physical planning of a library. They include interior decoration, colour concept, acoustics and furnishing, upholstering, carpeting, airconditioning, insulating, ventilation, etc. It is necessary for a librarian to be aware of possibilities of getting right effects of all these aspects in making a library attractive, inviting and comfortably. The main considerations are :

(i) Lighting

Lighting inside rooms are from two sources—natural and artificial. Natural light, while being the most comfortable for the human eye has its disadvantages. Its intensity is not always uniform depending to a large extent on weather conditions and the orientation of the windows. It also has the effect of producing very high intensity near the windows and a sharp drop a few feet away. Direct sunlight, moreover, is hot and has the effect of fading books allowed to come in direct contact with it.

It is no longer necessary to depend completely on natural light, and its intelligent combination with artificial illumination creates a very pleasing and psychologically satisfying environment. Shadows, contrasts and glare become disturbing and fatiguing should be avoided by careful study, selection and arrangement of fixtures. Walls and ceiling should be lighted but at a lower intensity than the reading surfaces. Dark walls and ceilings which result from recessed lighting fixtures or dark colour should be avoided. If the contrast or brightness ratio is too severe it causes strenuous and tiring readjustment of the eyes.

(ii) Physical Conditions

The most important aspect to be considered is the comfort to library users. Because of the extremely variable nature of the climate in tropical regions the creation of a cool comfortable space is essential. Air-conditioning is the best solution because along with cooling in summer and heating in winter it also controls humidity. However, provision of air-conditioning is very expensive and is usually done in very few libraries in this country.

Another important factor is humidity in tropical countries. Control of humidity is very essential not only for comfort of users but its adverse effect on books, manuscripts etc. It would be worth considering higher ceilings than those guided by stack measurements and provision of cross-ventilation in rooms. Care must, however, be exercised to prevent dust along with breeze inside the rooms. This problem can be countered by provision of mechanical exhausts. Landscaping around the building is also important.

(iii) Acoustics

Noise control is of utmost importance and can be achieved in several ways at once.

(a) In planning the location and orientation of the building mechanical noise producing features should be concentrated and isolated.

(b) Once the noisy areas are located, the problem of transmited noise can be overcome by use of partitions .of hard-dense materials of relatively high mass.

(c) Local subduing of noise i.e. local subduing of noise in particular areas can be best achieved by use of resident flooring, acoustic tile on ceiling and wall areas and draperies on windows.

It is also interesting to consider the effect of lowering sound levels too much. Casual noises which are generally camouflaged by the general noise level become annoyingly insistent. In stack areas, acoustic treatment is generally limited to the main aisles only.

STANDARDS AND SPECIFICATIONS

In the field of library work, most of the standards or specifications that have evolved over the years are more in the nature of "accepted practice". The national standardising agencies in many countries have thought it appropriate to formulate systematically these accepted practices and bring them out as national standards. In India, the Indian Standards Institution renamed as Bureau of Indian Standards has brought out standards. These standards provide the necessary guidance to the librarian in choosing the right design with functional efficiency. The National Institute of Designs, Ahmedabad, has also done considerable work in designing functional library furniture.

9
Collection Management

The collection in a library consists of the documents and non-documentary sources, collectively, both are known as Information resources, from which information or knowledge is provided to its readers. Documentary and non-documentary resources are discussed below :

DOCUMENTARY SOURCES

A document is a record of work on paper or other material for easy physical handling, transportation across space, and preservation through time. It may be said that the thought content of a document represents the information it contains. A document may be a macro-document like a book, monograph, thesis, dissertation, report, etc., or a micro-document like an article in a periodical. Documents have also been grouped as Conventional, Non-Conventional, Neo-Conventional, Meta documents, etc. As a matter of fact, these documents are available in various physical forms such as books, periodicals and also as audio-visuals.

NON-DOCUMENTARY SOURCES

Non-documentary sources include :

* Institutional sources
* Human Sources
    * Colleagues
    * Peers
    * Information Gatekeepers
    * Guides, Advisors, Consultants
    * Vendors, Contractors, Collaborators, etc.

CLASSIFICATION OF DOCUMENTS

On the basis of their physical characteristics, familiarity and usage the documents have been divided by Dr. S.R. Ranganathan into four classes.

* Conventional
* Neo-conventional
* Non-conventional
* Meta -documents

Conventional documents are those which are usually recorded on paper in a natural language by writing, typing, printing or some near-printing process. These are the most popular documents, in use. These include books, periodicals, maps, atlases, etc. *Neo-conventional documents* are a new class of micro-documents, such as standards, specifications, patents, data, etc. *Non-conventional documents* are a record in non-conventional size, shape or material. Audios, visuals, audio-visuals, microforms, etc. are included in this category. *Meta-documents* are a record of phenomena made directly, unmediated, by the human mind. They are an instrument-record of natural and social phenomena made possible by instrument technology, photography, radar, etc.

Ranganathan's classification groups documents in the chronological order of their development and does not take into consideration the information characteristics of a document. He does not make any difference between an ordinary periodical and an indexing periodical. Also a book and a periodical belong to the same category according to him.

BY INFORMATION CHARACTERISTICS

Whereas, C.W. Hanson and Denis Grogan have categorised these documents on the basis of information characteristics into three types:

(1) Primary Documents

These documents represent new knowledge or new interpretation of old knowledge. They are the first published records of original research and development. Often a primary document may be the only source of information in existence. According to Hanson, books, journals, reports, patents, theses, trade literature, and standards are the primary documents. Grogan adds to the list conference proceedings and official publications, but excludes books.

(2) Secondary Documents

Secondary documents do not carry new and original information but guide users to primary documents. They are compiled from primary documents. They organise the primary literature in a convenient form. These documents are of three types:

(a) Those which index selected portions of primary literature and help users in finding what has been published on a given subject, such as indexes, bibliographies, abstracts, etc.

(b) Those which survey selected portions of the primary literature to help users find the state-of-the-art knowledge on a given subject, such as reviews, treatises etc.

(c) Those documents which themselves contain the desired information collected and selected from primary documents. This information, such as biographies, facts, formulae, histories, procedures, theories, etc., is derived from primary documents and is arranged systematically in some convenient order in such secondary documents. Dictionaries, encyclopaedias, handbooks, manuals, etc., are some documents of this type.

(3) Tertiary Documents

Tertiary documents list secondary documents. Their function is to help researchers in retrieving secondary sources. Directories, Yearbooks, Bibliographies of Bibliographies, Lists of Research-in-Pro gross projects. Guides to Literature, Guides to Organizations, Guides to Libraries, and Textbooks are included in this category of documents.

Important documents' categories are discussed briefly :

(i) Books

Books form one of the primary sources of information. They provide a cohesively organised information on a specific subject of optimum depth. Since book writing, editing, processing and publishing call for a considerable amount of time, books can be said to contain ideas which are fairly well established. They form useful repositories of information both for teachers and learners in a particular field as they contain a crystallised presentation of ideas helpful to the majority of readers.

A book is a physically independent document as distinguished from a periodical publication, that is, it has been completed in a definite number of volumes. A book normally deals with a subject of great extension and less intention. It is thus a macro-document. Further, the books may be divided as under :

(a) **Single volumed book:** A book may be in a single volume or in more than one volume. The latter is known as a multi-volumed book. A multi-volumed book usually has a common index. It also has the same sequence of pagination continued in all the volumes if the set.

(b) **Simple book and Composite book:** A book, either by a single author or by two or more authors, that gives a continuous exposition of the subject, is known as a simple book. A book by more than one author, all contributions of which do not form a continuous exposition but have one title distinct and independent, is a composite book. If a composite book has a single generic title to denote all the contributions collectively, it is an ordinary composite book, otherwise it is an artificial composite book.

(c) **General book, Reference book and Textbook:** A book is either a general book, a text-book or a reference book. A general book deals with the subject in a general way. A book giving general exposition on the subject, or a biography, or a fiction is a general book. Examples of general books are: Ranganathan's *Five Laws of Library Science*, Girja Kumar's *Philosophy of User Education,* and Dhyaneshwar's *Gita: the Mother.*

A textbook is one that supports a teaching programme. It deals with the fundamentals of the subject using the language and style that suits the students. An author's newly propounded theory is usually not found in it. Different courses of study have different textbooks to support them. Guha's *Documentation and Information,* Prasher's *Introduction to Reprography.* Vishwanathan's *Cataloguing - Theory and Practice,* Krishan Kumar's *Theory of Classification* and Anil Dhiman's *Basics of Information Technology for Librarians and Information Scientists* are textbooks on documentation, reprography, cataloguing, classification and information technology respectively, meant for library science students.

Whereas a general book or a textbook belongs to the category of books that can be read through for information, education or inspiration, there is another class of books meant to be consulted or referred to for a definite piece of information. These are known as Reference books, and they provide information readily. Dictionaries, encyclopaedias, yearbooks, almanacs, directories, gazetteers, atlases, biographical dictionaries, etc. are all Reference books. *The Oxford English Dictionary, Harrod's Librarian's Glossary to Terms, Encyclopaedia Britannica, McGraw-Hill Encyclopaedia of Science and Technology, India - a Reference Annual, Imperial Gazetteer of India and Sen's Dictionary of National Biography* are some of the examples of Reference books.

(ii) Periodicals and Serials

Periodical publications form an important part of today's information world. It is one of the chosen forms of research communication. There are over 100,000 periodical publications which publish informative research articles. Most of these periodicals or journals publish papers sent by different authors after due referring and editing. An analysis of the titles listed in the Directory of Indian Scientific Periodicals shows that India is publishing 1323 primary periodicals containing research articles, review articles, news and notes, short communications, etc. It has also been estimated that there is an average increase rate of 50 new titles every year. However, considering the death rate of periodicals, it has been estimated that there are about only 2000 live periodicals in science and technology. An equal number is estimated to be published in the fields of social sciences and humanities. Of these, 500 are in regional languages, or are magazines for general circulation and targeted at readers who are not required to possess professional knowledge of the information presented. While magazine articles place great emphasis on what is happening and how it affects people, periodicals, on the other hand, place stress on how and why things happen and their influence on a particular profession or scientific community.

A periodical publication is that which appears in parts or volumes at regular intervals with the intention to continue its publication for ever. Besides, the element of periodicity and continuity, a periodical publication has a distinguishing number for each successive volume, known as its volume number. *Annals of Library Science and Documentation, ILA Bulletin, IASLIC Bulletin*, and *Journal of Library and information Science* are some important periodicals in library science. The periodicity of the first three is quarterly, and that of the last one is half-yearly. *Annals of Library Science* brought out its 49th volume in 2001, ILA Bulletin its 39th volume during 2003, and the *Journal of library and information science* was in its 27th volume during 2002.

A serial is also a periodical publication but each volume embodies more or less similar information but updated, mainly relating to its year or period of coverage, *India - A Reference Annual* is an example of a serial.

(iii) Government Documents

Government publications are the official documents brought out at government expenses. They are the records of activities of the (i) Executive, (ii) Legislature, (iii) Judiciary, and (iv) Research organisations sponsored by the government and similar others. The authority under which these documents are brought out, may vary, such as a ministry, a department, a government undertaking, an institute or any authorised agency of either central or state government; and this authority holds responsibility for the authenticity of the contents of the documents.

Government documents are a class by themselves, different from general publications. In size they range from pamphlets to voluminous books and in content they vary from an article with a popular appeal to technical treatises of value to scientists and academicians. These documents are generally divided into two categories:

(i) Parliamentary documents, and

(ii) Non-parliamentary documents

Parliamentary documents include proceedings, reports, etc., of legislative bodies, Acts of the Centre and the States, bills and statutory instruments, etc. Non-parliamentary documents include administrative reports, reports of transactions, rules and regulations, codes, gazetters, budget estimates, reports of committees or commissions, statistical data, notes and reviews, research papers, bulletins, monographs, maps, etc.

Government documents are an important part of any library collection. They are the primary and authentic record of the legislative, judicial and executive wings of the government, both for current use and for long term retention. Besides statistical data, a wealth of information is found in them on varied subjects.

(iv) Dissertations and Theses

Another important type of documents are post-graduate dissertations and doctoral theses submitted to the universities for degrees. They are valuable primary sources which report original work in specific fields. Besides yielding invaluable unpublished information on a specific subject, place or person, these documents have extensive bibliographies and footnotes which are usually of immense use to researchers. These documents often remain unpublished. Since they do not appear in any trade or national bibliography, their existence remains unknown. This creates difficulties in their selection and procurement.

Theses are primarily useful for their original contribution. Subjects dealt with in theses may not have commercial application. *Dissertation Abstracts International published by* Universal Microfilms Inc. usually covers doctoral theses in several subjects.

(v) Reports

Report literature is an important primary source of information, particularly for a research library. This new medium for communication of information came into being during World War II due to scarcity of paper, restrictions in distribution, and delay in bringing out periodicals. Reports not only solved the problems then, but proved quite useful to be continued after the war,

Reports originate in various research organisations and government departments and appear in a wide variety. Most of them are about research and development projects, in progress or completed. They may present quick preliminary information about the work in progress; or they may give complete information about the work just completed. In some subjects, such as nuclear science and aeronautics, a good amount of literature is available in the form of reports.

Technical reports may be issued ad hoc or in series periodically. Examples of reports are NASA reports, EURATOM reports, EEC reports, etc. Even in India, several institutions publish reports. National Aerospace Laboratories, Bangalore, publishes several reports every year. A special characteristic of a report is that it contains details of the project and includes a large amount of data. Information in reports is generally meant for internal audience. It may be said to be a nascent, unedited, non-formalised presentation of findings with a considerable amount of usage of jargon, acronyms and abbreviations, etc.

(vi) Pamphlets

A pamphlet is an independent publication, which is normally a document of a few printed pages, usually less than 49. Pamphlets cover an extremely wide range of subjects, but their uniqueness is that an individual specialised topic is dealt with in precisely and concisely. It is an ideal resource for anyone studying in depth a specialised topic. Further, much of the information appears in pamphlets before it is incorporated in books. Pamphlets are a current source of information and are indispensable to libraries because they may contain information not available from any other source. They are relatively less expensive than a periodical or book. Since they contain information on a narrow subject-field and are presented in a unique manner, they are very useful to specialised users. Their usefulness, increases if they are objective and balanced in presentation.

(vii) Standards and Specifications

Documents which are formulated by agreement, authority or custom of sponsors to define a product, material, process or procedure, quality, construction, operating characteristics, performance, nomenclature, and other like facts are called *Standards. Specifications,* on the other hand, are the documents that contain descriptions of the technical requirements of a product, material, process or service which are designed to meet the purchaser's particular needs.

The purpose of Standards and Specifications is to simplify production and distribution, to promote standardisation and quality control, to ensure uniformity and reliability, and to eliminate wasteful variety. Since Standards and Specifications play a vital role in manufacturing and commercial endeavours, these documents are indispensable for an industrial society. A library serving such a society must have these documents in its collection. In addition to international organisations who develop standards, every nation has its own standardisation body. In India, Bureau of Indian Standards (BIS), New Delhi is such an organization.

(viii) Patents

In science and technology, patents form an important source of information. It is a kind of legal protection for the inventor. A patent is an agreement between a government and an inventor whereby the latter discloses his invention to the public in exchange for an exclusive right of exploitation for a fixed period. Each patent presents a detailed account of a new manufacturing process, or an improvement of an existing process, a new product, a new method of testing and control, etc., which may not be available in this form in other sources. In addition to a detailed description, patent specifications include a statement of claim by an applicant regarding the scope of the monopoly he seeks to cover in his invention. The claim is relatively broad in nature, its purpose being to specify the range of products or processes that the patentee claims to monopolise. It, therefore, covers variations of the invention referred to in the patent. Thus, while a patent is a legal document, it can also be used as a source of industrial information.

Every nation has a Patent Office. India's Patent Office at Calcutta and its sub-offices grant Over 3,000 patents each year. The output of each developed nation is much more.

A comprehensive collection of national and foreign patents must be developed by all special and research libraries because of (i) they give technological information which is not found in any other source, (ii) in addition to the information on the general utility of the invention, they inform us about the practical application of the invention in industry as also some background material, and (iii) they reveal information on specific technological items more completely and earlier than other sources do.

(ix) Trade Literature

Trade literature consists of documents that give information on the processes and materials involved in the manufacture of a product, various types of product catalogues, compilation of trade data, manuals, guides, house journals, etc. Trade literature is issued by manufacture and dealers. The basic purpose is product advertisement. These documents normally provide accurate technical information about products and materials that are offered for sale. This information is usually not available from any other source. In a special library, trade literature is an important source of information.

The information contents of trade catalogues include details about uses, size and specification of products, the range of the products of a firm, properties of materials, design data, test results, operating instructions, etc. However, trade catalogues become obsolete quickly and are superseded by newer catalogues.

(x) Maps, Atlases and Globes

Maps illustrate the distribution of many things that occur on the surface of the earth. Information is presented by the use of a vast array of symbols, codes, and colours that attempt to communicate such features as shape, size, outline, pattern, arrangements, land reliever elevation, and the distribution of statistical values of an actual or relative quantity. Thus, the map user has the graphic means which make it easy and efficient to recognise, compare and examine patterns, relationships, surface features, locational data, scientific data, places, ocean currents, geological formations, climate, weather, demographic distributions, political boundaries, economic data, agricultural capabilities, industrial production, military development, etc. The communication should be made easier by adoption of familiar symbols and structures. The legend assignment, colour charting, relief protection planning should be symbolic to one another. There are a variety of ways in which maps are presented and stored. The following are some:

(a) **Atlas :** The atlas is a volume consisting of a collection of maps. These are available in various dimensions and they are intended for individual use.

(b) **Wall Maps :** Wall maps are considered to be entities, meaning they are unbound. They are usually 40-65 inches wide. Wall maps are intended for display and group use. They can be folded, mounted on spring rollers, or attached to dowels for hand rolling.

(c) **Bound Wall Maps:** Bound wall maps are designed to be attached to a tripod or slant permitting them to be flipped over.

(d) **Overhead Transparencies:** Maps on overhead transparencies are designed to be used exclusively on an overhead projector. Information can be added by the use of overlays or can be written on to transparencies with water-soluble ink.

(e) **Relief Maps:** Relief maps provide a three-dimensional perspective of the earth's surface. The relief, to be effective, must be grossly exaggerated in some of its proportions. For example, if a relief map of the world 72 inches square were to depict Mount Everest concretely (5 + miles high) in relief, it would be less than 1/60 of an inch high.

A map is a representation of a part or the whole of the surface of the earth or of a celestial body, delineated on a plane surface, each point in the drawing intended to correspond to a geographical or celestial position. It may be of a country, state, city, village or of a still smaller area irrespective of the scale or extent of area. Maps are of various types, such as physical maps political maps, thematic maps (historical, statistical, ethnological, etc). Indian maps are issued by the Survey of India, Dehra Dun.

An atlas is a volume consisting of a collection of maps, which may also contain photographs and other supplementary material. *The Britannica Atlas, Hammond Medalline World Atlas and Times Atlas of the World* are the important examples of atlases.

A globe is a spherical representation of the earth.

Maps, atlases, and globes form an important source of geographical information. These, therefore, form a useful part of any library collection.

(xi) Photographs and Illustrations

Photographs and illustrations are the documents which provide visual or pictorial representation of a person, place or situation which words fail to describe or find hard to depict. Words cannot tell what Mahatma Gandhi looked like, only his photograph can do that. Words cannot describe the Kumbha mela in progress at Hardwar or the Burning Ghats of Banaras or the Gateway of India of Mumbai as accurately as their respective photographs can. Similarly, a complicated subject may be easily explained by a simple illustration. Graphical representation is always helpful in making readers grasp textual matter easily. A radio, or television set cannot be assembled without the help of its drawings. Nor can a building be constructed unless the architect's plan is made available to the engineer. These documents therefore, also form an important part of a library collection.

(xii) Microforms

Microforms are those documents, which embody thought in a reduced form that cannot be read with the naked eye. They require some device for reading. They comprise of microfilms, microfiche, and micro-opaques and now common in libraries. The reasons for their popularity are: (a) Micro-forms reduce the bulk of documents and help the libraries save considerable space. (b) Out-of-print documents which are either not easily available or too expensive in the original form can be easily acquired in micro-form (c) documents in original are too bulky to be transported rapidly. Micro forms, greatly reduced in bulk are more suitable for easy and quick transportation, as also for airlifting (d) A readable photocopy can be prepared from a microform easily.

Microforms are available in different varieties and dimensions. Their organisation and maintenance also requires special care.

(xiii) Audio-Visuals

These documents consist of slides, gramophone records, phonotypes, cassettes, motion pictures, video records, and CDs etc. Through the use of these documents, one can hear the original voice or can see the incident as it happened. A gramophone record or a, phototape when played can bring to us the chirping of birds, the hissing of a cobra, roar of a lion or Rabindranath Tagore singing his own songs. Similarly, a motion, picture or a video record can bring back to us. Mahatma Gandhi and his followers taking part in the Salt Satyagraha. One can also witness a cricket match sitting right in your drawing room. No other form of document can provide this facility. These documents are being extensively used as teaching aids these days.

(xiv) Reference Books

A Reference book generally has the following qualities:

(a) It is a miscellany of information organised for quick, convenient use.

(b) Arrangement usually, but not always, follows some consistent, plan such as alphabetical order for encyclopaedias, tabular from for statistics, and chronological order in a history outline.

(c) It usually gives only a bird's eyeview of the topic, rarely considers it in any depth.

(d) It concentrates on facts. It is constructed for the reader who has definite questions, and does not raise questions of its own. For example, treatise on philosophy or science may be written with the object of raising questions without possible answers. A reference working the same fields serves to answer questions the reader brings to these works.

(e) The pragmatic test should not be whether the book can be taken from the library, but rather how consistently useful it is in answering reference questions. If it serves this purpose for either patron or librarian with any degree of regularity, it should be part of the reference collection— even if this means duplicating, the title in the main collection. For example, a book of etiquette may be frequently used to answer specific queries, and may also be a popular general reading material. In this case there should be two or more copies—one for the reference collection and one or more to be checked out on a regular loan basis.

Reference books are of several varieties; some are directory type, which give short answers to the immediate information requirement. The others can be bibliographies, directories of institutions, yearbooks, almanacs, time-table of events, dictionaries, glossaries, etc. They can be narrative texts such as Encyclopaedias, Annual Reviews, Synoptic Writing, etc. William Katz groups them in the following manner.

Direction Type	*Source Type*
(1) Bibliography	(1) Encyclopaedias
(2) Guides to Literature	(2) Directories
(3) Indexes	(3) Geographical Dictionaries
	(4) Yearbooks
	(5) Bibliographical Dictionaries
	(6) Dictionaries

Some of the sources are discussed here in brief :

Encyclopaedias : Encyclopaedias are the works containing informative articles on subjects in every field of knowledge, usually arranged in the alphabetical order and are used to answer specific questions. They attempt to present information in a concise and easily accessible form. They should be able to provide to an unfamiliar person enough details to make him familiar with the boundaries of a particular topic. The best known encyclopaedia is the *Encyclopaedia Britannica*. It was first published in the year 1768 and is now in its 15th edition, which was published in 1974 and reproduced in 1993. This edition is presented in three stages.

(1) Propaedia; (2) Micropaedia (3) Macropaedia

Propaedia gives a brief overview of wide subject areas and contains the outlines of knowledge a classification of contents of the encyclopaedia. Such a classification refers to article in Micropacdia on the basis of the name of the subject sought at any moment. *Micropaedia* is arranged in alphabetical order and gives brief information on specific subjects. It acts as an index to macropaedia. *Macropaedia* is also arranged alphabetically by the name of broader subject.

The text of the encyclopaedia is kept upto date by year books.

There are about 100 such general encyclopaedias in the English language. However, the most well known of them which one must find in a reference section of a large library are only few.

Dictionaries : Dictionaries primarily deal with all aspects of words from proper definitions to spellings. Webster's Third New International Dictionary is an example, another is the Oxford English Language Dictionary. There are a variety of dictionaries, monolingual dictionaries, multilingual dictionaries, specialised dictionaries, college dictionaries, and school dictionaries. The specialised ones are called glossaries. Harrod's Glossary of Library Science is an example. National standards organisations such as the British Standards Institution and the Indian Standards (now, Bureau of Indian Standards) Institution have published several glossaries on specialised fields.

Handbooks : A handbook is the source of knowledge. It normally emphasises recent advances in the particular field. It brings together comprehensively and collectively the latest information in a field of knowledge. It covers a field of limited scope or a mission. The presentation is brief, full of tables, graphs, symbols, equations, formula and jargon which normally experts and practitioners in the field understand. The *Handbook of Thin Films* and the *Handbook of Marketing* are examples.

Biographies : Biographical sources cover in varying details the personal and private life of a biographic. If information is needed on any person, a specialist or generalist one has go into a biographical sources such as *Who's Who, Current Biography, Dictionary of National Biographies, Webster's Biographical Dictionary,* and *National Encyclopaedia of American Biography*. A biography should cover in detail one's contribution to the field of knowledge, literature, social work, religious work, political work on any other aspect of relevance.

Bibliographies : Bibliographies are lists of books arranged by title, author, and subject or some other arrangement suitable for locating specific titles. These may be used for verification and identification, for finding materials in a given subject area of interest or as a help in selecting the best works in a particular area. *Indian National*

Bibliography, British National Bibliography, and *Books-in-print* are some of the examples.

Secondary Periodicals : Secondary periodicals are abstracting and indexing periodicals. They are the systematic listing of materials which help to identify and trace those materials. Indexes to contents of journals are the most frequently used secondary periodicals. In the field of library literature, *Library and Information Science Abstracts* and *Information Abstracts* are useful secondary periodicals.

Abstracting and indexing services provide a means for reading, assimilating much of technical communication published in the world today. The application of information technology is high in the abstracting and indexing services. It provides a mechanism through which a systematisation of knowledge is done on a continuous basis and at the same time provides for a multi-pronged approach to information.

(xv) Non-Documentary Sources

The non-documentary sources are institutional and human resources, both of which are important links in the information-transfer chain.

(xv) Institutional Resources

Institutional resources are produced by the institutes itself. Here, information usually lie in the form of statistical data, descriptive/ interpretive data or information, or directory type. To collect the information required, it is essential to know the information generating agency, i.e., the source of information. This would facilitate the location of the relevant sources and even if a published record is not available, raw data may be obtained from the concerned agency.

For example, the main sources of industrial / government information are the central and state governments and their various departments, learned and research institutions, international organisations, or associations, chambers of commerce, etc. In the context of planning for the establishment and development of small-scale industries, the following institutional sources of information would be very useful, especially in the preparation of feasibility reports:

* Ministries of the Government
* National Standards Bodies

* Small Industries Development Organisation and Societies
* Marketing Centres
* National Small Industries Corporations
* Factories Inspectorates
* Small Industries Services Institutes
* Employment Bureau and Exchanges
* State Directorate of Industries
* Sub-Contracting exchange
* State Bureau of Statistics
* Research Bureaus
* National Productivity Council
* Academic Institutions and Universities
* Chambers of Commerce
* Research Institutes
* Trade and Professional Associations
* International Organisations
* Commodity Boards
* Libraries & Technical Information Centres
* Banks and Financial Institutions
* Central Statistical Organisation
* Industrial Extension Centres
* National Sample Survey Organisation
* Census Office
* Directorate of Technical Development

Human Resources

These include -

- Colleagues in the organisation/institute
- Peers outside organization/institute
- Technological Gatekeepers
- Guide, Advisors and Consultants and
- Vendors, Contractors and Collaborators etc.

DOCUMENT SELECTION

The book selection or document selection is a very responsible job. It is conditioned by three factors; demand, supply and finance. Planning, therefore, must be mainly concerned with these factors. Demand and supply must be known, and finance secured. Further, men and materials required for the work need to be arranged. These aspects of planning can be discussed under four heads;

1. Ascertaining demand;
2. Finding resources;
3. Allocating funds; and
4. Arranging personnel

1. Ascertaining Demand

Since demand is a basic factor in selection so there is a need to develop a system for ascertaining the demand. Demand includes both expressed wants and unexpressed wants and unexpressed needs of readers. Similarly, needs of both the actual and the potential readers should be taken into account. The following sources can be made use of in ascertaining demand :

- Statistics relating to books circulated from, and consulted in, the library;
- Suggestions from library staff working in the service departments;
- Suggestions from readers;
- Indents from subject experts or departments;
- Findings of user need surveys conducted, if any;
- Syllabi and prospectuses of courses of studies; and
- Profiles of researchers.

The demands have to be assessed in terms of their volume, value and variety. The final rating of the demand showed conform with the selection policy of the library. Each library ought to have its own broad selection policy. Some libraries even have a written statement of this policy. In either case, the policy is the basic guideline in selection of documents.

2. Finding resources

As said earlier, supply is another basic factor. Supply means availability of documents or acquisition. Information regarding supply can be collected in the form of various selection sources or tools. Library will be regularly receiving various source materials. If not, they have to be acquired. A good source collection may contain the following :

* Trade catalogues issued by individual publishers and booksellers.
* Book trade journals.
* Previews and announcements issued by publishers.
* Book reviews appearing in newspapers and journals.
* Book reviewing journals.
* Book selection lists brought out by competent bodies.
* Lists of textbooks prescribed for various courses of studies.
* Published catalogues of book exhibitions.
* Published catalogues of important libraries.
* Subject bibliographies and subject guides to selection.
* National bibliographies.
* Comprehensive retrospective bibliographies like Books-in-print.
* Catalogues of second-hand booksellers.

The sources have to be sorted and stored for convenient use. Updating of the sources and weeding out of old ones should be done on a regular basis.

3. Allocating Funds

Finance is the most important factor in document selection. Proper planning of finance is basic to good acquisition work. Every library works according to its budget. The total budget of the library will include a separate provision for books. This amount will have to be apportioned among three heads, namely, books, periodicals, and binding. The amount thus set apart for books is the budget placed at the disposal of the Acquisition Department. This amount has to be used for purchase of books and other types of documents except current periodicals. For the balanced development of the collection the book budget should be allocated among different subjects and categories. This budget allocation is done by the library authority or its delegated body like the Book Selection Committee. The librarian and the acquisition staff are also involved in this process since they are the people to provide the information required for budget allocation to the authorities. Such information may relate to the actual and the potential needs of the clientele, the current and future programmes of the parent institution, the strength and weakness of the existing collection, the price range of publications in particular subjects, etc. These and other information can also be used by the library to obtain enhanced budget provisions. However, once the allocation is finalised, acquisition work has to conform to the financial discipline dictated by it.

4. Arranging Personnel

Planning for document selection should also cover the personnel or human factor. The people involved in selection process are the librarian, the acquisition staff, the subject experts and the library authority or selection committee. The ultimate responsibility for book selection rests with the librarian. The acquisition staff are there to help him, but neither the librarian nor his staff are experts in all the different subjects. Therefore, it becomes necessary to take help from subject specialists. The selection committee may or may not be composed of subject experts. Nevertheless, committee level decisions have the advantage of being more democratic and participatory. It is must to remember that document selection is not a one man job. It should be the outcome of good team work. Therefore, you must be very prudent in choosing the members of this team. This applies to both the acquisition staff and the subject experts. You need to maintain a panel of subject experts who will be willing to participate in the selection process by giving objective opinions and advice.

PROCEDURE OF DOCUMENT SELECTION

The actual process of document selection may be initiated in different ways. The acquisition staff take note of the desirable items and present them to the subject experts for approval. Alternatively the subject experts themselves or the subject departments may make indents for items they recommend. In both instances, the acquisition staff are responsible for the routine jobs connected with selection. It is their duty to collect, complete and correct information on the documents. So also it is their risk to allow all unnecessary and unintentional duplications. Therefore, adequate care should be taken to ensure that the items selected are not already available in the library. An acceptable selection procedure can be outlined as follows:

(i) Scanning : All the currently received sources should be scanned regularly. Old sources should be scanned only for specific needs.

Items found desirable may be ticked off in the sources. The knowledge about the existing collection and about the items already selected or ordered will help in avoiding duplication at this stage. If necessary, the marked items may be forwarded to the librarian and his concurrence obtained.

(ii) Scrutiny : The purpose of scrutiny is to rule out the possibilities of unnecessary duplication. This is done by checking the marked items with the following:

- Items selected earlier, by checking the 'Books Selected' card tray:
- Items ordered already, by checking the 'Books-on-order' card tray;
- Items already received, by checking the 'Books Received' card tray and the 'Books-in-Process' card tray:
- Items available in the library by checking the catalogue.

Only such items which are cleared after the above scrutiny are retained with tick marks. Others are scored out.

(iii) Recording : The purpose of recording is to make complete data available on each of the provisionally selected documents. The unit record can be a standard selection card of the size 5" × 3" with appropriate columns printed. The following are the essential data elements to be covered by a selection card:

- Broad subject name or class number
- Full name(s) of author (s)
- Full title with sub-title, if any
- Full name (s) of collaborator (s), if any
- Edition number, if any
- Imprint (place, publisher & year)
- Series name, if any
- Collation, like number of pages, type of binding, etc. size
- ISBN, if any
- Price

Other desirable elements, to be included, are:

- Reference to source/indent/suggestion
- Name of the subject export granting approval

- Order No. and date
- Name of the vendor with whom ordered
- No. of copies ordered
- Date of supply
- Bill No. and date
- Date of payment
- Amount paid and
- Accession number

All the essential information may not be found initially. One will have to use appropriate bibliographical tools and complete the columns in the selection card as far as possible. The desirable information listed above is provided for in the cards since they would explain the workflow regarding each item. The selection cards so prepared are then sorted out and arranged according to subjects or class numbers as the case may be and filed in a card tray labelled as "Books Selected".

(iv) Consulting : Consulting work can be done at prescribed intervals or as and when needed for placing an urgent order. For this purpose, subject lists are typed out from the cards in the "Books Selected" tray. Each list should be forwarded to the concerned subject expert with the request that he should return the list after considering every item and marking his specific recommendation as to whether "approved", "rejected" or "deferred". Once the list is received back from the expert the recommendations must be carry forwarded to the respective cards. Cards relating to the "rejected" items must first of all be removed and disposed off. Guards of the "approved" items must be duly noted and removed to another tray labelled as "Books Approved". Cards belonging to the "deferred" items may be separately kept in another tray labelled as "Books Deferred". These items can be presented again to the experts whenever it becomes necessary.

(v) Indents Passing : As and when indents are received from experts or departments they must be subjected to the process of scrutiny. Items found already available in the library or on order should be scored out unless additional copies are recommended. Clarification on this point can be sought from the indentor.

After scrutiny, the indent has to be posted. For this, the price of each item should be ascertained from proper sources and the total value involved estimated. The indentor should then be informed of the financial position through an Indent Noting Form. The following details should be included in the indent Noting Form:

- Number of items recommended
- Number of items already available or on order
- Number of items recommended for additional copies
- Estimated cost of items neither available nor on order
- Estimated cost of items to be duplicated
- Total estimated cost
- Total allotment for the subject/department
- Amount already appropriated
- Balance Amount available
- Remarks, if any

In the light of the above financial report, the indentor would be making suitable adjustments in the items intended or reconfirm the indent. In either case, the next job is recording the items and merging the cards in the "Books Approved" tray.

(vi) Sanction Obtaining : Book selection becomes final only when the formal sanction is obtained from the librarian or any other sanctioning authority. For this purpose, separate lists have to be typed out for subjects or categories of documents as per the classification in the Budget Allocation. Necessary financial report also should be prepared to accompany the lists including the total estimated cost, total allotment in each case, amount already appropriated, and balance budget available. Sanction is obtained for each list. If any alteration or deletion is made in the list the same should be entered in the respective cards also.

PROCUREMENT OF DOCUMENTS

Once the selection is finalised, the library has to proceed with the procurement of documents. This includes the work of procurement, its planning and procedure.

Planning

Procurement has to be planned with due regard to matters like different means of procurement, preparations and arrangement for ordering, like, the choice of the supplier and the terms and conditions of supply, the different types of orders to be placed, etc. These points are elaborated below:

Means of Procurement

The documents can be procured by any one of the following means:

- Purchase
- Gift
- Institutional membership
- Deposits
- Exchanges

Purchase : Purchases form the major means of acquiring documents in any library. Strictly speaking, purchasing must be resorted to only when no other means is open to the library. But, most of the required items will not be available through other means, and hence purchases against specific orders become the most usual practice in all libraries. Also because of this, ordering procedure becomes a matter of major concern in document procurement.

Gifts or Donations : Gifts or donations are always welcome in a library. There are many cases where personal collections bequeathed to libraries have become the main stay of collections. Such personal benefactions are to be explored and solicited by libraries. Gifts are possible also in the case of individual titles that are needed, particularly old and out-of-print books. Unsolicited gifts and gifts involving difficult terms and conditions need to be entertained with caution. Usefulness of the items should be the major deciding factor.

Unpriced publications that are distributed free make another important category in gifts. Timely knowledge and expedient action m acquiring them are important.

Institutional Membership : Institutional membership is another potential resource in collection building. The library may enlist itself as member of learned societies and institutions who publish useful materials. Often the membership subscription may cover the right to receive their publications either free of cost or at concessional prices.

Deposit System : Deposit system entitles some specially designated libraries to receive free copies of the publications brought out by governments, national and international organisations, etc. There are many university libraries and state central libraries enjoying these benefits. There are also the national and state level libraries designated to receive free copies of all publications originated in India, either under provisions of the Copyright Law or the Delivery of Books and Newspapers (Public Libraries) Act, 1956. In all these cases the recipient library should be continuously on its alert about the new titles and their timely receipt.

Exchanges : Exchanges may be another possible means of acquiring documents. In this case the recipient library or its parent body should have publications of its own to exchange with those of the other institutions. Exchanges are also possible between two libraries with spare copies against items needed.

Choice of the Supplier and Ordering Methods

The ultimate success of collection development programme will depend upon ensuring proper and timely supply of ordered items. Hence choice of the supplier is one of the most crucial matters. The different practices followed by libraries in the choice of the supplier and effecting supplies are:

(a) Inquiry/Tender method
(b) Quotation Method
(c) Standing Vendor method
(d) Books-on-Approval method
(e) Open purchases
(f) Direct ordering with publishers

A library may adopt one or more of these methods. A brief description on each of them is given here :

Inquiry/Tender Method : In Inquiry or Tender method, every book list of finally selected items is circulated among a number of booksellers who are invited to quote their lowest prices for each item. The order is placed for each item with the firm offering the lowest price.

Quotation Method : In this method, quotations are invited for various categories of documents along with trade discounts admissible in each case, and the conversion rates in the case of foreign currency prices. This is done usually prior to the beginning of the financial year. The supplier for each category is fixed finally on the basis of the most economic terms offered.

Standing Vendor Method : A Standing Vendor is one who is appointed as the authorised supplier to a library for a specified time, generally for a year or two, under prescribed terms and conditions of supply. The appointment is made on the basis of competitive quotations as in the Quotation method described earlier. But, in this case appointment will be based on expected total economy and efficiency rather than rates offered for separate categories.

Books-on-Approval Method : Supply based on Books-on-Approval operates in two ways. In first case, reputed publishers will be sending their new titles as and when published to the library directly. These items are accepted after due process of selection. The formal older will be placed with the local bookseller named by each publisher. If the book is not accepted it is returned to the same local bookseller. In the second ease, the local booksellers, at frequent intervals, bring some recent publications for approval and ordering.

The selected items are included in a formal order and accepted while the others are returned. This method of Books-on-Approval is a common practice.

Open Purchase : Open purchase is possible when the library has decided about the terms and conditions of supply like the trade discounts and conversion rates. In this case documents can be bought from any bookseller who is agreeable to these terms, through as in-shop selection, books-on-approval, or specific orders as the case may be.

Book fairs in major cities is a common occurrence now-a-days. Several publishers, both foreign and Indian including language books publishers take part in these fairs. It is a good opportunity to browse through and select good books.

Direct Ordering with Publishers : Direct ordering with publishers or their representatives is adopted by some libraries. This has definite advantages in the case of foreign publications, provided the publishers have their representatives or wholesalers in the country. Even in this case of direct ordering, publishers and wholesalers usually channelise the supply only through the local dealers. Where a foreign publisher has no trade representation in the country, direct ordering will pose difficulties of import licenses and foreign exchange regulations.

Terms and Conditions of Supply

The choice of the supplier is mainly governed by consideration of the maximum advantage to the library. Three major items are there in terms of supply, namely

- trade discounts

- conversion rates of currencies, and
- other conditions of supply

Trade Discounts : Trade discount is common feature in book purchases. The discounts may vary according to categories of publications. Normally a 10% discount is admissible on books. Indian language publications may have higher discount rates while law books, etc. are short discount items. Government publications carry no discount at all. The rates of discount admitted to libraries by booksellers is a part of the discount they themselves get from the publishers. Where competition is acute, booksellers may even underquote to the extent that actual supply will become practically impossible. To check this unhealthy competition standard norms would become necessary. One such measure employed in Britain is the Net Book Agreement.

Net Book Agreement is an instrument signed in 1929 revised in 1933 by the Library Association, the Publishers Association, and the Association of Booksellers of Great Britain and Ireland. This trade agreement prevents price cutting in books by prescribing a uniform commission for libraries. Almost a similar agreement is available in India.

Conversion Rates : Conversion rates can cause problems in buying foreign books. As exchange rates are always subject to fluctuations. Hence, current rates cannot be applied in fixing the price of books in all cases. Competitive rates will be offered by booksellers. Here again, standard norms are necessary to check the possibilities of underquoting. In India, such a standardisation could be achieved by the recommendations of a body known as tile Good Offices Committee. This is a voluntary organisation with representatives of publishers and booksellers organisations, professional library associations, major university and special libraries and documentation centres, University Grants Commission and representatives from the Ministry of Human Resource Development. The Committee meets at regular intervals to decide upon the conversion rates of foreign currencies to be applied in the case of tooks and periodicals, and the rate of discount admissible to libraries. It has among other things recommended a uniform discount of 10% on the published price of all books except the no-discount or short-discount items. The recommendations of the Good Offices Committee arc being increasingly accepted by all libraries in India.

Other Terms and Conditions : Regarding other terms and

conditions of supply, the library must ensure that the vendor is made legally and morally bound to supply only the ordered document, in its perfect condition, and at the correct price. A model set of terms and conditions of an agreement between the library and the vendor can be found in the book, *Library Manual* by Ranganathan.

Types of Orders

Book ordering practices cannot be the same in all cases. There are :

- Specific orders
- Blanket orders
- Standing orders
- Pre-paid orders.

The large bulk of ordering is for specific items, but others, may need a different treatment. Sometimes blanket orders may have to be placed to ensure that no new item published in a specialised subject area is missed by the library. Similarly, standing orders will be needed for the supply of all items belonging to a chosen publisher's series, or for receiving an unbroken set of multivolume books, or a book published in installments, or books like annuals and yearbooks. There are also items needing pre-paid orders. Government publications, subscription books and books supplied on pro-publication orders fall in this category.

Ordering Procedure

Ordering procedure relates to three stages:

- pro-ordering work
- order placing work
- supply receiving work

Pre-ordering Work

Pre-order work includes various jobs connected with:

- invitation of tenders or quotations,
- tabulating the quotations,
- fixing the suppliers or appointing Stanching Vendors, and
- Signing the contracts.

Order Placing Work

Order placing work consists of the following job items:

- Tallying
- Scrutiny and elimination
- Sorting
- Cost estimating
- Listing
- Transmitting
- Filing

Tallying means verifying the selection lists with the corresponding cards. Each selection list is then subjected to a final scrutiny. This has two purposes: firstly, to avoid unnecessary duplication, and secondly, to sort out items for different means of procurement and different types of orders. The first purpose can be achieved by checking the selection lists or their cards with the following:

- the outstanding orders, if any
- the standing orders, if any
- the blanket orders, if any
- the bills on hand
- the supply received
- the catalogue.

The second purpose is fulfilled by finding out such items in the selection lists as could be procured through other means like gift, Institutional membership, exchange and deposits. Also items needing standing orders or blanket orders are identified at this stage. The lists are then finalised for order after necessary eliminations. The cost incurred by each list is then verified and the amount noted in the Budget Allocation Register. Order Lists are then prepared, generally in triplicate. A printed order form can be used for forwarding the original of the Order List to the supplier. The order is transmitted with the signature of the librarian. The second copy of the Order List can be sent to the indentor or the department concerned for information. Such intimations should be sent to the individuals also in the case of items suggested by them. The third copy of the Order List is filed in the section. The cards belonging to the ordered items arc then taken, order details noted in, and arranged in a tray labelled as "Books-on-Order". Rest of the cards are separately filed for appropriate action.

Supply Receiving Work

Supply receiving work includes jobs like

- taking delivery
- tallying, collating and checking
- cards picking and noting
- transmitting for accessioning

Books may be supplied either by personal delivery or by parcel service, in the latter case the vendor would have sent the way-bills. Arrangements should be made with clearing agents for taking delivery of the parcels. In either case, supplies are effected along with bills. The books supplied should be first of all, checked with the bills. The bills and the books are then matched with the Order Lists. If discrepancies are noted either in the items supplied, or the physical condition of the books, or the prices given in the bills, they are notified to the supplier and got corrected. Extreme care must be taken to ensure that the books are in perfect condition. Possibilities of damages in transit, defects in binding, missing sections, etc. should not be overlooked. Once the supply is found acceptable after the tallying, checking and collating, the cards relating to the items supplied and accepted are picked out from the "Books-on-Order" tray and the supply date and bill number are duly entered. The books along with the bills and the cards are finally transmitted to the Accessioning Section.

ACCESSIONING OF THE DOCUMENT

The Accessioning Section is planned to perform two sets of activities, namely, accessioning or taking into stock all acquired documents, and passing the bills for payment.

The books are purchased and reach the processing section. The acquired book in the library passes through a chain of technical processes before it is available for use to readers. For example, preparation, classification, accession and shelving is done in accordance with modern methods of library practice. Acquisition Assistant may be assigned the following functions.

* To develop procedures to meet the needs of the library.

* To handle personally difficult or important correspondence problems relating to the ordering of books, serials, documents, periodicals, maps, pamphlets, films and other materials.

* To make recommendations to the faculty concerning book selection.
* To consult with Heads of other departments and divisions concerning book order.
* To ,notify the faculty of the non-expenditure of book-funds.
* To watch carefully rare books and secondhand dealers' catalogues for opportunity to purchase items on desiderata lists.
* To have materials filmed or otherwise reproduced when they are out of print or otherwise unavailable in original.
* To interview publisher's representatives, book-dealers, collectors and others, who are interested in building up the university's (higher institutions) book collection.
* To read and appraise books and other materials and make recommendations for their acquisition.
* To supervise the handling of all gifts and exchanges coming to the library.

Following may be the additional functions of acquisition section:

* Maintenance and use of bibliographic aids peculiar to acquisition work. For example, Dealers' catalogue, Trade lists, etc.
* Maintenance of order files, "In process' files, desiderata lists, and other records essential to acquisition work.
* Making up, despatching and filing of orders for books, and other materials ordered through department.
* Receipt, handling and inspection of incoming shipments.
* Packing and shipment of returns and exchange materials.
* Any preparation of materials ordinarily done by the Department. For example, stamping, perforating and plating of books etc.
* Preparation of bills for payment, bookkeeping and other financial activities assigned to the department.
* Preparation of accession lists.
* Informing individuals recommending the purchase of book about the status of such recommendations.
* Ordering and checking of periodicals and continuations.
* Follow up on items not promptly received.

Make-up and printed parts of the book

The make-up of all books is generally similar. The cover of a book is the outside binding and the book is made of several sections, which are sewn together. Generally a printed book has the following parts.

Title page : The title page has the title, author (s), publisher's name and the place, and year of publication. At the back of title page is mentioned the year of copyright and printer's name.

Preface : In preface, the author mentions the reason for writing the book with a summary of the contents. In some cases it is combined with the introduction.

Contents : It lists the chapters in the order in which they appear in the book, giving the page numbers on which each begins.

List of illustrations, maps and plates : It contains the titles with the corresponding page number.

Introduction : In this part of the book, the author mentions his viewpoint and describes his method of developing the subject. Sometimes, it is combined with the preface.

The Book : It contains all the prescribed parts, both text and auxiliary matter.

Bibliography : It consists ail references which supplement the information given in the book.

Appendix : It lists the information, which is supplementary to the general context of the book.

Index : It gives all the terms of subjects discussed in the book in an alphabetical order and gives page or pages on which references to each specific item appear. It is generally located at the end of the book.

Accessioning Procedure

Accession Register is the basic record in the library about each document forming part of its collection. The general practice in libraries is to have a single register in which all types of documents whether purchased or received as gift or on exchange or as deposit are entered. But some libraries have the practice of using separate accession registers for gifts and for deposited items. Still another practice is to have the accession list in card form. In this case, the card used at the stage of book selection will be converted into the accession card and filed in the

Accession Register

Date	Acc. Number	Author	Title	Publisher & Place	Vol.	Edn.	Yr.	Pp.	Source/Bill No. & Date	Order No. & Date	Cost	Remarks

accession number sequence and kept under safe custody.

The following jobs are involved in accessioning:

- Arranging the bills and the books in parallel sequence.
- Entering details in the Accession Register.
- Writing the Accession number on each book.
- Certifying the bills.
- Transmitting the bills for passing work.
- Transmitting the books for processing.
- Noting and filling the cards.

Documents are entered in the Accession Register date-wise according to their receipt in the library. All purchased books are entered in the order of the bills. For this purpose, the bills have to be first arranged in the ascending order of their dates. Books covered by each bill then have to be arranged and kept in the order in which they are listed in the bill. Book after book and bill after bill are then entered in the Accession Register keeping, the Accession Numbers running continuously. The Accession Number getting assigned to each document entered in the Accession Register will be a unique number which can identify that document. The Accession Number is then written legibly on the versa of the title page of the book and if necessary, on a clue page. The same number is then noted in the bill against the item. After entering all the items covered by one bill a certificate must be furnished on the bill which should read as

> "certified that all the books as per the bill have been duly entered in the Accession Register vide numbers from ....to............."

The- bills relating lo the books occasioned are then handed over for Bill Passing Work while the books are sent to the Technical Department for processing. The cards belonging to them, after noting the date of accessioning and the Accession Numbers are filed in a tray labelled as "Books -In-Process".

Passing of Bills

The various jobs involved in the Bill Passing Work are:

- Checking
- Certifying
- Passing

- Transmitting

A serious risk involved in Bill Passing Work is either double payment or over-payment. Sufficient caution should be exercised to avoid both. Every bill should be carefully scrutinised by checking the calculations and totals, the conversion rates, and the trade discounts provided. When verified and found correct a certificate to that effect should be furnished on each bill. This should read as:

> "Certified that the net published prices at the approved rates of conversion have been charged, and agreed rates of discounts have been allowed".

Each certified bill together with the Accession Register should be placed with the librarian for the final passing. He should satisfy himself after checking the bill and the corresponding entries in the Accession Register. He then should put his initials on the Accession Register and pass the bill for payment. This is done by writing at the bottom of the bill the words "Passed for payment" and putting his signature and office seal below. The passed bills are then transmitted to the Account Section for payment.

Problems in Acquisition

Acquisition work is not an easy task. It has got its own problems. Some are common to libraries everywhere while some are peculiar to India. Major problems are :

- conflicting factors of demand, supply and finance;
- the situation created by far-off book markets;
- the difficulties in dealing with local book suppliers',
- the problems relating to foreign publications;
- the special problems concerning Indian publications;
- publications needing pre-paid orders: and
- the question of out-of-print and rare books.

Conflicting Factors : Demand, supply and Finance are the three major factors governing collection development. Both demand and supply will be increasing while finance will be always inadequate, if demand is to be fully satisfied, a library will have to buy more and more items. This is particularly so since more items are being published every day. New items published will naturally stimulate more reading and in turn place more demands upon the library. In order to meet the growing pressures of demand and supply, funds at the command of the library also ought to grow. But generally, this does not happen. On the contrary, library budgets are very often subjected to severe cuts on account of other priority allocations. Even in cases where funds remain static, purchasing power of the available money may go down due to inflationary trends. To make matters worse, the prices of reading materials have always a rising trend. The ultimate result of this conflict of factors is that the library will not be able to buy all that it should. This is the case with even the richest library in the world. Therefore, every body must know how to utilise the available money in the most judicious manner. As advised by Dewey, your motto must be "the Best Reading for the Largest Number at the Least Cost". This principle underlies the balancing of the three opposing factors — books, readers and money. Every body has to ensure that the funds are expended in such a manner as to build up a well-balanced and purposive library collection. Strict financial discipline, therefore is needed in acquisition work.

Far Off Book Markets : Proximity to major book markets is an important factor in collection building. The book markets in India are concentrated in the cities of Delhi, Mumbai, Kolkata and Chennai. While libraries in these cities are in an advantageous position those in other parts of the country do not have easy access to these book markets and their large stocks.

Local Book Suppliers : Every library has to depend on the local book sellers for most of the supplies. Unlike the major outside book markets referred to earlier, local book shops do not usually stock many publications of interest to libraries. Their main aim may be casual readers and counter sales. Supply against specific orders will not be always prompt and effective since their investments in business will be small and machinery for procurement weak. As a result orders for many items may not he executed. They may even underquote and take the orders. But they will be more eager to push in their unsold stock to libraries than supplying the ordered items. Libraries also, after having waited too long for supply of ordered items, will be made to go in for whatever the bookseller has in stock, before the lapse of the financial year.

Foreign Publications : Libraries in India have to depend heavily on foreign publications. These are mostly expensive. They are not adequately stocked by Indian booksellers or even the publishers' own representatives. Procuring them from abroad against orders may take 3 to 6 months. Even then, the final supply will depend upon the bookseller's trade connections and credibility, various import regulations and formalities, and other factors. The situation can be overcome if you exercise sufficient caution in the choice of your supplier. Further, one will have to initiate your orders for foreign publications early enough taking into account the time factor.

Indian Publications : Publications of Indian origin have their own special problems. Firstly, publishing industry in the country is not fully organised. Although there are many well known publishing houses their total output is less than the total output of the unorganised sector which consists of numerous small-scale and newly emerging publishers. Secondly, it is a common practice in this country for authors to function as their own publishers and distributors. Thirdly, publishing in Indian languages is almost completely regionalised. Because of these and other reasons, it is difficult for libraries to keep track of all Indian publications. A large bulk of them, therefore, remains relatively obscure as they do not reach the booksellers in all parts of the country. As acquisition librarians everybody will have to be constantly alert and watchful about the announcements, advertisements, reviews and other information about these publications.

Pre-paid Publications : Atleast two categories of publications have to be ordered with advance payments. They are government publications and books on pre-publication sale. The first category is not marketed through booksellers. Orders have to be accompanied by advance payment in full. The second category represents a growing phenomenon today in Indian publishing. Pre-publication prices are usually lower than their catalogue prices and thus the library will be gaining some money in ordering with advance payments. The risk in not responding to pre-publication announcements is that such items will not be available for purchase later. The publishers in these cases have a tendency to print copies only to supply against advance orders. To acquire both the above categories of publications one must obtain the necessary financial sanction since the rules in force may not generally permit advance payments for books.

Out-of-print and Rare Books : No library can confine its collection to current publications only. In each of the subject areas there may be some old, out-of-print and rare documents of classical value.

Their inclusion would enrich the library collection, but these items will not be available for purchase through normal trade channels. One need to make special efforts to acquire them. There may be new book shops here and there which deal in secondhand books. You have to keep yourself in regular contact with these secondhand booksellers through correspondence or personal visits. Available items have to be negotiated and purchased. Personal collections are also a possible source io be explored. Useful items may be acquired if possible as gift or through outright purchase.

TECHNICAL PROCESSING

One of the important sections in a library is the Technical Section as it occupies a pivotal position round which all other activities take place. It is called by other names, such as, Processing Department, Technical Processing Section, Cataloguing Department, Technical Department, etc. Irrespective of the name by which it is called, the objective and functions of this section remain the same. While the acquisition is responsible for the building up of a good collection, it is the Technical Section that transforms the collection of documents into serviceable units. This it achieves mainly by performing two functions, namely, technical processing which includes classification and cataloguing, and physical preparation of the documents for circulation and use by the readers.

Need for Technical Processing

The need for technical processing has been brought about by a number of reasons/factors. They are:

(i) Accelerated growth of information resulting in the production of a large number of documents and, consequently, user problems of inadequate time for reading and assimilation.

(ii) Complexity in subject specialisation coupled with the interdisciplinary nature of information.

(iii) Demand from readers for better services, etc.

In addition, the pressures of the Five Laws of Library Science, especially the second and third laws have forced librarians to seek new procedures in the arrangement and management of the collection. This has resulted in the development of new tools called Vocabulary Control Devices— such as Classification Scheme, Thesauri, Catalogue Codes, Subject Headings Lists, etc — for the purpose of classification and indexing of information. Some of the advantages of technical processing are:

(i) It helps in the systematic arrangement of documents / information and thereby facilitates storage and retrieval whenever necessary.

(ii) It facilitates analysis of queries put by users.

(iii) It helps in the preparation of information services and products.

Organisational Structure

The Technical Section of a library, especially a university library, may consist of various units such as, Classification Unit, Cataloguing Unit and Book Processing Unit, etc., to carry out the routine work of technical processing. In the case of a small library, such a demarcation into different units may not be there, irrespective of the size of the library, however, it is necessary that this section be headed by a dynamic person with sufficient professional expertise and also be provided with staff to carry out the processing work.

Planning and Organisation

In this section, the major items of work are classification and cataloguing. They are of a highly technical nature and accuracy is the very essence of all technical processing work. It is suggested by Ranganathan that in libraries, especially large libraries, it will be a good policy to prepare atleast two copies of the catalogue to facilitate use by the readers on the one hand and by the classifier and the cataloguer on the other. In other words, one set of the catalogue should be in the Technical Section. This catalogue is described by some as "Official Catalogue".

Factors in Planning

The distinctive work of the Technical Section is to be planned with reference to the following factors:

- Classification
- Cataloguing
- Preparation of the volumes for public use
- Correction of call numbers and catalogue entries
- Binding
- Classification and cataloguing codes
- Catalogue cabinet

In the contest of the planning of the Technical Section, it is necessary to take certain decisions. These are related to:

- Choice of the classification scheme
- Choice of the catalogue code
- Choice of the internal form of the catalogue
- Choice of the physical form of the catalogue
- Adoption of a policy regarding classification and cataloguing
- Arrangement of personnel
- Acquiring the tools for use in classification and cataloguing
- Acquiring the necessary materials and equipment

Some of these matters involve policy decisions while others relate to the organisation of men and materials.

Classification

Classification is the foundation of librarianship. Classification, in common parlance, means arrangement. To state it more clearly, it means 'to bring order out of chaos'. The library partakes the nature of a growing organism. It presents problems of such an enormous growth that compels librarians to thick of devising certain methods by which they can bring order out of chaos and can maintain it. The same books are used time after again. It mean that if a permanent order is not brought in, the time spent in arranging, dearranging and rearranging will be so much that the readers will become sore about the libraries and they will begin to detest the library service. In this way, the purpose of libraries will be lost. In order to vouchsafe a permanent arrangement, librarians have invented many classification schemes. All these schemes have their own merits and demerits and have got universal applicability but may not suit all conditions at all times in all places. Therefore, while deciding the adoption of a particular classification scheme, we should take into consideration the various merits and demerits of all such schemes and their applicability to the book stocks of a particular library. The following are the important classification schemes which are used in various libraries of the world :

- Dewey Decimal Classification by Melvil Dewey
- Universal Decimal Classification
- Library of Congress Classification

- Subject Classification by J.D. Brown
- Expansive Classification by C.A. Cutter
- Bibliographic Classification by H.E. Bliss
- Colon Classification by Dr. S.R. Ranganathan
- Rider's International Classification by Fremont Rider

All these schemes of classification except Colon Classification Scheme are of foreign origin and have got bias towards Western subjects. Eastern subjects have been ignored to a great extent. Moreover, almost all these schemes are enumerative schemes. Bibliographic and Colon Classification schemes are analytico-synthetic schemes. Out of all these schemes, Dewey Decimal Classification scheme is widely used in all the countries of the world including India. Colon Classification scheme is the most scientific classification scheme devised by Dr. S.R. Ranganathan, an Indian who got world-wide fame for his insight into the various problems of Library Science. Colon Classification Scheme being of Indian origin treats all subjects, including Indian ones in detail. This scheme, though considered to be difficult, can suit the needs of all kinds of libraries. Generally speaking, only a tried and scientific scheme should be used which can stand the test of time. Efforts should be made to follow the scheme in toto without any amendments. If some amendments are to be made, these must be within the frame-work of the scheme in use.

Any of the scheme can be adopted. But Ranganathan has suggested the following points for consideration:

- Scope of classification
- Sequence of Basic/Main Subjects
- Provision for New Basic/Main Subjects
- Provision for "Systems" of exposition of a Basic Subject
- Provision for 'Specials' of a Basic Subject
- Crisp words to denote ideas
- Sameness of patterns in the sequence of subjects going with different Basic Subjects
- Objectively used postulate and principles
- Systematic procedure for practical classification
- Avoidance of the fault of alternative places for one and the same subject

- Inner mechanism to find a helpful place to a new compound subject
- Length of base of notational system
- Provision of connecting digits
- Hospitality in chain
- Hospitality in array, including extrapolation and interpolation
- Agency for promoting use
- Permanent organisation for development

He suggested the use of four scores: 0 Poor; 1 Passable; 2 Fair; and 3 Good in the scheme. Perhaps, this method would be very good for the choice of a scheme of classification, especially in special libraries.

Classification work is not only a technical job but it needs scholarship also. A sound subject background is essential for good classification, since the most important job in classification is the determination of specific subjects, it can be done only by subject experts because they know their subjects minutely. It is, therefore, essential that in 'the Classification Section of a library, subject specialists are appointed as Classifiers. The classifiers in a big library should include at least one person each for Sciences, Humanities, Languages and Social Sciences. In case of special libraries, the classifiers must be well-versed in the subject of specialization. The classifiers, in general, must have advanced education in various subjects. Besides, the classifiers should have advanced training in the art of classification. They should have an aptitude for classification.

Tools for Classification

The schedules of the classification scheme used in a particular library are the major tools of the classifier. In order to interpret the schedules of a particular scheme, other aids as given below can also be helpful for ensuring uniform class numbers for particular books—

1. Code for Classifiers by W.S. Merrill, 1939.
2. Indian National Bibliography 1957—.
3. British National Bibliography, 1950—.
4. Library of Congress Catalog 1898—.
5. The National Union Catalog (U.S.), 1948—.
6. American Book Publishing Record 1906—.

The classifiers can rely safely upon the above-mentioned standard tools because expert classifiers are responsible for classifying the books listed in these bibliographies and catalogues. It would be economical if class numbers are taken directly from these tools.

Classification procedure

The books are received from the Order Section after accessioning. The following jobs are performed for classifying the books :—

1. Duplicate checking.
2. Determining specific subject of the book.
3. Allotting class number by referring to the Classification schedules.
4. Assigning Book Numbers.
5. Assigning Subject Headings.
6. Checking of class numbers and subject headings by the Chief Classifier.
7. Maintenance of staff manual.

Duplicate checking : In big libraries, duplicate checking is the job of the Order Section. The Assistant of the said section gives the requisite information on the book selection cards which are ultimately sent to the Processing Section alongwith the books. As such the labour of the Classification Section is saved. All the same, in those libraries where this system is not in vogue, the under mentioned procedures are followed for duplicate checking:—

(a) All the books are divided into two main groups i.e. fiction and nonfiction. The latter group is further divided into various sub-groups representing various subjects.

(b) Books in each group/subject are arranged alphabetically by author.

(c) These books are taken to the public catalogue for checking, if official catalogue is not maintained.

(d) The Assistant first checks the books with the main entry/ author entry. If many title cards representing same author are found in the catalogue, then edition and year of publication are checked. In case of doubt, other entries are also checked. For pseudonymous authors, cards giving their real names are also looked for.

(e) The word 'Add' is written in pencil on the fly leaf of those books for which the catalogue cards are found in catalogue. Call numbers for these books are written on the versa of the title pages.

(f) The words "Main & Shelf" or letters "M & S" are written in pencil on the fly leaf of those books of which earlier editions are available in the library catalogue.

(g) The remaining books are taken back to the classifier for classifying.

Determining the specific subject : The books, the cards for which are not found in the catalogue, are taken over by the classifiers. They, first of all, find out the specific subject of each book by going through the following parts of the book in a successive manner :—

1. Title
2. Sub-title
3. Foreword
4. Preface
5. Table of Contents
6. Book Jacket's flaps
7. The thought content
8. Book Reviews

Generally, the specific subject can be found out by reading the title of a book but in cases where the specific subject is not clear from the title because of its misleading nature, the other parts of the book as given above are gone through.

Allotting class numbers : After determining the specific subject of each book, the classification schedules and other aids are used for allotting proper class numbers. The indexes attached to the classification schedules are also used to find out the class numbers, though complete reliance on the indexes is not advisable. In case of analytico-synthetic schemes, subjects are broken into various parts and the formulae for constructing Class Numbers are used for arriving at the exact class numbers.

Each library should make a policy decision as to whether close or broad classification is to be practised in the library otherwise there will be lot of confusion and inconsistency, especially in arrangement of books on the shelves. In general and small libraries, broad classification may be followed but in large academic, research and special libraries, close classification is desirable.

The Class Numbers so arrived at should be tallied with the other standard catalogues, if necessity arises, especially in doubtful cases. The Class Numbers are given in pencil on the upper half portion of the versa of the title page. It is given in pencil, because in case there is some change in the Class Numbers in future it may be corrected without any damage to the book, because the earlier Class Numbers can be rubbed off. This phenomenon is common because almost every classification scheme is revised periodically.

Allotting Book Numbers : After allotting the Class Numbers, the classifier assigns the Book Numbers. The following are the systems of allotting Book Numbers:

1. Cutter's Author Table.
2. Cutter-Sanborne Author Table.
3. Merrill's Author Table.
4. Author Tables of L. Stanley Jast.
5. Biscoe Time Numbers.
6. Ranganathan's Book Numbers System.

Generally, author marks constitute a Book Number. Cutter's Table or Cutter-Sanborne Tables are generally used to allot author marks. Suppose the Book Number for the book ''_An Introduction to Library Classification' by W. C. Berwick Sayers is to be allotted By using the Cutter-Sanborne Table, the book Number will be S 274 I. By analysing it, we find that 'S' is the first letter of the surname, 274 is the number given by Cutter-Sanborne Table for representing Sayers, and I stands for the first letter of the first word of the title of the book *i.e.*. Introduction.

But in case of Colon Classification, Book Numbers consist of language, form, year of publication, accession part no., volume no., supplement no., copy no., etc. But the year of publication is sufficient for most of the general books. For example, the Book Number is to be allotted for a book published in 1994, the Book Number will be N 94. N stands for 1900 and 94 for the actual year number. A decision is to be taken by each library as to which system is to be used for allotting book numbers.

Assigning subject headings : Subject headings are assigned by the classifier so that the cataloguer may prepare catalogue cards for the same. A classifier is in a better position to assign subject headings because be knows the subject of the book minutely. For assigning subject headings, the following tools may be used:—

1. Library of Congress List of Subject Headings.
2. Sears List of Subject Headings.
3. A.L.A. List of Subject Headings.
4. Ranganathan's Chain Procedure.
5. Classified Library of Congress Subject Headings, 1972.

Out of the above-mentioned tools the Chain Procedure method is most scientific and comprehensive one for deriving proper subject headings. It has been demonstrated by the British National Bibliography by its application. This system has been used generally by those libraries which are using Colon Classification and Classified Catalogue Code of Dr. Ranganathan. In this system, subject headings are derived by analysing the Class Numbers by the help of the classification scheme in use.

Those libraries, especially smaller ones, which do not make use of the Chain Procedure, may use the Sears List of Subject Headings or A.L.A. List of Subject Headings because in these libraries minute subject headings may not be required. But large, research or special libraries may use the Library of Congress List of Subject Headings which is a very comprehensive and standard one. But each library due to some local and special conditions has to adopt certain subject headings of its own in order to meet readers' demands.

On the back fly leaf of the book, the classifier writes down in pencil the subject headings. He gives other directions also *i.e.* whether main and shelf cards are to be prepared or cards for joint authors, series etc. are to be made.

Checking by chief classifier : If there are more than one classifier, as they are bound to be in bigger libraries, the classification work of the juniors must be checked by the Chief Classifier, so that consistency is ensured. Otherwise there will be chaos and the very purpose of classification will be defeated. After the Chief Classifier checks class numbers etc, the relevant books are sent on to the Cataloguing Department.

Maintenance of staff manual : If some modifications are effected in the schedules of classification scheme in use, these decisions should be properly recorded in a staff manual so that in case the classifiers leave the library or they are otherwise transferred to other departments of the library, the newcomers do not feel handicapped due to lack of proper guidance. The modifications, as already pointed out, should be decided in staff meetings after great thought and prolonged discussion so that wrong and hasty decisions are avoided. Such wrong decisions paralyse the whole system because it becomes very difficult to retrace the steps as the number of books to be reclassified and recatalouged becomes very large.

Cataloguing Department

Classification determines the place of a book on the shelves. Physically, book can be placed only at one place according to the subject contents of the book. But the readers seek book through various approaches such as author, title, series, and other collaborators like translators, editors, etc. Classification is not capable of fulfilling these approaches of the readers. The catalogue comes to the rescue of the readers. The catalogue is a guide to the blind alley. As a city without a map is difficult to be known about, so is a library without a catalogue. There is no matter connected with the administration of a public library which can view, in point of importance, with the character and the condition of its catalogues. However liberal its accessibility, however able its chief, however numerous and well-trained its staff, however large and well-selected its store of books, it will fall lamentably short of the true standard of a good library if its catalogue be not (i) well constructed, (ii) well kept up with the growth of the collection, and (iii) thoroughly at the command of its frequenters. It is needless to emphasize the importance of a catalogue because without it the whole purpose of libraries will be lost. Books will not be put to as best use as is desirable.

There have been significant developments in the bibliographical world during the last few decades which have profound impact on cataloguing.

In 1958—59, Cataloguing—In—-Source (CIS) experiment was made by the Library of Congress but was abandoned soon as it was considered impracticable from technical point of view, financing and utility. Under this scheme the complete main entry was to be printed on the back of the title page of each of the publications and thus the books could be processed and released for use after taking there equisete number of facimile copies of the main entry and after adding to them Book Numbers only.

A modified plan, known as Cataloging in Publication (CIP) was put through on in 1971. Under this project, the CIP entry does not contain coalition and imprint information but provides correct rendering of main entry, heading, title, series statement, bibliographical notes. Library of Congress subject headings, headings of added entries, Library of Congress Classification number, Dewey Decimal Classification number. Library of Congress Catalogue Card number and the International Standard Book Number.

Another major development in the bibliographical field has been the advent of ISBD (International Standard Bibliographical Description) in 1971 as recommended by the Working Group set up by the International Meeting of Cataloguing Experts. Copenhagen, 1969. It had been adopted by eight national bibliographies and other related agencies by 1974. It was originally meant for the description of monographic publications only but later on it was extended to serials, called ISBD (S) and to non-book materials, called ISBD (NEM) and ISBD for monographs was renamed as ISBD (M).

The ISBD (M) covers the following seven broad areas and the elements under them :—

1. Title and statement of authorship area
   - 1.1. Title proper
   - 1.2. Parallel titles, other title (s) and title information
   - 1.3. Statements (s) of authorship
2. Edition area
   - 2.1. Edition statement
   - 2.2. Statement (s) of authorship relating to the edition
3. Imprint area
   - 3.1. Place of publication
   - 3.2. Name of publisher
   - 3.3. Date of publication
   - 3.4. Place of printing
   - 3.5. Name of printer
4. Collation area

4.1. Number of volumes and/or number of pages

4.2. Illustration statement

4.3. Size

4.4. Accompanying materials

5. Series area
6. Notes area
7. International Standard Book Number, Binding and Price area.

7.1. ISBN

7.2. Binding

7.3. Price

Besides the ISBD, there have been two more developments *i.e.* ISBN (International Standard Book Number) and ISSN (International Standard Serials Number) in order to identify uniquely any publication.

For operating the ISSN system, two new concepts came into being is ISBD (S) and ISDS (International Serials Data System).

All these developments have much impact on the cataloguing of books and serials especially about the choice of main entry heading.

Cataloguing Tools : The Cataloguing Department needs various tools for effective and correct cataloguing. These tools include the Cataloguing Code in use and various important biographical dictionaries, dictionaries of names and dates besides the following :—

1. Indian National Bibliography.
2. British National Bibliography.
3. Library of Congress Catalogue/National Union Catalogue.
4. American Book Publishing Record.

Personnel : The Catalogue Department should be manned by a capable, punctilious, hardworking and intelligent staff otherwise the catalogue instead of serving as a guide will become a hindrance. For this purpose, the personnel should be well-qualified and experience in the art of cataloguing. The staff of the department should have good handwriting, it should prepare the entries with as much accuracy as is possible because accuracy is the essence of cataloguing. "No amount of training and no extent of study can make a person of are habitually inaccurate turn of mind a good cataloguer. Accuracy in transcribing, in compiling notes of authorities, in copying, in everything, in short, is the

Catalogue Card (5" × 3")

sine qua non of success". According to Stanley L. Jast "......to put a semicolon when the code requires a colon: to add extraneous marks to a class symbol; to change or miss-spell a word in a title; to do anything whatever except exactly what the code permits; this in a cataloguer is arson, high treason, burglary, every thing that is illegal or wicked."

These very strong words spoken by Stanley L. Jast emphasize the need of accuracy in cataloguing. Their implication is that the cataloguers should be very accurate in preparing entries. The handwriting should be as impersonal as is possible. It is better if training is imparted in a particular kind of handwriting. This handwriting should be disjointed one so that every letter used in words and phrases in transcribing the entries is crystal clear. There should be no ambiguity. The cataloguers should have practical training in cataloguing work. Inexperienced and raw hands should not be employed in the cataloguing department. Although the days have been gone with the introduction of computers. Now, printout of catalogues can be taken with help of library softwares but in many libraries manually preparation of cards is prevalent.

Kinds of catalogues and catalogue codes : There are many kinds of catalogues, but the needs of each library differ. For a public library, *simplified cataloguing* will do good but for a research library *descriptive cataloguing* will be useful. Similarly, for a big library, *selective cataloguing* will be in the interests of the library because the cataloguing costs are so enormous that if every bit of sheet received in the library is catalogued, an army of staff members and tons of stationery and cards are required.

It is also to be decided as to which kind of catalogue a library will use *i.e.* whether Classified Catalogue is to be practised or Dictionary type of catalogue is to be used. This also differs from library to library. For an academic library, *Dictionary Catalogue* may be useful because the readers, who are laymen, find it easier to consult it. Moreover, they do not require deep study of various subjects since their visit to the library is mainly confined to derive inspiration and information from the study of books. Conversely, for a research and special library, the *Classified Catalogue* would be more useful because the readers generally approach their reading materials through subjects and they expect to have atone place everything on a subject available in a library.

Again, it is to be decided as to whether a typed, handwritten or printed catalogue is to be maintained. This depends upon the size of the library. It is further to be decided as to which type of material is to be used for preparing the catalogue i.e. whether sheaf catalogue, card catalogue, or printed book catalogue or computer printout of the catalogue is to be prepared. This also depends upon the kind and size of the library for which it is to be prepared.

The next point of decision is the kind of cataloguing code according to which catalogue is to be prepared *i.e.* whether a library should adopt Anglo-American Cataloguing Rules-II (1978) or Classified Catalogue Code of Dr. Ranganathan ? This depends upon the kind of library for which the catalogue is going to be prepared. The provisions of each code should be studied minutely before decision in this respect is taken. Moreover, a stable and simple catalogue code should be used. The Classified Catalogue Code of Dr. Ranganathan is a new code which is based on sound principles and is very simple, scientific and logical. Libraries can adopt this code with profit. Now a days, in library softwares, entries based on MARC format are being made.

Cataloguing procedure

The cataloguing of books is an arduous job. It must be planned intelligently if it has to serve its purpose. Proper job analysis should be done and only those persons who can put their heart and soul into this work should be entrusted with this job. The following are the jobs which are involved in the Cataloguing Department :—

1. Preparation of the Main Entry.
2. Preparation of Shelf list.
3. Preparation of Added and Reference entries.
4. Label pasting.
5. Label writing and assigning location marks.
6. Checking of the catalogue cards by the Chief Cataloguer.
7. Alphabetization of Cards.
8. Card filing.
9. Maintenance of staff manual and authority file, and
10. Preparation of List of Additions.

Preparation of the main entry : In accordance with the rules of the cataloguing code in use, one of the cataloguers prepares the main entry card. This main entry card contains maximum information about the book. On the back of this card, tracing is done in pencil so that it can be changed without any damage to the card. By writing it on the back of the card, the readers are also saved from unnecessary confusion. This tracing provides guidance to the junior cataloguers as to how many and which added and reference entries are to be prepared. It is also useful at the time of withdrawing the cards of a book which is either lost or otherwise withdrawn from the stock of the library.

Preparation of shelf list : A Shelf List Card is a duplicate copy of the Main entry card. For each book, one shelf list card is prepared.

Preparation of added and reference entries : Division of labour and specialization of work are the order of the day. The industrial progress has amply demonstrated it. By specialization, both the quantity and quality of the work are improved. So is the case with the library work. Moreover, preparation of a main entry is a responsible job and the other added entries are merely duplication of the main entry with minor alterations and/or deletions etc. So it is better if this repetitive job is assigned to junior staff members. The tracings given on the back of the main entry card provide instructions to the juniors for preparing added and reference entries without any difficulty.

In case Unit Card method is followed, headings of various added entries are to be added on the top of the main entry card many copies of which are received in typed/printed form in the library. Suppose, a title entry is to be prepared according to the Unit Card method. One copy of the main entry card is taken and the title is added on the top of this card. Thus the title entry card is ready.

In case, Unit Card method is not followed, the added entries contain briefer information than that of the main entry card and these are prepared on blank lined cards separately.

Label Pasting : After the preparation of all the catalogue cards, the books are handed over to semi-professionals or unskilled workers who paste the labels in the books. The following labels are generally pasted in the books :–

1. **Spine Label :** Gummed white cloth is cut into round or square pieces of about 1.25" each. This label is pasted one inch above the bottom of the spine of the book. This is done so that the Call Number may be properly visible to the readers when the book is shelved in a book rack. Symmetrical arrangement can also be ensured. If the width of the book is much less and the spine label cannot be pasted on the spine, it should be pasted at the same level on the front card board. The specimen is given below:

Class No.
Book No.

Class No.
Book No.

Spine Labels

2. **Ownership Slip/Mark**

(a) **One Ownership Slip** is generally pasted on the inner side of the front card board at lefthand top most corner. The size of this slip may be about 3" × 2.5". The slip may be made of glazed paper. The specimen of the slip is given below : –

Name of the library
Class No.
Book No.
Acc. No.

Ownership Slip

(b) **Other ownership marks** are put at various places of the book by rubber stamps or embossing machines. A stamp, which contains the name of the library is put on the title page and another on the secret page, to be decided by each library. Third stamp may be put at the end of the book. Its specimen is given as under:

Name of the library
Location Place

Ownership Stamp

3. **Date Slip :** One date slip is pasted on the top most portion of the front or back fly-leaf of each book. But for Reference Books, manuscripts and other books which are not to be issued, this slip is not pasted, otherwise this would be a wastage of time, energy and stationery. The size of the said slip may be 5" × 3". Its specimen is given below :

Call No.	Name of the Library		Acc. No.
This book was issued/is due on the date stamped/marked			

Date Slip

4. **Book Pocket :** On the bottom of the inner right side of the front or back card-board cover, a book pocket of 5" × 3" size is pasted. Its specimen is given below :

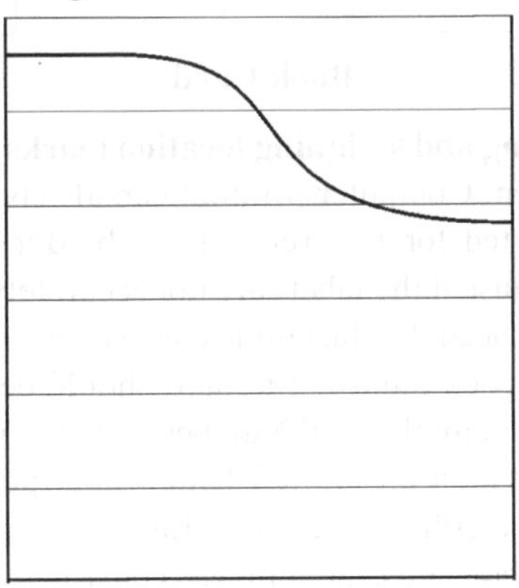

Book Pocket

For reference and other non-issuable books, this pocket is not pasted.

5. **Book Card :** One printed book card of 5" × 3" size is put in the book pocket of each book. But in case of reference and other non-issuable books, this card is not slipped in the book pocket. The specimen of this card is given below :

Call No.			Acc. No.
Name of the Library			
Author			
Title			
This book was issued/is due on the date last stamped or marked			

Book Card

Label writing and assigning location marks : The pasted labels are written with pen. Computer printout can also be used. Junior staff members are deputed for this repetitive job. But this job is a very important one because if the labels are not accurately written, the book is likely to be misplaced. So the employees who are entrusted with this job should have a good handwriting and should be accurate enough. The *spine labels* contain the Call Number and the location mark of the book. These are written on the left-hand upper portion of the label. Such marks may be either Reference, Rare, Text Book, Reports etc. These words are abbreviated and followed consistently. Their specimens are given below :

Rare 025 W 563 P	R 025 W 563 P	RR 025 W 563 P
For a Rare Book	For a Reference Book	For a Report used as a Reference Book

Location Marks

Catalogue cards checking by Chief Cataloguer : All the cards alongwith the catalogued books are submitted to the Chief Cataloguer for scrutiny and checking. In case of mistakes, the assistants are asked to correct the same. The Chief Cataloguer finds out as to whether all the cards have been properly made or not. Similarly, he has to satisfy himself to the effect that the label writing is done in an impersonal handwriting. It is better if the books are sent to the Librarian or other senior staff member for further checking. The books are thus, ready to be shelved and the catalogue cards are ready to be filed in the catalogue and shelf list cabinets.

Alphabetization : The catalogue cards to be filed in the public catalogue are alphabetized. For alphabetizing, there are two accepted methods *i.e.* word by word or letter by letter. In accordance with the practice of the library, these cards are alphabetized by junior staff members. The shelf list cards are arranged in a classified order. It is desirable that the persons deputed for this work should not be transferred very often, otherwise there will be chaos. But in order to avoid indispensability, many persons should be trained in this art.

Card Filing Work : After the Accession List is made the catalogue cards relating to the released documents are ready for merging with the catalogue. In the case of the Classified Catalogue, the Main Entries and the Cross Reference Entries are to be filed in its Classified Part while all the other Added Entries are to be filed in the Alphabetical Part. Since there is no classified part in the dictionary catalogue, all the entries are filed in a single alphabetical sequence. There are prescribed rules for filing. In the classified part of the Classified Catalogue, the ordinal values given to the various symbols in the Call Number will take care of this arrangement. Compared to this, the alphabetical arrangement will appear to be easier, but this is not true. There are many cases in alphabetical filing where definite rules arc needed for ensuring consistent in arrangement. Therefore, the library should have formulated rules of alphabetisation of its own, or have adopted some of the standard rules available, like the *A.L.A. Rules for Filing,* or the I.S.I. Standards for alphabetical arrangement. The Shelf-list Cards are filed in the Shelf-list-trays.

Catalogue Updating Work: The updating and maintenance of the library catalogue is the sole responsibility of the Technical Department. This includes, besides the filing of the entries relating to the newly processed documents, occasional work of corrections, consolidations and withdrawals. Labelling the catalogue trays and providing adequate Guide Cards inside the trays are also to be attended to. Since the catalogue will be growing corresponding to the growth of the collection there will be a continuous need for the movement of the cards from one tray to another. Parallel to this movement, the labels and guide cards also will have to be moved.

Releasing Work : Documents whose physical and technical processing have been completed are released for use at prescribed intervals, like once a week, once a fortnight, or once a month, etc. Releasing work also includes making lists of new additions or Accession List. For this purpose the Main Entries relating to the released documents are arranged in a classified order and sent for typing out the Accession List. The practice may vary from library to library with regard to the dissemination of information regarding new additions. The Accession List may be put up on the Notice Board, printed or cyclostyled and copies mailed to members, or published in the weekly editions of newspapers, etc. The documents released at a time are usually placed on display for a week or so before they are merged in the general collection. During this period the readers can examine the new documents and make reservation if necessary. The following procedure can be adopted for releasing work:

- Inserting the Book Card in the Book Pocket.
- Separating the Shelf-list Cards.
- Separating the Main Entry Cards.
- Separating the Added Entry Cards.
- Arranging the Main Entry Cards in the classified order.

- Typing out the Accession List from the Main Entry Cards.
- Noting the Date of Release on the Date Label of each document.

Shelving Book: Shelving of the books in the stack area requires special skill. In order to give satisfactory and prompt service to the readers, books must be kept in their proper place. According to *L. Marion Moshier* following pointers should be observed by any one shelving books:

- Shelve the books in the proper location. A book not in the proper location will be lost.
- Use books ends to keep books upright on the shelves, even with the edge.
- If shelf space permits, stand a book sideways to display a bright attractive cover.
- Fiction books should be arranged alphabetically by author; non-fiction should be arranged by classification number.
- Except for temporary displays of seasonal books or special theme books, the collections should be shelved in one arrangement.

ACQUISITION OF PERIODICALS AND SERIALS

Periodicals

According to A.L. A. Glossary' of Library Terms a periodical is defined as "a publication issued in successive parts usually at regular intervals and as a rule intended to be continued indefinitely. On the other hand, Ranganathan defines a periodical publication as a Conventional Document with the following attributes:

(i) A volume, or a small group of volumes of it, is intended to be published or completed normally once in a year (or at other regular intervals), though irregularity in interval is not ruled out.

(ii) Each successive volume, or periodical group of volumes, is usually distinguished by the year of publication and/or by a number belonging to system of simple or complex ordinal number. Such a number is usually called the *Volume Number*.

(iii) The intention may be to continue the publication of the volumes for ever, though not actually be carried out.

(iv) The intention may be to continue the same title in all the volumes, though this may not actually be carried out.

Where as, serial is defined as "a publication in printed form or not issued in successive parts usually having numerical or chronological designations and intended to be continued indefinitely". Thus, the term serial encompasses an extremely wide range of material including journals/periodicals, newsletters, newspapers, technical and research reports, yearbooks and annuals, and national and international government publications.

In modern times, it is necessary for the collection manager or librarian to be prepared to deal with periodical / serial literature published in a variety of physical formats in addition to the traditional print on paper. For example, microfilm and microfiche have, for many years, been popular serial formats. An important development in recent years is the increasing number of periodicals / serials available in electronic formats, either as full text on-line databases or on CD-ROM. CD-ROM is a particularly useful format for indexing and abstracting services, and the number of indexing and abstracting journals on CD-ROM is increasing. Core titles such as *Biological abstracts, Index medicus, Science Citation Index, ERIC databases* are widely available, sometimes from several different publishers.

The activities of the Periodicals Department include those pertaining to selection, ordering and receipt of periodicals / serials. To be efficient and effective, the Periodicals Department has to function in close cooperation with other departments, especially the Reference and Documentation departments which arc directly concerned with the promotion and use of the periodicals literature.

The management of periodicals include the following steps :

Periodical Selection

The selection of periodicals for subscription, exchange or as gilt is an important function of the library. This process is more difficult than book selection. While in the latter case, selection pertains to only one volume, selection of periodicals covers all the successive volumes to be published. Due to this standing commitment, great care is to be exercised in periodicals selection, This involves two aspects, namely, planning and procedure.

Planning : It is a task or activity that is required on a continuous basis for the management of all activities in an organisation, including libraries and information systems. It decides in advance what to do, how to do it, when to do it, and who is to do it. It is an intellectually demanding process and requires the conscious determination of courses of action and the basing of decisions on purpose, knowledge, and considered estimates. The selection of periodicals by the library depends on the following factors:

* Scope of the library
* Needs and demands of the users
* Needs of the collection — including availability and accessibility in organisation close to the library
* Personnel, their knowledge and skill
* Financial resources available

These factors are similar to those of book selection namely, demand, supply and finance. We can examine below these aspects of planning under four heads, namely:

(i) Ascertaining demand
(ii) Acquiring sources
(iii) Allocating funds
(iv) Arranging personnel

(i) **Ascertaining Demand :** The following criteria are recommended for the selection of periodicals:

    * Recommendations by subject specialists
    * Recommendations of library staff
    * Opinions of fellow librarians
    * Indents made by individual users
    * Announcements and reviews about new journals
    * Findings of users studies
    * Findings of bibliometric and citation studies.

Based on the factors mentioned above, the individual library should formulate its own selection policy which should serve as a guide to the collection librarian in selecting periodicals appropriate to the needs of users.

(ii) Acquisition Sources : Supply is another basic factor, which means availability of periodicals / serials for acquisition. Information regarding supply can be collected in the forms of various selectional sources or tools.

The selection tools which should be a part of periodicals collection of directories; lists brought out by major indexing and abstracting services like Chemical Abstracts, Science Citation Index, Engineering Index; trade catalogues issued by individual publishers; current issues of important book trade journals; previews and announcements issued by publishers; union catalogues of periodicals; National Bibliographies; Reports of citation studies and Reports of User Need Surveys etc.

(iii) Allocating Funds : The selection of periodicals is also governed by financial considerations. The finance available for periodicals is normally be decided by the library budget. Proper-budgeting should take into account the amount needed to continue current subscriptions as well as the amount available for new additions. The former should be arrived at after ascertaining the price increases which are not unusual in the case of periodicals. The amount set apart for the latter will have to be added every year. The selection of every new item is a commitment not only for the current year but also for succeeding years.

(iv) Arranging Personnel : Planning for periodicals and serials selection should also cover the personnel or human factor. The people involved in the selection process are the librarian, the acquisition staff, the subject experts and the library authority or selection committee. However, while the ultimate responsibility for periodicals' selection rests with the librarian.

The Periodicals Department should enlist the services of qualified and competent staff. They should be people who have intimate knowledge about the procedures and methods involved in the selection, ordering and management of periodicals. Since the work in the Periodicals Department involves estimating and accounting, including conversion of foreign currencies, there should be people with a flair for working with figures and people who understand the foreign exchange regulations and formalities. The staff in the department should be headed by a senior professional librarian who is well acquainted with the vagaries of periodical publications.

Selection Procedure

There can be two sets of operations in the selection of periodicals; those relating to continuing titles, and those relating to new titles.

(i) Continuing Titles : Every library will have a set of periodicals that are currently received. The subscriptions for them have to be renewed every year. The procedure involved in this renewal work is outlined as follows:

* Preparing the current list
* Reviewing the current list
* Consulting the cooperating libraries
* Reviewing the financial position
* Selecting items for deletion
* Consulting the experts, and
* Obtaining sanction

A complete list of currently received periodicals should be made with the new subscription amounts payable against each title. This list must then be subjected to a review by examining the desirability of continuing each item. Such a review and revision of the list will become necessary due to many reasons, like the worthiness of certain periodicals, the appearance of new and more worthy publications, the change in the requirements of the clientele, or inadequacy of funds. Although deletion of items once taken is an unhealthy practice, deletion would become unavoidable in certain circumstances. At the same time it must be remembered that periodicals have a permanent value. Even if a temporary decline in value can be found in the case of a particular periodical, it is more prudent to continue the title than cancel it. Collection building with regard to periodicals is a work that requires great forethought. Frequent deletions from current lists only indicate lack of this forethought in the original selection. There may be occasions when a cooperating library in the neighbourhood also is subscribing to the same journal. In such a case, an understanding should be arrived at between the two libraries to avoid duplication. Deletions effected through such arrangements can be replaced by new titles. In any case, necessary consultation with subject experts is a prerequisite in finalising the list. The final list is then presented to the sanctioning authority for ordering.

(ii) New Additions : The procedure in the selection of new titles is outlined as follows:

* Suggestions from experts
* Preliminary checking

* Details collected from sources
* Enquiries from publishers
* Finance
* Consulting experts, and
* Obtaining sanction

As and when specific titles of probable interest to the library are brought to notice, their particulars are taken note of. Announcements and advertisements, trade journals, entries in national bibliographies, suggestions from readers or indents from departments etc. are the varios sources for such titles in the library. These items are then subjected to a preliminary checking with the current list, and items available already in it are scored off. Complete details regarding the remaining items are collected from periodical directories or union catalogues. The correct title, name of the sponsor, if any, name and address of the publishers, periodicity, and subscription rate are the minimum details to be taken note of in each case. In the case of newly published journals, such details may not be found in published sources. Hence, enquiries have to be made from the publishers directly. Selection of periodicals will be more effective if specimen copies are available, which are generally sent or can be acquired from publishers free of cost. In some cases, specimen copies have to be paid for, or returned after examination.

The next step in selection is ascertaining the financial position and ensuring that there is enough money to pay for the new selections. Proposals for new additions have to be adjusted within the funds available. The experts arc then consulted for their approval of each item proposed. The approved items are then presented to the sanctioning authority and the final sanction is obtained for ordering.

Procurement of the Periodicals

The planning and procedure involved in periodicals' procurement are the steps covered under procurement of the periodicals :

(i) Planning : Procurement has to be planned with due regard to matters like different means of procurement, preparations and arrangement for ordering, like the choice of the method of ordering, and in case of the agency method, the terms and conditions of supply. These points are elaborately discussed below:

Means of Procurement : As in the case of books, the means for procurement of periodicals are the following:

* Gifts
* Exchange
* Institutional membership
* Purchase

Acquisition Through Gifts : Gifts constitute an important source for the acquisition of periodicals in the library. For example, many societies send their periodicals / publications to the library free of cost for the sake of publicity. Some publications also supply some of their periodicals for some time to make the libraries subscribe to them at a later date. However, the indiscriminate acceptance of gifts may create administrative problems pertaining to storage, processing, maintenance, cost, etc. Hence they should be accepted with much care and scruting after ascertaining their usefulness to the users of the library concerned.

Acquisition Through Exchange : Acquisition of periodicals through exchange is another mechanism by which collection can be builded. The two commonest forms of exchange are on a piece-for-piece basis or on a value-for-value basis. In the former method a publication has to be sent in exchange for another publication irrespective of its cost, while in the latter the exchange is based on the costs of the publications covered by the exchange relationship. The former has the advantage of not requiring much accounting provided that a reasonable and suitable item is sent or received in exchange. If the value of the item received is uncertain it may be advisable to insist on a closer degree of equality in respect of the materials sent.

For example Smithsonian Institution, USA, offers the exchange of their publications with those interested organisations of various countries. Similarly, there is an exchange mechanism between DRTC and IASL1C for exchange of serials/publications. Perhaps, exchange agreements between institutions concerned is a necessary prerequisite for a successful exchange programme.

Institutional Membership : Institutional membership is another potential resource of building up a periodical / serial collection. Learned societies generally publish one or more regular publications to communicate their activities, programmes and achievements to their members regularly. Hence, the library will do well to enlist itself as a member of learned societies and thus will be able to receive the periodical publications either free of cost or at concessional prices. For example,

ILA and IASLIC societies send their journals free on institutional membership.

Acquisition Through Purchase : Two different methods are available for ordering of periodicals. They are the *direct subscription method* and the *agency method.*

(a) Direct Subscription Method : In this case, the library places orders directly with the publishers of each periodical. There are several reasons why libraries resort to direct ordering of periodicals with the publisher.

* It is speedier than channelizing orders through agents.
* It is more economical since the library will not have to pay service charges to agents. In some cases, the publishers may even offer incentive discounts to libraries. The agents do not offer such benefits.
* It is more efficient since the periodicals are more promptly delivered to the library by the publishers than the agent. Mistakes in supply, if any, when pointed out, are immediately rectified by the publishers.
* It is less risky and more safe to pay advance subscription to the publishers than entrusting large amounts to the agent.
* There are some publishers who may not be willing to work through agents unless the agent in question has established business connections with the publishers.
* Many government and institutional publications are available only as gift or for exchange.
* Agents do not deal with these categories of publications.

Against the above advantages, direct subscription is more troublesome for libraries because of the administrative work involved in corresponding individually with the publishers in every case of ordering, reminder, mistake in supply, and settlement of claims regarding missing numbers. Further it is pointed out that the expenses of postage in the case of foreign periodicals will work out very high. Notwithstanding these extra costs in administration and postage, direct subscription ensures prompt and efficient service.

(b) Agency Method : In the agency method, the order is placed with an agent who acts as the intermediary between the library and the publishers. This is alternative to direct ordering with publishers is to acquire the periodicals. A subscription agent is a person or firm acting as a liaison between the subscribing library and the publishers. Such an agent may also be called a vendor or a dealer. The advantages of acquiring periodicals through agents are:

* Much paper work on accounting by the library can be avoided since orders arc placed in bulk and payment is effected against consolidated bills of the agent.
* Agents are more familiar with the peculiarities of individual publishers than the library, and they can act accordingly.

The disadvantages of this method are :

* Many agents do not honour the contractual agreements entered into between themselves and the libraries.
* Periodicals received through agents become more expensive for the library as they take handling charges, and do not allow the library the benefits of concessional prices or discounts allowed by publishers.
* There can be some time gap between the termination of one contract and the creation of another. As a consequence, timely renewal of subscription cannot be effected and the library is exposed to the risk of broken files.
* Some agents may not remit the subscription to the publishers in time although they have collected the amount from the library. So, the publishers resume supply of the journals only after payments are effected. Here again, there is the risk of incomplete volumes.

However, these disadvantages can be remedied to a considerable extent if proper care is taken in the appointment of the agent. Prompt, regular and reliable service should be the cnief criterion in the choice of the agent. There are agents with a good reputation and publishers are happy to deal with such agents. Therefore, the choice of the agent is the crucial factor in the agency method of periodicals' procurement.

Terms and Conditions of Supply in Agency Method : In case the library decides to appoint an agent for the supply of periodicals, there are different ways of choosing an agent, like inviting competitive quotations, or negotiating with reputed agents In either case the terms and conditions of supply have to be mutually agreed upon. These terms and conditions as well as the other points for consideration in the appointment of an agent are examined here :

The following aspects may be covered by the terms and conditions of supply.

* Trade discounts admissible
* Handling charges payable
* Conversion rates of foreign currencies
* Post-free supply of journals
* Supply of title pages, contents pages and indexes of completed volumes
* Supply of supplements, if any and
* Guarantee for the replacement of missing numbers or for refund of the cost of such numbers.

The library intending to appoint an agent should have prepared a description of its needs, including the list of periodicals, the period of subscription, etc. Quotations are invited and received on the basis of these needs. The library must gather reliable information about the financial soundness of the agents, their reliability and promptness in dealings, etc. Further, the appointment of the agent should come into effect before the period of expiry of the subscriptions already paid. As many subscriptions expire at the end of the calendar year, the appointment of the new agent should become effective during the months of September-October every year providing a sufficient margin of time for renewal of subscriptions before the beginning of the new year.

As pointed out earlier, when subscribing through agents the library docs not get the benefits of concessional rates and discounts from the publishers. Some agents, therefore, may be offering a flat discount rate on the bills. Agents usually take handling charges which may vary from 5 % to 20% of the subscription cost. Conversion rales can become arbitrary. This can be checked by enforcing the Good Offices Committee Recommendations. Postage, if payable, will be very high in the ease of foreign journals. The agent has to undertake the supply of periodicals postage-free to the library. He should also undertake to effect prompt delivery of the issues. But, as losses in transit are bound to occur, it is the responsibility of the library to take immediate action by notifying the agent. The agent in turn is bound to contact the publisher immediately and arrange for the replacement of the missing issues. Any delay in notifying the agent, or his acting upon it, can lead to non-replacement of the missing numbers since periodicals are generally published in limited numbers only. Irreplaceable cases lead to incomplete files which become an irreparable loss to the library. However, if all efforts at replacement fail, the agent should agree to refund at least the cost of the missing numbers. Another important point is the supply of the final section of every completed volume of a periodical including the title page, the contents pages and the indexes. As these are likely to be sent only after the last issue is sent, special care should be taken to ensure their receipt. The agent should also take the responsibility for the supply of the supplements brought out by each periodical.

The terms and conditions should form part of the agreement executed between the library and the agent.

(ii) Ordering Procedure

Here, the procedure relating to ordering the selected periodicals/ serials is done. They are not very much different from the procedures relating to procurement of books. In short, Ordering procedures relates to two stages:

* Pre-ordering work
* Order placing work

Pre-ordering work : It includes various jobs connected with:

* invitation for tenders or quotations
* tabulating the quotations
* fixing the suppliers or agents and
* signing the contracts

It becomes essential to call for competitive quotations from different agents/suppliers for the supply of selected periodicals for administrative reasons. It is not necessary to call for quotations individually for periodicals since it will not be possible for the agent to underquote the publishers' rates. The agencies would be required to finish their terms of contract in respect of; (a) conversion rates for foreign currencies; (b) advance payment of subscriptions; (c) percentage of trade discounts, if any, offered over subscription rates; (d) handling charges, if any, for periodicals coming under no-discount strategy; (e) supply of missing issues; (f) the executing of an agreement, etc. Apart from service, the financial status of the agent should to be considered while appointing him as a supplier for a fixed period of time, say one or two years.

In case of advance payment for subscription to foreign

periodicals, it may be a good policy for small libraries to subscribe through Indian subscriptions agents. Some of the advantages and disadvantages in placing orders through an Indian subscription agent arc highlighted below:

Advantages of Indian Subscription Agent

* Agents frequently allow a certain percentage of discount over the subscription rates of some periodicals where publishers do not offer any discount to subscribers.
* Agents get agency commission from most of the publishers which results in the saving of foreign exchange to the extent of 10% to 15%.
* Payments are made in Indian currency. There is, therefore, no need to apply to banks for obtaining bank drafts for payment of subscriptions in foreign currencies.
* Correspondence is restricted to one party, i.e., the agent concerned.
* Expenditure on postage and correspondence work will be reduced, if subscribed through an agent.
* The agent will act on the subscriber's complaint about "non-receipts" and arrange for replacement or refund of a proportionate amount for missing issues.

Disadvantages of Indian Subscription Agent

* When subscribed through an agent, it will not be possible to correspond with the publishers regarding the missing issues of periodicals in the absence of details of payment of subscription rates.
* It is necessary to check the subscription rates claimed by the agent for each and every title with the publishers rates which consumes the time and energy of the staff.
* The agents will not be able to know about the "non-receipt" till they are intimated by the subscribers, since the publishers supply the periodicals directly to the subscribers. Hence, some agents decline to undertake the responsibility of arranging replacements for the missing issues.
* There are the cases of some agents who have not remitted the subscriptions in time to the publishers leading to delay in the

supply of periodicals and resulting in incomplete volumes due to interrupted supply of some issues.

* Agents claim handling charges in case of periodicals published by learned societies and professional institutions, which do not offer agency commission.
* Institutions will remain in the dark about the non-receipt of subscription amounts by the publishers till they are intimated by the latter.
* The conversion rates for foreign currencies claimed by the agents have to be checked with the conversion rates circulated by the Good Offices Committee from time to time.
* There are cases of subscription agents who create complications by refusing to take responsibility over claims for missing issues in violation of the agreement. In such cases the execution of the agreement is no remedy unless supported by a security deposit.
* The subscription agent has to be appointed after calling for quotations and selecting the lowest. The work involved in calling for quotations and appointing the agent will take much time resulting in the delay of payment of subscriptions which can affect the regular and prompt supply of periodicals.
* Changes in the administrative set up and subscription agents cause interruption and sometimes complete stoppage of supply.
* Normally the lowest quotation is accepted, but it may prevent the selection of a reliable agent.

Order Placing Work : This work includes various jobs connected with the

* renewal orders for the continuing titles
* cancelling of unwanted titles, and
* ordering of new titles.

Renewal orders should be placed without causing any break in the continuous supply of the periodicals concerned. Cancellation of a current title should, as far as possible, be effected with the completion of the current volume. Similarly, new titles should be ordered with effect from the first issue of a volume. The jobs included in order placing will vary according to the method of ordering chosen, namely the direct subscription method or the agency method.

Direct Subscription Method

The jobs included in the case of the direct subscription method can be listed as follows:

* Sending letter asking invoices from publishers.
* Scrutinising the received invoices seeking and obtaining clarifications, if needed.
* Obtaining bank drafts.
* Sending orders with drafts.
* Noting the information regarding payment; and getting acknowledgements from publishers.

The Direct Subscription Method has some disadvantages too :

* Order placing work needs to be initiated 2-3 months in advance of the expiry of the subscriptions already paid. Letters should be sent to the publishers of each periodical selected for ordering, asking for their invoices in triplicate covering the annual subscription payable. If necessary, reminders should also be sent.
* As and when invoices are received they should be scrutinised and clarifications or additional information needed should be sought and obtained. The invoices may contain the subscription payable and the mode of payment proposed. Usually the payments have to be by demand draft. When the invoices are found to be in order, steps for making payment should be taken. The total amount involved in subscriptions should be estimated including the bank charges payable. Necessary procedures have to be gone through for releasing the amount required for this purpose.
* The next step is to obtain the bank drafts by remitting the money. Separate drafts have to be purchased in favour of each publisher. Foreign journals have to be paid for in the foreign currency. For purchasing the foreign currency drafts, an application has to be made to a bank dealing in foreign currency. Sometimes, the bank insists on the production of the original invoice for this purpose. The bank then issue a statement showing the rupee equivalent of each draft. The money is then paid and the draft is obtained.
* The drafts then are to be sent to the publishers concerned with a copy of the invoice in question with a covering letter. The covering letter should state the correct title of the periodical, the volume and number, and month and year from which the supply

should begin, and the name and address of the library. Details of the draft enclosed should also be given in this letter. It will be convenient if the library uses a printed form for this letter.

* Before sending the draft, the relevant details should be entered in the Subscription Register maintained for this purpose.
* The library should then wait for an acknowledgement from the publisher. The order placing work ends with the receipt of the acknowledgement.

One possible danger to be guarded against is double payment. Any carelessness or negligence in record keeping can lead to double payment. It can happen that publishers in the case of renewal of subscriptions may send their invoices more than once. It might be that the payment made in response to the first invoice had not reached the publisher when the second invoice was despatched as a reminder. The library by mistake can make a fresh payment in response to the second invoice also if proper records arc not maintained or available records are not duly examined. It is here that the Subscription Register plays a crucial role. It should have columns for entering the title of the periodical, the invoice number and date, the period covered by the subscription, the amount paid in Indian rupees and foreign currency equivalent, the draft number and date, the date of despatch, the date of acknowledgement, and remarks.

Agency Method

In the case of the agency method, following jobs can be listed:

* Sending list of periodicals asking for pro-forma invoice from the agent
* Scrutinising the received invoice
* Seeking and obtaining clarifications, if needed
* Estimating the cost involved
* Obtaining sanction for advance payment
* Making payment to the agent
* Getting proof of remittances made by the agent and
* Noting information regarding payments.

The library must prepare a list of periodicals to be subscribed to. This could be in two parts — renewals to be made and new titles to be ordered. In both cases complete details of every item listed should be given like the full title, the name of the sponsor, name and address of the publisher, the periodicity, the subscription for the previous year and the volume and year, and the month and year for renewal, etc. This list is sent to the agent asking for a pro-forma invoice. The agents sends the proforma invoice quoting the current subscription for each item in the list in the respective national currencies and stating the total amount involved in Indian rupees. The net amount payable and the advance amount required will also be indicated by the agent. On receipt of the invoice the library should check each item with the order list and satisfy itself about the correctness of the item invoiced and the total amount. Action must be initiated then for obtaining sanction for the advance payment to the agent and for the release of the required money. The advance is paid to the agent only after he has executed a bond on stamped paper incorporating the terms and conditions of supply and the details of the advance amount taken. The agent will be bound by the agreement to produce proof of the remittances made by him to the publishers. Necessary entries are made in the subscription register or card, as stated in the earlier section, upon production of satisfactory proof.

The operation to be performed in Ordering of Periodicals is similar to that for books discussed earlier. The distinctive work of the Periodicals Section is to be planned with following factors, according to Ranganathan:

* Standing vendors
* Current volumes
* Block volumes

The work in relation to the above factors consists of the following items:

* *Standing vendors* — This work consists of jobs similar to those mentioned for books.

In relation to the other factors of Current Volumes and Back Volumes, the work consists of the following items:

* *Current volumes*
    * Periodical Publications Selection Work
    * Periodical Publications Ordering Work
    * Periodical Publications Receiving Work
    * Completion Work

   * Cumulative Index Work
   * Rounding off Working
   * Periodical Publications Bill Passing
   * Loose Issue Sharing Work
   * Suspense Periodicals Publication

* *Back Volumes* — The jobs relating to the ordering and receiving of back volumes of periodical publications are similar in most respects to those of ordering and receiving of books.

Receiving of Periodicals

It is perhaps the most difficult activity in the Periodicals Department, which requires thoughtful planning and systematic routines and procedures. This consists of following :

Planning

Planning for the work of receiving periodicals has to do mainly with the methods for ensuring the prompt receipt and recording of the periodicals. The methods of recording adopted not only should account for the periodicals subscribed to and received, but also should alert the library about the non-receipt of any item after its expected date. It must enable the detection of the non-receipts so that follow-up actions like sending reminders and claiming replacements can be done as a regular routine. The system must also help in settling claims for non-supply and in avoiding overpayment. However, there are different methods in use among libraries, the most common being:

* Ledger System
* Card System
* Three Card System, and
* Kardex

(i) Ledger System : In this system, the record is kept in the form of a bound register wherein each page is allotted to a periodical. On top of the page usually, details like the name of the periodical, its periodicity, the name of the publisher/sponsor, the name of the supplier, the amount and period of subscription paid, etc., are written. Columns are be provided for year and months, volume and number, date of receipt and remarks. Entries are to be made in these columns as and when current issues are received. The chief advantage of this system is that each page will explain the receipt of the various issues of a periodical. This method may be found satisfactory for a small library subscribing to a few periodicals only. The disadvantages of the system are that each page has to be examined in order to take note of the non-receipt or overdue issues at a point of time.

PERIODICALS REGISTER

Title : .... Periodicity : ....
Publisher : .... Subscription paid : ....
Sponsor : ....
Supplier : .... Period covered : ....

Volume	Number	Date of Publication year month date	Date of receipt	Remarks

Ledger System

(ii) Card System : The Card System can overcome many of the disadvantages of the Ledger System. In this system, cards of a uniform size, either 5" × 3" or 6" × 4", can be used where each card can hold the data relating to a particular periodical. The card can contain all the details normally found in the Ledger System. If separate cards can be used for the different volumes of a periodical the card can contain additional information like the reminders sent, claims made, etc.

(Recto)

Title :- Periodicity :

Publisher : Supplier :

Vol. & year	Jan	Feb	Mar	Apr	May	Jun	July	Aug	Sept	Oct	Nov	Dec

(Verso)

Title :

Vol. & Year	Subscr-ibe Amo-unt	Bill No. & date	Vou-cher No. date	Remin-ders sent	Bound upto	Remarks

Card System

(iii) Three Card System : The Three Card System method was introduced by Dr. Ranganathan. In this system, three different cards of the size 5" × 3" are maintained for each periodical. They are called the Register Card, the Check Card, and the Classified Index Card.

Register Card: This is intended to record information about the name of the periodical, the name of supplier, the periodicity, the order details, the annual subscription, the payment details, details of issues received, etc. The Register Card enables the library to know the issues received and the dates of their receipt. These cards are arranged in a tray in alphabetical order so as to facilitate the title approach.

Check Card: The Check Card is the most important contribution of this system. It contains columns for volume and number, due date, details of reminders, etc. It is the arrangement of these cards which meet its very purpose, namely, watching the receipt of the issues for acting upon when found overdue. A check card will be prepared for each of the periodicals ordered. These cards will then be arranged in a tray behind Guide Cards indicating the expected week of its receipt. There will be 60 week guides in all, as there can be a maximum of 5 weeks in a month. The guide cards will be numbered as follows:

1.1	1.2	1.3	1.4	1.5	for the month of January
2.1	2.2	2.3	2.4	2.5	for the month of February
3.1	3.2	3.3	3.4	3.5	for the month of March
...	...	...	...	...	
12.1	12.2	12.3	12.4	12.5	for the month of December

As and when a new issue of a periodical is received, its check card is located from behind the appropriate Week Guide and information is entered in the columns. The Check Card is then removed to behind the Week Guide corresponding to its next issue. For example, the current issue of the periodical arrives in the library as expected in the second week of May. Its check card will be found in the set of cards behind the Week Guide numbered 5.2. After entering the details, this card will be taken behind the Week Guide corresponding to its next issue. For example, the periodical is a bi-monthly and therefore its next issue is normally expected in the second week of July. The number of the Week Guide behind which the check card is to be refiled is 7.2. At the end of every current week the check card remaining behind the corresponding Week Guide will be of those periodicals that have become overdue.

The Register Card

Title Vendor CN	Period in weeks Grace Weeks	Order No. & date	Payment	
			Vol or Year	Vouch No. & date
			Ann Subs	

Vol & Number	Date of Pub.	Date of receipt	Vol. & Number	Date of publ.	Date of receipt

The Check Card

Heading				Period Grace weeks			
Vol. & Number	Due Week	Week of Rem	Lbn	Vol & Number	Due Week	Week of Rem	Lbn

Classified Index Card

Cl. No. Ann Subs. per in weeks

Title

Vendor

Publisher

Vol Available

Indexes, etc.

Supplements, etc.

Cards in the Three Card System

The library can send reminders for them and do the necessary follow-up work. This is the great advantage of the check card. In fact, this has made the work of keeping track of the non-receipt of periodicals almost automatic.

The Classified Index Card : This card shows the volumes available in the library in the case of each periodical. It also gives details about the supplements, cumulative indexes, etc of the periodical. These cards, as their names imply, are arranged in a classified order according to the Class Numbers given to periodicals.

(iv) Kardex System : This system was introduced by the Remington Rand of India, Ltd. It is a type of visible record system maintained in a steel filing cabinet. Each unit cabinet contains seven trays in all providing more than 500 card holders. Each card holder can hold two cards, a Bottom Card and a Top Card. A Bottom Card is prepared for every journal when ordered, with its title and other particulars typed or written on the lower portion of the card. The Top Card is placed opposite the Bottom Card in the next Card Holder so that both cards become visible side by side. It is the Top Card that serves the purpose of keeping record of payments made to the suppliers while the Bottom Card helps to watch out for the receipt and non-receipt of periodicals. The system provides for single codes of different colours to indicate the issues received and the subscription due, etc.

Procedure

Periodical Receiving Work consists of three types of jobs — immediate, daily and weekly.

The *immediate jobs* pertain to receiving periodicals that come in the form of V P packets, and return of wrongly delivered packets.

On the other hand, the *daily jobs* include:

- Wrapper examining
- Sorting of packets into suitable groups
- Current issue collating -
- Current issues alphabetizing — Alphabetizing the collated current issues in each group
- Current issue registering
- Current issue cutting and stamping

The Top Card

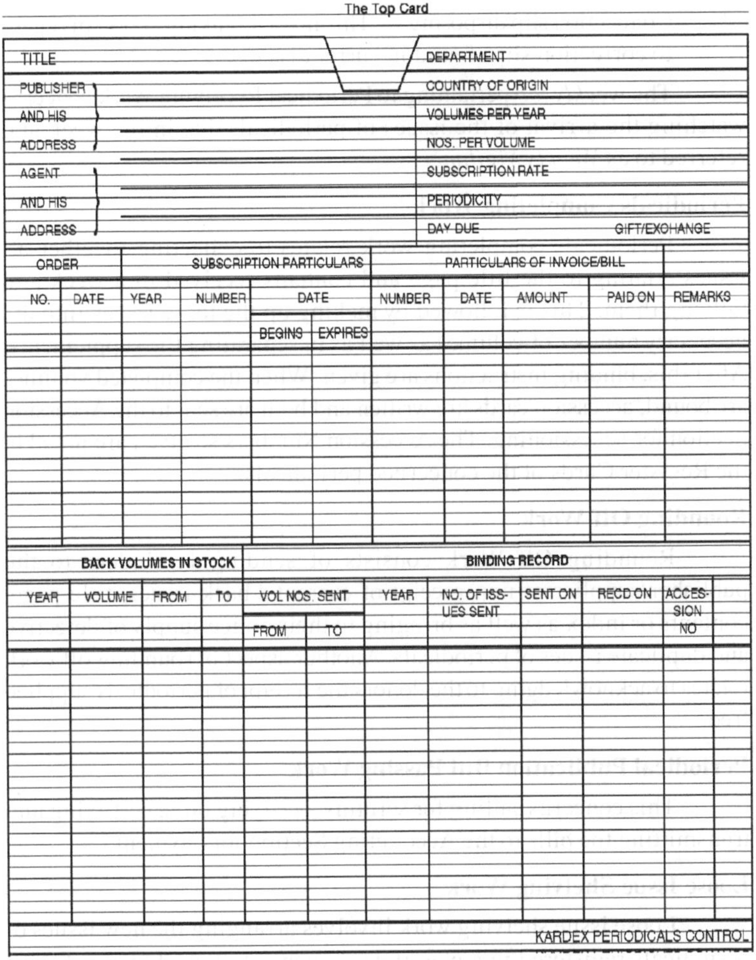

Karder Card

* Current issue perusing — to detect peculiarities and announcements, if any, in current issue
* Check card shifting — Shifting the check card of the periodical received behind the appropriate "Week Guide"
* Daily vigilance — This involves watching the arrival of the issues of the Dailies
* Loose sheets fixing — This involves fixing of any loose sheets, plates, maps found in any of the current issues

* Connection slip disposing — This involves taking action in regard to correction slips found in current issues.

The *weekly job* pertaining to Periodical Receiving Work concerns watching the arrival of the issues of periodicals due in the week and referred to as *Weekly Vigilance,*

Periodicals Completing Work

Periodicals completing work relates to collecting together all issues relating to the title page and contents received in a week and tallying them. This is followed by making up the loose issues into the necessary number of volumes as well as in separating the supplements. After this, binding instructions are given. When the completed volumes arc bound, accession cards are written and both are sent to the Accession Section for accessioning. The Accession Numbers so given are noted in the Register Cards of the concerned periodicals.

Rounding Off Work

Rounding Off Work consists of sending reminders to the publisher/supplier of non-receipt of current / back issues, title page, contents or index as well as bringing to their notice supply of defective and duplicate issues of periodicals. Another aspect of rounding off work relates to acknowledging to the donors the receipt of periodicals supplied free.

Periodical Publication Bill Passing Work

This concerns calling for scrutiny, verifying bills, certifying and transmitting the bills to the Accounting Section for payment.

Loose Issue Shelving Work

Loose issue shelving work involves arranging the new issues of periodicals registered in a classified sequence followed by displaying them on the display rack. As and when new issues are displayed, the old issues are shelved.

Servicing of Periodicals

This work comprises the jobs connected with facilitating the maximum use of current periodicals. Libraries adopt different methods to ensure the use of current periodicals. All libraries, for example, have the practice of displaying the latest issues of periodicals as and when they are received and registered. Some libraries circulate the issues among its specialist clientele. Many research and special libraries have the practice of bringing out current awareness bulletins in various forms based on the recent issues of periodicals.

Problems in Acquisition of Periodicals

Periodicals' acquisition work is beset with several problems and difficulties. There are problems in the selection, ordering and receipt of periodicals.

Problems in selection arise out of :

* the increasing number and variety of periodicals
* the increasing cost of periodicals
* the recurring financial commitment in the selection of a periodicals, and
* the vagaries of periodicals themselves.

Problems in ordering periodicals arise from:

* the scattered situation of publishers
* the difficulties with local suppliers
* the need to pay subscriptions in advance, and
* the involvement of foreign exchange.

Problems in receiving periodicals are:

* the delay in supply
* the chances for losses in transit, and
* the difficulties in getting replacements for non-received issues.

Problems in Selection

Periodicals are more important than the books for researchers and specialists. They contain more recent information in the form of research papers, news, reports and reviews which the researchers need. As research activities are world-wide and are increasing day by day more and more periodicals are being published from all over the world with a view to disseminating the growing research information. There may be around 100,000 periodical publications in the world. Not all these are alike in their standard and purpose. There are among them popular magazines and learned periodicals. Also there are primary journals and secondary journals like indexing, abstracting and reviewing periodicals. Selection of the most useful ones becomes extremely difficult. The cost of periodicals is also a threatening factor. The cost escalation in periodicals is of a higher rate than in books. If the budget remains constant, continuous subscription to the selected periodicals becomes difficult, sometimes impossible. Once a periodical is selected, it has to be acquired for years. If not, the library will have only broken files of periodicals and that will not serve the purpose of research. Therefore, selection of a periodical normally leads to a recurring financial commitment spread over the subsequent years. Selection of periodicals have to be therefore, very careful, deliberate and for long periods.

Problems in the selection and ordering of periodicals arise from the vagaries of the periodicals themselves. Periodicals are normally expected to be published under specific titles by certain publishers or sponsors with a prescribed periodicity and a numbering system leading to completion of volumes. But many periodicals do not conform to these essentials. There can be irregularity in publication like the non-publication of certain issues of a volume in certain periods. Some get out and some get resurrected. There can be a change in the title, in the sponsor or on the periodicity, or in one or more of the these. Two or more periodicals can be amalgamated to form a new one under a new title, also one or more periodicals can merged into another retaining the latter's title and sequence. Similarly, there can be splitting up of existing periodicals into two or more with their own titles. These vagaries can pose serious difficulties in acquisition work.

Problems in Ordering, Procurement and Receipt

Ordering and procurement of periodicals are very much inconvenienced due to different locations of their publishers. If the library wants to place an order directly with the publishers the extent of correspondence and administrative work arising would be very great. An alternative to this would be ordering through local agents. But here also there are many problems. To find an efficient and reliable local vendor would not be easy. Another peculiarity with acquisition of periodicals is that, unlike books, periodicals have to be paid for in advance, normally for the whole year. While subscribing through agents the advance payment involves risk. If it is direct subscription and if it is of foreign origin, there are involved the procedures and formalities of foreign exchange.

Receiving periodicals also has problems. Delay is inevitable in the case of foreign periodicals as they are often sent by surface mail. A more serious problem is loss in transit. Such losses may lead to incomplete volumes. Replacement of missing numbers will not be always possible since periodicals are usually printed in limited numbers. The library has to be constantly on the alert about the prompt receipt of periodicals and about timely actions to be initiated for getting replacements.

NON-BOOK MATERIALS AND ITS ACQUISITION

The term "non-book materials" (NBM) includes four categories of information sources drawn from the second edition of the Anglo-American Cataloguing Rules (AACR), namely :

* sound recordings;
* video recordings, including interactive video discs;
* graphic materials—photographs, illustrations, postcards and slides.
* micro-computer software, including CD-ROM

In addition, other forms covered by the term NBM are microforms–microfilms, microfiche, models, wallcharts, etc. As a matter of fact, microform dates back to the year 1839 when John Benjamin Dancer, an optician and professional photographer, produced the first micro-photograph. These microforms, perhaps, offer an alternative to book storage and help in solving the space problems encountered by libraries.

Commenting on the value of NBM, it was said by Leslie Gillert and Jan Wright as early as in 1971 that :

"NBM *have increased the range and means of obtaining and exploiting information for teaching, learning and research purposes, but to separate books from NBM is to divide information into false compartments. Hence, it is essential that books and non-books can he jointly identified and located to meet particular needs* "

In spite of this recognition, NBM have not become popular in libraries due to the following reasons:

(i) A lack of understanding or only recent concern with the learning processes by university academics and public.

(ii) The strong belief in the primacy of the printed word for research collections.

(iii) Little demand from users, who, perhaps, were dominated by the conventional information resources and with little exposure or access to NBM.

(iv) Lack of motivation and funds to build up NBM collections, etc.

Once it is decided that NBM will form a part of the collection of the library, efforts should be made by the librarian to make a planned selection of NBM that would satisfy the differential requirements of all the clients. But, it is not an easy task due to some aspects that are peculiar to NBM. Hence, the librarian should acquire the necessary expertise — i.e., knowledge and skill for identifying various sources of supply and a familiarity with problems hampering acquisition of NBM.

While the general procedure for selection and procurement of books would be applicable to non-book materials also, it must be remembered that since the physical attributes, production and publishing of NBM arc different, appropriate modifications should be effected in their acquisition. Unlike books which can be procured through local vendors, NBM producers distribute their own material and consequently there is no equivalent to the book shops in the NBM field. Further, since NBM are fragile, the publishers insist on the library paying for any material which is damaged during preview. In addition, NBM are not available on approval like books due to (i) their fragile nature; and (ii) perhaps, more important, due to the dishonesty of some librarians who copy the material and return the original. Another problem in NBM acquisition is the lack of bibliographic control which makes it difficult for the librarian to identify NBM available in the production and distribution agencies. Bibliographic tools for NBM are, perhaps, conspicuous by their absence, or, if they are present, they are very few in number. In other words, there does not seem to be any coherent bibliographic system for NBM. These are merely hundreds of separate publisher's catalogues and lists. Therefore it may be crucial for librarians wanting to build a NBM collection to establish contact with other librarians, to attend exhibitions and visit suppliers. It may also be useful to read the case studies of libraries in NBM published in the periodical *Audio-Visual Librarian*.

COLLECTION DEVELOPMENT

Encyclopedia of library and information science describes "Library Collection is the sum total of Library materials, - books, manuscripts, serials, government documents, pamphlets, catalogues, reports recordings, microfilm reels, microcards and microfiche, punched cards, computer tapes etc. - that make up the holdings of a particular library." Collection development in a library therefore means building up and improving the collection in that library.

Earlier librarians were concerned merely with acquisition and preservation of reading materials. At that time number of documents was more important than the information they contain. That means quality was given utmost importance in a library. There is change in this outlook now. User needs gain importance. The term Collection Development had evolved to emphasise the need to respond to user's needs. Bloomfield says "To meet the demands, librarians here evolved theories of collection development which imply a more active role is managing libraries collection and indicate that the role may change and develop in response to changing conditions."

With the change in our outlook towards and information services we are now more conscious of user needs ; usefulness of information, available with us, and exhaustive and expeditious dissemination of information.

Harrod's Librarians's Glossary defines collection development as "The process of plannings a stock acquisition programme not simply to cater for immediate needs but to build a coherent and reliable collection over a number of years, to meet the objectives of the services."

Collection development is sometimes considered as synonymous to "Collection Building" which means that there is already nucleus of collection in the library and the librarian is going to build up the collection. But collection development is a term other than collection building, since the word development implies qualitative improvement of the collection. That is why Shipman has said "Building a Collection may occasionally involve the selection and acquisition of ...... materials *ab initio*, but in most cases it is likely to mean the planned systematic development of an already existing collection."

Purpose of Collection Development (CD)

Collection development implies selection, acquisition and evaluation of the library collection in order to see that both print and non - print materials that are available a in a library are really useful to the clientele. Collection development therefore dispenses away with arbitrary selection and acquisition of documents. Similarly it envisages periodic evaluation of the library stock both to improve its collection as also to weed out the irrelevant, outdated and unnecessary document from the library. It also means that users's needs should be kept in mind while building up the collection.

Now, the purpose of collection development becomes clear. Its purpose is to find out the users information / documents needs to :

(i) fulfill the library's obligation to the user community to provide relevant and nascent information,

(ii) find out the users information / document needs,

(iii) select and acquire documents that are really useful to the clientele,

(iv) adopt systematic and judicious spending on document collection, keeping the objectives of the service in mind, and

(v) periodically review of the collection for weeding out unwanted and outdated documents a from it.

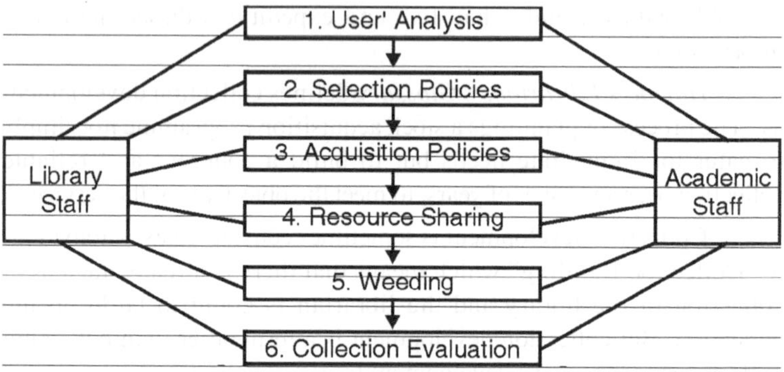

Purpose of Collection Development

Prerequisities of Collection Development

Collection development is an interplay of the library's aims and objectives and the strategies of the librarian and his staff in order to meet the users needs within the constraints of the library. For this purpose the library has to formulate a clear policy of the acquisition, periodic evaluation of the collection and the systematic weeding of documents.

Bloomfield observed that the collection development involves identification of some of the key issues like :

(a) Indentification of the purpose and mission of the library / parent organisation.

(b) Formulation of library's collection development policy by library committees or by library staff.

(c) Matching between users requirements and institutions aim and objectives.

(d) Budgetary provisions and the contingent problems.

(e) Working out the strategies for implementing the policies and programmes ; and

(f) Maintaining, revising and updating policy statements.

COLLECTION DEVELOPMENT POLICY

It is the course of action adopted for developing the collection or stock in a library. A policy can be unwritten convention or a written document.

The American Library Association's Collection Development Committee when preparing "*Guidelines for the formation of collection develpment policies*" assumed that "a written collection development policy is for any library a desirable tool which enables selectors to work with grater consistency towards defined goals, thus shaping stronger collections and using limited funds more wisely."

A written collection developments policy is preferred to non - written policy. Katz and others feel that Collection Development policy should be a written policy Futas states that a written policy "encourages stability and continuity in the library operation." Feng also feels that such a policy statement assures a consistent and balanced growth of library resources."

Advantage of Collection Development Policy

As mentioned earlier, it is always better that the Collection Development policy is in written form. From time to time the library may have to review its Collection Development policy due to policy changes of the funding agencies or the parental organisation, but, by and large many aspects may remain the same.

Several authors like katz, Magrill and Hickey mentioned the advantages of a written Collection Development policy. A Collection Development Policy :

(i) expresses openly its relationship with the objectives of the parent organisation / library.

(ii) forms the basis for planning collection development.

(iii) provides practical guidance in day to day selection of reading materials free from personal bias.

(iv) helps in determining the best method of acquisition.

(v) supports and assists in justifying the selection / collection. Collection Development policy offers some help against censorship by a clear statement of the type of materials to be purchased and indicating that the policy has the support of the library authority / committee.

(vi) acts as a rational guide for budget allocation and also helps in long range budget planning by stating priorities and outlining growth and development goals.

(vii) helps in making best use of resources.

(viii) facilities cooperative programmes like inter library loans, resource sharing and network.

(ix) assists in establishing methods of reviewing materials before purchase.

(x) Offers suggestions on types of materials to be sorted, weeded and discarded.

It is observed that a Collection Development Policy essentially state the policies of the library on :

(i) the selection and acquisition of reading materials;

(ii) the nature and method of periodic evaluation of the reading materials available with it ;

(iii) the storage and weeding of the collection ; and

(iv) resource sharing and networking.

The guiding principles for evolving the Collection Development Policy are :

(i) the goals and objectives of the organisation / institution;

(ii) the needs of the user community, real users as well as potential users ; and

(iii) the availability of financial and other resources.

Goals and Objective of the Institution

The institution or organisation of which the library is a part and parcel and for whose information needs it works keeping in mind its aim and objectives is known as the parent organisation.

For example, In the case of academic libraries the academic institution whose aims and objectives are the concern of the library will be the parent organisation. For example Delhi University is the parent organisation for the Delhi University library system. The system is supposed to keep in mind the aims, objectives and activities as the three important objectives of college, University and other institutions of higher learning, however in the case of school libraries the objectives can be identified as (1) Instruction (2) Recreation and (3) Extension activities. Though broadly common aims and objectives can be stead for academic library to another academic library even in the same category. This is because the parent organisation's priorities, specialisations and thrust areas may differ from one organisaiton to another. Even the same library may evolve new functions and new goals from time to time.

Collection Development policy of an academic library therefore should be guided by the aims and objectives of that type of library in general and of that library in particular.

The policy also needs periodic review to keep in tune with its changing objectives and goals. Even otherwise policy review is necessary to meet the changing situations and requirements.

Needs of the Users

For any library users are very important. A library gets its justification when the users are satisfied with its services. There is another aspect also. It is not sufficient if the library satisfies the regular users, it should also attract those of its clientele who for one reason or the other are not using the library regularly. That is how users of a library are classified as actual or real users and potential users. Potential users are those people who are not using the library and its services at present but who are likely to use them once they are informed and or motivated by the library about its functions and services. The clientele of an academic library can be grouped into three categories, namely, students, teachers and the supporting staff working for the academic institution. In the case of a university or an institute of higher learning the student community can again be classified as students taking there regular courses; and research scholars. Though recreational reading materials are not the prime concern or essential concern of an academic library; to meet the needs of supporting staff working same amount of such literature also should find place in an academic library for the administration.

Collection Development Policy should therefore strike a sensible and judicious balance between the various requirements of different users in different levels in a variety of disciplines.

Availability of Resources

The Collection Development policy is heavily dependent on the resources available for the library. The finance, the infrastructural facilities like library space and equipment, the book up with other libraries for resources sharing etc, determine the planning of CD policy. Above all the availability of documents is yet another constraint on the policy. Particularly if the relevant and useful documents happened to be foreign publications the CD Policy has to recognise the problems of foreign exchange, higher costs and time delay in collecting such documents.

Components of Collection Development Policy

It is seen that basing on certain guiding principle, a Collection Development policy should cover the selection and acquisition policies; the evaluation programme; the storage and weeding policies and the resource sharing and networking programmes.

In a summarised form, the various components of a collection development policy can be listed, as follows.

1. Objectives of the Library
2. Philosophy of the Library
3. Purpose of the Library
4. Brief description of the community
5. Who is legally responsible for the operation of the library and selection of materials.
6. Method of selection as well as limitations of budget served, different age groups of users and similar information.
7. Type of materials excluded.

8. An indication of how the collection is to be built in terms of (a) level of collection intensity (b) language (C) chronological period covered (d) geographical areas collected (e) form of materials collected, and (f) who is responsible for selection.
9. Acquisition of foreign language materials.
10. Statement of handling gifts.
11. Clarification on weeding and discarding practice; and
12. Statements regarding intellectual freedom.

The above points give the idea as to what items are to be covered when Collection Development Policy is prepared. It is already noted that it is better if the collection development policy is in written form.

WEEDING POLICY

Weeding policy is an important component of collection development policy. Weeding documents means removing documents which are found not useful or not serviceable from a library. The documents so removed from the library a may be completely discarded where they are not serviceable; are donated to some other library where they may be useful; or kept in a reserve place called a dormitory library. Weeding policy means a policy statement on (a) what materials are to be weeded? (b) when to weed? (c) who should weed? (d) how to weed? (e) what to do weeded materials?

With the explosion of knowledge documents are now being published in millions. New areas of knowledge are coming up and some of the earlier ideas and thoughts are becoming outdated. For a modern library it is a question of money and space to get all new documents which are relevant and useful. Particularly space for keeping the documents has become a major problem for university libraries. Solutions were attempted earlier and even now attempts are being made to find suitable solutions.

Saving place is not the only reason for thinking about weeding of documents. Some of the documents may get worn out because of continuous usage. Similarly some of the documents may became brittle and unusable by passage of time. But most important of all is that some documents may become the information in the document has become obsolete. In modern times, documents may be weeded out after transferring the information contained in them on to microforms and computer tapes and disks.

Report of the library committee of the University Grants Commission speaking on the need for weeding out says; "Many works lose their value within one generation, say in twenty five years. By that time, their thought content of same may even turn out to be wrong. In a service library no useful purpose is served by retaining such pedestrian books and providing shelf space for them after they have become obsolete. The proper course is to weed out periodically. They should give place to current variations of them."

Discouraging Factors

Inspite of the compelling reasons for periodic weeding out documents from a library many librarians hesitate to put it in practice, which is quite evident in our country. The following are some of the reasons for such a version :

(i) Love for Numbers : The glory for numbers in libraries is still there. Though modern librarians realise that it is quality of service that is more important than the quantity of documents in library even then they hesitate to weed out documents which are no longer useful. This is mainly because official reports to be submitted by them emphasize on numbers.

(ii) Sanctity of Collection : Many feel that very book however old it may be has its value. Sometimes they think that antiquity enhances the value of the book even though it exact reprint in a better physical condition is available in the market. But in service library documents loose their value and significance if they got mixed up with large number of outdated and useless documents.

(iii) Pressure of Work : Library being a dynamic organisation, a work pressure will always be on the library professionals. Since weeding implies careful, judicious and justifiable action, which needs time, librarians hesitate to weed out. Hindrance to or dislocation of the routine duties, due to time consumed by weeding out work, may not be appreciated by the clientele.

(iv) Fear of Audit and Clientele Comments : At the time of audit one may face objection that documents for which amounts were paid are not found in the library. Similarly, the clientele may also comment upon the documents weeded out of the library saying that some very useful documents were also discarded.

But a librarian need not get discouraged by these factors. A clear and well planned weeding out policy free form bias and approved by a committee appointed either for this purpose of the one looking after the library affairs will clear all hurdles. Katz says that the weeding is one of the best suitable techniques available to ensure long range usefulness of any collection.

What Materials are to be Weeded

The following are some of the types of materials that are to be weeded out periodically.

(i) Books that are mutilated by users because of constant use should be withdrawn.

(ii) Best sellers, fictions non-fiction used by hundreds of readers become worn out after sometimes. Such documents should be weeded out.

(iii) Text books and language books printed on inferior quality paper deteriorate soon. They can be weeded out once they are worn out.

(iv) In the field of science and technology, the developments are so fast that the books published twenty or thirty years ago become outdated. Such books have to be weeded out and replaced by latest edition or by new books on the subject.

(v) Reference books such as Year books, Annuals, Handbooks etc. that are published periodically have to be replaced by their new editions and the older editions are to be discardeed.

(vi) With the advent of microforms CD-ROMs and other space saving technology useful information can be stored in them. Some of the books and journals after the frequency of their use get reduced or even in the beginning itself should be replaced by such new form of documents.

(vii) Finally, a library should always keep in mind Ranganathan's Fifth Law "Library is a growing organism"; with the increase in the number of documents space becomes a problem. So, it is essential to weed out all unservieable materials to find place for new and urgently needed books and other documents.

When to Weed ?

At any time throughout an year the librarian may come across documents which may have to be stopped from circulation as they as are found to be worn out and unusable. Chopra says "In college and university libraries, if time permits each time a book is handled in the library is it should be examined from the angle of its physical condition and to its continued suitability. At least once a year the entire collection should be examined."

Who Should Weed?

Weeding out is an exercise which requires necessary judgement and expertise. The librarian has to personally involve in it. Sometimes members of library committee or the nominees of the library authority or members of a committee appointed for the purpose may take decisions and implement weeding out of materials from the library. The advice of subject experts or senior faculty members, whose judgement can be trusted, should be taken for this purpose.

Guidelines For Weeding

Weeding should not be arbitrary. Once we take out a document from the library we should think of

- Its replacement by a new copy or a new edition or a new book on the subject and
- What should be done if the same document is needed at a later date?

Several theories and guidelines on weeding have come out in the west. Fussler and Simon felt that past use is the best guide for future use of documents. Trueswell developed a technique for weeding a collection which would ensure a given degree of satisfaction in the future of by examining the past use. Raffel and Shisko suggested publication date should be the important criterion for weeding out documents.

The Council of American Library Association holds the view that in public libraries "Annual withdrawls from the collection should average at least 5 percent of the total collection" saying that "unnecessary items remaining in a collection can weaken a library as surely as insufficient acquisitions."

Sinha Committee Report (1958) holds a similar view in the case of Indian public libraries. The Report observed : Weeding out of worn out and out of date books is as important in a public library as acquisition of new books...... It is said a conscientious librarian should discard 5 percent of his fiction and 2 percent of his non-fiction every year...."

Ranganathan observes that "many" of the modern books get out moded in ideas expounded in them within 20 years. After that period such books should not be preserved in library but should be weeded out and written off.

What to do with Weeded Materials

The next problem is, what to do when materials are to be weeded out on sound principles? Of course, books and other materials completely worn out, mutilated and irreparable can be sold just like unpressured old news papers and other ephemeral materials. But if the books are in good condition particularly if they are older editions of reference sources like encyclopedias, hand books etc. they may have to be donated to other libraries which are not a position to go for such costly books.

Yet another way is to store the weeded documents which are otherwise useful in what may be known as "Book Reservoirs." At least one copy of a weeded document should be preserved at a place within a region of the country. According to UGC Committee on University and College libraries (1965) headed by Ranganathan "While weeding out, it is necessary in service libraries and generally modern university libraries or service libraries that it should not be done by the libraries of the country in an uncoordinated way for, it is necessary to preserve a few copies of every book somewhere in the country for the use of posterity and particularly for antiquarian and bibliographic research."

When documents are weeded out it should be done with the specific knowledge and sanctions of the concerned library committee or the library authority. The Accession Register, should carry the entry that the document is written off; quoting the relevant orders or proceedings of the concerned authority. Shelf list, catalogue and other records should be rectified by deleting the entries relating to the weeded out documents.

COLLECTION ORGANISATION

The organization of collection development activities in libraries varies with the size of the library, the purposes for which it was established, and the composition and location of the clientele it was designed to serve. In small libraries, all activities-from developing policy, allocating funds, selecting individual items, verifying bibliographic information, ordering and receiving, to fund accounting may be done by one person, or at least in one department. Observation of the evolution of library organizational structures indicates that responsibility for collection development may be retained by the library director or librarian longer than responsibility for cataloging or circulation or reference. When separation of collection development tasks becomes necessary, the director/librarian may delegate order preparation, book keeping, certain selection decisions, and liaison with users before finally relinquishing direct control of the budget. In large, complex libraries, the activities connected with planning, allocating, and selecting may be either highly centralized or widely dispersed, and may be separated both administratively and physically from the business activities of purchasing materials.

The administrative location of the collection development function also varies from one library to another. Collection development may operate as a department within either technical or public services, may actually be directed from the acquisitions department, or may be organized as a separate unit, parallel to public and technical services and reporting to the director/librarian. In large libraries, collection development often has closer ties to public service departments, particularly to the general reference department and departments that serve specific disciplines, than to the acquisitions departments.

In a 1987 review of the status of collection development organization, Bryant offered the following list while pointing out, at the same time, that "creative thinking can add to this list of possibilities."

1. collection development that is performed by a single librarian;
2. separate subject-oriented segments of the library, each of which has its own collection developer(s) who may or may not report to a collection development officer (other than the director/ librarian);
3. collection development that is the function of a committee that reviews suggestions from patrons and staff, making final purchase decisions;
4. a group of librarians who come together to perform collection development activities and then disperse to their primary assignments throughout the library;
5. a unit of full or part time collection developers that is subsumed by a larger division of the library;
6. a unit of collection developers that is separate from other divisions of the library; or

7. the collection development unit that subsumes one or more other library functions, such as acquisitions, special collections, or interlibrary loan.

One of the most significant factors affecting the organization of the collection development function in a library is the perspective - present or future - from which the collection is viewed. It the collection seen as a current resource, designed to meet the immediate needs of users and to be changed as often as those needs change? Or, is it seen as a permanent resource, a collection that will meet the as-yet-unknown needs of scholars far into the indefinite future? Although not all public library collections are built from the perspective of current needs, that is a common approach. As one public librarian expressed it: "In public libraries, every title that is purchased is expected to be used today." The emphasis in these libraries is on identifying popular materials as soon as they are announced for distribution, predicting the volume of local demand, and them buying quickly and in appropriate quantities. When public interest in certain authors, subjects, or formats wanes, the unwanted materials are removed from the collection to make room for those of rising popularity.

Educational libraries, particularly those serving students below the level of graduate or upper division undergraduate courses, may also be built from the perspective of current needs. In such cases, the demands of the curriculum play the role that popular demands and interests do in public libraries. Materials will be regularly selected and discarded from the collection in order to provide direct instructional support. Collections are most likely to be viewed as permanent resources when they are intended to support graduate instruction and scholarly research programmes. Research collections are seldom reviewed for the purpose of discarding materials and generally do not include multiple copies of the same item. Funds are spent in a way that will secure the greatest depth and breadth of coverage in the chosen subjects. As the collection development perspective varies from current demand to future needs, organization and participation in collection development may also vary.

Another factor affecting the organization of the collection development function in a library is the degree to which the library staff-as opposed to library users or those completely outside the library's community, such as book dealers - influences the development of the collection. Bryant has suggested that a library may represent one of three different postures in the organization of collection development: an *acquisitions* posture which acknowledges minimal staff investment; a *selection* posture which proclaims the library's intent to bear responsibility for new additions to its collections and for consultation with the library's patron community regarding purchases; or a *collection management and development* posture which perceives the library's collections as comparable in importance to its more visible services.

Since the basic characteristic of an acquisition posture is identified as being a reliance on external selection, many school, academic, and special libraries would fall into this category. Library collections in educational settings - from elementary schools to universities with graduate programmes - are influenced by the faculty and students who use them. In some college and university libraries, the faculty maintains tight control over departmental allocations and the selection of titles; in other libraries, the faculty is willing to leave these matters to the library staff. Special libraries try to respond so promptly to the demands of their users that librarians may find the range of their decision-making responsibility quite limited. Also falling into this category might be libraries where responsibility for initial selection decisions is turned over to publishers and book dealers, through standing orders, and approval-plan arrangements.

The rise of blanket order and approval plants has usually been credited to the sudden expansion of materials budgets between the late 1950s and the mid-1960s. Some librarians, particularly in developing universities, saw their materials, budgets suddenly double or triple, forcing them to drop traditional methods of selection and acquisition and try new approaches. In general, a blanket order plan is one in which a publisher agrees to supply everything published, generally without return privileges for the buyer; and an approval plan is one in which a dealer assumes the responsibility for selecting and applying all materials that fit with the library sprofile and needs, specified in terms of subjects, levels, formats, princes, etc.

A library with a selection posture toward collection development provides for some type of liaison with users, but decision making a assigned to librarians, who have the responsibility for building the collection. Academic libraries have formal arrangements for consolation with academic departments, while still retaining final collection development responsibility for the library staff.

The third of Bryant's categories - the collection management and development posture - requires a strong commitment of staff. Librarians are assigned specific subject areas in which to monitor publication, select new materials, evaluate the present collection, and remove unneeded materials. Attention may also be given to policy development, budget allocation, resource sharing commitments, preservation, and interpretation of the collection. The design and monitoring of approval and blanket plans may be among the duties of such specialists. In this type of situation, some proponents of blanket plans argue that a dealer's staff is an extension of the library's staff. If a detailed profile or plan for the library's collection has been provided to the dealer, then, theoretically, the dealer's staff should be able to match new publications with the library's needs in the same way the library staff does. When materials are needed in a language that few, if any, library staff members can handle easily, dealers can be instructed to select and ship. If, as supporters claim, blanket orders and approval plans mean that the library staff spends less time on current acquisitions work, then they ought to be able to spend more time evaluating the collection, identifying weak areas and doing retrospective buying.

Before collection development is planned it is necessary first of all to identify the types of documents that are to be kept in an academic library. It is seen that in modern times information may be available not only in the form of conventional documents like books and periodicals but in other forms also. Particularly in the case of a university library information available in non-conventional documents may also be required for teaching and research.

Similarly, the libraries may have to produce documents not only from within the country but foreign publications also. Sometimes documents published in foreign languages may also be required. Another way to looking at the type of documents needed is that documents may be of general nature or of reference type like encyclopedias, dictionaries etc.

Finally, documents in an academic library can also be classified as those that can be considered as basic documents like basic texts etc. and those that are concerned with micro level research in the subject, that is special subject areas.

The way in which the nature of the documents in an academic library can be classified is diagrammatically represented below.

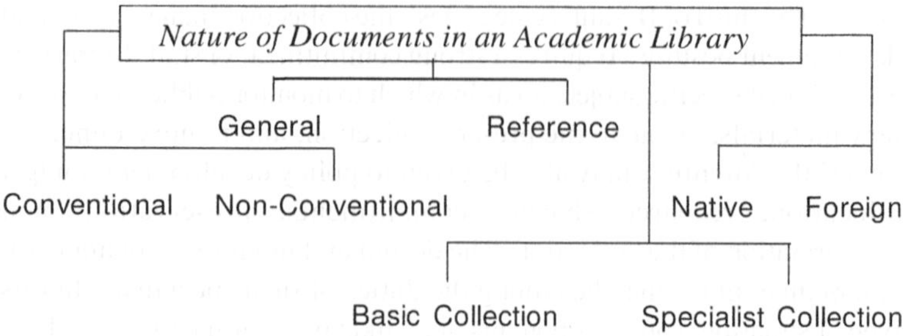

Ranganathan classified documents· that are needed for documentation work and services.

1. Conventional documents - Books and periodicals.
2. Neo-conventional documents - standards, specifications, data and the like.
3. Non-conventional documents - Microscopic, audio, visual and audio-visual documents.
4. Meta documents - records of National or social phenomenon got through instrumental and mechanical devices - unmitigated by human brain.

The Parry committee observed that "The policy documents of a university library shall considers all subject fields which are to be developed in relation to the needs of the students and staff of the university, all special collections and all types of materials whether printed or not. Some examples of the material which a university library may expected to collect and which pose different problems in their acquisition methods are : (a) students texts; (b) books currently published; (c) series; (d) currently published periodicals; and (e) other materials i.e. (i) maps (ii) sheet music (iii) microforms (iv) recorded sound on tapes and records (v) cine-films and other visual aids and (vi) cards and tapes for computers.

It is clear that in an academic library almost all kinds of information records are needed. The type of library *i.e.*, university, college or school and its objectives and functions decide which of these types of documents are needed most and at what level.

Selection

Speaking about a University library Ndegwa says "Selection for a university library collection includes not only books and periodicals but other print materials such as newspapers, pamphlets and maps. In most cases, it also includes atleast some non-print media such as microforms, tapes audio-cassettes, video-cassettes and so on." Where in case of public libraries, materials of public interest i.e., popular documents are needed. In case of special libraries, the materials of scientific interest are purchased.

Levels of Selection

So first thing is that some or many of the different types of documents are needed in an academic library. Next the library should identify the different levels of selection. That is to say for what level the documents are to be selected. *American Library Association's guidelines for formulation of collection development policies* recognises five main levels as follows:

(i) **Comprehensive level :** All significant works are required. This level is used only in "Special collections" whose aim is to be exhausitive.

(ii) **Research level :** This level includes the major source materials for post graduate and independent research with all important reference works and specialised monographs together with an extensive collection of journals and the major indexing and abstracting services in the subject.

(iii) **Study level :** It is expected at this level to provide adequate materials for undergraduate and graduate course work and for sustained study but at a lower level than the research level. It should contain the basic monographs by important writers, a selection of works by secondary writers and a representative selection of journals in the field.

(iv) **Basic level :** At this level of collection the documents define the subject indicating that more information would be available elsewhere. It includes major dictionaries and encyclopedias, selected monographs and bibliographies and a major periodicals.

(v) **Minimal level :** This is the level where the subject in question will not come into the scope of the library and where only the very basic reference tools and little else is acquired.

General Principles and Ideals

From the earliest times when libraries became service institutions the policy of selecting documents was there. The reasons are (i) not every document is useful for a library (ii) it should satisfy the objectives of the library and (iii) even if a document is useful sometimes the amount needed for its acquisition may so high that the library cannot afford its acquisition.

So certain general principles are enunciated for selection of documents.

Drury has enuciated the following principles of book selection :

(i) Apportion the library funds in such a way as to obtain books of high quality for the greatest number of people.

(ii) Secure any book which the library can use with advantage.

(iii) Fix upon a policy of selection and stick to it until it has been proved wrong.

(iv) Select books that represent any endeavour aiming at human development, material, mental or moral.

Ranganathan suggested the following ideals for book selection.

(i) The ideal is to select only after inspection and perusal. Conform to this ideal whenever facilities exist for it. Either in the form of the chief book centre being not far from the library or of booksellers or the agents for the publishers, taking the books from place to place.

(ii) Impeccable character and integrity should be brought to bear on the discharge of duties connected with book selection and assessment of potential wants of the readers free from any speaking tendency to please the whims and fancies of the members of the library committee.

(iii) Book selection should be the joint responsibility of the library staff and teaching staff. They should be guided by the probability of getting readers for the books selected. Book selection should never be vitiated by considerations of privilege.

(iv) Save the time of the staff by eliminating time lag in book selection. To eliminate time lag book selection may with due circumspection, base itself on the advance announcement of books by publishers of repute.

(v) Judge not hastily or light heartedly; reject not easily. Error on the side of selection rather than rejection.

Criteria for Selection

Keeping in mind the general principles of selection further step is to acquire different types of documents. They pose certain issues to be considered in their selection and acquisition. Some major issues and problems are being discussed in the following sections and sub-sections.

Selection of Books

Though electronic media have been entered in the area of recording information, books continue to be published and used in large numbers. For any library books form a major part of its collection. All the documents may not be relevant or useful in quality and contentwise. Sreepathi Naidu stated some principles for selection of books; reference works and non-book materials.

Books

The principles governing selection of books are:

1. Authoritativeness of author and publisher.
2. Significance of subject matter.
3. Accuracy of information.
4. Library value or artistic quality.
5. Importance to total collection.
6. Current and/or permanent values.
7. Scarcity of material on the subject.
8. Relationship to other materials in the collection.
9. Price, and
10. Format.

The criterion may slightly vary for certain categories of books; where specific evaluation principles are to be applied.

Reference Works

The following criterion for reference works are suggested.

1. Authority of the author, his credentials, biases and his previous work.
2. Scope of the work, its broadness of the topics or narrowness and limitations in the range of the subject.
3. Treatment of the subject.

4. Arrangement.
5. Format.
6. Indexing and bibliographical value.
7. Comparison with similar reference tools and whether it complements the existing collection.

Text Books

The text books are to be selected on the basis of:

1. Applicability to course of study.
2. Vocabulary.
3. Table of contents.
4. Index.
5. Appendix.
6. Glossary.
7. Graphics.
8. Clearly stated objectives.
9. Organisation of information.
10. Chapter arrangements.
11. Chapter summaries.
12. Supplementary material.
13. Physical quality, durability of binding and quality of paper, etc.

Fiction

Fiction are to be selected on the basis of:

1. Popularity of the author.
2. Style of the work.
3. Nature of the theme introduced.
4. Setting of the events.
5. Characters and
6. Reviewer's views.

Non-fiction Documents

Principles to be observed for selection of non-fiction documents are:

1. Accuracy and author's credentials,

2. Scope and authenticity of the book,
3. Quality of graphics when technical data are dealt, and
4. Bibliography at the end of the chapters.

Over the years libraries are familiar with books and periodicals. Problems of their selection and acquisition are more or less known. However, some general principles of selection have been evolved, which have already mentioned in the earlier Sub-section. The criteria suggested for selection of Non-Book materials are:

1. *Authenticity* : accurate facts; facts impartially presented; up-to-date information; other acceptable works of producer;
2. *Appropriateness* : vocabulary at users levels; concepts at users level; useful data; media subject correlation (e.g. are reprints to art, specimens to science) titles, captions etc. related to subject; narration, dialogue, sound effects related to subject; individual and/or group use suitability;
3. *Scope* : small coverage as indicated; superior concept development by this means; content to satisfy demands for current subjects;
4. *Interest* : relationship to user's experience; intellectual challenge; curiousity satisfaction; credibility; imagination appeal; human appeal; sensory appeal;
5. *Organisation* : logical developments; pertinence of all sequences; background elements; balance in the use of narration and dialogue;
6. *Technical aspects* : tone fidelity; clarity; intelligibility; in-focus pictures; true size relationship; unified composition; effective colour use; complete synchronization of sound and image;
7. *Special features* : descriptive notes, teachers/users guide; permanent accompanying material;
8. *Physical characteristics* : ease in handling for use and storage; minimum instruction for individual use; attractive packings; durability; ease of repair;
9. *Library potential* : relevancy that promotes communication; flexibility for many effective uses;
10. *Selection aids* : recommendation in evaluation sources; and
11. *Cost* : conforming to budget; less expensive for satisfactory

substitutes; average supplemental costs for replacement; repair; physical processing; storage.

As far as the selection policy is concerned a library has to first of all decide what should be its policy in relation to selection of materials. Each individual library has to take certain decisions on some major issues which will become the selection policy of that library.

Gelfand identified and discussed some of the issues as follows:

Instructions versus Research

The two important functions of an academic library particularly-a university library are instruction and research. Gelfand says "most university tend to place the needs of instruction before those of research in selecting books. But there should be no sharp lines of separation between the two needs in a university library." But, in case of a college library probably the emphasis has to be on instruction rather than research.

The institution should clearly formulate its present and probable future programme of teaching and research and provide an official statement of policy in some detail. For this purpose it may consult and take advice from appropriate academic sectors.

Foreign Books

Procuring foreign books is expensive and time taking. But if research and higher learning were to be the objectives of a university it will have to acquire major works in principal modern languages. "The library, accordingly, must select and acquire materials for each subject of university interest without primary regard to language".

Current versus Older Materials

A small academic library with limited graduate courses may perhaps prefer current materials over older materials. But "current publications are not easy to obtain by countries which are distant from the principal centres of the book trade, but out-of-print books and sets of journals - the two forms of older materials - are even more difficult to acquire. Co-operative acquisitions and inter library loans can provide a solution to the needs of older materials."

Research Materials

Basing on the research programmes initiated or sponsored by the parent organisation research materials useful and appropriate to studies should be acquired. It is most important in case of special libraries.

Text Books

Gelfand suggests the pressure for multiple copies of text books should be tactfully avoided by the library "since a diversion of substantial funds to this purpose will result in reduction in subject coverage, which will be harmful to teaching and research and therefore shall not be to the best interests of students and faculty. It is more appropriate for the university or the government, or perhaps for outside agencies to assist students" with their text book needs.

In our country the scheme known as "Book Bank Scheme" was introduced by the UGC to help students of weaker sections where multiple copies of useful text books are provided for. Also many university libraries and some libraries make provision for exclusive text book sections.

Popular Books

Gelfand says "libraries with insufficient funds for the purchase of basic required materials are hardly likely to spend appreciable amounts for popular fiction and non-fiction. They will tend to rely no neighbouring public libraries for these. In situations where the students do not have access to good public libraries, however, university library may find it desirable to form a small collection of popular materials. In case of public libraries, these form majority of collection.

Rare Books and Manuscripts

The selection and purchase of rare books and manuscripts should be done with great caution. "They are likely to be expensive, and unless they contribute directly to a course of study it is highly doubtful whether the small university library should acquire them." However, rare books and manuscripts of specifically local or national interest should be acquired.

Materials in Micro Facsimile and Related Forms

Many documents which are of great use for research and which may be out of print can now be made available in microform. "Sets of major scholarly journals, long runs of important newspapers, dissertations, government and international agency documents, manuscript collections and long out-of-print monographic literature may now be acquired in microform. In many instances the produces of microforms are also able to supply full-size paper reproductions. An increasing number of current publications is also available in microform. In general, it is best to acquire in microform the types of materials that are likely to be used for research by a few individuals rather than for general reading by many".

Aid to Book Selection

Today, there are various type of aids available for better book selection. The most useful bibliographical aid indicating all books published, in India is the *Indian National Bibliography* first published in 1958, in United Kingdom, the '*British National Bibliography*, published since 1950 and in America the '*Cumulative Book Index*' published monthly the list of every book in English Language.

Journals are also useful to aid current book selection, because generally they contain regular reviews of the books in the concerned subject. There are some aids, which are periodically published by these booksellers and publishers, containing information on the available books and also forthcoming books. However, following bibliographical tools are more useful in book selection.

Books published in America (U.S.A.)

1. *American Book Publishing Record,* New York, R.R. Bowker, Monthly.

The entries are arranged according to classified order by Dewey Decimal classification schemes. It includes all the entries of four issues of the 'weekly record' section of the publisher's weekly. It is also cumulated annually in a classified order. Author and title indexes are provided.

2. *A Reader's Guide and Bookman's Manual* : A guide to literature. New York, R.R. Bowker, 1960.
3. *Books in Print* : New York. R.R. Bowker, 1948—— Annual.

It gives details about the books published in U.S.A. in a limited time period, in which the entries of publisher's trade list are rearranged under author, title and series sequences. Now it is published in two volumes. In Vol. I - entries are arranged by author and editor and in Vol. II - entries are arranged by titles and series.

4. *Book list and Subscription Books Bulletin*, Chicago, American

library association, 1905 -, Fortnightly, (monthly in August) .

It gives the information of the selected books as recommended by the ALA for public libraries, in which entries are arranged by classified order of Dewey Decimal Classification scheme. An author and subject index is also introduced. However an annual index for author, title, imprint, series is also available. In 1956, the subscription books bulletin was merged with the book list.

5. *Book Review Digest*. New York, H.W. Wilson, 1905 Monthly (Except in February and July).

It lists more than 4,000 book reviews, published in 70 English and American journals. The entries of books are arranged alphabetically by author's name, with separate title and subject index. It gives the complete information of the book alongwith annotation. Its half yearly and five-yearly cumulative volumes are also available.

6. *Cumulative Book Index* : World list of Scientific Books of English languages. New York, H.W. Wilson, 1898 - Monthly (Except July, August and December).

It includes all the books of world published in English language, except government publications, pamphlets and ephemera. The entries are arranged alphabetically by subject, author, collaborators, title, series in one sequence. Each entry gives the detailed information of the book alongwith library of Congress card number. It is also cumulated into half-yearly and two yearly volumes.

7. *Library of Congress Catalogue, Book, Subject*, Washington, Library of Congress, 1950 -, Quarterly.

It includes the books recently published and also available in the annual and quinquennial cumulative volumes. The entries are arranged alphabetically by subject.

8. *Library Journal*. New York, R.R. Bowkder, 1878, Fortnightly (Monthly in July and August).

It publishes the annotation list of various useful books for libraries and also a list of children's books. The entries are arranged alphabetically by subject.

9. *National Union Catalogue*. Washington, Library of Congress, 1948 - (Monthly).

It includes the books received in the Library of congress, excluding books of the National Library of Medicine Catalogue and the

Bibliography of Agriculture. The entries are alphabetically arranged by author and cumulated into quarterly and annual volumes.

10. *Publishers Trade List Annual*. New York, R.R. Bowker, 1879-, (Annual).

It publishes the trade lists of numerous publishers of America. The entries are arranged alphabetically by author.

11. *Publisher's Weekly*. New York, R.R. Bowker, 1872 -

It includes the new books of the week published in U.S.A. and each entry provides detailed information with annotation. The entries are arranged in alphabetical order by author. It is monthly cumulated as a title index.

12. *Scientific, Medical and Technical Books*. Edited by R.R. Hawkings 2nd ed. Washington, National Academy of Sciences, National Research Council, 1958.

It includes selected books published in America on scientific, medical and technical subjects.

13. *Subject Guide to Books in Print*. New York, R.R. Bowker 1950-, Annual.

It publishes information of the American books in print. Each entry gives bibliographical details and entries are arranged in alphabetical order by subject.

Books Published in Great Britain

1. *ASLIB Book List*. London, ASLIB, 1935 - Monthly.

It publishes a monthly list of more than 70 recommended books on scientific and technical subjects. Each entry gives the detailed bibliographical information along with annotation. The entries are arranged in a classified order by U.D.C. in four parts; Elementary, Intermediate, Advanced and Reference Books.

2. *Book-seller*. London J. Whitaker and sons, 1858 - 1908, Monthly; 1909 - Weekly.

It covers all the published British books of each subject. Each entry gives full bibliographical details and is arranged in an alphabetical order. It has monthly, quarterly and yearly cumulations.

3. *British Books in Print : The Reference Catalogue of Current Literature*. London, Whitaker, 1887 - Irregular, Annual.

It was previously known as '*Reference Catalogue of Current Literature*, but now it is called '*British Books in Print*. It contains information on about 2,00,000 British books, which are in prints and available at a particular time from about 3,000 British book-sellers. It has two volumes as under:

Vol. 1 - Author index, i.e. author, editor, and other collaborators.

Vol. 2. - Title index, i.e. Title and subject forming part of the title.

4. *British Book News*. London, British Council, 1904 - Monthly.

It publishes 250 important selective books published in U.K. and Commonwealth, each month. The entries are arranged in classified order.

5. *British National Bibliography*. London, Council of British National Bibliography, 1950 -, Weekly.

It publishes the British publications received at the British Museum of a week under Copyright Act. Dewey Decimal Classification scheme is followed for arrangement of the entries. The alphabetical indexes of a author and title are also provided. The entries are catalogued according to the A.A. code. The cumulation of author index is published every month. BNB has monthly, quarterly yearly and quinquennial cumulations.

6. *Times Literary Supplement*. London, The Times (Daily News paper), 1902 - Weekly.

It reviews British Books on humanities and social sciences by subject specialists.

7. *Whitaker's Cumulative Index*. London, Whitaker, 1924 - Quarterly and Annual.

It contains all British Books published during the quarter period. Each entry gives bibliographical details and class number according to the Dewey Decimal Classification scheme. The entries are arranged in the classified order and alphabetically by subject. The author and title indexes are available separately. Annual cumulation is also available.

Books published in India

1. *Documentation on Asia*. Edited by Girija Kumar and V. Machwe. New Delhi, Allied Publishers, 1963—Vol. I — 1960 — Annual.

It publishes a Bibliography of current literature on Asia, in which the entries are arranged according to the geographical areas and subarranged according to subjects.

2. *Indian National Bibliography.* Calcutta, Central Reference Library, National Library, 1957 —. Quarterly. 1964 — Monthly.

It contains all books in English and Indian languages, received in the National library under the *Delivery of Books and Newspapers Act* 1954 (as amended in 1956).

3. *Indian Books in Print.* Complied by Sher Singh etc. Delhi, Indian Bureau of Bibliographies, 1981.

It contains details of English books and imprint in India. Each entry includes the bibliographical details along with price.

4. *The National Bibliography of Indian Literature.* New Delhi, Sahitya Academy, 1962-

It includes all Indian books of literary merit and abiding value, in four Indian languages, Assamese, Bengali, English and Gujarati, published in India in four separate volumes. The entries have bibliographical details in Roman script with an annotation in English language.

5. *Indian Press Index with Book Review Supplement.* April, 1968—.

It contains the bibliography of the books reviewed in newspapers indexed in the Indian Press Index.

6. *Indian Scientific and Technical Publications*; A bibliography complied by National library. Council of Scientific and Industrial Research, New Delhi.

It is a selected bibliography of scientific and technical books in English and other Indian languages published in India. The entries are arranged in a classified order in two parts. Part I. Indian languages, published work. Part II. English Books.

7. *Impex Reference Catalogue of Indian Books.* New Delhi, Indian Book Export and Import Co. 1960 —.

It is a comprehensive list of valuable books published and printed in India. The entries are arranged in two sections. Section. I - Under broad alphabetical subject groups. Section II - Under author, title, catchwords title and series.

8. *Publisher's catalogues.*

Several publishers publish the periodical catalogue of their publications. Shree Publishing Books catalogue by Ms. Shree Publishing

Delhi, Book News by Jain Book Depot, Hathras and Delhi branch by M/s D.N. Publishers monthly by M/s. Chand & Co. (Delhi), Asia Bulletin by M/s. Asia Publishing House (Bombay) monthly. Oxford University Press Catalogue by M/s Oxford University Press, New Delhi and Library Refresher by Ess Ess Publications, New Delhi.

9. *Bookseller's Catalogues*

It is published by many big or small booksellers, the books available in their stock e.g. UBS's catalogues, Indian Book House's catalogue, Shivalal Agrawal's catalogue and Bishen Singh Mahendra Pal Singh, Dehradun catalogue etc.

Selection Tools for Non-print Materials

Use of non-print information materials can be possible only if the library acquires the necessary and appropriate equipment. Selection of equipment also is as important as selecting and collection of non-print materials. There are two important factors in the selection (1) standardisation and (2) changing media field. These two factors combine to make equipment buying too hazardous to risk collection of non-print materials. However, this aspect is given the greatest attention by all concerned, nationally and internationally. Some of the tools that might help selection of equipment are listed below:

Sound Recordings : *National Sounds Archive's Directory of Recorded Sound Resources in United Kingdom.*

Video Recordings : *British National Film and Video Catalogue (BNFVC); British Universities Film and Video Council Catalogue (BuFVC Catalogue); The Video Gallery; Educational Film/Video Locator Lists; Library Video Magazine, etc.*

Videodiscs : *International Bildplatten Katalogue; The Videodisc monitor; Interactive update.*

Graphics : *Illustrations Index*

Microcomputing Software: *Directory of Hardware and Directory of Software (National Computing Centre); Personal Computer World; Educational Computing; The Computer Users Yearbook and Software Users Handbook.*

CD-ROM : *CD-ROM Directory; CIMTECH; Library and Information Briefings (from Central London Polytechnic Library and Information Technology Centre), Publishers Catalogues (Silver Platter, Multi-lingual, UMI)*

COLLECTION EVALUATION

Webstar's Seventh New Collegiate Dictionary describes evaluation as an attempt to determine either the relative or intrinsic worth of something in terms other than monetary. It is an integral part of library management and administration. Evaluation of the document collection is an essential and inevitable component of the collection development policy. Through evaluation only library can improve its quality of service.

For this purpose the library may take up a survey by its own personnel or entrust it to an outside library consultant. Such a survey can be limited or comprehensive covering or formore of the areas like: book collection, technical services, readers services, use of the library, the personal, administrative organization, co-operative activities, financial needs, obstacles to library development, operation of special services etc. "A comprehensive survey might will include all these areas. But even a limited survey may need to cover several related areas." For collection evaluation some quantitative measures like adequacy of the documents can be used but the emphasis should be on the appropriateness of the collection in terms of quality and scope of the materials acquired. The faculty and research scholars and even students may be helpful for measuring quality and appropriateness of the documents produced.

Standard bibliographics - both general and specific subject bibliographies; checklists of selected reference books and periodicals can be used as guides.

Questionnaire surveys eliciting opinion from the faculty to find out the adequacy of the collection for their class lecture preparation; individual research needs and student guidance can be conducted. Similarly, research scholars evaluation of the usefulness of the stock can be ascertained through surveys.

Another way of knowing about the collection is by going through borrowers records; books borrowed on inter library loan; and records relating to the requests made by the library users for books which are not available in the library.

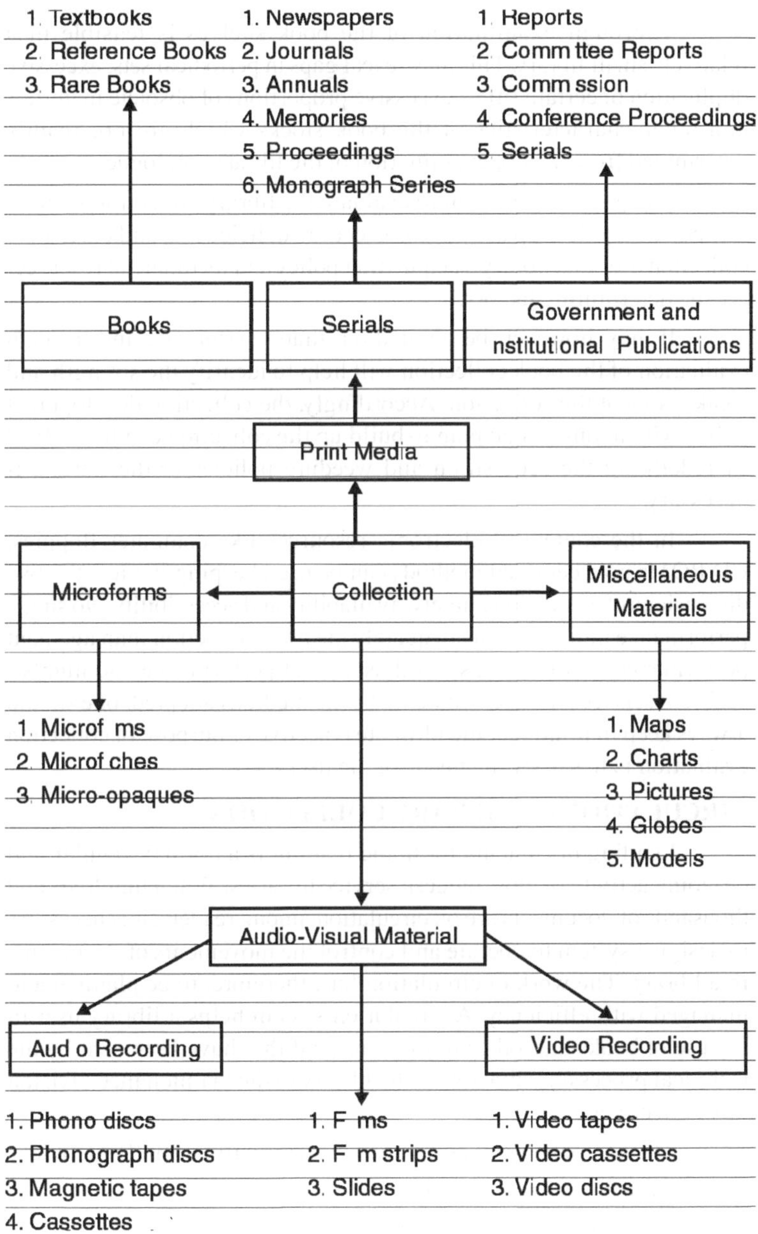

Collection Evaluation

Thorough examination of the book shelves is feasible in a relatively small library. This may reveal gaps in periodical sets, excessive duplication of certain titles, excessive proportions of obsolete materials and other characteristics of the book stocks which are not readily determined from a mere examination of the library catalogue.

It is just not sufficient to evaluate the library collection without any positive follow up action to correct the deficiencies and enrich the collection. For this library's acquisition policy and its financial resources are the determining factors.

It may, however, be pointed out that a systematic and through evaluation of the book collection will help to identify the strength and weaknesses of the collection. Accordingly, the collection development policy with a long-range plan to build up the collection can be evolved by redefining the acquisition and weeding policies of the library, if necessary.

In the context of electronic resources like computer floppies, CD ROMs user centered methods can be used keeping in view the two dimensions of evaluation namely, availability and accessibility. No single performance indicator can adequately measure collection man agement performance, as there are several aspects of performance and number different services. Hence, whatever be the methods adopted, one should always keep in mind that the ultimate objective or purpose of collection evaluation is to satisfy the needs of the users.

CIRCULATION OF LIBRARY COLLECTION

Lending documents for home reading is a normal, regular and on-going activity of most modern service libraries. When hundreds and thousands of documents are on circulation among readers, it is necessary to design a system to operate and control the movements of documents in a library. The work of circulation has, therefore, to be planned and managed with efficiency. A circulation system helps a library user in the use of books and other library material that have been sent by the technical processing division of the library to the maintenance division most effectively.

The components of circulation systems will normally include :

* a file of registered borrowers,
* a record of all loan transactions,
* a system of charging and discharging,

* a renewal mechanism for extending due dates for return of books, and
* reservation of books already on loan for members who need them.

In addition to these, the circulation division may be required to take responsibility for the shelving of materials, recording and maintenance of circulation statistics and protecting the collection to ensure its fullest long-term use. It also helps to remove any obstacles between the individual user and the library material.

The charging system which presently exists in libraries, has evolved over a period of time. From a simple register system of recording loan transactions, circulation systems have now evolved into sophisticated computer - based system. These can be broadly grouped as under :

(i) Register systems
(ii) Card systems
(iii) Semi-mechanical systems
(iv) Automated systems

Register Systems

The earliest method of charging books for home use was a relatively simple one of writing the author, title and borrower's name in a 'Day book'. A 'Day book' was a register that recorded all daily transactions sequentially in a register. Later, this method was superseded by the 'Ledger system' with separate pages for each registered borrower. Each borrower's transactions were recorded, in his/her respective page. This avoided the tedium of searching through the 'Day book' for a single entry. The 'ledger system' remained in use until the middle of the nineteenth century.

The disadvantage of both the 'Day Book' and 'Ledger' systems was the absence of a mechanism to locate the whereabouts of the books, A solution to this shortcoming was found in the 'Dummy System'. In this system a block of wood or cardboard about the size of an ordinary book was covered with sheet of ruled paper on the back of which was entered the number of the borrower, call number, title of the book and date of issue. The wooden dummy was filed on the shelf in place of the book that was withdrawn. This method eliminated the need for going through lists of names and titles to find a specific book. This method made possible, for the first time, to identify of both the borrower and the book charged out.

The next step forward was the development of the 'Temporary Slip System'. In this system, a slip is prepared at the time of issue of a book, with the particulars of the book such as the call number, author title, and the particulars of the borrower, i.e., name registration number, address, etc., and the date of issue. These slips were arranged at the counter either datewise, or by alphabetically in the name of the borrowers or the registration numbers of borrowers. These slips were either destroyed or given back to the reader as a receipt upon the return of the books. The main advantage of this system over the 'Dummy system' was that it kept the circulation record together at the circulation counter instead of scattering throughout the shelves. These temporary slips were later replaced by a permanent slip or a card for each book.

Card Systems

With the increase in the number of readers using libraries, it became necessary to devise some method of identifying both the book and the borrower. Thus the two card system, one card for the book and one for the borrower came into existence. First, identification cards were used, which were later substituted by borrower's card on which all book transactions were entered.

Semi-Mechanical Systems

The next stage saw the replacement of human labour by machines when mechanical charging systems were developed, essentially most subsequent systems, involved the use of cards with prepunched holes around the edges, one of which could be cut to indicate the date on which an item is due. The cards are arranged by call number in a single sequence. The insertion of a knitting needle through a given hole will allow all the books overdue for a given date to fall free of the bunch of punched cards. This system is characterised by inventory and date access but placed a greater burden on the borrower. A borrower had to write the borrower's name and address and the call number, author and title of a book borrowed.

The next system to be developed was the photocharge system. In this system microphotos were taken of the borrower's card, the book card and a sequentially numbered date of issue or date due slip. This due date slip contained all the necessary information about the book as well as the borrower. Nevertheless this also had many drawbacks as the availability entire information on loan transactions was limited to a roll microfilm which introduced major operations difficulties.

Automated Circulation System

For several decades now, ingenious librarians and library equipment manufacturers in western countries have designed circulation systems using the latest technology. The advent of the computer in the 1960s and microcomputers in the 70s and 80s radically altered ground rules. Now all sequences of encoded elements are possible and information on any management data can be derived. Important statistical data pertaining to collection use and library users can be obtained by manipulating the data accumulated in the circulation process. However library automation extends beyond circulation functions into the more integrated systems of cataloguing, acquisitions, decision support systems and virtually all other library operations. Advantages of speed, the ability to manage large amounts of data, and the long term trends of increasing computer power and decreasing cost have attracted libraries to automated circulation. In the developed countries of the world, it is now possible for all but the smallest libraries to have access to and control their material through the current range of computers. The situation in India may not be as promising; however a slow process of change is taking place in at least the libraries towards computerisation. The computers were expected to enter other types of libraries too by the next decade or so. An increasing number of university and college libraries already are to be moving towards automated circulation systems. The libraries are switching over to automation. There are available various libraries softwares through which automated circulation can be adopted. Namely few are Libsys, Troodon 3.0, and Libman etc.

CIRCULATION FUNCTIONS

* User registration,
* Charging and discharging,
* Control processes like renewals, recalls, holds, overdues and notifications,
* Additional lending operations like inter-library loan,
* Maintenance of records and statistics,
* Clearance,

* Miscellaneous functions like gate register, property counter, vigilance at entrance and exit gates, etc.

User Registration

An obvious first step in any circulation system is to register the users or borrowers. This is a time consuming and somewhat expensive procedure but mandatory for several reasons. This procedure establishes the potential borrower as a legitimate member of the library. Registration identifies the borrower as a member of the community in the case of public libraries or as an enrolled student or faculty staff member in a typical academic environment. This identification is necessary for the accomplishment of the controlling processes like holds, recalls, fines, etc. Apart from this, it also serves as a useful point for informing the clientele of the library policy and procedures. It is one of the initial contact points with the user community. Another important purpose of registration, particularly in the case of public libraries, is that it provides an accurate statistical description of the user population.

Registration Procedure: The registration procedure is fairly well standardised. The borrower to be, is given an application form to fill, which may preferably be in a card form, so that the same is alphabetically filed to serve as an alphabetical registration record. The information usually requested is the name, address, telephone number, occupation, business address and telephone number. If it is a public library, the occupation, name, address and telephone number of a referee or a guarantor is sought. The signature of the applicant and the guarantor is also insisted upon.

College and university libraries grant borrowing privileges to all faculty, staff and registered students. The method of student identification differs among institutions. The student may be asked to show his identification card issued at the time of entry into the current academic session. Another alternative is to require the borrower to show his admission receipt. The third alternative requires the student to get the head of his institution or Department to countersign his application and in case of faculty or administrative staff a copy of the appointment letter. It is important to establish the bonafides of the student or faculty. Registration enables the user to make use of the privileges of the library. The form of registration is directly influenced by the type of circulation system. The borrowing privileges of members are also indicated in the borrowers' register. Borrowing privileges refer to the types of documents that can be borrowed, the length of retention, recall right of the library, etc.

Charging and Discharging Functions

As we know, circulation is an activity whereby library materials are lent to borrowers and records of such loan transactions are kept in an orderly way. It is noted that this is an important basic activity of a service library. It is this service that brings users into direct contact with the operating system of the library. Librarians have, therefore, spared no efforts in designing and developing efficient and economical charging systems to give borrowers excellent service. Not only it is necessary to provide efficient service to borrowers, but it is also crucial to maintain a reliable record of loan transactions to know where a book is at any given point of time. This is essential in all types of libraries but more so in academic libraries where certain titles are in constant demand.

An ideal charging system, should therefore have the following capabilities. It should be able to:

* identify the books that are charged, i.e., be able to ascertain whether a book is in the library or out;
* identify the borrower of a particular book;
* identify when a book is due back in the library;
* measure the extent of use of books, i.e., provide a permanent record of the number of times a certain book has been circulated;
* indicate the extent to which a reader is making use of the library's borrowing facility, i.e., indicate the number and type of book a user has borrowed, etc.; and
* indicate the number of books circulated per day and also other subject-wise circulation statistics.

There are three categories of records on which circulation control is based. These include:

* items of documents that are on loan;
* borrower's list with all details including books borrowed;
* time record linking the above two records.

The quality of operational competence is evaluated with reference to:

* speed, i.e., the issuing and returning of books should be earned out with speed without sacrificing efficiency;

* economy, i.e., the system should economise on staff, time, money, materials, plant and stationery;
* its being foolproof, i.e., versatile in terms of identifying the whereabouts of a book;
* the smooth flow of traffic, i.e., no congestion at the counter at any time;
* a minimum backlog, i.e., all the filing should be done on the same day; and
* a minimum need for preparatory work.

A minimal circulation model is a set of procedures of record keeping with respect to only their category, i.e., records of the materials held by a borrower. A total or complete system is one that provides for all three categories of records. The earliest system, the 'day book' met the minimal circulation requirements of recording the transactions. The 'ledger' system was an improvement in that was a more orderly control of charges as opposed to the former. However this also did not provide for identifying the books borrowed. It was the 'dummy' system which provided for complete inventory control. Most of the later systems like Browne, Newark have incorporated features which meet most of the requirements directly but the rest only indirect. It is only the computer based system that can meet all requirements.

Controlling Processes

The controlling processes further regulate the circulation of library materials. These function include:

* renewals
* reserves
* recalls
* fines or overdue charges
* notifications.

(i) **Renewals:** Renewals represent an extension of the loan period by recharging the same item to the same borrower. Some books are required by readers for a longer period for various reasons. Books may be renewed if there is no demand for the same book, as indicated by the reserves record. Books may be renewed by presenting the book in person or by telephone depending on the library policy. However renewal is allowed on condition that the book will be returned immediately if recalled.

(ii) **Reserves:** The reserve procedure is also known as hold procedure. In this, library materials already on loan are identified and held or reserved upon request for other patrons, A record is then made at the circulation desk that serves to identify the user making the request and the book in question. The next step occurs upon the return of the book. When the book in question is returned the charge record indicates that the book is now 'on hold' for another user. Such 'On hold' books are separated and a notification to the requesting patron is sent to the user who made the request.

In academic libraries, textbooks and other related materials are in great demand by the students. Due to paucity of funds or non-availability of the item, college and university libraries are not in a position to acquire multiple copies to satisfy the demand for use same books by several students. With fixed book funds, a balance has to be struck between multiple copies and ensuring equitable access to certain titles for all users for home use. Information regarding 'holds' for specific titles can also be used as an effective selection tool for 'multiple copies'.

(iii) **Recalls:** Another important controlling activity concerns circulation is recalls. This is the activity of calling books back into the library so that they can be lent to the other person is known as recall. Thus, a request for a hold or reserve initiates a recall of a book on first loan or already renewed.

(iv) **Reminders:** Sending regular reminders for overdue books is one of the most important jobs of counter staff. Readers may not return books in time either for selfish reasons on due to forgetfulness. The library's inability to locate the book promptly and ensure availability may also prompt the readers to retain the books with them for a long time. To avoid such monopoly of books by a few persons and to give every reader a fail chance to use these books, reminders should be sent at regular intervals. A record of the overdue books, the concerned readers' name and address must be made regularly. Printed reminder forms may also be used.

(v) **Fines / Overdue Charges:** It is a general practice in libraries to collect overdue charges fines for books returned after the due date. The policy of fines/over dues is primarily measure of control for the proper use of books. The policy of over dues is mainly to dissuade the practice of cornering certain books in demand. This also results helps to enforce discipline. The fines activity is also closely related to the charge and discharge activities. The amount of fine and the ways of cumulating fines varies and depends on the library's policy. Fines are normally cumulative upto a certain amount per book and then stay at that maximum amount.

The procedure of collecting overdue charges is either by issuing regular receipts or by keeping a conscience box for this purpose. The procedure depends on the library policy. Considering the cost and time involved in issuing receipts some libraries prefer the conscience box method. A conscience box is a method by which the defaulter puts the amount of overdue charge in a locked box with a slit on top. The total collection for the day is taken out and entered in the cash book of the library.

All these control activities of recall, fines, etc., can be more complicated, if multiple copies, multiple branches, multiple patrons, varied loan periods for different patron types, media types are involved. All these activities are dependent upon the library's ability to send notices to users. The proper functioning of the notification process largely depends on accurately maintained user registration files, clearly defined policies of loan periods and fines and finally the response of the user to the notice itself.

As for as the Charging and discharging systems are concerned, the f ollowing two system are in vogue.

Browne Charging System

The Browne Charging System was devised by Nina E. Browne who was librarian of the Library Bureau in Boston and served as the secretary of the Publishing Board of the American Library Association.

Even though the system originated in the United States, it is not much in use in the country of its origin, but it has become quite popular in India.

(i) Equipment and material used: The special equipment and stationary material required to operate the system are the following:

(a) Registration cards of all borrowers arranged alphabetically.

(b) Borrower's tickets or pockets. Each borrower is given as many tickets/pockets of manila or rough paper as he is entitled. This ticket is in the shape of a pocket of 3" × 2" size with openings on two sides. This ticket bears the names and address of the borrower, the date of expiry of membership. In many libraries a code number is devised and written/typed on the top of the card to represent category/ subject of interest and date of validity of the membership. It also bears the signature and stamp of the librarian and the signature of the borrower on it.

(c) Book cards of size 4" × 2" bearing the call number; accession number, author and title of the book.

(d) Book pockets of size 5" × 3" which are pasted on the inside back/front cover of the book. The book cards are kept in these pockets when they are not in circulation.

(e) Date slip on which the date due or date of issue are stamped, to be pasted on the back or front flyleaf of the book.

(f) Date stamp and ink pad

(g) Date guide cards

(h) Charging trays

(i) Circulation statistical sheets

(j) Reminder cards, reservation cards, overdue fine slips, etc.

(ii) Charging Routine: Charging is the issue of books that are presented at the circulation counter to borrowers. This routine involves the following steps:

(a) The book to be borrowed and the borrower's ticket are presented by the user to the assistant at the circulation desk counter.

(b) The counter assistant after the identification of the reader either by familiarity through the identification card/ membership card, takes the book card out of book pocket and slips it into the borrower's ticket/pocket.

(c) The due date is stamped on the due date slip pasted on the back or from the fly leaf of the book and the charged book is handed over to the patron.

(d) The book card coupled with the reader's pocket is filed in the charging tray behind the respective due date card by call number.

(e) The call number and the borrower number are recorded in the daily circulation statistics sheet.

(iii) Discharging Routine: Discharging is the work of securing books borrowed and reaction the borrower's tickets. This routine involves the following:

(a) When the book is presented at the counter for return, the due date/issue date is ascertained from the due date slip.

(b) The book card coupled with the reader's ticket is picked up from behind the appropriate date guide card from the charging tray.

(c) The due date/issue date is cancelled on the due date slip and the reader's ticket is returned to the reader.

(d) The book card inserted into the book pocket and the book is thus discharged and the reader is absolved of his responsibility.

(e) If the book is returned after the due date, due overdue amount is computed and an overdue charge slip is given. The reader's ticket is returned only after the receipt for the overdue charge is presented.

(iv) Reserves : Reserves constitute a facility of a circulation system by which a reader can reserve a book that is out on loan. This facility is built into a charging system. The routine involved is explained below:

If there is a request for reservation of a book in circulation, the reserve ticket is filled up by the reader and the reserve ticket containing the details of the book and the reader is inserted into the reader's pocket in the charging tray. When that book 'on hold' is returned the reserve card along with the book card will be slipped into the book pocket and the book will be kept in a special sequence and intimation will be sent to the reader who has reserved the book.

(v) Advantages:

(a) Being simple the procedure results in economy of time and efforts. It is estimated that at least 300 books can be issued per hour.

(b) The issue of reminders and calculation of fines/overdues is simplified.

(c) The statistics of issue can be prepared easily.

(d) Reserves and Recalls can be carried out promptly.

(e) No signatures are required at the time of issue or return,

(vi) Disadvantages

(a) No permanent record of issue is available.

(b) It is difficult to ascertain the number of books issued to a person as the borrower's tickets are scattered.

(c) In case of loss of tickets, misuse is possible as the signature of the reader is not necessary.

(d) Caution and vigilance are necessary while inserting book cards into the readers' pockets as there is only one record of issue. Otherwise book cards and readers pockets may be mismatched.

In spite of these limitations this system is very popular in Commonwealth countries including India because of the simplicity of the procedure. This system saves the time of the staff and reader to a great extent. To overcome some of its limitations many modifications are incorporated into the system in many libraries in India.

CALL NO.		ACC. NO.
NAME OF THE LIBRARY		
The following books were issued/are due in the library on below mentioned dates		
Date of Issue/ Due date	**Date of Issue/ Due date**	**Date of Issue/ Due date**

Size: 12.7cms × 7.6 cms

Date slip

Brief Library Rules And Instruction

Size 12.7cms × 7.6 cms

Book Pocket

CALL No.	ACC. No.
Author : ____________	
TITLE: ____________	

Size: 10.25 cms × 5 cms

Book Card

NAME ADDRESS DATE OF EXPIRY	
	SIGNATURE OF THE BORROWER

Borrower's tickets

Newark Charging System

This system was developed by John Cottan Dana and was firstly introduced in the Public Library of Newark of New Jersy State. It is similar to Browne System but some modifications were incorporated in this system.

(i) Equipment and materials used

(ii) Charging routine

(iii) Discharging routine

(iv) Reserves

(v) Advantages of the system

(vi) Disadvantages of the system

(i) **Equipment and materials used:** It requires following equipment and materials. They are as follows :

(a) Registration files of all borrowers, which are composed in an alphabetical file of the application blanks of registered borrowers and also a numerical file of numbers assigned to each borrower usually tipped on sheets in a loose-leaf notebook or the form of a register.

(b) Borrower's cards bearing the name, address and registration number of each register borrower with space for recording transactions.

(c) Borrower's cards bearing the call number, author and short title of the book.

(d) Date slips which are pasted on the back or front flyleaf of the book.

(e) Book pockets giving the call number, author and short title of the book.

(f) Pencil, dater, date stamp and ink pad.

(g) Date guide cards for filing the day's circulation.

(h) Fine record slips.

(i) Circulation statistical sheets.

(J) Overdue reminder cards, reserve cards, etc.

(ii) **Charging routines:** Charging routines are a little more elaborate and time consuming in this system than in the Browne Charging System. The steps involved in charging are follows:

(a) Borrower's Cards are presented by the user to the assistant at the circulation counter.

(b) The due date or date of issue, whichever is used, is stamped on the date slip in the book by the assistant.

(c) Similarly the due date is stamped on the book card taken out of the book pocket and the borrower's card.

(d) The borrower's number is written opposite the date in the book card and filed behind the concerned date guide card.

(e) The borrower's card and the book are returned to the patron. Thus, the book is duly charged.

(iii) **Discharging routines:** The steps involved in discharging routines are:

(a) When the book is presented for return along with the membership card, date of return is stamped on the borrower's card, thus cancelling the charge for the book. The borrower's card is returned to the patron.

(b) The book card is located in the circulation file from the date on the date slip and placed in the book pocket.

(c) If the book is returned after the due date, the fine is computed and collected. The date of return is stamped only after the fine is paid.

(iv) Reserves: Reservation procedure in this system is similar to the Browne Charging system. The reserve ticket filled in by reader is attached to the borrower's card in the charging tray. When the particular book 'on hold' is returned, the reserve card along with the book card is pinned with the borrower's card and the book is kept in a special sequence and Intimation is then sent to the reader who has reserved the book.

(v) Advantages

(a) There is a permanent record of the number and type of books circulated and the kind of books borrowed by each reader.

(b) It is possible to know at all times, where a given book is, to whom it is charged, and when it is due.

(c) The record of the number of times a book has been circulated is available even when the book is not in the library.

(d) Since the transaction is recorded both on the borrowers' card as well as on the book cards the danger of dislocation is minimal. If the borrowers' cards are lost, the record on the book cards is available and vice-versa.

(e) Several assistants can carry on the routines simultaneously.

(f) The borrowers can be allowed to borrow books from any branch library of a larger library system, provided there is a central registration file at the main library where an alphabetically arranged copy of all branch registrations is available.

(vi) Disadvantages

(a) Routines are slow, and cumbersome. The procedure of

writing/stamping of the date of issue/due date and the borrower's membership number on the book cards and writing/stamping of issue/due date on the borrower's cards are time-consuming.

(b) There are chances of inaccuracies creeping in, especially when transcribing borrowers' card numbers. This is particularly true during rush hours.

(c) Two registration files are necessary: an alphabetical file by borrower's name and addresses and a file of registration numbers assigned to each borrower.

On the whole, the Newark System is considered to be foolproof and safe. This advantage may not always be available.

CALLNO: ACC NO: NAME OF THE LIBRARY This Book was issued/ due on the date last stamped or marked

Size 5" × 3"

Date Slip

OPEN FLAP
NAME OF THE LIBRARY BRIEF LIBRARY RULES 1 2 3 4

Size: 5" × 3"

Book Pocket

NAME OF THE LIBRARY
CALL NO:
ACC. NO:
AUTHOR :
TITLE:
This Book was issued/is due on the date last stamped or marked.

Size: 4" × 2"

Book Card

NAME OF THE LIBRARY			
Borrower's No: ______________________________			
Date of Expiry : ______________________________			
NON-TRANSFERABLE			
The following books were issued to me.			
Signature			
Due date/ Date of Issue	Date of Return	Due date/ Date of Issue	Date of Return

Borrowers' Card

Inter-Library Loan

It is neither desirable nor feasible for a library to be totally self-sufficient. They need to depend on other cooperating libraries in the city or region, to obtain books and other library materials required by the patrons. The resource sharing networks and programmes of libraries facilitate activities like borrowing material not available in a specific library from other participating libraries. Such loans between libraries is known as an inter-library loan. The inter-library loan is perhaps the oldest form of cooperation among libraries.

Inter-library loan operations can be divided into two: those relating to borrowing and those relating to lending. Both these activities are a more complicated variation of the general circulation functions.

When a reader makes a request for an item not in the library, efforts are made to identify other libraries which may be having that particular item in their collection. This procedure is simplified if proper tools like union lists and union catalogues are, available. Once the libraries are identified, depending on the policy and procedure of interlibrary loan arrangement a request is sent to a library owning the material through a standard form or letter. After the receipt of the requested book, the user is notified of its arrival and the item is charged on to him. In many libraries books acquired in a library on inter-library loan are not allowed to be taken out of the borrowing library to ensure its prompt return oh requisition by the lending library as also to safeguard against possible damage due to negligence. Once the user return the book at the end of the loan period, it is in turn sent back to the owning library. The lending activities for the inter-library loan are initiated upon receipt of a requested be from a borrowing library. Then the availability is checked using the library catalogue and other bibliographical tools. Once the item is located, it is sent to the requesting library. A record of these inter-library loan transactions are usually maintained separately the form of a register.

Records and Statistics

The maintenance of records in the circulation department is very important because these records form the basis of collecting statistics on documents taken on loan, the types of users and what they have been borrowing, how often a particular title has been borrowed, defaulters, etc. These statistics are invaluable in providing useful indicators to the library to plan its acquisition policy, nature of services, the range and type of users, etc. Such analysis go into the annual reports of the library. Various registers like 'patron register' 'interlibrary loan register', 'overdues and fine register', 'suggestions register' 'gate register' are maintained by the circulation department.

Clearance

When a reader leaves the institute or withdraws his membership from the library, he has to obtain no-dues or clearance certificate from the library. The issue counter after checking the record of a reader that no book or document is pending against particular reader, issue clearance to the reader.

Miscellaneous Jobs

As the circulation counter is usually located close to the entrance/ exit gate, the circulation department is entrusted with the task of maintaining of the gate register and the property counter.

(i) Gate register : A record of the daily visitors and their purpose of visit to the library in maintained in the form of a gate register. Each visitor is the library is asked to enter the details of personal information in the specified columns of the gate register which is kept at the entrance of the library. This is a useful record to know the visitors. Analysis of the gate register may throw light on the patrons of the library. However it has limited value in university and college libraries where the users are a defined group who remain the same daily and visits the library many a times in a day.

(ii) Property counter : As users are not allowed to bring books, other materials and their belongings inside the library a 'property counter' is usually installed near the entrance. In small and special libraries the property counter staff can also do the vigilance job which is necessary to eliminate the unsocial habit of some members walking away with books of the library.

PLANNING AND MANAGEMENT OF CIRCULATION

One of the most important aspects of any library service to its users is the circulation process. Planning is essential in this area to insure quick, efficient, and convenient procedures. The organisation of a circulation department depends on the size library, scope of its work and the degree of departmentalization. However, the circulation department should be well organised in order to provide quick and efficient service to advance the instruction and research programmes. Since the contact made at the circulation desk is the only one for many readers, the circulation process becomes an important public relation factor for the library. The library management must be concerned with the development of an efficient circulation system.

Factors in Planning

In planning the circulation process, there are following factors that the management must consider.

(i) **Multiplicity of materials:** It is necessary to provide for a multiplicity of materials like conventional books, periodicals, media, etc., as well as the special equipment needed to utilize these materials. The process must be planned to handle the size of the collection, daily volume expected and types of material circulating. The larger the collection and volume of circulation, the larger and more involved the circulation process.

(ii) **Multiplicity of users:** A public library, for example, caters to a more heterogeneous group of users, while a special library would have a more homogeneous group with an identifiable nature of interests. As it is possible to have more control and access to patrons in a special library, the circulation process can be much simpler.

(iii) **Degree of service:** It is an additional factor that needs careful consideration while planning. Are all materials to be circulated? Should specialised materials like cassettes, films be circulated? If so, is the equipment to be made available to the patron for home use? Limited circulation of some items is necessary for a variety of reasons. The length of time for which materials may be charged out or to whom is another matter to be considered. In academic libraries, for example, specialised materials like non-print materials and reference materials, are loaned to faculty staff only. Books under categories such as manuscripts, personal papers of eminent scholars, standard reference books are normally not loaned even to faculty. Usually a varying loan period relevant to the format of material and the type of patron is followed in many libraries. Certain materials may be available only to faculty for overnight borrowing only.

The old problem of overdues and fines is another area which needs to be clearly spelt out. Professional literature is full of pros and cons relating to this problem. To fine or not to fine for overdues is a controversial issue. Circulation regulations usually describe the parameters which apply to circulation. Many libraries have limits on the number of items and the length of time the materials may be kept. Other considerations include whether materials may be renewed and if so, whether renewals may be made by telephones; whether books on loan may be reserved etc. All these questions need to be carefully considered before arriving at a decision. The goals and specific objectives of the library must be considered as the basis for any decisions reached.

(iv) The choice of charging system is a very important factor that needs to be considered while planning a circulation process.

(v) The provision of personnel is another factor that management must consider. The circulation process can be operated quite adequately be semi-professionals, clerical personnel and others. Professional involvement is generally restricted to determination of basic policies and procedures and general supervision. Once the basic process including policies has been established a "semi professional" or clerk can handle the day-to-day supervision.

Many modern management techniques like cost benefit analysis, system study are made use of in evaluating circulation systems. These methods identify the relative costs of systems and attempt to balance these costs against the relative advantages of each choice. Capital equipment labour and material are weighed against such benefits as patron satisfaction, operational efficiency and economy, and statistical information.

10
Maintenance, Preservation and Stock Verification

The ultimate success of various functions in a library like acquisition, classification and cataloguing rests on the efficiency of maintenance work. No matter how well a collection is classified or catalogued, books cannot be serviceable to users unless proper care is taken to organise and maintain the book collection. It is one of those less glamorous, nonetheless, very important tasks in a library. Maintenance work involves continuous monitoring of the proper stocking, arrangement and display of books on the shelves in the stack rooms and taking care of them. This essentially implies two aspects:

(i) Organisation of the stack room and arrangements of books on the shelves.

(ii) Conservation of books i.e. overseeing and supervising the physical conditions of books, overall cleanliness of the stack areas, etc.

(i) Organisation

In an open access library which allows users to browse, choose and select books of their interest, shelf organisation and arrangement of books are of primary importance. Books on different subjects that are constantly on demand are to be easily accessible to readers. This means that the professional classification schedules arc rarely in tune with the layman's expectations of sequence of books on shelves. In a public library books of fiction, travelogues, biography may be more popular from the readers point of view than the more serious books on literature, sciences and social sciences. A classification scheme does not provide the sequence of subjects of books on their its popularity.

Besides, reference books like encyclopaedias, dictionaries, year books, directories, etc. should be kept in a separate place for easy reach and uninterrupted use by readers.

Recent arrivals and books on current interest must be displayed at a prominent place to attract the attention of readers.

Other books must be stacked according to their popular use with reference to the subjects.

(ii) Conservation

The second aspect of maintenance work is book conservation. Those books which are in good physical condition should be allowed to stay on shelves. Constant shelf checking would remove torn, solled and damaged books from shelves for repair, rebinding or to be withdrawn from circulation. This is a healthy practice and should never be underestimated. The stacks must be cleaned regularly to protect books from dust, dirt and insects. Airconditioning of stack rooms would be ideal to protect books from dust, heat and moisture.

All these efforts are to aid the fundamental task of locating a book when it is wanted and returning to its assigned place when it is no longer needed; maintaining the order of books and taking care of the books that they are wanted again.

All these tasks are usually entrusted to a maintenance section/ division in addition to the other functions.

Responsibility Areas of Maintenance Section

The main areas of responsibility of the maintenance section or division are:

- Taking responsibilities regarding (a) the method of stacking and type of storage equipment; (b) the arrangement of the collection, including special arrangement for category of materials — oversized books, non-book materials, etc., (c) the effective and efficient use of the architectural features of the building for stacking books.
- Maintaining orderliness and cleanliness in the stackrooms;
- Training and supervising the work of the maintenance section/ division staff;

– Decisions regarding the conservation of material, repair, binding, etc.;
– Maintenance of records pertaining to stock control.

Functions of Maintenance Section

The specific functions of the maintenance work include:

* shelving
* location of documents
* shifting of collections
* dusting and cleaning
* preparation and maintenance of guides
* maintenance of documents
* shelf rectification
* maintenance of shelf list or register
* stock verification
* binding
* vigilance and
* conservation

Management of Maintenance Work

Like all other work in the library, the magnitude of maintenance work depends on the size and complexity of the library and the quantum of operations. Decision regarding whether to have a separate maintenance section or not depends mainly on the intensity of operations. In small or medium sized libraries maintenance may be under the circulation section. Apart from the size, another contributory factor is whether the library is open access or closed access. In a closed access library, shelving work is relatively less, while paging work is more, which involves the job of locating the requisitioned book on the shelf and bringing it from the shelf and giving it to the reader. This work of paging is an integral part of the circulation function of a closed access library.

In open access, users quite often remove books from the shelves for browsing or consultations and they are not, as a rule, allowed to replace the books on the shelves as they are not likely to know the exact position. This task is invariably taken care of by the library staff. In an actively used library, this work may keep the staff continuously busy throughout the day, making shelving a major function.

It is a common practice to have a separate maintenance section/ division with one or more assistant librarians in large libraries like university libraries. The number of junior staff needed for shelf work depends upon the size of the collection and the number of books circulated and the number of users. In larger libraries, having multistoried stacks, at least one shelf worker should be provided for each wing of the stacks.

STACKING PRINCIPLES

Ranganathan's Laws of Library Science give clear guidelines to the ways of organising stack rooms and the arrangement of books on shelves. Use of documents, rather than preservation being the main concern of libraries leading to the introduction of open access system, increasing attention has been given to library architecture and buildings with specially designed stack room, specifically designed furniture for improving stacking facility and display, etc. All these have contributed to improved facilities for the user of books.

Apart from these facilities, there are also some useful guiding principles regarding stacking of documents in libraries. They are:

* Ensuring maximum capacity with minimum wastage of space;
* Facilities for accommodating books and also other book-like and non-book materials;
* Easy accessibility to books and also other related areas like Library catalogue, Circulation desk, etc;
* Proper ventilation for adequate flow of fresh and dust-free air, along with temperature and humidity control;
* Adequate artificial lighting; and
* Provision for future expansion.

STACKING SYSTEMS

The main consideration in stacking is to achieve economy of space while ensuring ease of accessibility for the readers to the contents of the shelves. Space is at a premium in almost all libraries and the problem of space is faced by libraries with a large and growing collection. This problem can be solved using different methods of stacking.

(i) Double Rows on Fixed Shelves : In this method, books are arranged in double rows on normal fixed shelves. While this increases capacity, it hinders access to the rear row. A modification of this is to use two separate shelves for 'two layers' with the facility to swing one layer to the side to have access to the rear row.

(ii) Hinged Stacks : In this method two shelves are joined together with hinges at one side. One shelf is fixed, while the other is mounted in front of it at the hinges. In this system, the whole shelf can be opened as a door to reach the books on the rear shelf. In order to facilitate the operation of the hinged shelf a roller is attached to the bottom edge, running on a curved metal rack on the floor.

(iii) Rolling Stacks : These are metal stack units mounted on ball bearing wheels which are placed side by side. The ball bearing wheels help the individual units to roll easily when they are pulled aside.

(iv) Multitier Stacks : The multier stacks consist of wooden stacks, supported by metal framework extending from basement to the roof. The load of books and shelves rests on the basement which has a strong foundation to bear the load. The vertical extension of stacks is economical than the horizontal one. In this method, as the floor on each stack is a temporary one, which may be either a wooden framework or a lighter steel or concrete framework. This type of multitier stacks is used in many libraries in India.

(v) Compact Storage : Compact shelves are a special type of storage equipment which makes possible a substantial increase in the capacity of storage space through various arrangements of units, sections and complete shelving systems, as well as adaptation of the shelf loading surface themselves. The construction, organisation, and the method of employment of this equipment differ from the traditional shelves and traditional storage equipment.

The storage of collections shelved with this equipment is known as 'Compact Storage' because of the higher degree of compactness achieved. Compact shelving falls into the following types:

(a) Stationary shelves combined with movable revolving segments,

(b) Stationary shelves with movable drawers, and

(c) Movable sliding shelves.

All revolving compact shelves use a suspended construction with vertically hung hinged sections of various types usually combined with a guide rail arrangement. It could be either double faced or single faced. The essential principle of compact shelving results in firmly packed collections as against more dispersed fashion of shelving. While traditional shelves use up only 30 per cent of the floor space, the different methods of compact shelving are said to increase the capacity of the stacks having the same area from 50 to 65 per cent.

However, compact storage in addition to decreasing the accessibility, it has disadvantages too. They are: 'Cost of the shelving equipment' — as the cost of fixtures themselves are reasonable; 'increase in building costs' — for most of these equipment requires buildings designed' specifically for their use; mechanical functioning and safety features. But Librarians have to be judicious in the matter and ensure that compact storage has sufficient advantages to offset its obvious disadvantages.

(vi) Conventional Shelving : In this selving, the books are kept on open shelves which are usually arranged in parallel rows with passages from 75 to 80 cm in width between the rows. The normal height of the shelves is 190 to 205 cm which permits taking books from the uppei most shelf. Single faced shelves are placed along the walls. Within the rooms themselves, between the aisles, the shelves are double-faced. Single faced sections have six or seven one metre shelves. While double faced sections have twelve to fourteen one metre shelves. Under these circumstances, taking into account all aisles and gangways and approaches only about 30 per cent of the floor space's is actually used for shelves themselves. The conventional shelving system is high on accessibility, but quite low on economy.

The degree of usage of different parts of the stacks of a library must become the basis for selecting the most rational arrangement of shelves. For collections which are in active use or those that are open to free use by readers, the conventional shelving is considered to be more suitable.

For collections that are rarely requested or used, a more compact arrangement of shelves must be undertaken - with a view to increase considerable to the capacity of the area of the stacks in which they are stored. A recent trend is to combine stacking of reading materials with provision for reading space.

(vii) Storing, Shelving and Arrangement of Current issues of Periodicals and Non-Book Materials : Most libraries have periodical collections, the current issues having to be display for reading. Back numbers of them for a year stored along with current issues. Special display racks are available for this kind of storage and display.

Special storage facilities are also required for storing Audio-visual materials, microfilms of newspapers, CD-ROMs, etc. which are acquired by university, research and other types of large libraries.

The problem here are their preservation and storing for case of retrieval. They cannot be browsed and hence their shelving and storage need special attention. Depending on the size of these collections, storage and arrangements aspects of these materials have to be considered. Special storage shelves are available which have to be throughtfully acquired, satisfying all functional ans service aspects.

ARRANGEMENT OF LIBRARY MATERIALS

The collection of a library is first broken into sequences irrespective of the category to which a library belongs. Depending upon the size of a library collection may be arranged only under two sequences-books and periodicals or more than two sequences. Once the material has been grouped by sequence the question of arrangement on shelf comes up.

The arrangement of library materials will include:

(1) Sequence Arrangement

(2) Shelf Arrangement

(1) Sequence Arrangement

The distribution of library materials in the library in sequence arrangement may be based on any one or more of the following features.

(i) Access Consideration: The library may divide its collection into open access and closed-access. Generally microfilms, manuscripts, art books, and the books which are very old and become rare, are placed under closed sequence. Similarly classified documents, personal papers are also placed in closed sequence. Some libraries have a policy of putting publications upto a certain date of printing in closed sequence.

(ii) Size of Books: Dividing books into different sizes — normal, over size, under size — helps more efficient use of shelf space. The normal book size is demiquarto (5.5" × 8.75"). Books much smaller than this are placed under undersize sequence and much larger under oversize sequence.

(iii) Purpose: In an academic library, the collection is arranged by purpose for which patron will use them. Books with brief ready information such as dictionaries, encyclopaedias, bibliographies are kept in reference sequence. A set of books prescribed for various courses of study is placed in text book sequence.

(iv) **Category of Materials :** Here the books are grouped by level or style of treatment in sequences such as children books, adult readings etc.

(v) **Physical Aspects:** Since material such as manuscripts on palm leaf, on clay tablets, or on chemically prepared base material such as gramophone record, tapes, films, paintings etc. present their own problem of preservation, they are arranged in a separate sequence.

(vi) **Special Sequence:** Sometimes a library specialising in a specific field may arrange books in the field concerned in a separate sequence e.g. Gandhiana, Nehruana Publications of the parent institution, etc.

(vii) **Arrangement by a Combination of Sequences:** In order to satisfy the varied and complex approaches to documents, the arrangement cannot be unitary, based on subject alone. Normally a shelf arrangement based on a combination of the characteristic features of the books is followed. The combination depends largely on the nature of library service. For example, in a public library, it is common practice to have a separate sequence for children or juvenile books, while in a university or college library such a sequence is not at all relevant. It is a usual practice in most of the libraries to have separate sequence for Periodicals, Reference works, Microforms, Reports, etc. Another norm is to have separate collections based on purpose or service status i.e. books for lending, for reading, etc. Within these separate collections, different types of sequences are followed. While it is common to have classified arrangement for books and also for reference works, periodicals are, as a rule, arranged alphabetically by title when the broad subject groupings. Specialised collections are arranged on certain criteria which are characteristic of that type of material.

(2) Shelf Arrangement

Once the library has a taken decision on the number of sequences in which the total collection is to be organised the material in the shelf in each sequence is arranged.

(i) Alphabetical by Author/Title : In small libraries, it is more helpful to arrange books by the alphabet in the name of the author or title. Generally books of fiction are arranged in a separate sequence by author of the book. Author arrangement in large libraries does not satisfy laws of library science.

(ii) Classified Arrangement : The subject is the permanent and more useful basis for the arrangement of books. Size, title, sometimes even author may change from one edition to another edition of the book, but the subject remains basically unchanged. Hence books must be arranged systematically by subject if the aim of library service is to be achieved. Arrangement of books on shelves has to be in accordance with the majority-approaches to the documents. Approaches of the users to documents can be conveniently grouped as 'searching for known documents' and 'searching for unknown documents'. Documents whose existence is known to the user i.e., the user knows that there is a document written by such and such authors, with such and such a title, are called as known documents. When the user is not aware of the existence of the documents, such documents are called 'unknown documents'.

Approaches to the known documents - which are relatively less, are usually through author title etc., and approaches to the 'unknown documents' is invariably the subject approach. Approaches to known documents are termed as Specific documents approach and approaches to the 'unknown documents' is termed as 'specific subject approach'. The subject approach is the most predominant approach and thus a classified arrangement is very useful for the readers as they can find all the related materials at one place, browse through them and select the ones that they need.

(iii) Block Arrangement : This is the method of shelving books in a regular shelf to shelf, case to case order according to the classification scheme. In some busy public libraries a variant of this method is followed by having a rack of non-fiction books in between busy congested fiction racks. However, there is always the danger of mixing fiction and non-fiction books by the reader while browsing.

(iv) Broken Order Arrangement : The common practice of breaking away from the order of the chosen classification, for various justifiable reasons, is known as the broken order. This practice leads to a more efficient shelf arrangement, due to the following reasons:

- To shelve books, belonging to certain frequently used 'classes' like fiction, at the beginning of the stacks.
- To bring two thematically related but classificatory separated groups of books together, like 650 Management Science and 380 Commerce, or 400 Languages and 800 Literature.

(v) Accession Number : Arrangement by accession number could also be very effective in providing access provided (a) that the stacks are closed and readers have no access to the stack, (b) there are a very detailed and in-depth subject and author catalogues providing access to content of the materials, (c) that the requests are for specific documents whose existence is known to the user. Since these conditions are difficult to fulfil, arrangement by accession number is not usually preferred.

STACK MAINTENANCE

The maintenance of stacks work implies the organisation of stack rooms, arrangements of books on shelve in stack rooms and conservation. The maintenance of stack rooms involves the following work:

* Preparation and maintenance of stack guides
* Maintenance of shelf register, shelf list
* Maintenance routines
* Tools needed in maintenance section.

(1) Stack Guides

Guides are to be put up at different places in the library in order to enable a user to find his way into different parts of the library with minimum of assistance from library staff. In a stack room, the following guides will have to be provided.

(i) **Tier Guide:** Each tier of stacks should have one tier guide showing the arrangement of books on the shelves in that tier. These should show the subjects covered in the respective tier giving the inclusive class numbers and their verbal headings.

(ii) **Gangway Guide:** Each gangway should be provided with a gangway guide, indicating the subjects covered in the particular gangway with the help of class numbers and equivalents in the form of verbal headings.

(iii) **Bay Guide:** Every bay of shelves be provided with a bay guide containing the concerned class numbers and their verbal headings.

(iv) **Shelf Guide:** Every shelf should be provided with a shelf guide giving the class numbers to denote the subject on which the books are found in a particular shelf.

(vi) **General Guide:** A guide giving an overall view of the stacks and the arrangement of books has to be provided preferably in the lobby or somewhere near the entrance.

(vii) **General Instruction Guides:** The maintenance section should provide the following guides:

(a) 'No Smoking Please'

(b) 'Talk and Walk Softly'

(c) 'Silence Please'

(d) 'Do not shelve the books. Leave them on the table' etc.

(2) Shelf Register/Shelf List

Shelf register or shelf list is an important record of books, which shows the position of any book on the shelves. A shelf list is usually maintained in standard size cards. These cards are arranged parallel to the corresponding arrangement of books on the shelves. Books in the library are kept in multiple sequences. Therefore, there would be many groups of shelf list card. The shelf list enables the library to maintain correct sequence on the shelves and also indicate immediately the position of any book on the shelf. Shelf list is nothing but a stock register and therefore comes in handy for stock verification purposes. Since the shelf list is an important record, it should be kept under the safe custody and also kept up-to-date.

(3) Maintenance Routine

Besides, the responsibility related to the different functions like stacking, shelf arrangement and stock verification, the maintenance section/division should also attend to day-to-day routines. The duties of routine maintenance work are the following:

* dusting and cleaning of the shelves;
* shelving the newly processed books from the processing section;
* shelving the books returned by borrowers sent by the circulation section;
* shelf study and rectification;
* identifying and separating the torn and otherwise mutilated books for mending or for rebinding;

- shifting and resifting books whenever warranted;
- locating particular books on the shelves upon request by readers when they are unable to find them; and
- maintenance of book tags, etc.

(i) Dusting and Cleaning of Shelves: The dusting and cleaning are important and indispensable routines of libraries which have to be attended meticulously. Books have to be protected from dust and dirt. No room should be given to readers to complain about dust and dirt oh the shelves. In a library where stack area is very large, cleaning can be done by using mechanical devices like vacuum cleaners.

(ii) Shelving: Books received from the processing sections of the library need to be displayed for a week or ten days on the latest additions shelf, before are taken to the stacks for shelving. This may be a weekly activity, but books received from borrowers must be returned to the shelves regularly, preferably the same day so that they are readily available for use by others.

(iii) Shelf Study and Shelf Rectification: The maintenance staff at all levels in a library would do well to devote their free time to studying the books on the shelves so as to develop a fair knowledge of their contents. This knowledge is of vital importance to the efficiency of their work, particularly in their relation to the reference section. An intimate knowledge of the book collection would be invaluable in answering reference enquiries which involves prolonged search.

Books are very often misplaced on the shelves by readers who browse through them. Readers are to be strictly instructed not to replace books on shelves but still it may happen quite often. A book wrongly placed is as good as lost. Hence restoring order among the books is absolutely essential. This work is referred to as shelf rectification.

(iv) Damaged Books: Shelf study and shelf rectification would also enable the maintenance staff to identify books that need mending, repair, rebinding, etc. Unsocial elements could also mutilate books which can be discovered during shelf study or rectification. These books have to be withdrawn from circulation temporarily till they are repaired or replaced by a fresh copy if they are important.

(v) Shifting and Reshifting Books: In order to take away the monotony of appearance of shelf arrangement and to introduced an element of novelty, books have to be reshuffled to keep in tune with the changing popularity of subjects with the reading public. While this cannot be done too frequently, the entire library may be reshuffled once in five years.

(vi) Assistance to Readers: Readers often need advice and help in locating and identifying books of their interest. Although reference assistant may do this job, the maintenance staff who have a closer knowledge of the contents of the library could also go to the rescue of their colleagues in the reference section.

(vii) Maintenance of Book Tags: Book tags carry call number of books fixed at the bottom of books or on their spines. This helps the arrangement of books on the shelf. These tags get damaged or worn out after repeated use and they have to be refixed if they get soiled. In many libraries, book tags have been replaced by tooling, a process by which call numbers of books could be written on the spines or at the bottom of the covers. This will reduce the work of the library.

(4) Tools needed in Maintenance Section

The maintenance section needs to be provided with the following tools:

* At least two *book supporters* are required for each plank of the shelves to ensure that the books are standing upright.
* In a multistoreyed library building book *lifts* are needed to carry books from one floor to another. Similarly *book trollies* are needed to transfer books from one end to the other end of each floor.
* *One table* for sorting out books for shelving should be made available on each floor of stacks.
* A number of *stools* for short persons to browse books kept on top shelves and also for easy replacement of the books.
* *Two step* or *three step ladders* for reaching upper shelves for shelving, cleaning and dusting.

PRESERVATION OF BOOKS AND READING MATERIALS

The preservation of reading materials in the library is very important aspect of Library Management which generally find a neglecting aspects and the least attention is paid by the library authorities to this. It is generally acknowledged that in the present day circumstances the main attentions are laid down only on the use of library materials but its preservation aspects has received little attention. The books and other reading materials which contains and deals with the developments of our ancestor's civilization and history of human beings are precious. It, infacts, not only preserves but also mirrors of a country's cultural heritage. The ancient and old cultural heritage of any nation can be traced out only from reliable source of literature in the form of books and other kinds of non-book materials. So the books and other reading materials stocked in the library should be preserved for posterity as it has a significant values. Books are regarded as the life blood of great thinkers of the past and present. We find life long labours and researches under taken by our ancient thinkers, scientists, philosophers, sages and other such heores who have contributed lots for the sake of development of human civilization and built up a society.

Preservation of books, the treasure of knowledge, is most difficult task for the librarian. We know that a considerable proportionate of library budgets are apportioned for the purchase of books and journals in the library. It is imperative that due attention should be given so that it should not be damaged by its enemies. The money spent on its are not vital things but its values are the point of consideration. It conserve the knowledge. The role of the librarian therefore becomes significant. He is entrusted with the preservation of the books and publicizing them. However a book may get damaged or defaced due to certain causes such as:

(i) Climatic factors

(ii) Light

(iii) Moisture

(iv) Dust and Dirt

(v) Insects

(vi) Human being, the readers.

(i) Climate factors : Sudden variations in temperature is important factor responsible for the deterioration of the reading materials. They should be kept in a comparatively uniform temperature. Various scientific methods can be employed for this purpose.

(ii) Light : Direct sunlight reduces the softness of paper and binding. Therefore efforts should be made to avoid direct sunlight.

(iii) Moisture : Moisture, humidity, dampness, etc. are the different factors, which damage the books and journals. The moisture in air can be removed by proper ventilation in the stock room. Dampness ruins the paper and also becomes a breeding ground of many injurious insects.

(iv) Dust and Dirt : Dust and dirt are also harmful to books. To avoid these dusting should be done in a warm and dry weather.

(v) Insects : Several kinds of insects earth into wooden articles. These insects thrive in this dampness and dust. Some of the insects are- Cockroach or Black Beetles; Termites or White ants; Silver fish; Book lice; Book worms and Fish insects etc. Besides, the Fungus too may prove destructive to the books.

- **Cockroach or Black Beetles:** These are normally found in warm countries. They eat away the binding and other gummed parts of the bock. To kill these insects Gemmaxene or D.D.T. powder may be used. Alternatively these insects can be repelled by camphor and naphthalene. Fumigation and naphthalene bricks are more effective to kill bookworms.
- **Termites or White Ants :** These are the most injurious enemies of books. They eat wood, books, files and other valuable picture and catalogue cards of the library. Once these termites start destroying the books, it becomes very difficult to stop the process, as they based very fast. There are two categories of termites.
  - Earth dwelling termites.
  - Wood dwelling termites.

  To eliminate these termites chemically, carbon bisulphide or carbon tetrachloride are used. Solignum oil may also be used in stock rooms as a precaution.
- **Silver fish :** These also destroy the binding paper and starch at night. They perforate papers, prints, photographs, catalogue cards and card board boxes. These insect can be removed, if a mixture of simple boric acid and flour is spreaded near the books. A mixture of sodium flouride and flour (12 : 100) would also be effective to remove them.
- **Book lice :** Book lice are very small sized insects and may be present in thousands of numbers between two pages of a musty book. Book lices can be avoided by using ethylene, carbondioxide and formaldehyde vapours.

- **Book worms :** Book worm is a generic term that includes the larvae of different beetles. These are mainly found in tropical and semi-tropical parts of world. They generally lay their eggs on the edges of books generally on the bottom edges and shelves. Books damaged by beetles should be removed from the shelves immediately.
- **Fish insects :** These damage the books by eating the coloured parts of binding and damaging maps and other illustrations. To remove these, ethylene, carbondioxide and formaldehyde vapours are used.
- **Fungus :** Though not in the category of insects, fungus is also injurious to books which grows in humidity. It forms a thin whitish coating consisting of fungi of many kinds. Fungus destroys the paper and leather leaving white scars on the book. It can be removed by proper ventilation system. A loose shelving of books should be done to avoid the fungus. Hot air circulation may also be used to heat the shelves. A mixture of thymol crystal (100 grams), mercuric bichloride (4 grams), ether (200 c c.) and benzene (400 c.c.) can also be used to destroy the fungus layers.

In case the books are severely attacked with insects, the best means of eliminating it is to fumigate the infected materials with thymol. Besides, other methods are also used to remove the insects.

(i) Thymol Fumigation : Thymol chamber is used for fumigating infected materials by fungus and insects. Though thymol is a powerful fungicide, it may be quite safely used in museums and libraries.

A suitable wooden rectangular air tight box of plywood is known as thymol chamber. The measurement of the wooden chamber is 6' × 4'. The size may be bigger or smaller according to the requirement. This chamber is rendered airtight by lining it with black board cloth. At a height of 8" from the bottom four brackets are fitted, inside the box at four corners. A movable wire-net shelf is placed on the brackets. At the bottom inside below the shelf, two electric points are fitted (one vertically in the middle and the other horizontally at one side) on which two 60 watt electric bulbs are placed. Immediately above the bulbs two thin gloes dishes containing thymol crystal and carbon tetrachloride 2 oz. to 4 oz. are placed for heating.The objects which are to be treated in this chamber are mostly of fabric such as textile, painting, manuscripts, leather, parchment vellum, palm leaves etc.

The infected objects are kept on the wire-net shelf and the chamber is shut for three days. In every 24 hours, the bulbs are to be switched for two hours. By this the thymol crystals will begin to melt and the fumes will envelope the intected materials kept on the wire at shelf. The materials is removed from the chamber after three days.

(ii) Carbon-disulphide Chamber : It is also called fumigation chamber. It is a airtight ply-wood box. The measurement of the chamber is 6' × 4' × 4'. It is covered by a lid measuring 6' × 4' × 2'. There is also a locking arrangement in the chamber and the ceilingis attached with the lid. At four corners, at a height of 8" from the bottom four brackets are fitted inside the box on which a movable perforated tray is placed to keep the objects under treatment. The chamber has three stands fixed in a triangular fashion in the box below the shelf. Three dishes or glass cups with 2 oz. of carbon disulphide are kept over three stands. The infected materials is placed on the perforated shelf to be exposed in carbon disulphide vapour for a week. To ensure further protection the specimen is re-exposed to the vapour for a week more in the chamber.

Precautions must be taken while using the chamber. When the infected material is kept in the chamber for treatment lid should be tightly covered. Proper care should be taken so that there is no leakage in the chamber, otherwise the fumigation vapour will go out and the material will remain as it were. Brittle objects like old manuscripts should be carefully kept in the chamber and taken out with precaution.

The vapour is highly inflammable and no lighter should be lighted near the chamber. As the vapour is injurious for human health, it is desirable to keep the chamber open for sometime and then the material should be taken out.

(iii) Fumigation by Formaldehyde solution : This method is very helpful even in a small library. Formaldehyde fumes are very effective for cotton, silk, wool and paper goods. The fabric or book should be properly cleaned and dusted before putting them for fumigation treatment.

20 oz. of water and 2 oz. of commercial formaldehyde solution (i.e. 40%) are to be put in an ordinary canister having size of 18" × 9" × 9". The top of the canister will be kept open. At a height of 6" from the bottom four brackets are welded at four corners. A movable plywood box with a hole of 5" diameter at its bottom and opposite lid completely open is placed on the brackets. A sheet of wire-gauze is placed on the

opening of the box to protect the infected books from falling down. The infected materials are kept on it and canister placed over a bunsen burner or a spirit lamp on a stand. The top of the canister is closed by a wooden lid. The fumigation is done for 8 to 10 minutes in the case of a Bunsen burner or 12-15 minutes with a spirit lamp. The specimen is taken out after 24 hours.

In course of treatment the specimen absorb little moisture hence it is necessary to dry it up in open air but not in direct sunlight. After that the specimen be placed in its original position.

Important chemicals used to kill the Insects

Insect	Chemical used
1. Cockroaches or black beetles	Thymol hydrocyanic gas, D.D.T., flit tick-20 and belgoan carbon disulphide
2. Termites or white ants	Solignum oil
3. Silver fish	Dry heat. A mixture of Sodium fluoride and flour (12:100)
4. Book lice	Ethylene and carbondioxide
5. Book worms	Napthalene bricks, solignum oil.
6. Fish insect	Ethylene and carbondioxide, formaldehyde vapours.
7. Fungus	Fynoil. hot air circulation. A mixture of thymol crystals (100 gm), Mercuric bichloride (4 gm), Ether (200 c.c.) and benzene (400 c.c.).

(vi) Human beings, the readers : Some readers are in habit of stealing and mutilating the reading materials. Thus they damage the library reading matter by:

- **Misplacement:** Some readers are in habit of placing the books at places other than the shelves they are supposed to be, thus other readers find it difficult to find the desired books at the right time and place.
- **Mutilation :** A book made unfit for reading either wholly or partially by dog earing the pages, plates and pictures is termed as mutilation of the book. The act of mutilation of books by the readers is traceable broadly to
  - (a) Shortage of time at the disposal of reader
  - (b) Idleness and sluggishness
  - (c) Vengeance and

(d) Mental ill health of reader.

- **Theft:** Theft of reading material from library is a major problem throughout the world. A theft may be defined as carrying away of the reading material without prior permission of the librarian. In order to prevent the theft, manually controlled entrance and exit gate, strict vigilance in the stacks, reading rooms and other important places in the library and a through checking and search in at the exit are essential.

Generally, it is observed that the readers who are not capable of copying the graphs and art plates etc. are tempted to take away them even against their conscience. Therefore, if there is a provision of reprographic service, this wrongful act may be avoided. Some more precautions are also suggested such as:

- To be alert and check all visitors coming to library.
- To keep an eye on doubtful readers.
- No personal belongings should be allowed inside the library.
- Pocket sized and other such smaller books should be kept under lock and keys.
- The windows and doors of the library should be made theft proof as well as rat proof i.e. a netwire of steel meshes should protect books from being thrown out of the library.
- Only one door should be kept open for exit and another of for entrance.

Overall, the safty and preservation of library books and other reading materials are the responsibilities of librarian and its staff. They are appointed for this purpose. But it is surprise greatly that staff are the chief enemies of the books. Incapable and unexperienced staff are most dangerous which damages the books by doing some foolish activities. When the books purchased in the library the books are sent to Technical Section for its technical process. In this process, the books are stamped pasted the labels, date slip and monogram of the library. These should be pasted on a proper place. Some time a little mistake causes damage of books as the wrong pasting disturbed the necessary information which irritate the readers.

After technical processing of the books are transferred in the circulation section. In a big library the distance of circulation section from the technical section has a long distance. So the book should be carried over on a Book Trolly. During the shelving of books on the shelves, it should not be shelved too tightly no too loosely. The former damages the binding when other books are forceful inserted and latter causes large books to sag and to strain the sewing.

It is often found that the staff threw the returned books on the ground or floor of the circulation section which will creat misapprehension among the readers. The readers will not respect books or keep them carefully if the staff are seen throwing the books carelessly into heaps, or casually dropping them on the floor. A frequently overlooked point is the need for caution in opening new or newly bound books. If these books are too abruptly opened the glue on the spine or even the stitches will be strained and permanent weakness will result.

Besides, the books received from the processing section of the library need to shelved properly on the shelves by the staff after cleaning and dusting of shelves.

MENDING, REPAIRING AND BINDING

Old books or manuscripts are very useful especially for research purpose. Special precautions should be taken for their preservation. The *mending* and *repairing* processes imply the following.

- **(i)** **Mending :** Minor restoration not involving replacement with any new material or the separation of book from cover.
- **(ii)** **Repairing :** Partial rehabilitation of a worn volume, the amount of work done being less than the minimum involved in rebinding and more than maximum involved in mending.
- **(iii)** **Reinforcing :** Strengthening the structure of weakened volume usually by adding material.
- **(iv)** **Recasting :** Replacing the cover on a volume which has come out of its cover or has loosened in its cover, the sewing and cover, being still in good condition.
- **(v)** **Re-backing :** Attaching a new shelf back on a volume without any other binding.
- **(vi)** **Resewing :** The process of making a new cover and attaching it to the volume.
- **(vii)** **Recovering :** The process of taking out the volume out of its cover, removing the old sewing and replacing in the same cover.

BINDING

The purpose of binding has been the preservation of the written word. Prior to the modern book, the earliest library materials of the Alexandria-Assyrian clay tablets with their cuneiform inscriptions, were enveloped in outer clay shells. Early Egyptian Papyrus rolls were preserved in rectangular grooves cut out of wood. The rolled up scrolls of vellum, papyrus of paper were encased in cylinders or similar shape. With the advent of manuscripts in book form, came the development of fine bindings, splendid work in leathers and metals, ornamented with jewels, enamels, and covered ivory. It became the art work of great craftsmen. The development of printing brought in publishers' binding which is often of poor quality and workmanship. Thus binding was transformed from an art to a mere craft.

The main objective of binding is to build strength into a book, subjected to the rigorous and abuses of library usage. Binding ensures the preservation of written, printed or near print material. The objectives of library binding are:

(i) to enhance the life span of library materials by insulating against wear and tear.

(ii) to improve the durable quality of library materials i.e., maintaining them in good shape while being used, and

(iii) to improve their aesthetic qualities by creating a new book and thereby attracting readers to them.

Binding Policy for Libraries

Binding does not present a serious problem when library materials are not used heavily, where periodicals are not kept permanently and where special materials are not collected. A library need not bind every item it acquires, however, every item should be maintained in such physical condition that it can be used by patrons without injury to the material. Neglect of binding activity in libraries would result in issues of periodicals getting lost or mutilated, books being used beyond repair, rare volumes being needlessly damaged, leather bindings being allowed to deteriorate, and special materials being destroyed.

The guiding principles of binding documents are the type of material in terms of their physical quality and content value and extent and nature of use. All materials do not necessarily need the same type of binding in all libraries. Estimates of their useful life and of the extent of use that will be made of them, will help determine the best policy.

Materials of heaviest use should be bound according to prescribed standards and specification; those that are of less use but which for historical or research purpose will be valuable over a period of time, will also need this type of binding. Usually large or heavy volumes and those which receive extra-ordinary use should have reinforced bindings. Indexes, bibliographies, dictionaries, encyclopaedias, book catalogues and similar reference works need this type of binding.

Periodicals Binding

Periodicals constitute a very significant part of library collection, especially research libraries and university libraries. The binding of these materials in a research library represents an important element of conservation. They should be carefully checked at intervals all through the year for completeness and due care should be taken to obtain for every periodical its tittle page, contents and index from the publishers when available. The checked sets may then be bound according to the use anticipated. The advent of their wear and tear is comparatively less. Thus libraries can save space and money by going in for light storage bindings, that is, a cloth binding with boards of strength adequate to save unnecessary expense. It is not advisable to bind permanent materials which are fragile, rare items, archives and newspapers. For their protection, they should be laminated. File envelopes and specially sized flat storage boxes are more suitable for archival material. Special collections, rarities and other beautiful works may be bound with special 'fine bindings'.

Newspapers Binding

Of all the library materials, the newspaper is probably the most comprehensive, the easiest to collect and the most vanishing type of a source. The newspapers reflect the conditions, events and forces of its time and the information contained in a newspaper is valuable.

Since newspapers are printed on newsprint 'a type of paper' they disintegrate very fast, therefore, they have to be conserved in an appropriate manner. Temporary bindings may result in some savings but such method are usually not satisfactory for long rangeconservation. Microfilming offers the best available solution to the problem of conservation of newspapers. Newspapers can be bound in canvas covers or in an economy-binding consisting of stout boards covered with a paper like material with cloth of leather spines.

Documents not considered as permanent to the collection need not be bound even if their initial use is heavy enough to warrant it. Some libraries prefer to acquire multiple copies to satisfy heavy initial demand and bind only one copy for the occasional request later. To this category belong current fiction and textbooks which are frequently revised.

Fiction Binding

Fiction needs most careful consideration in view of heavy demand and use and its ephemeral nature. Still its heavy use may prompt librarians to decide on binding, but at the same time has to retain a large stock to avoid complaints from readers that there are no fiction books available on the shelves. Binding a worn-out fiction is no less expensive, if not more expensive than purchasing another copy. Fiction has also been given the same treatment as other books in the past, resulting in over-binding. As a reaction against this policy many librarians today advocate cessation of binding for fiction which they claim can be purchased as cheaply as the cost of binding, with an improved psychological effect on readers. However some librarian believe that in order to keep continuity of actual volume of book stock, binding is still necessary.

Materials of temporary value and limited use can be bound according to the specifications or the library and binder together can develop a type of suitable binding. However, such material does not need more durable binding.

Pamphlets Binding

Pamphlets are paper covered materials of fewer than fifty pages. Most libraries collect pamphlets and if these materials are to be used effectively and efficiently, considerable attention must be given to their proper care. They are treated in several ways. One of the earlier methods was to bind a suitable number of these pamphlets into a book form. This practice is not at all satisfactory from the point of arrangement, although it has the primary advantage of ease of handling and economy. Another practice is to place pamphlets in vertical files, boxes or envelops or wire-staple them into manila covers. Another alternative is to use modern suspension filing system. This method has the great advantage of permitting very close subdivision, of giving visual indexing.

The decision as to which method a library should follow, depends upon the emphasis given to preservation of pamphlet materials, upon the nature of the pamphlets and also the size of the pamphlet collection.

Handling of special material needs careful consideration. The specifications have to be clearly spelt out. Technical reports have to be stored in some form of pamphlet or storage boxes. As standards and specifications and some other materials, are subjected to frequent revision they require some form of loose binding.

BINDING PROCESSES

The production of binding completes in two parts. All the processes of binding books before lettering and decoration, are known as 'Forwarding', which is a craft, requiring a high degree of technical skill and also a good knowledge of materials and processes used in book production. 'Finishing' i.e. decoration of the cover in various styles, is an art in which some figted binders of the past have attained substantial heights of achievement, comparable to artistic creativity. In contrast to finishing which embellishes a book with artistry, is regarded more difficult, but forwarding is the most important. Though the lettering and decoration contribute nothing to the life of the binding, they however identify the book and make it pleasing to look and handle. Apart from the utility value of a good binding, forwarding gives pleasure in the compactness of the book the way in which it opens and the precision of execution, while finishing delights the eye by the brilliance of gold, the harmony of the colours and the form of decoration. The forwarding finishing include the following eight processes:

(i) Collation
(ii) Sewing
(iii) Attaching covers
(iv) Endpapers
(v) Gilding
(vi) Headbands
(vii) Hollow Backs
(viii) Finishing

(1) Forwarding

This include the following :

(i) Collation : It is the first step in the binding processes. All the parts and the pages of a volume have to be correctly sequenced. In the case of periodicals, it is very important as it involves correct sequencing of the separate issues and insertion of usual title and content and index pages in the proper places. While binding worn out, torn, soiled and damaged books, special care has to be taken while collating. It is to be ensured that the paging sequence is in order and that no page is either defective or missing. Collation is a difficult job in the case of manuscripts and other printed books as they are generally not paged.

If a book is to be rebound it must be 'pulled'. Pulling is the process of separating cover from text and removing old threads, tapes and glue which is often a tedious process. If folds of old books are damaged, a 'guard' would be necessary. 'Guard' is a narrow strip of paper used to repair a damaged for or to attach a plate or a single leaf. Special techniques are employed in guarding and mounting maps and folded sheets.

(ii) Sewing : Before sewing, the pages of a books must be pressed firmly, to expel air and also to crease the folds of the sheets. Books are to be trimmed before sewing. There are various styles of sewing. Stabbing is the most primitive of these. Oversewing or overcastting or whipstiching was developed in the eighteenth century to hold heavy plate books together firmly. It is a method for making a series of sections, then sewing all along them. Oversewing machines are the mainstays of modern library binders.

(iii) Attaching Covers : After sewing, the sewn book must be "knocked up" to be square at head and spine. By hammering along the back edges, the expansion resulting from the sewing can be reduced. The spine is glued with a thin hot glue diluted with some insecticide such as DDT. The book again is "knocked up" to round the spine and the spine, line. Preparation of cover boards for the book case requires exact measurements. To prevent the deposition of colouring matter of the boards from showing through the end papers, the boards are to be lined up and marked for sewing and for fixing tapes. The board is then attached to the book and pressed and the glue is let to dry.

(iv) Endpapers : Sheets before and after the text of a book arc called endpapers and they may or may not be decorated. Marbling is the classic type of decoration used and commercial binders often use maps, engravings or pertinent photographs for endpaper illustration. The endpapers perform a protective function and thus require leaves for good quality paper.

(v) Gilding : Gilding or colouring edges may be done either at the time of trimming the edges or after cutting the boards. The purpose of gilding or colouring is primarily or protect the books. Gilding or colouring of the edges gives a smooth solid surface that will prevent dust accumulation. Secondly, the gilding or colouring enhances the 'looks' of the book.

(vi) Headbands : Headbands function as decorative pieces. The back is lined up using different methods of lining up. However the different methods of lining up have one thing in common, that is, smoothening of the surface of the spine by gluing a soft kraft paper over it.

(vii) Hollow Backs : Hollowbacks help save the spine from cracking. This kind of back is achieved by marking a kind of 'tube' with heavy wrapping paper. A paper three times the width of the spine is taken and one thickness is glued with the spine and two thicknesses apart from the spine.

The binding is covered either wholly or partially by leather, cloth or paper. All the above processes described so far are known as 'forwarding'.

(2) Finishing

Finishing is the final process of making the binding more artistic and attractive which includes :

* preparation of the leather covering.
* imaginative design for the cover.
* tooling i.e. fixing the title, call number of the book, etc. on the spine or at any other place on the cover.
* decoration i.e. giving the final touches to get a finish.

Generally leather is used to provide fine covering for the bound book, but cloth or canvas is also used for this purpose. These covering materials have to be prepared for tooling. Tooling is the process of fixing the letters of titles, call numbers, etc. On the leather or cloth binding with special lettering tools. This is done to make the lettering on the spine stand out in relief not only to make the binding more attractive but also to read them easily when they are kept on library shelves. When tooling is done through gold leaf, it is called 'gold tooling'. When neither gold not any colouring matter is used, it is called 'blind tooling'. Lettering may also be done by writing individual letters using an electric stylus.

Finally the outer leather or cloth binding is given a polish and the lettering is given an embellishment needed to get an artistic finish.

KINDS OF LIBRARY BINDINGS

The different kinds of binding required for the different types of documents in a library are :

(i) Publishers' casings and paperbacks

(ii) Library reinforced binding

(iii) Library binding: Full leather binding; Half leather binding; Full cloth binding; Half cloth binding.

(iv) Perfect binding and

(v) Plastic covering for books.

(i) Publishers' Casings and Paperbacks : It is a light straw-board cover, over which an attractive coloured cloth is glued. This casing is attached to the book itself by narrow tapes projecting beyond the spine to which they are glued. This is usually reinforced by mull fabric and protected by the end papers pasted on the inside of the cover. As a rule majority of fiction, popular editions of books, student editions and others are published in this form of binding. These kinds of books are meant for public and hence their price has to be within their reach. It is possible only if the paper and binding is of inferior type. The paper used in such books is a bit stronger that that of newsprint and the binding is of hard paper only.

(ii) Library Reinforced Binding : Reinforced binding means strengthening the book by adding some material. It could be strengthening of the hinge with cloth or the reinforcing a page with some tissue. The Council of the American Library Association, the Library Binding Institute (L.B.I.), the Joint Committee of A.L.A, have prescribed the standards for Reinforced (pre-library bound) binding of new books as follows:

> All 'reinforced' new books shall be completely reserved in accordance with the minimum specifications for class 'A' Library Binding. (Most books having proper inner margins and suitable paper shall be sewed by machine, all sections shall be pasted. No oversewing shall extend more than 3/16 inch in from the back edge of the volume, and no nearer to the head and tail than 1/2 inch).

(i) With the exception of the cover, all other parts, construction, processes and materials shall be in conformity with the minimum specifications,

(ii) Three types of cover shall be permissible:

Type I Class 'A' Cover : Cover similar in appearance to the publishers' original cover but made of heavy weight library buckram (starch filled or pyroxylin-filled) or pyroxylin coated fabric as required by the minimum specification, and with the publisher's original design imprinted thereon.

Type II Publihser's light-weight buckram cover : Cover similar to that of Type 1, but made of a light-weight buckram, with the publisher's original design imprinted thereon.

Type II Publisher's original cover : This refers to the cover which would be on the book if bought in its original form, non-reinforced, through the usual channels. A reinforced book of this type would have the publisher's original cover taken off by the binder, who would then resew and otherwise reinforce the book and replace the original cover on the volume.

Reinforced new books which conform to A.L.A. standards, shall be designated as follows:

(i) Resewed and reinforced in class 'A' cover or "cover 'A' pre-bound" (Corresponding to Type I above).

(ii) "Resewed and reinforced in publisher's buckram cover" (Corresponding to "Type II' above).

(iii) "Resewed and re-inforced in publisher's original cover" (Corresponding to "Type III" above).

Only books reinforced in accordance with "Type I" shall be designated "Class A" or referred to as conforming to the minimum specifications:

For books which are to be either rebound or which are bound for the first time, Ranganathan's specifications are given below in brief:

- **Collation:** All books received by the contractor are to be examined and collated and any found to be imperfect or seriously damaged are to be returned unbound to the Librarian.

(i) A periodical shall not be held to have been collated properly nor to be perfect, unless all the parts of a volume are bound in correct sequence or pagination and the usual title.

(ii) Wrappers and advertisements in periodicals and books are to be bound in, if the contractor is instructed to do so; otherwise, they are not to be bound in.

– **Sewing:** Books printed on paper of good quality are to be sewn one sheet on 'except where thinness of paper makes it necessary to sew two sheets on' with unbleached thread of suitable thickness over unbleached linen tapes. Books printed in soft, spongy or brittle paper are to be lined at inner and outer folds with strips of thin but tough paper before they are sewn. All sections broken at the back are to be lined with tough paper on linen strips, and where necessary neatly overcast on modern methods of cross stitching before being sewn to the tapes. The first and last sections of all books are to be enclosed at back in linen strips. All separate leaves, plates, maps, plans, etc. are to be mounted on guards of linen, or tough thin paper and to be sewn in. Pasting on is not to be permitted. Two of the tapes are to be placed within one inch of the head and tail of each book. Straight-line machine stitching will not be accepted.

– **End papers:** End papers are to be of good tough opaque paper of approved mild colour, with at least one plan white leaf between each of them and the printed matter. The end papers are to be made with strong liner of cloth and to be sewn on as a section.

– **Cutting edges:** Unless other wise instructed, the contractor is to cut edges of books accurately and to take care to leave margins as wide as possible.

– **Forwarding:** Unless otherwise directed, all books should have French joints and tight or close flexible backs with the covering material attached directly to the back-tapes firmly inserted between split boards.

Leather is not to be unduly paired down or unduly stretched in covering. The covering material of back is to extend over boards to at least one-sixth of the width of the book. All books should open un freely and lie flat.

– **Lettering:** Lettering is to be impressed in best gold directly on to the material which covers the book.

- **Sizes:** The size of a bonk is to be determined by the measurement of the board, the square of which must not exceed one eighth of an inch in books upto the crown octavo, and proportionately for larger sizes.

(iii) Library Binding

Binding should be appropriate to the type of material and to the expected use. Early binding for libraries stressed strength, appearance being only a secondary consideration. Books were generally bound in half leather with cloth sides. Magazines and newspapers were generally bound with leather backs and corner and with cloth sides lettering was stamped in gold. Scarcity of leather during World War I led to the use of cloth for entire cover.

In 1935 the American Library Association issued its minimum specification for Class A Library Binding' followed in 1939 by its 'Standards for reinforced (Pre-Library Bound) New Books' issued with the Library Binding Institute. These standards have been combined and have been revised as needed, to reflect new materials and new processes by the Library Binding Institute. These standards which are useful are given below:

(i) All books shall be careful collated before being taken apart to detect any missing or damaged leaves or any peculiarities of paper or constructions that might take rebinding inadvisable.

(ii) All tears through print shall be mended with Japanese tissue or onion skin bond, and all tears in margins with bond paper of suitable weight.

(iii) Books unsuited for over sewing shall be prepared and reinforced through their folded sections.

(iv) Books that are to be oversewed shall be divided into uniform sections, each section not-to exceed .050 inch in thickness, except flexible pulpy paper which may be thicker sections not to exceed .606 inch each.

(v) All end papers shall consist of three functional parts: a paste-down or outward end-leaf which becomes the cover lining; at least two free-leaves, and reinforcing fabric.

(vi) The construction of end papers shall be such that the sewing will go through the reinforcing fabric the same as through the sections of the book.

(vii) Most books having proper inner margins and suitable paper shall be sewed with thread by oversewing method, either by machine or by hand. If sewed by machines, all sections shall be pasted. No oversewing shall exceed 3/16 inch from the back of the edge of the volume and no nearer to the head and tail than 1/2 inch.

(viii) All books shall be trimmed as slightly as possible.

(ix) Edges shall be sprinkled, stained or left plain as instructed.

(x) Backs of books shall be glued with approved flexible glue, well rounded and backed, and lined with approved canton flannel extending to within 1/4 inch of head and tail of books and well onto each end paper, approximately 1½ inches.

(xi) Covers shall be made of heavy weighty starch-filled or pyroxylin-filled buckram or drill base pyroxylin-coated material of a quality at least equal to the standards set forth in part v of these specifications.

(xii) Covers shall be made cover hard-rolled binders board, with uniform squares, in a neat manner. The thickness of the board shall be suited to the size and weight of the book.

(xiii) Books shall be cased in with glycol paste and pressed between metal-edged boards until thoroughly dry.

(xiv) Lettering shall be done after proper sizing in clear tape of a size appropriate to the book in style and position as instructed, using X.X.23 carat gold deeply impressed to insure long adhesion to the cover.

(xv) All books shall be sprayed or treated with a protective material evenly and lightly applied over their lettered backs.

(a) Full leather binding: Full leather binding means that whole of the card board is covered by leather. Books which are very expensive and are rare may need this kind of binding. Usually reference books such as encyclopaedias, dictionaries, atlases, etc., are given full-leather binding.

(b) Half-leather binding: In this type of binding, half the board is covered with leather and the rest by cloth or buckram. The back and the corners are covered by leather as they are the portions which need protection. Backruns of periodicals and magzines, may need this kind of binding.

(c) Full cloth binding: In this type of binding, the cover boards of books are covered completely with cloth. Generally this kind of binding is given to standard books and textbooks which are very heavily used.

(d) Half cloth binding: The spine and corners of the board are covered by cloth and the rest of the cover boards is covered by cheaper materials such as paper and other decorative materials. Books which are slightly cheaper are given this kind of binding.

(iv) Perfect binding: The need to find a less expensive process for binding paperbacks led to the development of the 'perfect binding'—considered as the most imperfect. This substitutes an adhesive for sewing. Development of new materials has made these adhesive bindings almost as durable as oversewn bindings. However, they are not suitable for large or heavy volumes or coated papers. They are, excellent for cheap and porous papers, for publications with narrow inner margins and where it is desired for a books to open flat without undue strain on the spine.

Binders are able to make up special variations on any of these bindings suitable to the individual need of their customers.

Because not all library material needs quality binding the ALA has also approved minimum specification for little used materials. These are referred to as LUMSPECS. For these, Class A specifications are followed in relation to materials, where applicable, but covers consist of hard rolled binder's boards with buckram spines.

(v) Plastic covering for books: Librarian are always interested in attempts at preserving the freshness of newly purchased books for as long as possible, particularly those with artistic and decorative dust jackets. The most effective method is to attach transparent plastic covers to the book. These covers are reasonably priced and can be easily fitted. The book is also protected from the elements, thereby achieving the objectives of conservation. They are sometime available in prepared 'sleeves' and the foil is available in rolls of various gauges of thickness.

BINDING: ORGANISATION AND MANAGEMENT

Binding has not generally received the attention that has been given to acquisitions, cataloguing, circulation and reference. In some libraries binding is combined with acquisitions while in others binding may be the responsibility of the periodical department, the maintenance section, the circulation department or the cataloguing department.

The scope of book conservation covers a series of tasks from the time of receipt or even before or a library materials to the time of discard. The tasks include — selection of material keeping in view its usability and useful life; examining conditions of all materials acquired; providing proper storage and housing in accordance with its conservation needs as well as its use; assuming responsibility for its condition at all times: ensuring its proper handing by staff and patrons; inspection and supervision of collection in order to identify the materials needing conservation; deciding on the proper treatment of all material needing attention; supervising the treatment and deciding on storing and discarding.

The binding is the concern of the library and not of any one department. It is for this reason that binding is not easily integrated into the standard organisational pattern and so has not received the systematic approach given to other aspects of library services. Recognition of binding as a part of a total programme of conservation would result in giving appropriate status for the binding work/division.

The responsibility of a Binding Division/Section/ Department in a library is towards the newly accessioned and catalogued books received in an unbound state or with unsuitable binding. The division must prepare for rebinding the previously bound volumes in the collection which have become worn out or damaged. The activities of a Binding Division may be summarized as :

(i) Identification and preparation of materials for binding.

(ii) Recording of all such materials requiring binding.

(iii) Specification of the style of binding, lettering and special instruction to the binder in accordance with the library binding policy.

(iv) Reviewing materials, especially periodicals and other special materials prepared for binding.

(v) Maintaining current records of material in the process of binding and permanent records of materials bound.

(vi) Compiling statistics of binding in terms of the style of binding and of the divisions/sections of the library from which the materials was received.

DIGITAL PRESERVATION

"Digital preservation" or "digital archiving" essentially aims at taking steps to ensure the longevity of electronic documents. It applies to documents that are either "born digital" and stored on-line or on CD-ROM, diskettes or other physical carriers or to the products of analog-to-digital conversion, if long-term access is intended.

The fundamental problem of preserving electronic documents or "digital objects" arises from the fact that the the objects unlike non-digital formats are accessible only by using combinations of computer hardware and software. In market competition, this hardware and software can become obsolete in cycles of less than three years. Ensuring ongoing access, therefore requires currency with technology changes, and moving digital objects from obsolete to current file formats, storage media, operating systems and so on. A number of other technical, social and legal issues add to the difficulty of the task. These include :

* the increasing complexity of digital objects incorporating text, images, audio, video in various formats and their increasing software dependence (e.g., storage in databases);
* the rapidly increasing number of digital objects and proliferation of document standards and formats;
* the lack of planning to incorporate preservation needs in systems and lack of availability of off-the-shelf products supporting preservation needs;
* the lack of consideration of long-term access requirements when creating digital products;
* the absence of widely-accepted standards which will assure access over time;
* copyright/intellectual property rights that may interfere with the ability to preserve digital objects through systematic copying;
* unstable storage media (e.g., diskettes) whose life span is limited;
* a lack of technical expertise in collections managers and preservation experts;

Preservation Requirements

Preservation measures ensure that a document digital or otherwise is accessible in a usable form over time. Maintaining the accessibility of digital media however, is much more complex than with such non-digital media as paper. For example, when a book is preserved in its original format, all aspects of the book are preserved. It is practically impossible to extract individual elements (e.g., content without layout) because they are inextricably linked. Even reformatting to paper or microfilm does not completely divorce content from layout as page sequences and physical appearance, for instance, can still be captured. Digital objects, in contrast, are easily decomposed into individual elements, and significantly more effort must be made to preserve them as a "whole." For example, one can retain the content of an electronic document, while losing the layout. Further, one can keep its physical presence i.e., a file, but fail to preserve its readability.

In the digital world, the first task is to identify the multiple aspects of a work that must be preserved. Next, to succeed in the preservation of digital objects, preservation measures must ensure that as many of these aspects as possible persist over time. In preserving a digital object, we aim to:

* **Integrity of Object :** A book is a book, or it exists in a set, but what are the boundaries of a document in a hypertext environment? The boundaries of digital objects are less clear, especially if they are compound objects created by assembling different media or by linking to resources from around a network.
* **Physical Preservation :** The physical presence in this case refers to the computer file, the series of "1"s and "0"s that are the basis of a digital object.
* **Content Preservation :** This aspect refers to maintaining the ability to access the content at its lowest level, such as ASCII text, without the embellishments of font variations and layout features.
- **Presentation Format**. Content is typically rendered in some presentation, format or layout, that includes different font faces and sizes, the use of white space, columns, marginalia, headers, footers, pagination, and so on. In many types of digital documents (e.g., SGML, XML, and some forms of PDF), the layout specifications are separate from the content. To retain the original look of a document, these layout specifications must also be preserved, especially when they contribute significantly to the understanding and interpretation of the content.

* **Functionality :** Digital objects have a functionality that goes far beyond traditional paper documents. They can contain multimedia components (i.e., text, graphics, audio, and video), exist in hypertext format.
* **Authenticity :** An individual accessing the object must be able to verify that it is the one he wants, and that the transformations to keep it accessible have preserved its original form. Thus, activities to guard authenticity include securing digital objects against unauthorized changes and monitoring digital objects through multiple "copying" cycles to ensure that each copy is an acceptable rendition of the original establishing authoritative depositories would also help achieve this goal.
* **Location and Reference :** Digital objects can be readily altered, copied or moved. An individual must be able to match a citation to a digital object, and to distinguish it from other versions or editions.
* **Provenance :** Provenance is an archival concept that asserts the origin and chain of custody of an object and contributes to defining it as a whole. Imprint statements and bookplates, for example, partly fill this role for formally published items. Establishing an object's origin and history help confirm that the work is authentic and its content is intact.
* **Preserve context :** Digital objects are partly defined by their hardware and software dependencies, their mode of distribution and linkages to other digital objects. Preserving digital objects may mean weaning them from some technical dependencies, changing the mode of distribution, and deactivating links. In these circumstances, preserving context is a particular challenge.

Preservation Strategies

Several strategies attempt to address the primary digital preservation problem of technological obsolescence. These include migrating information through successive generations of technology; using software to emulate the behaviour of older machines preserving original hardware and software to run obsolete programs, and creating hard copies in paper or microform of digital objects. Each of these strategies meets some, but not all, preservation goals.

(i) Migration and Transfer : Migration is the primary strategy articulated by most organizations that plan to preserve digital objects. It covers a range of activities to periodically copy, convert or transfer digital information from one generation of technology to subsequent ones. Migration may involve copying digital information from a medium that is becoming obsolete or physically deteriorating to a newer one (e.g., floppy disk to CD-ROM), and/or converting from one format to another (e.g., Microsoft Word to ASCII), and/or moving documents from one platform to another (e.g., VAX to UNIX). Migration certainly preserves the physical presence and the content of a digital object. However, it may not preserve presentation, functionality and context. For example, presentation elements such as bolding and italics may disappear, and the functionality and context provided by links between database entries may be lost because the links break. Successive migrations may eventually result in unacceptable data loss. The focus is on limiting the loss and retaining the content in a usable form. Migration is undeniably an important strategy for preserving digital objects. However, it has yet to be tested and proven as a mechanism for managing complex multimedia objects over the long term.

(ii) Emulation : Emulation refers to creating new software that mimics the operations of older hardware or software in order to reproduce its performance. Thus, not only are physical presence and content preserved, but digital objects could display original features; e.g., layout and functionality available with the older software. Emulation has recently attracted attention as a potential strategy to assist preservation, recognizing that some electronic material that is highly dependent on particular hardware and software will not lend itself to migration.

Emulation is used to provide "backward compatibility" for video games, and to model how future systems might run. Emulators exist for some obsolete systems, however, emulation for preserving digital objects over the long term has not been widely tested or priced.

(iii) Output to Paper or Microfilm : Outputting a hard copy of a digital file is a "low tech" solution that can result in a well-standardized product with a life expectancy of several hundred years. Certainly, this strategy could fix the object as a whole and preserve content and to some extent layout. However, a decreasing number of publications (flat files, printable formats) lend themselves to such methods. For example, output to paper will lead to great functional loss for hypertext documents, and cannot capture multimedia. Despite these drawbacks, a "hybrid strategy' of creating both microfilm and digital copies is gaining support as a technique for reformatting paper originals. The digital copy enhances access and functionality, and the microform copy acts as an archival surrogate.

(iv) Preservation Technology : Another method for ensuring ongoing access to digital objects would be to simply keep older technology available for use. Although this would preserve content and enable future generations to view digital objects in their native format with original layout and functionality, creating hardware or software "museums" is prohibitive in cost, space and technical support requirements. At best, this method is an interim measure when migration is not possible.

Control

To increase the probability that digital objects will be preserved, organizations need to lay appropriate groundwork. One way is to develop and implement the most effective practices in acquiring, describing and managing digital resources.

(i) Standards : To facilitate preservation, the best practice is to adopt a three-part approach:

(a) use current standards to create digital objects;

(b) monitor standards as they change;

(c) migrate to new standards as they are established.

Most digital preservation guidelines advocate collecting digital objects in standard formats. Unfortunately, while standards are well defined for text (e.g., ASCII), images (e.g., JPEG, TIFF) and encoding documents (e.g., SGML. HTML), standards have not emerged for some other types of information (e.g., databases). In addition not only do standards change rapidly, but vendors seeking to increase their market share incorporate "value-added" features to accepted standards. Institutions performing the digital preservation activity can also be subject to standardization.

The International Standards Organization (ISO) has produced a reference model (CCSDS 650.0-W-4.0), for an Open Archival Information System (OAIS). The model establishes the minimum requirements for a digital archive to ensure long-term preservation of digital information, and provides a framework for describing and comparing archival architecture and operation.

(ii) Developing Digital Preservation Guidelines : Archives and record-keeping bodies in Europe, North America and Australia have taken the lead in developing best practices and functional requirements that address some preservation issues. Common elements include.

* Recognizing the creator's responsibility to preserve his work initially;
* Identifying responsibilities of the archive;
* Adopting appropriate selection guidelines which emphasize standards when a choice of formats exists;
* Securing archived items from intentional or unintentional alteration;
* Providing contextual documentation including a history of creation, transmission and use, and audit trails; and
* Describing digital objects completely.

Some libraries have developed similar guidelines, but most digital preservation guidelines focus on creation, receipt and capture of digital objects, and do not satisfactorily address their long-term preservation.

(iii) Documenting Resources : A recurrent theme in digital preservation guidelines is documentation and description of electronic resources. The need for such deliberate subscription stems in part from the fact that digital objects do not carry the visible evidence of creation and use, e.g., imprints, bindings bookplates, marginalia, or Scotch tape of non-electronic formats. Such clues guide preservation decisions. They also help users to establish that the work is whole and intact, and to understand its provenance and the context in which it was created.

- **Metadata :** A description of a digital object is "data about data" or metadata. Such descriptive data should include the contextual information crucial to the long-term management of electronic information. Metadata elements useful in preservation might include;
  * Identifiers;
  * Hardware, operating system and software required to access a document;
  * Physical details of tangible format publications such as CD-ROM, floppy disks;

* encoding standard and version;
* migration history and its success;
* data to assist determining authenticity;
* rights management information;
* versions and dates.

Conversion projects would employ additional metadata elements such as the capture device, resolution, compression, source material, and producer of the digital document. Existing metadata schemes (e.g., MARC, Dublin Core) provide some such information capture, but there is no consensus on which approach will work best for preservation purposes. In MARC, for example, some of the necessary data is captured in notes' fields that may not use sufficiently detailed or consistent language for subsequent search and retrieval.

- **Unique identifiers :** One element of describing a digital object is to assign it a unique and persistent identifier. An identifier is a number, like an ISBN, which is associated with a particular instance of a digital object. Unlike an URL, it is independent of the location of that object. A unique, widely supported identifier for digital objects would help establish the authenticity of the object by confirming to a user that the resource he is accessing is the one cited. It could also help establish the relationship between copies or versions of digital objects, as any modification of the original would result in a modification of its identifier. Some organizations involved in digital preservation are currently using PURLs (Persistent Uniform Resource Locators), URNs (Uniform Resource Names) or modified Digital Object Identifiers. As yet, no single digital identifier has achieved widespread; international acceptance.
- **Linking Metadata with Content :** Metadata can be stored either as an integral part of the document it describes (e.g., embedded in an HTML header) or as part of a separate file of information (e.g., a-MARC record). One way of linking metadata and the digital object is to package them together. To this end, the aforementioned Reference Model for an Open Archival Information System (OAIS) proposes an "information package" comprised of "content information" and "preservation descriptive information". Along similar lines, a working group of the Society

of Motion Picture and Television Engineers has developed a Universal Preservation Format (UPF), a data-file mechanism that uses a container structure to incorporate metadata into digital media objects. Although primarily developed for audio-visual data, the principles underlying the UPF may have wider applicability.

(iv) Establishing Infrastructure : A final way in which libraries are gaining control over the preservation of digital objects is by building preservation requirements into systems development. The Australian National Library, for example, has started a Digital Services Project to develop systems to manage its digital collections and to support cooperative shared access.

The National Library of Canada has incorporated preservation requirements in its Digital Library Infrastructure Project. The next step is to develop the systems. To reduce the uncertainty surrounding digital preservation, one can encourage creators to use practices that will aid long-term preservation, such as creating valid documents in standard document formats and address the question of which preservation strategy will work best by testing migration and emulation and identifying associated costs and tradeoffs in each case.

It is noted that rapid technological obsolescence combined with relatively shortlived media means that collections must be actively managed. Simply "collecting" and "shelving" important works, a passive strategy that works to some extent for paper-based publications, is insufficient to ensure digital objects will survive in perpetuity.

STOCK VERIFICATION OF COLLECTION

Stock verification implies the physical check - up of the articles on record. It is a common practice in big business houses and government departments to resort to annual stock-taking in order to assess the profit or loss. They try to find out as to what has been sold out and what has been left behind so that a proper quantity of a particular item may be procured for future sale. There is a practice to differentiate between stock and store articles. More importance is attached to stock articles since these are of permanent value and are likely to remain longer in use whereas the store articles are consumable. An analogous example can be cited by referring to two kinds of leaves i. e. earned and casual leaves allowed to employees. The former can be cumulated whereas the latter cannot be cumulated since it is consumable and lapsable.

In the present day context the Stock Verification may be defined as "An yearly compulsory mechanical exercise of orpetitive nature required by auditors causing inconvenience to library users by the libraries' closure as well as acting as drudgery for the unwilling library staff and finally yielding unreliable results without any monetary gain leading to unnecessary harrassments and punishments to mostly innocent library staff."

The concept of Stock Verification is as old as the very concept of preparation of inventories of objects having a physical entity, namely stores of different kinds and descriptions. Since books also have a physical entity, these are treated as stores for that purpose and since all stores are subject to audit control, so are the books and consequently libraries. Annual Stock Verification has therefore been an audit requirement in all libraries and the purpose is to find out the loss, if any and to fix the responsibility for the loss. Thus, the whole idea of Stock Verification in libraries emanates from the concept of treating libraries as mere stores of books. However, with the development in the paper industry, its production of books at cheaper rates, the changes in the concept of functions and use of libraries as well as the services offered to clientele have made the task of Stock Verification very difficult and cumbersome, rather making it impossible to meet the audit requirements of losses found in stock taking on any one as losses depend largely on the moral tone of users rather than the library staff. Moreover the losses are not worth the amount of labour and headache involved in doing Stock Verification. Todays, most of the documents in the libraries are kept open to make their maximum use. Hence in open access system the books are allowed to be handled freely and it is natural that some percentage of the loaned books are bound to be lost.

Causes of Loss of Books/Documents

1. Loss is due to the nature of human beings. There are following three kinds of human beings :-
   (i) Those who will never steal even if they come across a valuable article and have got ample facility or opportunity to steal.
   (ii) Those who must steal, irrespective of the fact, that many hurdles are placed in their way and many other precautions are taken against them. B. S. Kesavan, once addressing an annual conference organized under the auspices of the

Punjab State Library Association at Chandigarh, disclosed that a reader was caught red-handed while stealing a volume of the Encyclopedia Britannica. This fact shows that such a person was an incorrigible thief.

(iii) Those who are not regular thieves, but if proper, vigilance is not taken, they are also tempted to steal. This type of readers may steal due to the fact that very strict and discouraging rules are prescribed for the use of books and other kindred material. In other words, when they are not allowed to make use of certain essential reading material, they perforce resort to stealing.

2. The second reason, which may encourage certain persons to steal, is the poor vigilance arrangements made in the library. Such persons are in a majority and are on the borderlines. It is the first and foremost duty of a Librarian to ensure that all these persons are made good citizens and are dissuaded from stealing, by providing constructive programmes.

Responsibility for the loss of books

As regards loss, though in Indian Libraries the Librarians are made responsible for the loss and they are asked to pay for it but the trends suggest the proper remedy. The Panjab University in 1961 on a representation from the Punjab College librarians Association, Jullundur, recommended to its affiliated college to consider a loss of 3 books per thousand of stock as normal loss which should be written off. The Advisory Committee for Libraries, appointed by the Government of India in its report published in 1959 stated that.

"In many places he (Librarian) is even held responsible for paying the cost of books lost during the time he was in charge of the library. We have no hesitation in saying that such practices are iniquitous and unheard of in the library practice of any advanced country in the world. In the first place, the safety of library books depends on the moral tone of its users and no Librarian, unless he is to restrict severely the use of books, can prevent the depredations of unsocial elements. Secondly, since no Librarian is adequately paid, the effect of asking him to pay for the loss of books would be that he will place all books in his charge under lock and key and thus nullify the fundamentals of a good public library. We, therefore, strongly recommend that the practice mentioned here should be put an end to, and no State Government should require a librarian to furnish security or to pay for the loss of books, unless gross negligence or dishonesty is proved against him."

The same provision is found in the Model Public libraries Bill circulated by the Ministry of Education, Government of India, for eliciting the opinion of State Governments and Library Associations in the country. The Model Public Libraries Bill, prepared by the Working Group on Libraries also contained a similar provision. The Report of the UGC (India) Library Committee forcefully recommends to write off an inevitable loss @ 2 for every 1000 books issued. However, in an open access library an annual loss of 3 volumes for every 1000 issues should be considered as a normal loss in normal circumstances as recommended by Dr. Ranganathan. The latter is being followed generally by various educational and public library authorities in India.

In foreign countries, the lost books are written off and no Librarian is held responsible for such losses. Dr. S. R. Ranganathan very forcefully pleads the case of Librarians as regards their responsibility for the loss and mutilation of books in libraries when he remarks :-

1. Mutilation of books is the result of the inherent criminal impulse in a few readers. This is exactly as stealing is an inherent criminal impulse in a few people in a society.
2. It is as improper to make the librarian pay the cost of all mutilated books as to ask the policeman to pay the cost of all property stolen.
3. It is for the college authorities particularly the principal and the members of the teaching staff to wean away the student population from this criminal tendency.
4. Neither equity nor social justice, nor any kind of propriety can make it the librarian's duty to be the sole agent in a college to reform the conduct of students.
5. I appeal to the Government and the authorities of any kind of libraries in the country to reexamine their attitude in this matter and not exercise the power, they have in a blind way.

Necessity of Stock - Taking

If some books are lost, it is essential to replace them so that no gap is created in the usual library services. This would be possible only if periodical physical check up of the library stock is made. But, on the other hand, it is suggested that those books which are important and popular and which must be replaced, can earsily be found out since such books will be demanded constantly and if not found on the shelves and are not issued out can be deemed to be lost and can be replaced and so no special purpose may be served by regular stock - taking. Though, theoretically it may not be very essential to resort to regular stock- taking in view of the above mentioned suggestion, yet, in practice, it is both essential and desirable to have some kind of checking so that inherent defects in the administrative policies may be detected and possible remedies may be devised to eradicate these maladies.

The desirability or otherwise of stock - taking also depends upon the size of the book stock of a library. In big libraries, it becomes difficult, if not physically impossible, to do thorough checking at regular intervals and it also dislocates the regular rhythm of the library routines since some staff members working in essential services sections of the library are engaged in stock verification. There are libraries which close the library during stock - taking period or curtail some service. This practice runs counter to the basic principles of library service. In a library having less than 20,000 volumes, annual stock – checking is recommended and in the libraries with more than 20,000 volumes, sample – verification in every 3 years should be commenced.

Advantage and Disadvantages

Since every action has got some good or bad points, now the question arises whether in the present context it is desirable to do stock verification every year as a ritual or completely abandon it as is being done in American and British Libraries. There are both good and bad points for both the views. According to E. R. Carbett, R. L. Mittal, P. K. Banerjee and others, Stock Verification has following advantages and disadvantages.

Advantages

(i) It makes it possible to bring the catalogues and other records uptodate, thus improving the reservation and Inter- Library Loan procedures and reducing irritation to both readers and staff.

(ii) It may reveal large scale losses and suggest additional security and precautionary measures.

(iii) It permits a general overhaul of the book stock and its physical condition and thereby old and damaged books lying on the shelves can be got repaired, written off or replaced by new copies of the lost titles.

(iv) It clears up many of the "quarries" which be set even the best run libraries.

(v) Books are properly arranged on the shelves and the misplaced books are restored to the current places.

(vi) It satisfies the auditors and authorities that stock is being properly controlled.

Disadvantages

(i) It takes up a considerable amount of staff time which might be better employed.

(ii) It's results are largely negative and unreliable.

(iii) It is virtually impossible in large libraries.

(iv) It causes unnecessary inconvenience to library users by closure of library or disruption in normal library activities and facilities.

(v) Innocent library staff is put to unnecessary harassments by library authorities and some times it is used as an excuse for taking vengeance from certain staff members due to some past grievance or ill - will against them.

(vi) The amount amount of labour, time and money involved in stock taking is not worth the trouble as the monetary loss revealed by stock taking results is generally very meagre as compared to the overall expenses incurred by libraries on it.

Stock - Taking Methods

The prevalent methods of Stock - Taking are given below:

(i) Stock - Taking by Accession Register.

(ii) Stock - taking by using a separate register with Accession Numbers.

(iii) Stock - Taking by preparing separate sheets which contain Accession Numbers in a consecutive order.

(iv) Stock - Taking by Numerical Counting.

(v) Stock - Taking by the Shelf List having special columns on the cards for stock taking record.

(vi) Stock - Taking by Shelf List without any specific columns on the cards.

(vii) Combining of stock rectification and stock - taking processes.

(viii) Stock Verification with the help of computer.

(ix) Sample Stock Verification.

(x) Stock - Taking by Duplicate Set of Book cards.

(xi) Stock - Taking by Master Record.

Important methods are being discussed here :

(i) By Accession Register : This method is very simple. The Accession Register is taken to the shelves and one person calls the particulars of the books from the shelf alongwith the Accession Number and the other person ticks the concerned Accession Number in the Accession Register. When all the books are checked, a list of untraceable items is prepared and efforts are made to trace out the missing books.

This system though looks very simple, is very cumbersome and time consuming and it spoils the Accession Register. It is cumbersome because each time the particulars of a book are called by the person on the shelf, the other person which with the register has to find out the exact Accession Number by lifting many pages at a time. As such, there is a danger of mistakes. It is time - consuming because it takes a lot of times in finding out the exact Assession Number from the Accession Register since the books on the shelves are arranged according to the Accession Numbers but are arranged according to the Call Numbers which represent the subject of the books. It also spoils the Accession Register because when some mark either by pencil or pen is a made, it leaves behind some impression even though these marks are erased. Thus, the whole of the Accession Register is spoiled and a day comes when the Accession Register becomes unintelligible.

(ii) Stock - Taking by using Separate Register with Accession Numbers : If the Accession Register is used for stock - taking it is likely that it may be disfigured and even the life of the Register may be shortened because by constant handling, the paper will give way and an essential record may be lost. To prepare duplicate Accession Register, especially when the number of accessioned books runs into thousands and lakhs, is a stupenduous task. An alternative method is suggested by which a separate stock - taking register is prepared with the following columns :

Acc. No.	1996	1997	1998	19991	2000	2001	Remarks
25726							
25727							
25728							
25729							
25730							

In this method, the Stock - Taking Register is taken to the shelves. One person speaks out the Accession Number from the book and the other one ticks the relevant year column from the register against the spoken Accession Number. At the end of stock taking, a list is prepared on separate sheets, tracing of the untraceable books is done and the items found afterwards either from the Issue Record or binding Section or from the shelves are crossed from this list. The remaining items are noted down on a separate paper for getting them written off. All the relevant information about the books is given on this sheet and the price of these books totalled so as to find out the actual loss. The crossed items are tick marked in the Stock - Taking Register. In this way, stock-taking is completed.

This method, no doubt, is better than the previous one since it saves the Assession Register from wear and tear. The danger of speaking out wrong Accession Number or crossing out wrong number always remains there. This method also is very slow and it takes much time in stock verification. Hence, this method is not suitable for big libraries. Moreover, the Stock - Taking Register will be used for a limited number of years and again a new register will have to be prepared afresh every time the year columns are ticked. This is an unnecessary wastage of money, time and energy.

(iii) Stock-Taking by Preparing Separate Sheets containing Accession Numbers : In order to obviate the necessity of getting printed the new Stock - Taking Register after some years or of preparing fresh Accession Register, a new and simple method can be used for stock verification by preparing separate sheets which have Accession Numbers upto the last item acquired in the library in a consecutive order as under:

1.	~~11~~	21.	31.
2.	12.	22.	32.
3.	13.	23.	33.
4.	14.	~~24~~.	34.
5.	15.	25.	35.
6.	16.	26.	36.
7.	17.	27.	37.
8.	18.	28.	38.
9.	19.	~~29~~.	39.
10.	20.	30.	40.

Specimen Stock - Taking Sheets

This means that the books with Accession Numbers 11, 24 and 29 have been traced out. Similarly, all the traced items are to be crossed out and the remaining items are checked with the Charged Tray, Binding Tray and other sequences in the library such as Withdrawl Register etc. and the items found in these sequences are crossed on these sheets. The rest of the Accession Numbers are transferred on to separate sheets and detailed bibliographical information is noted against these Accession Numbers. These sheets are either got typed or the numbering is done by a numbering machine. In this method, the sheets can be multiplied and many persons at one time can do the stock - taking work. Thus, the whole of the work can be finished within a short time.

(iv) Stock - Taking by Numerical Counting : Another simple method of stock - taking found in foreign libraries is the mere counting of books on the shelves, charged trays and other sequences and the total thus arrived at is deducted from the total number of books accessioned according to the Accession Register. The balance indicates the number of books not traceable. This method gives a rough idea of the amount of loss and is adopted by those libraries which do not give undue importance to physical checking of each and every item in the library. As such, this system does not serve the basic purpose for which stock - taking practice has been stated.

(v) Stock - Taking by Register or Shelf List with Special Columns : All the above methods do not help in stock rectification since their approach is through Accession Numbers whereas the books are generally arranged subject wise and so it can not be found out easily as to whether a particular book was shelved at its proper place.

The present method of stock verification presupposes the maintenance of an up - to - date and accurate shelf list on cards. If it is in register form, it will not be handy and the problems of Accession Register methods will recur to some extent. The card form is flexible and ensures speedy stock - verification. In this system, proper arrangement of shelf list cards is essential otherwise lot of time will be wasted in tracing out the exact titles. These cards, besides having the necessary information which is given for a main entry of a book, must contain some columns for recording stock - taking entries.

The particular drawers are taken to the shelves and the person on the shelves speaks out the call number of each book and the person with shelf list checks the call number. After tick marking the relevant year column goes on pushing forward the cards which have been checked. The cards bearing those a call numbers which are not spoken out by the person on the shelves are made to stand on their shorter edges and each day a list of standing cards is prepared after these cards are checked from other sequences such as those of the issue counter, binding, withdrawal register etc. These cards represent those books which are not traceable. This list of books is got written off and proper remarks are given in the Withdrawal Register. The shelf list cards of the

<table>
<tr><td>0251.1
N242</td><td colspan="2">Narayana, G.J.</td></tr>
<tr><td>5492</td><td colspan="2">Library and Information Management. New Delhi : Prentice Hall of India Private Limited, 1991,
307 p, 22 cm.
<table><tr><td>1994</td><td>1995</td><td>1996</td><td>1997</td></tr><tr><td>1998</td><td>1999</td><td>2000</td><td>2001</td></tr></table></td></tr>
</table>

Specimen of Shelf List with Special Columns

withdrawn books are filed in a separate sequence called withdrawal sequence.

This type of Stock - taking is efficient and speedy but because one column is to be tick - marked on the shelf list cards, it takes some time. Moreover, the limited number of columns can be drawn on the face of the cards, so these cards become useless after some years and necessity arises for preparing fresh cards. If descriptive cataloguing is in vogue, it is difficult to provide such columns on the shelf list cards.

(vi) Stock - Taking by Shelf list Cards without Special Columns : This system is almost same to the previous one except that no specific columns are provided for tick - marking. Simply, the cards are pushed forward as soon as the call numbers of their respective books are spoken out by the person on the shelves. The cards of those books which are not found on the shelves are made to stand on their shorter edges and are marked with soft lead pencil. These cards are listed in the evening after these are checked with the charged trays, binding and withdrawals sequences and then the standing cards are put in their normal position. The specimen of shelf list card is given below be employed to do this job at one time. Moreover, since the books and cards are in one and the same sequence, checking is easier. The final is again checked

0251.1 N242	Narayana, G.J.	
5492	Library and Information Management. New Delhi : Prentice Hall of India Private Limited, 1991, 307 p, 22 cm.	

Specimen of Shelf List without Special Columns

with the shelves and those books which are found there are crossed from the list.

(vii) Sample Stock Verification : Another alternative method is the sample stock - verification. It means that only few sections which are mostly in use are checked thoroughly and an estimate of loss of books is made on that basis. The shelf lists can be for used checking while the items chosen by inches of material rather than a fixed number of cards per drawer. In larger university libraries, in India, sample stock verification is very common because there a complete stock verification can not be done at once.

(viii) Stock - Taking by Duplicate Set of Book Cards : In this system, duplicate book cards of different colours are prepared at the time of processing of books. One of the book cards is slipped into the book pocket while the other one is arranged in a classified sequence in a catalogue cabinet.

At the time of stock - taking, the book cards are exchanged from the catalogue cabinet to the books. The book cards of particular colour which remain in the catalogue cabinet indicate the loss of books after ascertaining the books which are issued or have been withdrawn already or have been sent for binding. This system also entails lot of work and time.

(ix) Stock - Taking By Master Record : The Library of the Institute of Armament Technology, Giri nagar, Pune (India) started an experiment of stock - taking without a shelf - list in 1961 - 62, but with a master Record containing had written Accession Numbers on separate sheets of paper. A record was prepared i. e. 'Shelf Record' besides preparing multiple copies of Master Record containing Accession Numbers printed columnwise with the help of a numbering machine. Many pairs of persons were put on the job and each of them recorded on a sheet of paper the Accession Numbers of books found on the shelves and later on the relevant Accession Numbers from the Master Record were scored.

But this was found clumsy and tiresome and was not fool proof. Therefore, the formats of the Master Record and Shelf Record were changed into booklet forms, each page of which corresponded to a thousand Accession Numbers arranged in column of 50 while the thousandth number was indicated by the page number. Each page accommodate 1,000. However, the Shelf Record contained 400 and only the first three digits of the Accession Number of the book called out were to be written down. Later on, the numbers from the Self Record were scored off from the Master Record and the unscored numbers indicated the ultimate loss. But later, the sheets of Master Record and Shelf Record were loosened so as to allow more pairs of persons to do the stock - taking work. Secondly, instead of writing 3 digits of an Accession Number in the Shelf Record, they were written in the order of their hundreds i. e. all numbers occurring between 900 and 999 were written under column 9 while the numbers between 800 to 899 under column 8 and so on.

However, this method involved the speaking of Accession Numbers twice i. e. at the time of preparing the Shelf Record and again while scoring off from the Master Record. So, slips of 5" × 3" were prepared and at the time of stock - taking, the Accession Numbers were written and at the time of stock - taking, the Accession Numbers were written on them and these were visible. Under this system, 8 persons were able to write down 29,000 slips and to complete the work in 5 to 6 days. But the method was also handled 29,000 slips.

In 1974 - 75, the final method was adopted in which the Master Record was maintained while the Shelf Record was eliminated. However, the Accession Numbers 0 to 999 were arranged in 10 groups, each having number indicated the thousand number. The cyclostyle sheets containing members were pasted on double foolscape sized sheet and were converted into registers. The Accession Numbers called by one of the two persons were scored off from the registers and the unscored items indicated missing books.

However, in order to facilities easy transfer of the scored items, the registers were loosened and the sheets having same page numbers i.e., same thousand were grouped together. Some more changes were incorporated in the Master Record. Firstly, the space between numbers and groups of hundreds was reduced in order to overcome the inconvenience caused by the turning of pages. The size of the sheets was also reduced. These were stepped to form booklets. But it was decided that the numbers were rearranged in groups of fifties instead of hundreds in order to avoid strain to the eyes.

It is claimed that the method for stock - verification without shelf list evolved at the Institute of Armament Technology, Pune had the following advantage :-

(i) For a book stock of about 40,000 volumes and other kindred materials, the library is to be closed for about 3 to 4 days.

(ii) The number of untraced items is between 300 to 600 only out of a book stock of 40,000 i.e. ¾% to 1½% only.

(iii) Errors due to fatigue are reduced.

(iv) Proper records of stock - verification are maintained.

(v) The job is performed in an orderly manner.

(vi) The job of verifying a stock of 40,000 volumes takes about 200 man - hours.

But this method can be found suitable for small libraries only.

STOCK RECTIFICATION AND STOCK VERIFICATION

The above mentioned methods dislocate normal circulation work. It is experienced that doing the entire checking at high pressure in a few weeks results in much dislocation in the work of the library. The dislocation will increase with the size of the library. The modern spirit, of library service has led the library profession to give up the old practice of closing the library for checking purposes.

Dr. S. R. Ranganathan has suggested a new system for stock taking purpose. He says that stock rectification and stock verification processes should be combined. In an open access library, though the readers are directed not to shelve the books by them selves, yet it is found that books are very often misplaced. A misplaced book is at least temporarily lost. Moreover, selfish and criminal minded readers do resort to such practices. They hide the books where nobody can ordinarily reach. For example, a student of 'Economics' may hide a book of Economics in 'Useful Arts' Section. A student of 'Economics' is unlikely to look up the section of Useful Arts' for his book on 'Economics' and so, for him, the book in question is temporarily lost. Second and Third Laws of Library Science are thus, violated. The importance of regular stock rectification cannot be overemphasized. Stock verification itself becomes easier and speedier if the books are placed at their proper places as indicated by the arrangement of the shelf list cards. He further suggested that this work should be done in a phased programme. The work of the Circulation and the Maintenance Sections should be so combined that proper stock - rectification and stock verification goes on smoothly. In this way, lot of time is saved. Moreover, if this method is followed, the library need not be closed for the readers.

For successful implementation of this method, the classification scheme in use should be such which provides individualized class / call numbers so that each book is identified by reading the class / call numbers only.

Procedure for Stock Rectification and Verification

The whole length of stacks is divided into convenient parts and each part is allocated to a party of two persons. It is estimated that about 25,000 books can be rectified and verified within one month's time. One person goes to the Counter and asks the Counter Assistant to read out the Call Numbers of the books of particular region selected for checking for the day out of the Charged Tray. The cards of books not found out of this sequence are made to stand.

In the meantime, another staff member is asked to rectify the shelf pertaining to books to be checked for the day. The person who had gone to the Counter for checking comes to the shelves and asks the other person to read out the Call Number from the spine labels of the books. He himself goes on pushing towards himself the cards of the books, the Call Numbers of which are called out by the person on the shelf. At the end of the day's appointed quota, the cards of books of which the Call numbers are not called out by the person on the shelf are taken out and are placed in the Investigation Box. The cards which were made to stand on their short edges are turned to their normal position.

The cards in the Investigation Box are then checked with the Bespoken or Reversal Book Sequence, Binding Sequence and the books which are waiting to be shelved. The cards of the books which are thus found out are replaced in the Shelf List Cards Tray as usual. The remaining items are reported to the Librarian.

COMPUTERS AND STOCK VERIFICATION

Now-a-days, various software of Library automation like Libsys, Troodom etc. are coming with inbuilt facilities for stock verification. One can either feed the list of presently available books on shelf manually or scan with Data capturing unit. The program automatically match the accession numbers from this list along with issued books, numbers and give a comprehensive list of missing books.

This automatic stock verification is done very fastly rather than all manual verification as discussed earlier and give correct and accurate results.

Stock Revision and Weeding out

In a good library, a policy of continuous revision of book stock should be followed which means that not only enough number of copies of those books are procured which are required by the readers but all the subjects are also represented in the book - stock. This can be achieved only if new editions of books are purchased by constantly keeping watch over the publication of the new editions of books through careful search of book reviews and other bibliographical tools and journals containing announcements of new editions. However, care should be taken that reprints and editions are differentiated and before the reprints/ new editions are purchased these should be thoroughly checked in order to avoid unnecessary duplication.

Similarly, old editions of books which become out - dated, as their new editions have been published should be weeded out besides other torn and spoiled books unless it is found essential to retain the old editions. The catalogue cards of the books of new editions should contain a note that the books of old editions have been retained. The weeding out of books is essential in order to make enough space for the usable stock. The weeded out material should either to be sent to Regional / State / National Depository Centres or these should be distributed to the local school and public libraries provided these are likely to be used. Otherwise, these should be burnt or sold out as waste - paper or should be kept in the tertiary sequence if at all these are considered essential.

Losses of Books in the Libraries

Even with the best of safeguards, the most human treatment possible and vigilance of a high order, certain percentage of losses of books in all libraries are bound to occur. Just as we accept the loss of merchandise in operating department stores and in other business and discount a certain amount of loss as unavoidable similarly in the libraries, the authorities should be prepared to accept some losses as a fair price for the enormous increase in the use of books.

The books in a library are bound to be lost even if there is closed access. It is a social evil and it must be eradicated like other antisocial activities in society by contacting the library clientele individually and occasionally collectively and creating a public opinion against this evil. This method no doubt is slow in results. It requires persistent efforts on the part of library and library authorities and it seems to be the only practicable method.

A comparative chart is being given to cases of loss of books with their possible remedies for the working librarians.

Comparative Chart

Causes for losses of books in Libraries	*Remedies for overcoming these causes*
1	*2*
1. Pilferage of big sized books under the garments, over-coats, pants and even shirts.	No fool proof method is possible. However indecent methods of searching of the person may prove useful.
2. Pilferage of bulky books by removing their hard board covers and then taking away the books in piece meal on different occasions and then getting the part of books stitched together. This can be easily done by keeping the books in parts in the inner pockets of garments or hiding them inside the garments.	No remedy except that of creating better civic sense.
3. The small sized books, pamphlets, college catalogues, loose issues of journals etc. can be stolen by hiding them inside the files and note books which the reader brings in the library.	Insistence on checking the personal files, note books and portfolios at the gate of the library by the janitor.
4. The readers bringing personal books inside the library for reference and consultation purposes and then under the garb of personal books take away the library books after removing their library ownership markes such as book plate, seal, etc	Personal books should not be permitted to be taken inside the library.

1	*2*
5. The ordinary rubber stamps used by the libraries for issuing books can be easily procured from the market and anti - social elements of the society can put the issues stamps on the library books and take them away form the library even after proper checking at the gate.	1. Special type of automatic daters may be used in the Library. 2. Token system can be introduced. Along with each book a token may be issued to the borrower which may be deposited with the janitor at the gate while leaving the library. The three records namely that of number of tokens issued by the library assistant, the book cards collected by the issue assistant and the number of tokens collected at the gate by the janitor should be tallied every day before closing the library.
6. Insistence by some senior staff members on issuing books to them on slips resulting in the loss of slips and issue record and the book ultimately getting untraceable.	Books should only be issued against cards and not on slips. Browne system should be strictly adhered.
7. By the connivance of the library janitor a reader may take away a book even without getting it issued.	1. Token system. 2. Wicket gate at the exit door which may be operated by the man at the issue system, or 3. Both combined into one.
8. During rush hours the janitor may fail to check each and every book taken out of the library by a reader and this may result in loss of books.	Token system can overcome this difficulty.
9. The library staff at the issue	1. No remedy. However a

1	2
counter may himself destroy the issue record after having issued the books to a reader.	strict vigilance and checking of issue record daily and that of over - due books can minimise such chances. 2. By maintaining a duplicate record issue of books the chances of losses of books by this method can be minimized but it would prove expensive and time consuming. 3. Only persons of known integrity should be kept at the counter but it is extremely difficult.
10. By issuing through oversight books on lost cards or outdated cards by the issue assistant.	No remedy except the staff to be more vigilant.
11. In the case of Departmental Libraries books are issued against the signatures of lecturers or readers and later on when the lecturers leave the university service, there is no one from whom the books may be claimed.	The books for the Departmental Libraries should be issued only against the specific requisitions from the heads of the department and against the signatures of either the Head of Departments or the O. C. Libraries who may be duly authorised by the Head of the Departments for doing on their behalf and there should be proper handling over of the charge by one O. C. Library to another in case of change over of O. C's.
12. Teachers after borrowing library books go abroad or leave university service and do not bother about returning the library books.	No teacher should be permitted to proceed abroad or leave the university unless he obtains a clearence from the library.

1	*2*
13. Losses of books from the Department Libraries are likely to take place by not entering the books taken from the Central Library into the Stock Register of the Departmental Library.	The entry should be made immediately on the receipt of the book in the Department and it should be signed by the O.C. Library.

PROBLEMS WITH ELECTRONIC PUBLICATIONS

The CDs are acquired in the libraries through two processes. First, the CDs which come free along with the printed material. These are common in case of computer science books. Second, the CDs which libraries subscribe against a payment, as in the case of journals on CDs For example, CDs of Library & Information Science Abstract (LISA) in the field of library & information science and Medicinal & Aromatic Plant Abstracts (MAPA) in the field of plant sciences.

The following problems are faced by the libraries regarding the stock verification of these electronic publications.

(i) Issue/Return of CDs : The question arises whether the CDs should be issued or not? If yes, then what should be the criteria to follow? The CDs coming free are to be treated as a part of book or separate entity and for how much time these should be issued? If these are considered a free entity and readers do not return, or CDs get non - operational, can these be ultimately treated as written - off material?

(ii) Life of CDs : The second question is related to the life of CDs. In the case of books or other printed material, the librarians can just read and use them even after 50 years of its publication, But, as the manufacturers of CDs claim, the life of CDs is 12 - 14 years which in practice could be determined as only 2 - 2.5 years, Moreover, the CD can get non - operational very soon if mishandled which does not happen at all in the case of printed documents. Are we in a position to weed out a CD costing 1 lakh or more just after 1 or 2 months or immediately after acquiring it for the library.

(iii) Checking out CD's Content : If CDs are allowed to take out from the library by the users as printed material, one needs to check its content again when it is returned to the library. It is observed that many libraries do not have necessary computer facilities to check the viability of CDs operation as to whether these have not been spoiled by the users? Even if the computer infrastructure is there, how much trained staff is available in the library for sparing time to check and verify the contents of these CDs? Moreover, in many cases, the libraries are just running single handed by the clerical staff who is generally not aware of technical problems.

(iv) Criteria of Use : Generally, in the case of printed material, a loss of 3 books per 1000 consulted or issued books to the readers is permissible and is well within the limit of a librarian, under the approval of competent authority to write off the same. But what will be the criteria to determine the loss factor for CDs? - the number of uses of CDs, whether 1000 times actual use in library or merely just handling it 1000 times in the library?

(v) Responsibility of Maintenance : Who can be held responsible in case of mishandling of CDs - librarian or the staff actually handling the CDs in the library? Again, if the staff or librarian is held responsible it will demoralize them and ultimately will affect the library services.

These are some of the problems which the library professionals may face while working in the library presently and in future.

For the solution, following measures can be taken :

(i) Issue - return of CDs etc. should be made restricted to avoid their misuse.

(ii) If these are issued, at the time of returning their functionality should be check at the return - counter.

(iii) For costly CDs, a duplicate set can be prepared which is made available to the readers. This will also reduce the burden of mishandling.

(iv) An independent person should be appointed to look after the non-book materials in the library separately.

If these measures are taken, the librarian can overcome of the problems.

11
Library Authorities, Committees And the Library Rules

Library is said to be a social institution charged with the function of preserving and disseminating human culture and civilization contained in the books/documents. It serves as a centre for providing recreation which is vital for mental development, for enabling people to utilize their leisure time for engendering in them love of books and humanity and to be on enviable medium for helping all - round development of the community. A library can rightly be called as an index to the human development in the fields of Humanities, Social, Physical and Biological Sciences. The functions of libraries broadened gradually so that libraries might serve as storage places of knowledge to be disseminate and that they might get true and sustained knowledge.

Every organisation needs to establish a system of authority, so that the objectives of the organisation may be given practical shape. The 'word' authority implies a person having power to do something. The purpose of authority is to perform some kind of service by means of administrative process.

MEANING OF AUTHORITY

New Webster's Dictionary of the English language defines Authority as "Power of Right to command or Act" or Domination; Control a person or persons exercising power of command."

C. G. Frederich says that "authority is a quality of communication which makes a command or opinion worthy of acceptance because it can be elaborated reasonably."

Alfred G. Meyer writes "authority cover the field of human relationship, in which communications by actor are accepted as or binding another". Authority implies the right or power to control, command, regulate or resolve disputes.

Need For Authority

The very existence of an organisation or institution essentially lies in the nature and effectiveness of the authority. It is the guiding, controlling and actualising force, for managing an organisation or institution. The term authority implies a person having power to do something. He is powerful enough since he has been authorised by a competent agency to do a certain job such as library authority, or board of management etc. on the other hand a committee means a body consisting of certain persons, which assigned particular job. Such committees mostly supervise and advise the librarians in matters in which public participation is essential.

Structure of Authority

Authority is a management concept. A manager's authority in all institutions consists of the right to do such things as to make decision, assign work to do subordinates, review the work of subordinates under recommended retention or release of subordinates on the basis of performance. Most institutional authority resides in the formal positions or officer rather than in the office holder. Authority is legitimated by the processes of socialisation.

According to Hicks and Tillan the structure is as follows.

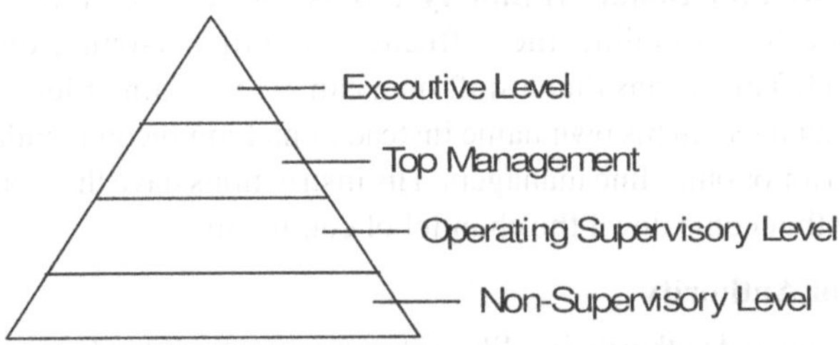

The above illustration shows the levels of authority. The vertical dimension - showing levels of authority and responsibility and horizontal dimension showing the function, as units at that level,

- Policy making
- Supervising and
- Non - Supervising

Kinds of Authority

The authority may be divided broadly into three kinds.

(i) Line authority

(ii) Staff authority

(iii) Functional Authority

(i) Line Authority : It is clearly defined the role to play in the organisation which requires understanding of the nature of line authority. Line authority exists between superior and his subordinate. In the organising process, activities are assigned to the individuals making them responsible for the proper performance of these activities. Authority is delegated to these individuals to perform the activities. These individuals, in turn, assign some of the activities to persons working below them in hierarchy and delegate them authority. The process goes on creating superior-subordinate relationship in the organisation.

(ii) Staff Authority : Staff authority is exercised by staffman over line personnel. The exercise of this authority depends on the degree of authority delegated to a staffman or department. The staff authority may further can be divided into the following categories.

(a) Advisory staff authority.

(b) Concurring staff authority.

(c) Control staff authority.

(iii) Functional Authority : It is the most extreme formal technique for extending the influence of staff personnel over line personnel. This means that a staff man can give certain orders directly to line managers in his own name instead of making recommendation to his superior or other line managers. His instructions have the same force as those that come down the channel of command.

Limits of Authority

Limits of authority in a library/organisation can be shown through the following figure. The quantum of authority decreases at successively lower levels and it is maximum at the highest level and minimum at the lowest level.

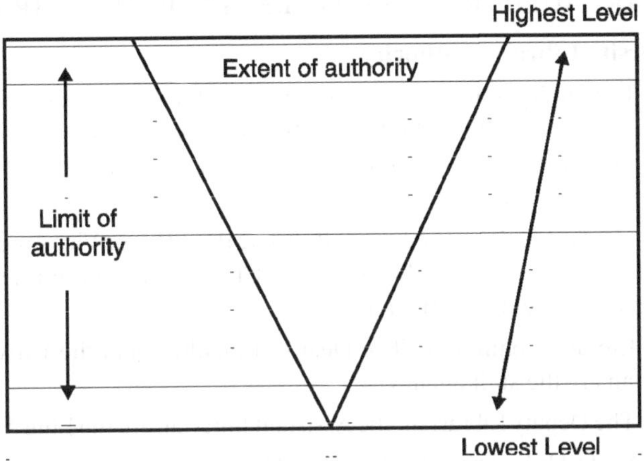

The above figure shows that authority is not absolute. It enjoyed by an organisation/library and is exercised subject to various social, legal, political and economic factors. Similarly, the use of authority by a superior over his subordinates is restricted by various factors.

Delegation of Authority

We may define delegation as the assignment to another person of formal authority and responsibility for carrying out specific activities. It implies that the Chief Executive surrenders some of his powers to his immediate subordinates. Here authority may be downward. The delegator does not surrender his overall responsibility but retains the power of control. He can even revoke his delegation and take back all the authority. In university library, Librarian delegate certain powers to the Deputy Librarian. Assistant Librarian and also the section heads, for smooth disposal of the work with higher sense of responsibility.

Powers of Authority

As stated earlier, authority is a Chief Executive person having power to do something. The following are the powers of authority.

(i) It has an administrative process, to implement the functions and fulfil the objective.

(ii) Administrative process to be tested with certain powers.

(iii) To test certain power to carry on certain functions.

(iv) Authority should have status. Both are inseparable.

LIBRARY AUTHORITY IN DIFFERENT TYPES OF LIBRARIES

University Library Authority

University is an autonomous body. For the Central Universities, the President of India is the Chancellor and for state universities the Governor of the concerned States. The University authority is divided into two types. They are :

Central University Authority : The President or Vice - president of India and Senate - Syndicate, Vice - Chancellor are the Executive Authorities of Central University.

Library Committee, The Deans of faculties and the University Librarian are the staff agency.

The Deputy Librarian, the Assistant librarian are the Line Agency.

State University Authority : The Governor of the particular State, (Chancellor), Pro - Chancellor, Senate, Syndicate, and the Vice - Chancellor of the concern University are the Executive Authority.

Library Committee and University Librarian are the staff Authority.

The Deputy Librarian and the Assistant librarian are the line agency. In University the Administrative Board (Syndicate Executive Council) provides the library committee to assist the libraries in the allocation of book funds and in the formulation of board, general policy of library development.

College Library Authority

Every College has got a managing body which is concerned to be the college library authority. It constitutes the library committee. The library committee is mainly concerns with the executive planning of the administration of the library. It is constituted of Heads of Departments, and Senior Lecturers, with the Principal as Chairman, and Librarian as the Secretary.

In Government Colleges, Director of Collegiate Education. Principals of Concerned Colleges, Library Committee and Librarian are in the structure of authority whereas in private college, the College Managing Board is the supreme authority.

The administrative hierarchical structure of the college library is given below :

Principal of the College
↓
Administrative office | Librarian | Library committee
Librarian
↓
Assistant Librarian (technical services) | Assistant Librarian (lending service) | Assistant Librarian (reference services)

Public Library Authority

In case of public libraries, Director of public libraries or chairman of the city constitutes the library authority.

Special Library Authority

Here, Director of the research institute or chairman of the organization forms the library authority.

LIBRARY COMMITTEE

The library committee means of body consisting of certain persons, which is assigned a particular job. Such committees mostly supervise and advise the libraries in matters in which public participation is essential.

The words 'Library Authority' and 'Library Committee' have been used at several places in the Acts. Hence it is necessary that the distinction between these two words be understood clearly to avoid any unnecessary confusion. The word 'authority' implies that a person having authority would be powerful enough and authorised by a competent agency to perform a certain job. Libraries authorities have the power to govern the libraries. A committee means a body, consisting of some persons who may be assigned particular powers to perform the job, such committees have got mostly advisory and supervisory powers.

A Library Committee is responsible for policy making and the librarian is to implement the policy. The librarian generally acts as the secretary as the committee and his duty is to prepare the agenda for the committee meetings. The librarian should prove himself as a reliable guide to the committee. The committee should not interfere in the internal working of the library except through librarian.

Advantages of a Committee

(i) It helps the librarian in carrying out the administration of library more efficiently.

(ii) It serves both as co-ordinating and policy making body.

(iii) It adds to the prestige of the library.

(iv) The Librarian with the help of committee members can get the important and complicated 'works done in a easy way.

(v) The administration needs support arid this is possible by the Committee.

(vi) The committee members may assess the financial needs of the library and finally they may arrange for more and more funds.

(vii) It ensures better understanding between the management and the readers.

(viii) It can convince the government and the people about the needs of the library service for the well being of the community.

(ix) It can explore and use modern methods for broadening the library resources and facilities.

Qualities of the Members of Library Committee

The Library Committee members should possess the following qualities.

(i) They should be willing workers.

(ii) They should be ready to attend regularly the meetings of the library committee.

(iii) They should not be very busy persons.

(iv) They should be Literary - minded persons.

(v) They should be specialist in various branches of knowledge.

(vi) They should have fair knowledge of the purposes and aims of libraries so that they may be able to fulfil these aims properly.

Need for Library Committee

The followings are the need for library committee:

1. The Librarian requires the committee to serve as a buffer agency

and an interpreter of the needs of the library to the higher authority.

2. It is a general belief that the Librarian alone should not carry the whole burden of a big institution like a library.
3. In the absence of a library committee, the librarian would find himself defenseless and unprotected.
4. In the absence of the committee, there may arise some financial troubles. Usually the representative of Vice - Chancellor and a member from Syndicate will be in the committee. Therefore, they can successfully and convincingly appeal for more funds.
5. The committee members being laymen keep the librarians at his guard at all times.
6. The committee ensures the financial needs of the library in accordance with the national library standards.
7. The committee ensures a better understanding between the reader and the library policies.
8. The Librarian always needs the help of library committee.
9. The committee having strong voice, can easily convince the authorities and the public.

Kinds of Library Committee

A library may have a numbers of committees depending upon its size and nature of activities and operations. However, committees are usually constituted according to requirements. Generally we find the following kinds of library committees are in practice :-

1. Executive Committee
2. Adhoc Committee
3. Nominated Committee
4. Reporting Committee
5. Recommending Committee
6. Self Perpetuating Committee
7. Sub-Committee

1. Executive Committee : It is a committee with delegated powers by the authority. This committee can be said the most powerful committee. The local authority cannot interfere in its work and it need not report its decisions to the library authority. It is autocratic in action.

2. Adhoc Committee : It is the special committee for the supervision and control of libraries functioning. It is speedy in its decisions and it can accommodate coopted members of performing a specific job. This committee is more or less independent and it has nothing to do with the Local Government Bodies. This committee is also called statutory authority committee. It has the advantage of being independent of politics. It takes the decision very fastly. It can coopt men of intellect and foresight. But some times it may come into clash with the Local Government Bodies specially in the matter of collection of taxes.

3. Nominated Committee : Nominated or elected committee is constituted by a larger committee or the authority to look after the works and matters of the library. It delegates certain function to such a committee. The provision of such type committee was made for the first time in the Andhra Pradesh Public Libraries, Act. 1960 under chapter II. It is an effective committee.

4. Reporting Committee : It is an effective and powerful committee who has got powers to decide the policies within certain limits. Its decisions and action taken are simple and are to be reported to the authority only for the information. It does not require the confirmation from the supreme authority. It is co-operating and helpful to the librarian.

5. Recommending Committee : This type of committee has no powers but it can recommend certain proposals for governing the library which are subject to the approval of the library authority. This type of committee is found only in England. It is very slow in action.

6. Self-Perpetuating Committee : It is created and exists in case of libraries operating under special character of statutes. Such committee has sole authority and is independent as regard the control and management of libraries under it. It need not to report its activities to the higher authority. In USA and South Africa, we found such type of committees.

7. Sub-Committee : In addition to the above committee, the authority appointed sub-committee according to the needs to look after the functions like maintenance of accounts, purchase of books, physical verification and other such important matters. It depends on the size of the library system.

Duties and Responsibilities of Library Committee

The duties and responsibilities of the library committee are manifold but it should be concerned mainly with library policy than with library administration. The administrative matters, involving planning, location and distribution of departments; staff duties, technical works etc. should be left to the librarian and the committee interference in these matters should be minimum. In order to avoid confusion and better performance of works the powers and obligations of the Library committee and the Librarian be clearly defined.

	Duties and responsibilities of Library Committee	*Duties and responsibilities of of the Librarian*
1.	Appoint a competent and qualified librarian and staff so that effective library services are given to the readers.	Work as advisor to committee/ board on all technical and professional matters.
2.	Determine and adopt policies to govern the management and programme of the library.	Place the draft of needed policies for committee's action.
3.	Must know the needs of the library in relation to the community keep abreast of standards and library trends.	Recommend for creation of posts and appointment of library personnel and supervise their work.
4.	Define- the purposes of the library and secure adequate funds to carry on the library's activities.	Implement the policies of the library as adopted by the Committee/Board.
5.	Maintenance of library building and keep watch on other properties of the library.	Advise the committee for extending the library's services.
6.	Establish, support and participate in social welfare programmes at local state and national level.	Prepare Annual Reports of the library for placing before the committee.
7.	Assist in the preparation of the annual budget and exa-	Examine the current progress of work and future needs and

	Duties and responsibilities of Library Committee	*Duties and responsibilities of of the Librarian*
	mine incomes and expenditures.	to prepare plan accordingly.
8.	Compile and revise Library rules and regulations.	Prepare annual budget for the library in consultation with the committee.
9.	Extend further library services by opening branch libraries, mobile libraries, and deposit centres.	Know local and state laws and support library legislation.
10.	Appoint such sub-committee as may be required for carrying on the committee's work more expeditiously.	Select suitable books and other library material and place orders.
11.	Receive donation and gifts for the Library.	Attend all committee and sub-committee meetings-other than those in which his own salary, tenure or leave matters are under discussion.
12.	Meet regularly at fixed intervals for transacting the business as mentioned in the agenda and placed before it.	Affiliate with professional organizations and attend workshops, seminars and meeting at local, state and national level.
13.	Must be aware with the local and state laws and support library legislation in the state and nation.	Build contacts with other local educational cultural and research institutions.
14.	Establish co-operation among libraries and similar other organisations dealing with books for better utilization of resources scattered in different places.	Work as liaison between the committee and the staff for better understanding and harmony.

Duties and responsibilities of Library Committee	*Duties and responsibilities of of the Librarian*
15. Provide adequate, proper and attractive library furnitures and fittings,	As Chief Executive of the Library he must be firm, strict and vigilant in all matters and on all occasions.

Power and Functions of Library Committees

The powers and functions of library committee, vary according to its nature. Almost all the proposals for discussions at the library committee meetings are put forth by the librarian who generally acts as an Ex-officio Secretary to the committee. These functions are broadly to the following items.

(i) **Library Building :** A library committee ensures that a library building could be functional and modular if proper library services are to be provided. Necessary arrangements should be made for the proper maintenance of the library building.

(ii) **Library Furniture and Fittings :** The other important function of a library committee is to ensure that adequate, proper and cosy library fittings and furniture articles are made available in the library.

(iii) **Library Staff:** A library committee should employ qualified and adequate staff for the library. So that standard library services are provided to the readers. The library committee should keep in mind accepted norms for fixing the number of staff members and their salary scales with sufficient opportunities for promotion so that the staff members stay there for fairly long time.

(iv) **Library Finance and Book Collection :** A library committee should provide enough funds for establishing the basic book collection and for adding latest books in a library. It should appoint a sub-committee should be experts in various fields of knowledge who keeps themselves in touch with the growing literature.

(v) **Library rules :** A library committee should form a set of library rules which are not rigid but are flexible and suit the needs of readers.

(vi) **Library Accounts & Audit :** A library committee should appoint an account sub-committee for auditing the accounts.

(vii) **Library Acts and Rules :** A library committee keep the library acts and rules up - to - date.

(viii) **Standard Library Service :** A library committee should put in its best efforts to secure full coverage and standard library service.

(ix) **Library Co-operation :** It should find out ways and means for securing co-operation among educational institutions for cordial relationship between users and libraries.

(x) **Library Policies:** The library committee should lay down a policy for the guidance of the librarian for the general day-to-day administration of the library.

Library Committee Meetings

The committee should meet either monthly or after longer intervals as the case may be. To conduct a meeting there must be some presiding officer. A Chairman to be elected by its members provided there is no ex- office Chairman. Vice-Chairman may also be elected to preside over the meetings in the absence of the chairman. Librarian generally serves as the Secretary of the Committee.

Agenda of Meeting

The Librarian should always discuss the agenda with the chairman before it is issued to members. While sending an agenda for a committee meeting, care should be taken to supply the members all the requests information about the items on the agenda so that the decisions are arrived at expeditiously and properly. The agenda should be accompanied with a forwarding letter in which the members are informed regarding the time, date and venue of the next meeting of the committee.

The agenda should provide for the following items :

(i) *Minutes of the last Meetings* : The decision taken by the committee in the last meeting and it is presented in the next meeting for having formal approval of the committee.

(ii) *List of Books for Approval*: The Librarian should submit a list of books to be purchased for the library. If there is a sub -committee on Book Selection, Librarian gets its approval and presents a report to the library committee.

(iii) *Purchase of Stationary and Other Equipments* : The librarian submits detailed list of requirements for the next year along with comparative statement of rates if the items are costly.

(iv) Bills for various articles purchased.

(v) Estimate of heavy plans of alterations in the building.

(vi) Librarian should provide true picture of the financial position.

(vii) Estimates for the provision of additional services and staff or opening of new branches.

Librarian's Report

The Librarian should submit a monthly report to the committee about the working of the library during the previous month. This report consists of staff and services.

The Chairman and the Secretary of the committee must be fully briefed by the librarian in all matters likely to arise from minutes of the last meeting and from the current agenda. The Librarian should take note of the deliberations and decisions in the meeting and at the end a draft of the minutes be prepared. The minutes of the meeting should be brief as well as clear.

COMMITTEES IN DIFFERENT TYPES OF LIBRARIES

It is now a universal practice in libraries to have well constituted committees built in to the management structure. Usually one or more committees function to aid library management. The constitution and composition of the committee may vary, depending upon the statutory provisions governing the different types of libraries. In public libraries, particularly those that operate under the Public Library Act, the government of the respective states, constitute the committees according to the provisions of the act. In universities, the statutes of the universities prescribe the procedure for the constitution of the committees and in special libraries, their parent bodies constitute the committees in accordance with their statutory procedures.

Public Libraries

In India, the states, those have a public library system, are governed by their respective public library acts. As these public library systems are supported by public funds, the democratic structure of the systems enjoins them to function under committees at different levels of the library system. Although there are variations in their constitution, composition, number of members, nomination of chairpersons and member-secretary, powers, etc., the general pattern is that committees are constituted at the state, city, district and lower levels, functioning independently but with a general policy of the state governments as stipulated by their library acts. In general, the committees comprise public men of standing, scholars and bureaucrats, as ex-officio members. The state library committee advises the government on all matters of library service, as envisaged by the library acts. Generally, librarians who head the state, city, district and other unit levels serve their corresponding committees, as member-secretaries and governors. These committees enjoy authority and powers to plan, make policies, evaluate and oversee the activities of the library system in the state.

University Libraries

In universities, the statutes of the universities have the necessary provision for constituting library committees. Usually the university Library Committee is the highest committee, comprising Deans of faculties, university teachers, Principals of colleges and a few university officials with the Vice Chancellor of the University as the chairperson. This committee is the most authoritative committee vested with powers of approving the budget, framing policies and programmes, rules and regulations, evaluation of library and documentation service and others. The university librarian is generally the member-secretary of the committee who is responsible for convening meetings and maintain all records relating to committee work.

This Library Committee may constitute other sub-committees or standing or ad hoc committees for specific activities such as book selection, library and information services, special projects. The librarian or his nominee may be a member of these committees who convenes meetings, record the minutes of meetings, maintain all official records of these meetings. For the internal management of the library, the librarian may constitute a few committees to advise him on specific matters.

Special Libraries

Special libraries are invariably constituents of larger institutions such as research laboratories, industrial undertakings, business organisations. For library and information services of these institutions, usually an advisory committee is constituted, comprising seniors of the organisations, a few outside experts, with the Director of the respective institution or his nominee as the chairperson. The Library/Documentation Officer is the member-secretary of such committee who convenes the meetings and takes care of all committee work. Most of such committees function in an advisory capacity. A number of sub-committees may also function to advise the Director and the library/documentation officer on collection building, information services, evaluation of activities, introduction of new services, etc. The library officer is always a member of such committees and does all the work of the committees.

LIBRARY RULES

As the Libraries are being social institutions, their managements have a special responsibility to see that the use of their resources, facilities and services be regulated properly so that there is no room for misuse, discrimination or scope for obtaining any special favours to an individual or group. It is, therefore, a general practice for libraries, to lay down rules and regulations in the use of the library, applicable equally to all categories of users, without any discrimination.

The rules may vary according to the nature of the Library and these variations may occur in :

(a) Working hours and holidays .

(b) Enrolment of members.

(c) Reading room facilities.

(d) Lending facilities.

(e) Research room facilities, etc.

But the purpose of rules and regulations, common to all types of libraries, are to :

* provide guidance and direction to users, aiding them in the use of the library's ' resources, facilities and services;
* protect documents and other properties of the libraries and facilities from damage and misuse; -
* inform users of their privileges and limitations in the use of the library;
* empower library staff with authority to enforce the rules and regulations.

While equal privileges, facilities and services are made available for all categories of users in all libraries, the libraries reserve their right to offer any special service to select categories of users, keeping in view their nature of work, duties and responsibilities. Rules and regulations are framed to suit the requirements of specialised users.

Contents of Rules and Regulations

The general framework of library rules and regulations for all types of libraries is more or less the same. The contents include:

* Name, address, telephone, telex and the such other data of the library
* Working hours
* Admission, to visitors and members
* Borrowing privileges
* Interlibrary loan facilities
* Use of reference materials
* Referral services
* Document supply
* Preparation of bibliographies
* Literature search for current references
* Other special services like obtaining a copy of a translation of a research paper in a language other than English
* Generalities

Some of the services mentioned above like referral services, document supply, preparation of bibliographies, literature search, special services have been introduced in libraries in recent decades, particularly in academic, research and special libraries. These services are offered on a selective basis to those who need them most. Sometimes they are available only on request and at a nominal price.

Referral services direct users to sources of information which documents may be available in other libraries, or an agency or institution which may have the information or an expert in the field. The library which offers this service must have the information on the sources.

Document supply services include search and identification of bibliographical details of a requested journal article or a report, locate the libraries that may have the article of report, obtain a photocopy to the requester.

Literature search service provides current lists of bibliographical citations with or without abstracts on a given topic.

These services are increasing in demand and many libraries are responding to these demands, gearing its own capabilities. There is, however, no uniformity in framing rules and regulations for these services nor is there any standard for price fixation.

Library rules in different types of Libraries

While the general purpose of library rules and regulations remain very much the same in all types of libraries, their contents and the details are bound to vary according to the kinds of users they serve and the nature of services they offer. The variation may be expected with reference to:

* working hours of the library -
* admission to the library
* borrowing privileges
* nature of services.

In public libraries, factors that would determine framing of rules and regulations may be: (i) the locality in which the library functions; (ii) the type of clientele they serve; (iii) the nature of document collection they have; (iv) facilities they have for different types of services.

In a large city central library, the working hours, admission to the library, borrowing privileges and the services it offers would be distinctly different from what one may obtain in a district central or a taluk library. Hence rules and regulations have to be framed orienting them towards meeting the requirements of the residents concerned.

But, in district central and taluk libraries, serving a smaller population, library services cannot be expected to be as extensive as they are in a city central library. Naturally rules and regulations will have to be framed to meet the requirements of a smaller clientele.

An important character of public libraries, we should note with reference to their clientele, is that they enjoy the same privilege and therefore there cannot be any difference in their treatment. Rules and regulations apply equally to all.

In a university library, the users are a homogeneous group of educators, learners and researchers. Each group may have special facilities and privileges but there may also be limitations. For instance, a text book collection may not normally be available to a faculty member, particularly at the time of the university examination. A current issue of a research periodical cannot be borrowed by a student under normal conditions. This implies that the privileges, facilities and services offered by the library would vary in accordance with the specific functions of the clientele in the university.

Rules and regulations relating to working hours, number of days the library is open in a year and the, facilities and services will have to be conducive to serve the best interests of the community of users. Some university libraries, particularly in smaller towns, are open to the public, but borrowing privileges may be limited. Services like document supply, interlibrary loan, bibliographical compilation, literature search may be undertaken in university libraries on certain conditions to special categories of users.

Therefore, rules and regulations in university libraries would be framed in accordance with different needs of their community of users.

In a special library, the clientele is also homogeneous as in a university library. All members of the parent organisation of the library would enjoy equal privileges, facilities and services. Information being the unit of service in special libraries, requirements of books may be minimal but Documents supply, literature search, compilation of bibliographies and such other services get greater emphasis and attention. Admission to these libraries is highly restricted. No person outside the parent organisation is generally permitted to use the library. The working hours and the number of days the library works in a year will be in accordance with the functioning of the parent organisation.

Therefore rules and regulations of special libraries have to be framed in conformity with the needs of the users, and in keeping with requirements of the parent organisation.

The following is a set of model library rules governing circulation work and a few other matters connected with the use of a public library:

Name of the Library:

Address:

Telephone: Telex:

(1) Hours of opening		The hours, when the library will be open to the public, shall be fixed by the Library Committee from time to time. The Library Committee has decided as follows for the time being. The library shall be open to the public on all days from 8 a.m. to 9 p.m. *Note*: The loan counter shall be closed half an hour before the closing of the library.
(2) Admission to the Library	21	No person, who is not of sound mind, nor clean in person, nor properly dressed, shall be admitted into the library. *Note*: The decision of the librarian, or his deputy during his absence, in regard to these mailers shall be final The Rules may provide for admission by special permit in the case of specified classes of persons.
	22	A person desirous of using the library shall enter his name and address legibly in the gate register kept for the purpose. Such entry shall be taken as an acknowledgement that the person agrees to conform to the rules of the library.
	221	Sticks, umbrellas, boxes and other receptacles and such other articles as are prohibited by the circulation staff shall be left at the entrance at the property counter.
	222	Dogs and other animals shall not be admitted.
(3) Conduct within the Library	31	Silence shall be strictly observed in the Library.

32 Spitting and smoking are strictly prohibited.

33 Sleeping is strictly prohibited.

34 No person shall write upon, damage, or make any mark upon any book, manuscript, or map, belonging to the library.

35 No tracing or mechanical reproduction shall be made without the express permission from the librarian.

36 A person shall be responsible for any damage done by him to the books or other property of the library. He will be required to replace such books or other property damaged or pay the value thereof. If one book of a set is damaged, the whole set shall be liable to be replaced.

37 Before leaving the library each person shall return to the circulation staff any books, manuscripts or maps taken by him for consultation.

38 Cases of incivility on the part of library staff, or other failure in the service, should be reported immediately to the librarian or his deputy during his absence.

(4) Loan privileges

41 *Membership*: In a public library any of the following is entitled to take out books on loan on enrollment as a member of the library:

(i) Any person living within the area of the library and guaranteed by another known resident within the area of the library.

(ii) Any person employed in an

institution within the area of the library and guaranteed by the head of the institution.

42 *Enrollment*: To get enrolled as a member, a person shall fill up and sign a Form of Enrollment, which can be had free of cost at the library counter (and make a deposit of ...)

Note: The portion of the above rule shown in brackets varies from library to library. Some libraries prefer to omit this clause.

43 Reader's Ticket: Each member shall be given as many reader's tickets as the number of volumes, he is entitled to have with him on loan at one time.

431 The tickets of a member will be valid for twelve months. They can be renewed by filling up a fresh form of Enrollment and returning to the librarian all the expired tickets along with it.

432 A book will be lent to a member only in exchange of the tickets. This will be handed back to the member when the person returns the book, unless it is returned after due date, in which case the ticket will be handed back only after overdue charge is paid.

433 A week's notice shall be given before a deposit is withdrawn. No deposit shall be repaid until all the books outstanding against the member and all his member's tickets have been duly returned and all the dues from the person are paid.

Note: Rule 433 will be deleted if the

portion of Rule 42 shown in brackets is deleted.

44 *Loss of Tickets*: A member who has lost a ticket shall make a written report of the same to the librarian.

441 Three months' time shall elapse (or any stipulated period) after the date of such notice, before a duplicate can be issued. During this period, the member shall attempt to trace and recover the ticket if possible and send a second report at the end of the period, stating the result of his endeavours.

442 If the ticket has not been traced, the member shall give an indemnity bond in the prescribed form and pay a prescribed fee for each duplicate ticket required.

443 After the receipt of the indemnity bond and the fee, the duplicate ticket will be issued.

444 If a member, who has lost one or more tickets, applied for withdrawal of deposit amount, no action will be taken on such application till the expiry of six months after the report of loss of tickets. If the ticket is not recovered by the member before the end ,of that period, the member shall give indemnity bond in the prescribed form in respect of the lost tickets. After the receipt of the indemnity bond, the application for withdrawal will be dealt with in the usual way.

Note: This rule will be deleted if the

portion of Rule 42 shown in brackets is deleted.

(5) Conditions of Loan

51 Each member may borrow on loan not more than (state limit) separate volumes at one time. The person must make his own arrangement for the conveyance of books to and from the library or any of the delivery stations, except that in the case of handicapped members, books may be delivered once a week at their residence on payment of an advance quarterly subscription of (state fee).

52 Before leaving the counter, the member shall satisfy as to whether the book lent is in sound physical condition; and if not, the member shall immediately bring the matter to the notice of the librarian or his deputy in his absence; otherwise the member is liable to be held responsible for the replacement of the book by a sound copy.

53 If one book of a set is damaged or lost, the member concerned shall be liable to replace the whole set.

54 Periodical publications, directories, works difficult to replace, and such other works, as may be declared reference books by the librarian, shall not be lent out.

55 Members are not allowed to sub-lend the books of the library.

56 All books on loan shall be returned at the expiration of a stipulated period from the date of issue.

57 Books temporarily in special demand

may be lent for such shorter period as may be necessary or may be temporarily declared reference books under Rule 55.

58 Loans may at any time be terminated by order of the librarian.

59 If a book is not returned to the library when due, an overdue charge of (state fee) per volume per day shall be levied.

591 Loan may be renewed for a further period, provided:

(i) The renewal application reaches the librarian not less than three and not more than five clear days before the date on which the book is due;

(ii) No other reader has applied for the book in the meantime; and

(iii) Not more than three consecutive renewals shall be allowed for the same book without its production to the library for inspection.

In case of condition (ii) is not satisfied, the librarian shall sent a letter to the member concerned and the book shall be returnable on the due date.

592 A member against whom any overdue or other charge is outstanding shall not be allowed to borrow books (or withdraw the deposit) until the person has paid the amount due.

(6) General

60 The librarian may refuse, under special circumstances, admission into the library to any person or the use of any book without assigning

any reason thereof.

61 The Library Committee may refuse, under special circumstances any application for the privilege of loan of books without assigning any reason thereof.

62 The Library Committee may grant special loans on such conditions as it may prescribe.

63 Any infringement of the rules will render the privilege of admission to and of borrowing books from the library liable to forfeiture.

LIBRARY BROCHURES

In modern libraries, as a part of their users' service or user education programmes, well designed brochures describing the major functions and activities of the library, are prepared and produced to be distributed to all the users of the library. These library brochures are attractively printed with coloured photographs and pictures, maps and other illustrations to guide users in the use of resources, facilities and services of the library. Such brochures contain:

* a topographical plan of the library indicating its various units, in particular, its service units such as reading rooms, open stacks, periodical display and reading room, reference room and reference counter, circulation counter, the public catalogue/ research cubicles, reprographic unit, audio-visual room, if any, etc.;
* description of the document collection of the library with its subject ramification, their organisation and location;
* details of library, bibliographical, documentation and information services the library offers;
* facilities for photocopying, special reading rooms for microforms;
* the publications of the library; its current accessions, indexing and abstracting bulletins; special bibliographies, etc.;
* names of senior officers of the library who will be available for assistance and help or consultation, or service, including the head of the library;

* any other special feature of the library which the user should know;
* extracts of important rules and regulations such as library hours, list of holidays, registration of members, borrowing and reference facilities etc.
* Price list of publications and services.

In addition to printed brochures, modern libraries prepare and produce tape-slide kits or video programmes to be shown to users, introducing them to the resources, facilities and services of the library. Display boards in many libraries is a common feature. All these efforts are aimed primarily to achieve the basic objective of promotion of the use of books and library services and make aware the users with the library rules and regulations.

12
Computer and Internet and the Library Management

The word *Computer* has been derived from the latin work *Compute,* which means to calculate. Therefore, the word computer can be applied logically to any calculating device. A computer capable of accepting information/data automatically, applying a sequence of prescribed process to the information data and supplying the results of these process. It usually has an input and out put devices and central processing unit.

The computer is a device that accepts information and manipulates it for some result based on a programme or sequence of instructions on how data is to be processed. In view of its potentialities, government departments, agencies institutions and other organisations make use of computers in a variety of activities such as data processing and management information system. For the last many years, computers are being used in airlines operations, railways, networks in the banking sectors and other industrial fields. The library and information centres have also became aware of the potential of computer as a powerful tool, which is used to improve both the operational efficiency of library and information personnel and the quality and range of services provided to the users.

There are available various types of commercial softwares through which Acquisition, Cataloguing, Circulation work and Serial control can be managed in effective way in a library. Some to name are Libsys, Alice for Windows, Troodon etc., which can be used for automated management of library working. Besides this, the computers can be used in documentation work also. The indexing of micro and macro documents, Thesaures construction, Abstracting work,

Compilation of Union Catalogues/Lists, Bibliographic work, Searching and Print-outs of queries of users etc. can be better done with the help of computers.

As far as Internet in concerned it is the world wide network of network which is conglomeration of smaller networks and other computers spreading over the entire globe creating a virtual web like structure. It is the resources of information, which is accessible to public from any computer connected to internet. It is composed of a large number of smaller inter connected networks called *Intranet.* These intranets may connect tens, hundreds, or thousands of computer enabling them to share information with each other and share various resources, such as powerful super computers and database of information. The internet has made possible for people all over the world to effectively and inexpensively communicate with each other.

In internet, usually different kinds and varied technologies are put together in such a way that they appear as a single network. It is the global computer and communication system linking millions of business, organizations and private users. A user having Internet access can communicate to another user on the Internet anywhere in the world just like one communicate with the help of ISD telephone call. A huge amount of information can be accessed through the Internet from any where in the world, that is why Internet is also known as '*Internet Super Highway*'.

As the uses of Internet in Library services is concerned, it can assist a reader in the pursues of knowledge learning, research, and increasing their capacity for social interaction. Internet is seen to promote enquiry and creativity through interaction of various forms of knowledge such as text, multimedia, graphics, photos, music, video, sound, animation etc. Use of Internet in Library Services has become indispensable need. It will help as additional tool for library professionals for providing various types of information services to the users. Some of the important applications are :

* Internet has created profound impact on Library and Information Service by offering new modes of information delivery and a vast information sources.
* Due to Internet not only is our world of leadership becoming an inter connected global community, but the early use of internet has changed fundamental roles, paradigms and organisational culture of libraries and librarians as well.

* Inovative uses of Internet technologies enable us to reach both local and distant users much more easily and effectively than higher to possible.
* Technologies such as e-mail and Web provides tremendous opportunities for Library and Information Scientists to deliver the information to the desktops of out users.
* Realising the potential, many libraries are rushing to getting the connectivity.

Internet plays a vital role in library related activities. The main library activities in which Internet can assist, are :

1. **Acquisition :**
   - Suggestion from users
   - Correspondence with Bookseller & Publishers
   - Reminders, Price verification
   - Bibliographical details downloading of records
   - Ordering billing
   - Book shops are online
   - On-line Catalogues searching
2. **Classification :**
   - BUBL-User DDC
   - Cyber Dewey Decimal
   - Math Classification System
   - Engineering Electronics Library Classification
   - Internet Public library and Gateways Users Classification System
   - DDC : www.oclc.org/dewey
3. **Cataloguing :**
   - Cataloguing network resources
   - OPAC – Website
   - MARC–21
   - OCLC : http://www.oclc.org
4. **Serial Collection :**
   - Acquisition or Subscription process

- E-Journals
- Different models
- Web access etc.

5. Resource Sharing :

- Union Catalogues
- Access, adding, downloading
- Access to database over network
- ILLINET, WLN, OCLC, BIB (UK)
- Full text journals access etc.

6. Reference Services :

- Linking of useful sites
- Subject guides
- How to search
- Directing for right sources
- Answering for short range and long range questions
- List of Reference Book on Website

7. Services :

- Document Delivery Service
- Reference/Information Service
- Current Awareness Services
- Science Directory
- Recent Additions
- Content Pages
- SDI Services

8. OPAC :

- Library Cataloues
- University Press, etc.

9. Database Access :

- Bibliographical
- Full text

10. User Education :

- E-mail
- Web
- Setting Internet

The Internet is the world's largest library network containing millions of books, images, documents, maps etc. The libraries have simply know the source to locate the information. Some of the Internet sites are mentioned here for general reference purpose :

1. General Reference Resources

(i) Reference Desk
(http://www.refdesk.com)

(ii) Caltech General Reference Page
(http://Library Caltech.edu/refere.htm)

(iii) Internet Public Library General Reference Collection
(http://www.ipl.org/ref/RR)

2. Dictionaries

(i) Dictionary.com

3. Encyclopaedias

(i) Free Internet Encyclopaedia
(http://clever.net/cam/encyclopaedia.htm)

(ii) The WWW Virtual Library
(http://hom.istar.ca/obyhom/encyclopaedia)

4. Geographical resources

(i) World fact book 2002
(http://odcl.gov./cia)

(ii) Date and Time Gateway
(http://www.bsdi.com/date)

5. Biographical Resources

(i) Biographical Dictionary
(http://www.s9.com/biography)

(ii) Cambridge Biographical Encyclopaedia
(http://www.biography.com)

6. Articles and Printed books :

(i) Uncover

(http://uneweb.carl.org)

(ii) Find Artciles.com

(http://www.findarticles.com)

The above discussion give us the general ideal about computer and Internet and their usage in Library Services. As far as the management aspect is concerned, management Information system can be generated with help of computers for better management in library environment.

MANAGEMENT INFORMATION SYSTEM (MIS)

The term Management Information System (MIS) is of relatively recent origin and is widely adopted following the accelerated use of computers in the early 1960's. The Management information System to business is what is the nervous system is to the human body. It is described as "informational blood stream" of an organisation, which encompasses a wide range of subject matters like management theory communication theory, human processing of data and information technology. Often the concept of Management Information System is splintered and confused by touting new ideas like decision support system, management reporting system, office information system, transaction processing systems, office automation, information resource management and database management system as replacements for Management Information System. However, a brood interpretation of the concept of Management Information System includes all the above.

The Management Information System can be defined as collection of data processing equipment, procedures software and people that integrates the sub-systems of the organisation and provides information for decision making planning and control operates. In other words, Management Information System is an integrated approach for obtaining relevant and timely information on which base management decision.

Characteristics of Management Information System

Management Information System captures data and information from the environment as well as the transactions and operations of the system. Data have to be obtained both from the internal environment like marketing, production, finance and other functional areas as well as from the external environment like competitors, unions, labour force, government policies, legal considerations, suppliers, customers, society, market etc. The internal information is generated from the operations of the organisation at various management levels in the various functional areas. The information gets processed within an organisation as it travels from the clerical level to the top levels of management. That is, the internal information always pertains to the various operational units of the organisation and gets summarised and processed as it gets from lower level to the top level. Only summarised internal information is consumed at the top level and other internal information is consumed by lower and middle level managers. The external information which is from the environment affects the performance of the organisation from outside.

In any organisation two basic approaches possible to Management Information System which are :

(i) Organisational functional sub-systems like-marketing, production, materials, personnel and finance.

(ii) Processing activity sub-system at four different levels:

(a)	Transaction processing	(Clerical staff)
(b)	Operational control	(Junior level managers)
(c)	Management control	(Middle level managers)
(d)	Strategic planning	(Top level managers)

The major processing functions in Management Information System are:

(i) Processing of business transaction

(ii) Updating of master files

(iii) Generation of information reports

(iv) Processing of interactive enquiries

(v) Providing interaction analytical support

The important characteristics or attributes of quality information from an effective Management Information System are timeliness, accuracy, precision, completeness, conciseness, relevance and appropriateness of form.

It may also be noted that an organisation can have information sub systems like accounting information system, office management system, marketing system, human resource information system, etc. The physical components of MIS are hardware, software, database, personnel and procedures. A database (i) which avoids data redundancy and inconsistency, (ii) which is programme and data independent, (iii) which provides flexible access to shared data, (iv) which ensures centralised control of data and v) which provides data privacy, security and confidentiality against fraud, theft, system errors, maliciousness, accidents, disasters, computer crime and abuse, etc. The essential functions carried out in the transaction processing are data capture, validation, classification, sorting, retrieval, calculation and summarisation. In order to achieve its set objectives Management Information System has to have many desirable characteristics apart from the attributes of quality information mentioned above.

An MIS has to be management oriented as well as management directed.

It must posses attributes like accessibility, comprehensiveness, accuracy, appropriateness, timeliness, clarity, flexibility, verifiability, freedom from bias and qualifiability.

It has to be highly selective and capture only relevant data and information. It must integrate all functions, departments and levels of management in the organisation so as to ensure both synergistic effects as well as the impact of one function on the other.

It must systematically synthesise the information requirements of each manager based on his position, responsibilities and scope for decision making.

It must differentiate the kind of information required for planning, decision making and controlling purposes.

MIS is designed for job positions rather than for individuals keeping in mind the job responsibilities and for needs of different levels of management in different functional areas.

It must be highly responsive to changes caused by organisational and experimental changes.

It must have some flexibility, ease to use, adaptability and an in-built contingency nature.

Management Information System must consider the full effect of a decision in advance by supplying the required data. The information provided should have degrees of details just needed for the level of management, minimum need for further analysis and interpretation, uniform presentation and identified significant past relationship and forecasted future relationship.

Management Information System should be integrated by way of a database with single point data entry and updatation and no data redundancy.

Types of MIS

Information systems could be of two different types, i.e., structured and unstructured. Formalisation and publication of information lead to structuredness in information processing activity. Information systems could also be characterised as formal and informal. Formal systems follow the hierarchical structure of the organisation, whereas systems where unauthorised people pass on public or private information from one level to another level are called informal systems.

Advantages of MIS

An efficient Management Information System has many advantages. Some of them are given below:

(i) It quickly provides all sorts of information required for decision making at different levels of management.

(ii) In the process of capturing data forms, one may find gaps, incomplete and incorrect data. The same are likely to be rectified or completed or filled in the process.

(iii) It makes decision making easy, accurate and less risky.

(iv) Information flow from either direction is ensured and encouraged in the rank and file of managers.

(v) Continuous monitoring and updating of information become imperative.

(vi) It greatly helps long range planning with accurate forecasting trend analyses and preplanning information in budget preparation. Even operations planning and tactical planning are provided with information inputs by MIS. Plan modelling, consisting of premising, identification and comparison of alternative courses of action, is greatly aided by MIS.

(vii) It plays a crucial role in controlling managerial operations, monitoring performance and decentralised decision making through performance report, break-even analysis, financial ratios, etc. MIS calculates variations between budgeted and actual results, triggers revised forecasts and acts as an early warning systems for monitoring activities. In other words, MIS provides for control of information which was not previously available and for information sharing across departments.

(viii) MIS helps in planning additional new facilities.

MANAGEMENT INFORMATION SYSTEM FOR LIBRARY AND INFORMATION MANAGERS

Though MIS is playing well in business organization but it is surprising to note that a fully computerised and comprehensive Management Information System is yet to be seen in libraries and information centres. However, the underlying principles are followed in manual, mechanical or semi-automated way to gather, process and use information mostly from within the organisation required by library managers. Information from the external environment is rarely collected and processed. In most cases, use of periodic reports and statistics can be seen, but they cannot match the characteristics of Management Information System. It is really an interesting area to know how the information requirements of decision makers and managers of information are scuttling. As examples, one may think of the following simple situations in a typical library and how equipped Management Information System of libraries are to face such decision making situations.

(i) Monitoring and feedback on need for procuring additional copies of certain books based on heavy demand.

(ii) Change of policy regarding entitlement of number of books to be borrowed by customers as well as the number of days (period) for which books can be kept.

(iii) Taking a decision regarding a sudden cut or a windfall of budget for journals.

Though library statistics and annual reports cannot be considered as substitutes for MIS, they serve the major purposes of providing a base for performance assessment of libraries, decision making and public relations. They are aimed primarily at users, library authorities and taxpayers at large rather than library managers and staff. They also serve the purpose of knowing the activities of the year, comparing libraries and comparing performance over the years.

Comprehensive, accurate, well planned and uptodate library statistics help gauging the progress of a library, formulating policy and procedure, measuring the efficiency of various sub systems, planning a new service or improving an existing service, measuring the output and performance of library staff and planning reward and salary structure. As statistics have all the potential for abuse, misuse and overuse, due care and precaution should be taken on using library statistics. Properly compiled annual reports of libraries help in determining the progress, providing publicity, evaluating the library, and taking remedial measures where needed, apart from serving as a way of seeking public funds, providing feedback to top management, comparing performance with standard as well as other libraries and finally serving as historical records.

A typical MIS for library and information centres with reference to Users, Use, Use time. Collection, Services and Personnel is given below, indicating how such an MIS may be useful in decision making for library managers.

Users

Regular members who have borrowing privileges and use the library well. Visitors not regular but use intensively the library. Casual visitors.

Analysis of data relating to their position, duties and responsibilities in their respective organisations, purpose of use and how used, frequency of use, etc.

Information obtained from data analysis may provide useful indicators for extending support to intensive users, offer them special facilities and thus fix priorities for attention to different categories of users.

Use

What materials are heavily used, by whom, materials used within the library, and such other things. These data may be obtained from statistics kept in the circulation division and Reading and reference rooms.

Use Time

When is the library heavily used - during a day, during a specific period, etc.

Information on this will enable staff deployment during rush hours and satisfy customers.

Collection

Collection analysis in terms of subject distribution, types of material within a collection and such others will throw light on the quality of collection, if properly assessed.

This information will be vital for collection, planning and building and thus improve usefulness and the image of the library.

Services

Services like circulation, reference service, literature search, Current Awareness Service, and Selective Dissemination of Information, etc.

These services may be assessed for cost effectiveness, cost benefits, and such others to give indicators for fixing priorities, allotment of financial resources, deploying personnel, improvements in quality, etc.

Personnel

Assessment of performances, promotion to deserving persons, control deployment, upskilling capabilities, harmonious development, etc. will lead to a better organisational image and performance. This information if systematically collected, organised and stored and available for retrieval through multiple access points will be of invaluable support to decision making.

MIS can be developed, collecting all data mentioned above, which can be accessed by authorised person, providing facilities of access through LAN (Local Area Network) and also integrated appropriately so that data collected in one operation can be used for other purposes, if necessary.

The characteristics of MIS, benefits, problems and pitfalls, etc., are all relevant to such a MIS for library and information centre management.

BIBLIOGRAPHY

Ansari, M.M. 2003. Textbook of Library Management. Shree Publishers and Distributions, New Delhi.

Banerjee, S.R. and Radhakrishan, G. 1970. Physical Verification of Stock in the Library. *ILA Bulletin. 6:* 177-78.

Brown, C.R. 1989. Selecting Library Furniture: A Guide for Librarian, Designers and Architects. Orya Press, Arzona.

Bryson, J. 1990. Effective Library and Information Centre Management. Gower, London.

Chakrabarti, A.K. 1983. A Treatise on Book Selection. D.K. Publications, Delhi.

Cohen, A. and Cohen, E. 1979. Designing and Space Planning for Libraries: A Behavioural Guide. R.R. Bowker, New York.

Corbett, E.V. 1978. Fundamentals of Library Organization and Administration. Library Association, London.

Creth, S. and Duda, F. (Eds.). 1981. Personnel Administration in Libraries. Neal-Schumann, New York.

Dhiman, A. K. 1997. Computers and their Applications in Libraries. *Lucknow Librarian.* 29 (1-4): 11-15.

Dhiman, A.K. 1998. Modern Technology in Resource Sharing for Information Handling. *Library Progress.* 18(1-2): 19-21.

Dhiman, A.K. 1999. Implementation of TQM in Library and Information Centres. In J. L. Sardana edited 'Library Vision 2000: Indian Library and Librarianship in Retrospects and Prospects' (45th All India Library Conference Papers). Indian Library Association, New Delhi. Pp. 663 - 68.

Dhiman, A.K. 2000. Stock Verification : Some Problems of Electronic Publications. *DESIDOC Bulletin of Information Technology*. 20 (6): 3-5.

Dhiman, A.K. 2001. Usefulness of Performance Appraisal in Library & Information Centres. In S.M. Dhawan edited 'Quest for Quality : Strategies and Applications in Library and Information Services'

(46th All India Library Conference Papers). Indian Library Association, Delhi. Pp. 333-39.

Dhiman, A.K.2001. Role of Library Professionals in the Era of Information Technology. *Indian Journal of Information, Library & Society.* 14 (1-2): 81-85.

Dhiman, A.K. 2001. Impact of Information Technology (IT) on Library Management. In Kalpana Dasgupta edited 'Library Practices for Effective Management' (47th All India Library Conference Papers) Indian Library Association, Delhi. Pp.191-202.

Dhiman, A.K. 2002. Resource Sharing in Digital Environment through Internet: Problems and Prospects. In H. Anil Kumar, P. Upadhyaya, S.R. Ganpule and P.C. Shah edited 'Internet Engineering for Libraries and Information Centres (Ninth CALIBER-2002 Papers). INFLIBNET Centre, Ahemdabad. Pp. 43-54.

Dhiman, A.K. and Sinha, S.C. 2002. Academic Libraries. Ess Ess Publications, New Delhi.

Dhiman, A.K. 2002. Libraries in Self-financed Academic Institutes: Realities, Problems and Prospects. *UPLA* Seminar held at Institute of Management and Technology, Ghaziabad. Pp. 68-72.

Dhiman, A.K. 2002. Management of University Departmental Libraries. *Library Progress.* 22 (1): 59-64.

Dhiman, A.K. and Gupta, S. 2002. Library Legislation: Need and Importance in Uttaranchal State. *Indian Journal of Information, Library & Society.* 15 (1-2): 38-43.

Dhiman, A.K. 2003. Internet Based Library Services. In Pandey S.K. Sharma edited 'Electronic Information Environment and Library Services: A Paradigm' (48th All India Library Conference Papers) Indian Library Association, New Delhi. Pp. 99-106.

Dhiman, A.K. 2003. Data Mining and its Use in Libraries. In TAV Murthy edited 'Mapping Technology on Libraries and People (CALIBER-2003)'. INFLIBNET, Ahemdabad. Pp. 568-74.

Dhiman, A.K. 2003. Basics of Information Technology for Librarians and Information Scientists. 2 Vols. Ess Ess Publications, New Delhi.

Dhiman, A.K. 2004. Cataloguing of Non Book Materials. Ess Ess Publications, New Delhi.

Dhiman, A.K. and Arya, C. 2003. Leadership Qualities for Information Professionals. *International Library Movement.* 25 (1): 25-32.

Dhiman, A.K. 2003. Intellectual Property Rights in Digital Environment. In Y. Singh et al., edited 'New Challenges in Information Management and E-learning in the Age of Globalisation (SIS - 2003 Paers). Central Library, IIT Roorkee. Pp. 292-98.

Evans, G.E. 1983. Management Techniques for Libraries. 2nd Edition. Academic Press, New York.

Godden, I.P. 1984. Library Technical Services: Operations and Management. Academic Press, Glencove.

Goswami, B.P. 1972. Personnel Motivation and Work Efficiencies in Libraries. Radha Krishna Publications, Varanasi.

Goswami, B.P. 1996. Motivational Factors in Library Management. Radha Krishna Publications, Varanasi.

Immelanan, R.F.M. 1947. Foundations of Library Management. Cape town.

IGNOOU. 1999. B.L.I.Sc. Materials on Library Management. Booklets 1-5. IGNOU, New Delhi.

Issac, K.A. 2001. Glimpses of Library and Information Science. Ess Ess Publication, New Delhi.

Jetkins, C. and Morley, M. (Eds.). 1996. Collection Management in Academic Libraries. Jaico Publishing House, Bombay.

Jourdon, P. 1987. Staff Management in Library and Information Work. Gower Publishing Ltd., Hampshire.

Kanter, J. 1990. Management Information System. 3rd Edition. Prentice Hall of India, New Delhi.

Katz, W.A. 1980. Colletcion Deveoplment. Holt, Renhart and Winston, New York.

Kaula, P.N. 1971. Library Buildings: Planing and Design. Vikas Publishers, New Delhi.

Kishore, J. 1981. Personnel Management in Libraries. Ess Ess Publications, New Delhi.

Kchochar, R. S. 1999. Electronic Media and the Library Services. Discovery Publication House, New Delhi.

Koontz, H. and O'Donnell, C. 1998. Essentials of Management. Tata McGraw Hill, New York.

Kumar, K. 1987. Library Organization. Vikas Publishers, New Delhi.

Kumar, K.1987. Library Administration and Management. Vikas Publishers, New Delhi.

Lovecy, I. 1984. Automating Library Procedures: A Survivor's Handbook. The Library Association, London.

Marchant, M.P. 1971. Participative Management. *Library Trends. 20:* 49-58.

Mittal, R. L. 1983. Library Administration. 5th Edition. Metropolitan Book Company (Pvt.) Ltd., New Delhi.

Mayer, P. 1978. Periodicals: Administration in libraries. Clive Bingley, London.

Mookerjee, S.K. and Sengupta, B. 1972. Library Organization and Administration. World Press, Calcutta.

Mukherjee, B.B. 1973. Preservation of Library Materials, Archieves and Documents. World Press, Calcutta.

Murdick, R. G. and Ross, J.E. 1983. Information System for Modern Management. 2nd Edition. Prentice Hall of India, New Delhi.

Prasher, R.G. 1991. Managing University Libraries. Today & Tomorrow's Printers Publishers, New Delhi.

Prasher, R.G. 1994. Personnel Problems in Indian Libraries. Medalion Press, Ludhiana.

Prasher, R.G. 2002. India's University Libraries: Organizations, Operation and Services. Medalion Press, Ludhiana.

Ramayana, T.V. 1980. Elements of Library Organization and Management. Andhra Pradesh Library Association, Hyderabad.

Ranganathan, S.R. 1960. Library Administration. 2nd Edition. Asia Publishing House, Bombay.

Ranganathan, S.R. and Gopinath, M.A. 1966. Library Book Selection. 2nd Edition. Asia Publishing House, Bombay.

Sayer, W.C. Berwick. 1949. Browns Manual of Library Economy. 6th Edition. Grafton, London.

Sharma, B.K. and Tripathi, B.P. 1989. Information Handling in Libraries in 21st Century. Ess Ess Publication, New Delhi.

Sharma, C.K. 1983. Library Management and Organization. Shree Publishing House, New Delhi.

Shimmon, R. (Ed.). 1976. A Reader in Library Management. Clive Bingley, London.

Sinha, S.C. and Dhiman, A.K. 2001. Citation Analysis of the Research Field and Information Technology Development. Ess Ess Publications, New Delhi.

Sinha, S.C. and Dhiman, A.K. 2002. Prolegomena to Universe of Knowledge. Ess Ess Publications, New Delhi.

Sinha, S.C. and Dhiman, A.K. 2002. Research Methodology. 2 Vols. Ess Ess Publications, New Delhi.

Sinha, S.C. and Dhiman, A.K. 2002. Special Libraries: Technical and Research Libraries. Ess Ess Publications, New Delhi.

Singh, R.S.P. 1981. Glimpses of Librarianship. Janaki Prakashan, Patna.

Taylor, F.W. 1911. Scientific Management. Harper, New York.

Terry, G. 1988. Principles of Management. Irwin, Homewood.

Tauber, M.F. 1954. Technical Services in Libraries. Columbia Press, New York.

Thompson, G. 1973. Planning and Design of Library Buildings. 2nd Edition. Architectural Press, London.

Steuard, R.D. and Morgan, B.B. 1987. Library Management. 3rd Edition. Libraries Unlimited Inc., Littleton.

Zwans, V. 1992. Management Information Systems. WCB Publisher, Dubuque.